COWBOY CULTURE

COWBOY CULTURE

A Saga of Five Centuries

David Dary

University Press of Kansas

Published by arrangement with Alfred A. Knopf, Inc., by the
University Press of Kansas (Lawrence, Kansas 66049), which was
organized by the Kansas Board of Regents and is operated and funded
by Emporia State University, Fort Hays State University, Kansas
State University, Pittsburg State University, the University of Kansas,
and Wichita State University

Library of Congress Cataloging-in-Publication Data

Dary, David.
Cowboy culture: a saga of five centuries/David Dary
p.   cm.
Bibliography: p.
Includes index.
ISBN 0-7006-0390-5
1. Cowboys—West (U.S.)—History. 2. West (U.S.)—Social life and customs.
3. Cowboys—Folklore. 4. Folklore—West (U.S.)
I. Title.
F596.D29 1989   88-30449
978—dc19   CIP

Printed in the United States of America
10 9 8 7 6 5 4 3

Drawings on pages 17-18, 32-3, 49, 148-53, 204, 243-5, 283, 316
by Al Napoletano

Grateful acknowledgment is made to the following for permission to
use illustrations from their collections:

Jose Alvarez Del Villar, Mexico City: Illustrations on pp. 19, 20
California Historical Society, San Francisco: Illustrations on pp. 57
(below), 65
California State Library: Illustration on p. 57 (above)
Colorado Historical Society: Illustrations on pp. 81 (above), 203
(above right), 257 (above), 288 (below), 337 (left)
Denver Public Library, Western History Department: Illustrations on
pp. 34, 287 (below), 323 (below), Beldon photo
Kansas State Historical Society: Illustrations on pp. 81 (below), 108,
143 (above), 165 (above), 175, 185, 186, 189, 194 (above), 203 (above
left), 207, 208, 219, 224, 236, 246, 257 (below), 259 (above), 260, 277
(above), 282 (left), 288 (above), 295 (below), 300, 337 (right)
Library of Congress, Erwin E. Smith Collection of Range-Life
Photographs: Illustrations on pp. 143 (below), 144, 161 (below), 162,
165, 194 (below), 270 (below), 293, 295 (above), 299
Montana Historical Society: Illustrations on pp. 247 (above),
282 (right)
Nebraska State Historical Society, Solomon D. Butcher Collection:
Illustration on p. 323 (above)

*Owing to limitations of space, all further acknowledgments
of permission to use or adapt previously published material
will be found following the index.*

To Sue

Contents

Maps

Maps drawn by Lewis A. Armstrong
Art and lettering by Al Napoletano

Foreword

THE YEAR 1994 will mark the five-hundredth anniversary of the arrival of the first cattle in the Western Hemisphere. Several years after that historic event occurred in 1494, the Spanish conquered New Spain and cattle ranching developed in what is today Mexico. It was then that the vaquero, or cowboy, was born. He moved northward as cattle ranching spread into modern California, portions of New Mexico and Arizona, and Texas, where Texians adopted and modified many of the vaquero's tools, techniques, and customs and thereby created their own cowboy culture. Following the Civil War the Texian cowboy culture spread throughout much of the American West. This book traces the culture of the cowboy from its roots in New Spain to modern times in the American West.

The word "culture" means different things to different people. To some, it denotes good books, paintings, poetry, classical music, opera, and other artistic endeavors. For others, it refers to high society or the well-educated person. And to still others, the word implies something vaguely foreign and not understood. How the term is defined usually depends upon those who are asked to define it, their education, way of life, worldly experiences, and *their* culture.

If one applies the dictionary definition of culture to that of the cowboy, his culture might be defined as "the totality of socially transmitted behavior patterns, beliefs, institutions, and all other products of human endeavor and thought characteristic of those human beings involved in cattle raising." But that academic definition is dry. It lacks the color and flavor of the cowboy's culture— his horse and saddle, his lariat whistling in the air, the red-hot branding iron, the smell of burning hair and flesh on a calf being branded, sleeping under a blanket of stars, the taste of dust on a long trail drive, the smell of hot coffee on a cold morning, a new pair of handmade boots, or the fine wines served to wealthy cattlemen in the Cheyenne Club.

These and countless other things constituted the culture of the cowboy, a culture that was learned. It was a culture based on mobility, custom, and the survival of the fittest. It was influenced and shaped by many things. It was a culture with little permanence. It was a frontier institution, and it died when the frontier died.

Untold numbers of books and pamphlets have been written about the cowboy. Many are fiction, but there are a surprising number of factual accounts by old-time cowboys and cattlemen, and they are primary sources. Most of these have been consulted along with other primary and secondary works. Many are included in my notes and selected bibliography, but the majority focus on one period of time or on the cowboy in one geographic region or on one aspect of the cowboy's life. This book is different. It traces the culture of the cowboy for nearly five centuries. To do this it has been necessary to follow a historical thread. It would be impossible to understand the culture of the cowboy without considering his history. They go hand in hand.

This work, however, is not intended to be a definitive history of the cattle industry. Such a history has yet to be written. I hope that the combination of history and the cultural aspects, especially the tools and techniques, of the cowboy will provide the reader with new insights and erase misconceptions that exist about the American cowboy and his culture.

I am indebted to many people whose names appear in the text and notes. But I owe a special debt of gratitude to the following: Joe B. Frantz, retired professor of history at the University of Texas, Austin; Jeff Dykes of College Park, Maryland; Joseph Snell, retired executive secretary of the Kansas State Historical Society, and Nancy Sherbert of that Society, Topeka; Wayne and Elizabeth Rogler of Matfield Green, Kansas; Sheila M. Ohlendorf of Austin, Texas; John D. Gilchriese of Tucson, Arizona; Floyd E. Risvold of Minneapolis, Minnesota; Gene M. Gressley and Emmett D. Chisum of the University of Wyoming, Laramie; Al Napoletano, who has since retired to Oregon; Dr. Larry Day of the University of West Florida; Lurton Blassingame and Eleanor Wood of New York City; and especially, my editors at Alfred A. Knopf, Inc., Angus Cameron and Ann Close, for their helpful advice, suggestions, and guidance. I also want to thank the University Press of Kansas for making the book available in paperback.

David Dary

Along the Kaw
Lawrence, Kansas

COWBOY CULTURE

CHAPTER 1

The Spanish Roots

*And God made the beast of the earth after his kind, and
cattle after their kind, and everything that creepeth upon
the earth after his kind; and God saw that it was good.*

—GENESIS 1:25

SPRING is a glorious time to be in the Kansas Flint Hills, especially
if the rains have been plentiful. The bluestem grasses lose their winter
gray and brown in favor of deep rich green, a color that will soon fade
with the coming of the hot summer sun. Even if spring is brief, as it is
in some years, it is sufficient. The clean sweet smells carried on the gentle
warm breeze blowing up from the southwest carry a freshness that the
nostrils have not sensed since the Indian summer days of fall. "The hills,"
as the local cattlemen call the land, have none of the flaming beauty of the
forested New England mountains or the majesty of the Rocky Mountains.
Rather, the gentle contour of the rolling carpet of grass stretching from
horizon to horizon is soft and restfully inviting. It is peaceful because the
hand of man is little in evidence. Most of the Flint Hills are still virgin
prairie much as they were a century or more ago when the Indian's
cattle—buffalo—grazed on the tall grasses. Today the white man's cattle
have replaced the shaggy monsters of the past.

Cattle are big business in the hills that stretch from north of Manhattan, Kansas, southward into Oklahoma where they are known as the
Osage Hills. Many cattlemen consider them the best large grazing area in
the world. They comprise about four million acres in eastern Kansas.
Geologically, the Flint Hills are nothing more than a series of closely
spaced, relatively high ridges formed by ancient ocean currents and glacial
movements. And their name is really a misnomer. The hills do not contain
ledges of flint. Only nodes of flint can be found in the softer limestone.
Although it is scarce, early Indians found enough flint of sufficient size
to make arrow points. Because the topsoil is thin, the roots of the grass

easily tap the lime and absorb it. In turn the predominant grasses—big
bluestem, little bluestem, and the side oats grama—are more productive.
Cattle gain weight fast on the grasses of the Flint Hills. One can find the
identical grasses growing elsewhere in Kansas and on the ranges of New
Mexico, Colorado, and other western states. But aside from the black-earth
region of central Texas, only here in these Kansas hills do the coarse
grasses feed on the lime which makes them so palatable and so nutritious
for cattle.

It is probable that Francisco Vásquez de Coronado and his party
touched the region while searching for Quivira in the sixteenth century.
Although they did not find the fabulous riches of which the Indian called
Turk boasted, Coronado and his men recognized the fertility and beauty
of the land and its resemblances, real or imagined, to Old Spain. Jaramillo,
a member of Coronado's expedition and perhaps the first "booster" of
what would later become Kansas, was pleased with the country and pre-
dicted that it would be very productive. He wrote that many cattle existed
there, "as many as anyone could imagine." Jaramillo, of course, was referring to the immense herds of buffalo then common to the plains and
prairies. His prediction held true, but it was nearly two and a half centuries later before white men returned with their own cattle.

Although the Spanish spent little time in or near the Flint Hills, their
influence is still felt today by the ranchers who graze their cattle on the
lush grasses that sometimes grow as high as a man on horseback. Like cattle
ranchers throughout the American West, those of "the hills" owe much of
their vocation's traditional culture to the Spaniards who first introduced
cattle to the New World and who first developed cattle ranching in this
hemisphere more than a thousand miles south of the Kansas Flint Hills.
To the motorist driving through the Flint Hills today, the Spanish influence is not outwardly evident. The ranch houses are not of Spanish architecture. Most are frame or stone, and in appearance they reflect more
the English or Scotch or German ancestry of their residents. But when
you go beyond the barbed-wire fences to where men, young and old, may
be seen working the cattle, the influence of the early Spanish is evident
in many of the cowboys' saddles, their lariats, and even their horses, or it
is heard in some of the words sprinkled through their daily speech. The
same, of course, is true throughout the American West.

To understand fully this influence, one must go back nearly five
hundred years. The roots of Spanish influence were planted in 1494 when
Christopher Columbus returned to the New World for a second time. He
set anchor off the north coast of Hispaniola near present Cape Haitien,
Haiti, on January 2, 1494, and unloaded twenty-four stallions, ten mares,
and an unknown number of cattle. They were the first such creatures in
the Western Hemisphere. They and their progeny were destined to change

the face of the New World and bring about a revolution comparable in impact to that of the Industrial Revolution nearly three centuries later.[1]

Horses and cattle had long been an intricate part of the way of life in the Old World, especially in Spain, where Spaniards had bred horses for centuries before the Moslem invasion of Europe. The Spanish horse was well-known for its speed and quality a thousand years before Taric el Tuerto led his forces into Spain. Horses not only provided transportation but were vital to soldiering; cattle were a source of food, and their hides and tallow were staples. When, after his first voyage, Columbus reported that he had found no such animals in the New World, seed stock was transported across the ocean to Hispaniola. But the task was not an easy one. It took about two months for the small, light Spanish caravels to sail from the Iberian Peninsula to the Canary Islands 900 miles away, and then 2,500 miles across the Atlantic to the West Indies. Horses and cattle were carried in stalls on the decks of the ships, since there was little room below. In prolonged calms, when water ran short and all of the fodder was consumed, many horses and cattle died and were cast overboard or butchered and the flesh added to the crew's meager gastronomical fare. The area where calms were frequently encountered—about 30 to 35 degrees north and south—became known as the "horse latitudes," because of the many horses cast into the sea.[2] Such losses, together with the expense of transporting supplies from Spain to the New World, soon convinced the Spaniards that their settlements had to be self-sufficient. Stock raising and agriculture were essential.

It is not surprising that the cattle, horses, and other livestock that survived the long ocean journeys prospered on Hispaniola, as did the grains, vegetables, and citrus fruits introduced by the Spaniards. The warm climate was conducive to growing things. Beginning in 1498, small cattle ranches or royal villas were established to increase the supply of breeding stock. And by the early 1500s, as the Spaniards settled modern-day Puerto Rico, Jamaica, Cuba, and other islands in the West Indies, the practice of agriculture and stock raising was extended to each of the new settlements—much to the delight of the Spaniards, who had an aversion to the beefless diet of the natives. Conditions were so favorable that soon the supply of cattle increased beyond the needs of local consumption. Many cattle roamed free on the islands and became wild. In some instances Indians began hunting the wild cattle and selling smoked meat to passing ships. The flesh was smoked over wooden racks or frames, which were called *bocanes*. From this term sprang the French word *boucanier* after the French invaded the islands in the seventeenth and eighteenth centuries and copied the Indians' way of smoking meat. Later many of these Frenchmen became pirates and were known as "buccaneers."

As the Spanish became firmly entrenched in the West Indies early

in the sixteenth century, a young man with a strong will set out to conquer New Spain in the name of God, country, and gold, and not neces-
sarily in that order. He was Hernán Cortés. Educated as a lawyer, he used
religious fervor as his excuse for almost any excess, including killing and
robbing. Cortés was spurred by a seemingly insatiable desire for gold and
pleasure, and his double and deceitful dealings with the Mexican Indians
are infamous. Yet he was able to do what many might believe impossible:
he took a few hundred men and conquered a nation of many thousands.
Those who knew Cortés described him as a man of pride. This was one
of the salient marks of sixteenth-century Spaniards, who believed they
were a superior race. Historian John Bartlett Brebner, writing in 1933, concluded that Cortés won "because he exploited not only every known and
half-known element of the Spaniards' inherent prestige, but as well every
fissure and weakness in his opponents and their position which his remarkable perception revealed to him."

Even so, Cortés and his followers probably would not have won without their horses. The Indians feared the "Big Dogs," as some called the
horses, and many Indians believed that man and beast were one. Jose de
Acosta, writing in 1590, quoted an unnamed Spaniard as saying: "Although
the people of this country resisted, they were soon defeated by the cavalry,
which they held in great fear." Another Spaniard, Bernal Díaz del Castillo,
wrote tenderly of the Spanish horses, calling them comrades and friends
and describing their individual characteristics and abilities as though they
were human. He and other writers leave little doubt that Cortés and his
followers realized almost from the start of their conquest that their horses
were something special.

It is ironic that when Cortés brought the first horses to what is today
Mexico—the memorialized sixteen: eleven stallions and five mares—the
species had come full circle in the New World. When Cortés's horses
were landed at Vera Cruz in 1519, the Spaniards were unaware that they
had reintroduced horses to a continent where the species may have originated sixty million years earlier and then vanished. But, unlike the first
horses that probably roamed Mexico and much of North America, those
introduced by Cortés and his followers were Andalusian, descended from
grays and roans that existed in a primitive state in Old Spain before Stone
Age man settled there, and from Moorish horses brought to Spain by the
conquering Moslem invaders. Although the Moorish horses had some
Asiatic blood from Syria, Egypt, and Arabia, the horses brought by Cortés
to the New World were not truly Arabian, as some writers have suggested.
They had been bred in Spain. As one authority has noted: "In spite of the
fact that it is offensive to the Spanish people and to scholars who have
made a thorough study of the ages-old Iberian hippology, self-proclaimed

authorities persist in writing that the Andalusian horse is an 'Arabian,' and that the horses brought to the Americans by *conquistadores* were also blue-blooded 'Arabians.' No statement was ever made on thinner evidence."[3]

The Andalusian horses were bred by Spaniards in the basin of Guadalquivir in the provinces of Cádiz, Huelva, Sevilla, Málaga, Jaén, and Córdoba. By 1492, when the Moors were expelled from Spain, the Spaniards were riding the small, swift, and hardy Andalusian horses, but they had adopted Moorish saddles with short stirrups and the Moors' Arabian style of riding and fighting. This Moorish style of horsemanship was called *a la jineta*, and Cortés and his men brought it to New Spain. The short stirrups forced the rider to stand and lean back against the cantle of his saddle when galloping. The *jineta* style was one of two schools of riding that existed in sixteenth-century Spain. The other was called *a la brida*, an ancient mode of riding dating back to the knights of old. This older style used a saddle with long stirrups, and the rider did not have to stand in the saddle.[4]

Six months before Cortés captured what is today Mexico City and conquered the Aztecs, another event occurred that was to have lasting impact on New Spain: an expedition led by Gregorio de Villalobos landed several head of cattle—one account says they were all calves—on the banks of the Pánuco River near present-day Tampico. These apparently were the first cattle in what is now Mexico.[5] In less than a year Villalobos became lieutenant governor of New Spain and from Vera Cruz coordinated the arrival of Spanish settlers, supplies, and an increasing number of horses and cattle. So many cattle and horses were brought to the mainland through Vera Cruz that stock raisers on the islands soon feared the loss of their monopoly. They raised the prices of their cattle and other livestock, and then placed restrictions on exporting such animals, invoking the death penalty against anyone selling livestock to persons on the mainland. However harsh such actions seem today, they point up the importance placed on horses and cattle by sixteenth-century Spaniards. Cortés was angered when he heard the news and ordered an end to the slaughtering of cattle and other livestock on the mainland. Just as farmers and ranchers might write letters today to their senators and congressmen complaining about import or export quotas, Cortés wrote such a letter in October 1524 to Emperor Charles V in Spain pointing out that if the settlements in New Spain were to survive they must have livestock. It took months for the letter to reach Spain, but Charles responded favorably and lifted the ban by royal decree late the following year. The flow of cattle and other livestock from the islands resumed.

It is unfortunate that Spanish chroniclers failed to describe the kind of cattle first brought to Hispaniola by Columbus and later to New Spain by Villalobos and others. There is only passing reference to cattle in documents of that period. It may have been that the chroniclers viewed cattle as impersonal objects associated with wealth. The word "cattle" had been, in many European tongues, synonymous with the word "capital," meaning a man's wealth. Until about 1500 a man's wealth in Europe was often reckoned in cattle. Wilfred Funk, in his book *Word Origins and Their Romantic Stories* (1950), points out that a *chattel* mortgage "is really a 'cattle' mortgage, and up to the 16th century the English spoke of 'goods and cattals' instead of 'goods and chattels.' "

Regardless, sketchy bits and pieces of information suggest that there were at least three strains of Spanish cattle brought to the New World. One was the piebald, or *Berrenda*, with white body and black markings about the neck and ears. Another was the Jersey-tan-to-cherry-red *Retinto*, with its long narrow head. The third strain was the ancient black variety, the *ganado prieto*, commonly known as the Andalusian fighting bull, or *toro de lidia*.[6]

While the Andalusian fighting bull would be trained for the bull ring, the other strains provided the foundation herds for what would be known decades later as Texas longhorns, cattle known for their long, low-swinging heads, admirable horns, narrow sides, long legs, and nasty disposition. Such cattle, unsuited for dairy or draft purposes, became valued for their hides, tallow, and stringy beef. And on the plains and in the valleys of New Spain these cattle prospered. Stock-raising conditions in the West Indies were good, but they were even better on the mainland for these strong and tough cattle. Many Spaniards compared the flora and fauna of Old Spain to that of New Spain. The country from Vera Cruz to near what is today Mexico City provided excellent grazing and good watering. And the mild climate aided their propagation. As one Spanish writer, the secretary to Franciscan Father Alonso Ponce, observed: "They reproduce as in Castile, only more easily, because the land is temperate and there are no wolves or other animals to destroy them, as in Spain."

In all likelihood, Cortés was one of the first white men to realize that Mexico's great variety of topography and climate could accommodate almost any crop known in Old Spain and was ideally suited for stock raising. Cortés may have realized this soon after he and his men moved inland from the coast to conquer the Aztecs, although one can imagine that his attention was then focused on finding gold. But the promise of instant wealth was not fulfilled. It may have been then that Cortés decided to let the land—the league after league of fine country—produce his wealth, for soon after the conquest he turned his attention to stock raising, horse breeding, and agriculture.

Cortés chose the lush valley of Mexicalzimgo, more than 8,500 feet above sea level. This beautiful valley, south of modern Toluca, became the chief center of experimentation in cattle breeding.[7] Here the grasslands were stocked with cattle that soon multiplied in number. His cattle brand, three Latin crosses, may have been the first such brand used in New Spain. And his men probably used branding irons constructed of iron with perhaps wooden handles. Whether the three Latin crosses were shaped on the end of the iron is unknown; his men may have used instead what later became known as a "running iron," something similar in appearance to a fireplace poker in the shape of a long L: the man doing the branding would heat the iron in an open fire until it was cherry red, and would then use it like a pencil to "write" the brand into an animal's hide.[8]

Continuing to do as he wished, Cortés divided up much of the Indian population in central Mexico and placed the natives under the control of different Spaniards, including himself. As might have been expected, Cortés took the largest number, at least 23,000 souls. Each Spaniard granted one of these encomiendas, or trusts (the grantee being styled an "encomendero"), was to see that his Indians were converted to the Catholic faith, fed, and clothed. In return, the Indians were expected to provide labor. The Indians became something like the feudal vassals of the Old World.

Soon other Spaniards began to graze cattle on land south and west of Mexico City. Within a few years cattle became plentiful there and eastward to the grass-covered plains and valleys near Perote and Tepeaca. The Spaniards let most of their cattle wander at will, but Indian farmers soon began complaining about trampled fields of maize and other crops. They demanded that cattle should not go unattended while crops were in the fields. Although the crown had insisted that Indians were to have rights, many were driven from their lands by the cattle, leaving the Spaniards quarreling over land rights and disputing ownership of cattle, many of which were not branded. It became commonplace for a Spaniard to claim all unbranded strays and to brand them as his own. Centuries later this practice would be called "mavericking," first in Texas, then elsewhere in the American West.

In an effort to resolve such problems and keep peace among Spaniards and Indians alike, the town council of Mexico City, which was composed of several cattle raisers, ordered the establishment of a local stockmen's organization called the Mesta. It was established on June 16, 1529, and was patterned after a similar institution in Old Spain. The Mesta was to become the granddaddy of all organized stockmen's groups in the Western Hemisphere. The town council ordered that "there shall be two judges of the Mesta in the city who shall, twice annually, call together all stockmen who should make it known if they had any stray animals in their herds."[9] The town council further directed each stock owner to have his own brand, which would be used in the future to identify all his animals. Stock owners were then directed to register their brands in what undoubtedly was the first brand book in the Western Hemisphere, kept at Mexico City. Later, the use of such brand books as a public record of all registered brands would spread northward and throughout the American West, just as branding would be used to mark ownership of cattle.

It could be said that the first population explosion in the New World was that of cattle. As the Mesta began to solve some of the problems resulting from this explosion, the crown, reacting to social changes occurring in Europe and desiring to centralize control in New Spain, gradually began reducing the power of the encomendero. This gave more freedom to the Indians and created small farms and common grazing lands around Indian villages in a pattern similar to that then found in Old Spain. While this was happening in the early 1530s, a number of Spaniards appropriated grazing land some distance west and northwest of Mexico City and established their cattle herds in what is today southern Querétaro, northern Michoacán, and southern Guanajuato. In these areas disputes soon erupted between Indian farmers, who claimed much of the land, and the cattlemen who, in typical conquistador fashion, had taken it without asking. There are also accounts of disputes between sheep owners and cattle raisers over grazing rights.

Many of these arguments became lawsuits and were taken to the *audiencia*, or supreme court, which had been established by the Spaniards in Mexico City. But the court was slow, and it became so overwhelmed by cases involving cattle and other livestock that the crown itself finally moved to solve the problem of grazing rights: in 1533, soon after New Spain was officially proclaimed a Spanish colony, a royal ordinance established common grazing lands for livestock owned by Spaniards and Indians alike. The first such range was located at the southern end of the central plateau region north and west of Mexico City. There, on the broad swath of gradually rolling grassland, Indians began to graze their livestock. At first, the Spaniards boycotted the common range, but then Don Antonio de Mendoza, first viceroy of New Spain, ordered the Spaniards to take their cattle from their old estancias, or land grants, and place them on the common lands. The Spaniards complied.

Don Muñoz Camargo, from whom we learn much about the early cattle industry in New Spain, recalled that the old cattle-raising valleys were stripped of cattle, and all the *estancias de vacas*—grants for cattle—were in the lands extending some 200 leagues (500 miles) from the San Juan River beyond the valley of Guadiana. Having common grazing lands away from farming areas appears to have reduced the number of disputes over grazing rights and encouraged further growth and development of the cattle industry in New Spain. It also created new problems. More cattle were stolen from the common grazing lands by rustlers, who sometimes changed brands in hopes of concealing their crime. These might be considered the first cattle rustlers in the New World. But even poor people, and that included most of the native population, did not hesitate to steal cattle and slaughter them for food. They would either keep or sell the hides and tallow.

The Spanish cattlemen reacted much as ranchers in Texas, Kansas, or Wyoming would today. They asked the authorities to put a stop to the rustling. The crown responded in 1537 and ordered Don Antonio de Mendoza to establish the Mesta *throughout* New Spain, and "to enact ordinances to benefit and increase the herds, and to remedy and punish frauds and crimes which are committed with much frequency." The first code of the Mesta, drawn up on July 1, 1537, included three regulations which served for nearly forty years as the foundation of the Mesta system and would later be adopted by the cattle industry north of the Rio Grande: *First*, all brands had to be different, so that animals could be quickly identified. No person could have the same brand as another. *Second*, where two stockmen did then have the same brand, the Mesta arbitrarily gave to each a distinct brand. *Third*, cropping the ears of an animal for identification was prohibited. Such marks could be easily changed and were viewed as an invitation to fraud and deception. Any stockman who cropped an animal's ears was liable to have his herd confiscated by the council of the Mesta.

The Mesta code of 1537 required all persons owning three hundred or more sheep, goats, and hogs or at least twenty burros, mules, cows, or horses to become members. In this manner the crown forced nearly all livestock owners to join. Once they were members, each was obligated to attend meetings in person or to send a representative. Initially there were two meetings annually, one in February and the other in August, and they were well advertised. All owners of livestock were expected to bring stray animals found with their herds to the Mesta meeting in their locality. The strays were then identified by their brands and returned to their rightful owners. If their owners could not be found, the animals were sold and the money placed in the royal treasury.

The Mesta controlled the collection of penalties and fines from persons violating its ordinances and handled the conservation of grain supplies. It even regulated the kind and number of dogs that each sheepman could have. For example, only mastiffs—large dogs with short fawn-colored coats—could be owned by sheepmen; three dogs for each one thousand head of sheep. Because dogs could do much damage to cattle as well as to sheep and other livestock, all owners of dogs were subjected to Mesta regulations. Even Indians living in villages within 3 miles of seasonal pastures were permitted to have only one dog at their homes.

There is no question that the Mesta served the special interests of the livestock owners, especially the cattle raisers. In a real sense it was a cattlemen's protective association, much like those that would develop centuries later in the American West. And the Mesta's ordinances were similar to modern American laws relating to ranching; today's laws, in fact, are essentially variations and adaptations of the regulations first established in New Spain more than four centuries ago.

The Mesta in New Spain, while modeled on a similar institution in Old Spain, never achieved the political influence of its prototype. The New World Mesta was not used by high officials to gain political power and prestige, nor was it a huge monopoly under royal protection, as was the Old World institution. Small stockmen and farmers fared equally well with the large ranchers in early New Spain. In Old Spain the Mesta and the crown worked against the small livestock raiser.

CATTLE WERE SO PLENTIFUL in New Spain by 1540, nineteen years after the first seed stock arrived, that Coronado had no difficulty in gathering a herd of perhaps five hundred cattle plus innumerable hogs, goats, and sheep for an "on the hoof" commissary to support his fabled Seven Cities of Cíbola expedition. Starting from Compostela, the expedition headed north and northwestward, eventually passing through territory that is today the state of Sinaloa. There Coronado left a number of exhausted cattle. Many apparently survived, because twenty-five years later Francisco de Ibarra found thousands of wild cattle in the same area. Coronado continued northward, entering what is today southeastern Arizona and traveling through portions of modern New Mexico, Texas, Oklahoma, and into Kansas. It is possible that Coronado reached the Gila River in modern Arizona with some cattle, in which case they were the first such animals in what is today the American Southwest. But it seems unlikely from his accounts that the cattle survived the journey beyond that point. They probably met their intended fate and were devoured by Coronado and his followers.[10]

IN OUR HIGHLY MOBILE and push-button world of rockets and missiles, it is difficult to imagine the horse as a superior weapon of warfare. But for the early Spanish in New Spain, the horse was their best weapon, both psychologically and physically. Cortés and his men realized that they could remain superior as long as they kept the horse from the Indians. Perhaps they even sensed that Indians on horseback would be formidable antagonists—as was proven true before the end of the sixteenth century. Thus it is not surprising that following the conquest of Mexico only Spaniards were permitted to own and ride horses. Gradually, as the cattle population swelled from Pánuco and Nautla in the northeast to Vera Cruz and the Grijalva River in the south, and in areas north and west of Mexico City, this changed.

Muñoz Camargo recalled that cattle were "being born and multiplying unbelievably; you cannot exaggerate their numbers or imagine the spectacle before your eyes." With so many cattle on the common grazing ranges, rustling was on the increase, and it became necessary for the Spaniards to watch their cattle. Most Spaniards viewed such work with disdain. It was beneath their dignity; others provided the labor that produced the wealth. Even the padres in the increasing number of missions with their own herds of cattle had a similar belief. These men of God, many of whom did not like to ride horses, viewed the handling of cattle as menial work. It appears that the padres were the first to find a solution to the problem: they chose to teach their new converts—Indians, Negroes, and other non-Spaniards—to ride horses and to look after cattle. Gradually the vaquero, the Mexican cowboy, was born.[11]

The early vaquero was not a very romantic figure. Spaniards and Mexicans have never viewed him as Americans north of the Rio Grande later viewed the traditional cowboy. The vaquero was, in the eyes of most sixteenth-century Spaniards, nothing more than a poor laborer on horseback. He was about as far down in the social order as one could get.

The first vaquero undoubtedly wore what clothes he had on his back, but in time he found certain kinds of dress more appropriate than others for his work. During the decades that followed, his dress became a blend of that worn by the Spaniards and that of the natives of New Spain. Working on horseback in the hot sun eventually brought about the adoption of the Spanish sombrero, a hat similar in shape to the planter's hat of the American Old South a few centuries later. It had a low flat crown and straight stiff brim, and was constructed of leather, cheap felt, or woven palm fiber. But unlike hats worn by wealthy Spaniards, which were decorated with gold and silver ornaments and sometimes heavy gold and silver braid, the vaquero's sombrero was usually plain. Few vaqueros could afford such fancy decorations.

Under their hats many vaqueros wore bandannas tied over their heads. Their hair was parted in the middle and brushed back into long single braids much like those of some young people of the counterculture today. And long sideburns probably graced both sides of the vaquero's face, a face that might be shaved once a week, if at all.

In the warm climates the vaquero might wear cotton shirts year round, but in the temperate regions he might change to a wool shirt during the cold months of the year. Both cotton and wool were in good supply in New Spain. The Aztecs had produced cotton long before the Spaniards arrived with the first sheep. Tradition says that Antonio de Mendoza, the first viceroy of New Spain, introduced Merino sheep into the country and emphasized sheep raising for many years, thereby ensuring a plentiful supply of wool. But where the vaquero could not obtain or afford a wool or cotton shirt, he probably turned to cowhide and made his own shirt from tanned leather. Leather was waterproof, and wind-resistant in the colder altitudes.

By the late sixteenth century many vaqueros had chosen leather for their *chaqueta*, or jacket, and their knee breeches. These pants, or *sotas*, usually laced up the sides and would fit tightly enough to stay up by themselves, or else would be held up by a sash at the waist that also kept the vaquero's belly warm in cold weather. If the knee breeches were not of leather, they probably were wool or cotton, perhaps hand-me-downs from some Spaniard. Underneath the breeches were long drawers, once white but now probably soiled. From where the breeches ended and the long drawers could be seen, the vaquero sometimes wore wrapped leather leggings, or *botas*. They covered the lower leg to about the ankle, where the tops of his buckskin shoes, which might have leather soles and low heels, could be seen. But shoes were not common with early vaqueros. Most vaqueros went barefooted, especially in the warmer regions. Cowboy boots, as we know them today, were still nearly three centuries away, although a handful of vaqueros may have had heavy jackboots. If so, they were likely hand-me-downs from wealthy Spaniards, or perhaps stolen. It would have been a rare vaquero who could afford the expensive boots worn by wealthy Spaniards, which were made of the finest cordovan and morocco leathers. Such boots were exceedingly wide at the top, often lined with silk or velvet, and made to be worn with silk stockings, something few if any vaqueros owned or had ever worn.

A pair of large iron spurs would be strapped to whatever footgear the vaquero wore, or even to the ankles of bare feet. The rowels—rotating disks, with sharp points, at the end of the spur—were very large, often 8 inches in diameter. These spurs were similar to the type that had been worn by Cortés and the other conquistadors. The large rowels made walking very difficult, but then the vaquero never walked when he could ride, a trait he would pass along to the American cowboy of the nineteenth century. When a vaquero did walk, the rubbing heel chains and the pendants attached to the rowel pin—these were later to be called jingle-bobs—gave off a bright ringing sound. To the vaquero, the spurs were a badge of his calling.

Spurs were already centuries old when the vaquero began wearing them. Some historians believe early goad spurs first appeared about 700 B.C. By the fifteenth century, spurs were a mark of rank for old World cavaliers, knights, and caballeros; the right to wear spurs was then awarded only by a feudal lord or king. By the sixteenth century, they naturally found their way to New Spain with the conquistadors, and subsequently onto the feet of vaqueros.[12]

History does not record what kind of men these first vaqueros were. Undoubtedly they were not fools but intelligent and practical men capable of learning by doing and by observing the Spaniards. They learned early of the gullibility of most Spaniards and had, from the beginning, taken advantage of this trait whenever possible. Accounts of how these early vaqueros lived are nonexistent, but since many of them a century later lived an almost primitive life, it seems safe to assume the same was true of vaqueros in the middle sixteenth century. Cleanliness was not next to the godliness taught by the fathers. Most vaqueros had no ranch house to shelter them. In fact, few ranchers built buildings on their encomiendas. Their construction outlays went instead for town houses well into the seventeenth century. So when tending the herds, the vaquero slept under the stars or in a crude lean-to constructed near water and wood. Such huts consisted of nothing more than two forked poles stuck upright in the ground with another pole laid across the forks. Still other poles were then placed against the cross pole with their lower ends touching the ground. Straw or grass might be spread on the ground to form a soft floor. On top of the hut cattle hides, straw, or shingles would be laid on the sloping poles, thereby completing the shelter. If available, stone might be used for the walls. The back side of these shelters usually faced the prevailing winds. At the front the vaqueros would build their fire and cook their meals, usually *atole* (corn meal mush) when beef or wild game was not available. It was not a very comfortable life.

The need for vaqueros increased after the Spaniards discovered rich silver deposits at Zacatecas in 1546 and hurriedly moved into the frontier region of New Spain. Herds of cattle were driven north, and many of them were placed on new grazing areas established on the central plateau. The demand for beef in the mining camps and new settlements was great. Ranchers hurried to take advantage of the high prices being paid for beef. This pattern would be repeated later far to the north when American cattlemen in the nineteenth century drove cattle half a continent away to capitalize on high meat prices paid by hungry gold miners in California and later in the gold fields of Kansas Territory (now Colorado). The large herds of *ganado vacuno*—beef cattle—not only fed the miners, but their tallow was used for making candles to provide light in the mines. The hides were made into bags to carry ore to the smelters and to pack the refined metal to the cities. Of course, hides also provided the raw material for clothing, harnesses, saddles, hinges, water bags, and numerous other leather products.

While many ranchers were given land grants in the new region to graze cattle, some were not satisfied with what they had received. They seized huge chunks of land, some covering more than 200 leagues (about 450 miles), from the Rio San Juan to Zacatecas, and even farther into the valley of Guadiana, deep in country inhabited by nomadic and warlike Indians who did not like the Spanish encroachment. These Indians, the Chichimecas, began raiding Spanish settlements, ranches, and supply trains, killing Spaniards, burning, looting, and stealing cattle. The Spaniards reacted by building presidios, or forts, in the region to protect the settlers and by sending soldiers to patrol the roads leading to the mining region. Here again the Spanish were setting a pattern for the settlement of the land, a pattern that would be repeated by Americans three centuries later as they moved onto the plains and prairies of the western United States.

Cattle became so abundant in New Spain that by the early 1550s the supply outdistanced the demand for meat. Cattle prices began dropping. Meat was so plentiful that every person, whether he worked or not, had food and creature comfort. Soon the hides and tallow of cattle were more valuable than the animals' flesh, and ranchers began raising them primarily for these purposes rather than as food. Such operations, to be profitable, demanded huge herds, vast grazing areas, and a large labor force of vaqueros. By then the silver strikes at Zacatecas (1546) and Guanajuato (1554) had created new wealth for many Spaniards. Churchmen, government officials, and miners could find little in which to invest except land and livestock. As they invested heavily in both, especially along the northern frontier in a region that became known as Nueva Vizcaya in 1562, a rancher aristocracy began to develop. Soon many large ranches were owned by men from Mexico City, Puebla, and Queretaro. William H. Dusenberry tells much of their story in his book *The Mexican Mesta*. He describes how these men chose to live in towns in large houses where they could enjoy the luxuries that great wealth provided. To run their ranches they hired estancieros, or overseers. These estancieros, a notch or two above the vaquero in social ranking, worked for either fixed wages or a small share of the profits. Most estancieros were Spaniards who hired a labor force of vaqueros, some of whom were mestizos (of mixed Spanish and Indian parentage) or mulattoes (of mixed black and white parentage). Many Negro slaves had been brought from Africa by way of Spain, and many of the free males became vaqueros. The sole possessions of each were often only an old saddle, a horse—sometimes stolen—and a short lance.

These early vaqueros of the mid-sixteenth century used any one of three kinds of saddles. A few had stock saddles, developed by Spaniards in the West Indies, that were well suited to their work, but most of them used saddles brought from Old Spain. The old *silla de montar*, or war saddle, was heavy and cumbersome in appearance. The cantle and pommel wrapped around the rider, and the stirrups were usually high, causing the rider to crouch when riding. The *jineta* saddles were similar in construction, but the stirrups hung closer to the ground and the cantles were lower and only partly encircled the rider. The fact that *la jineta* is a feminine form suggests that these saddles were made for comfort, something the soldiers using war saddles were not provided. These older saddles were not satisfactory for the vaquero's work. They were heavy and did not offer much security or comfort for someone who spent most days from sunrise to sunset in the saddle, with perhaps a break in the middle of the day when the sun was the hottest.[13]

The horses ridden by these early vaqueros were descendants of those brought to New Spain by the Spaniards. Most were stallions—the vaqueros, like their Spanish masters, believed stallions were more powerful than mares. They usually judged a horse's strength by the size of its *huevos* (testicles) and the loudness of its neigh.[14] Because it was then a Spanish custom to leave stallions uncastrated, and there were many strays, wild horses were so plentiful after about 1550 that a man did not have to steal his mount unless he was lazy. A horse could be had for little more than the trouble it took to capture and break the animal. Even if the Spaniards had wanted to keep horses from the natives, it would have been impossible

OLD SPANISH SADDLE (*silla de montar*)

to do so by the middle of the sixteenth century. The sheer numbers of wild horses roaming the countryside enabled anyone to own a horse. One account tells of wild horses roaming the swampy meadows of the Rio Lerma, on the road to Toluca, only 10 leagues southwest of Mexico City.

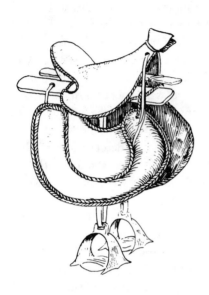

OLD SPANISH SADDLE (*la jineta*)

Wild cattle were even more plentiful than wild horses. There were so many wild cattle in New Spain by the 1550s that it was not uncommon for a calf not to see a human being until the animal was full-grown or even several years old. In 1555, seventy or eighty bulls were captured in isolated areas far from any settlements for a bullfight to be held during a celebration honoring Viceroy Luis de Velasco. Some of the bulls were twenty years old and had never seen a human until they were captured. Having lived in the wild for so long, these bulls must have been vicious when men sought to end their freedom. They were, in the true sense of the word, *wild* animals.[15]

The temperament of these cattle made them so difficult to handle that ranchers began to round them up regularly so they could become accustomed to humans. This regular activity began during the 1550s and became known as the *rodeo*, a word that comes from the Spanish *rodear*, meaning "to go around" or "to surround or encircle." The rodeo was simply a roundup and may have been inspired by a form of Indian hunt, but it was nothing like its modern-day cousin in the American West. There were no flags or banners or bands, nor was it held in a stadium or arena. It was not a spectator sport. Vaqueros would drive cattle toward a ranch from all directions, or the cowboys might head the cattle to some other fixed point, where they were sorted. New calves would be branded and strays would be separated from the herd. The vaqueros would use their long, iron-tipped poles or lances to separate the cattle and check their brands. These lances were similar to ones used in Spain.

The lance was of secondary importance to the vaquero after cattle became more valuable for their hides than for their flesh during the 1550s. It was then that the hocking knife or *luna* grew to prime importance. The knife—shaped something like a scythe—was a steel blade about a foot long.

It was sharpened on the concave edge and then attached securely to the end of a stout pole about 10 or 12 feet long. This tool was called a *desjarretadera*. When the pole was held in a horizontal position the points of the knife aimed forward. With a *desjarretadera* in his right hand, a vaquero mounted his horse, and holding the shaft forward so that the knife was about 2 feet above the ground and to the side, he steadied the shaft under his arm. The knife would then be ahead of the horse. The vaquero spurred his horse and chased the bovine he wanted. Nearing the animal he would thrust the knife end forward until the animal's right hind leg struck the razorlike edge of the knife. As the animal's large tendon was cut, it became helpless and fell to the ground. The vaquero then dismounted and drove one end of the knife into the animal's head just behind the horns, severing the spinal cord. Once the animal was dead the hide was removed and pegged out on the ground to dry.[16]

Today this procedure is called hamstringing, and by our standards it is an ugly process; but it was accepted practice during the sixteenth century. The vaquero's first slaughterhouse was the open range, unlike today, when the killing of beef for flesh and hides is done behind closed doors and in a more humane fashion. François Chevalier, who scoured the provincial archives of Mexico and Spain in more recent times for facts about life in colonial Mexico, wrote that horsemen using *desjarretaderas* "acquired such dexterity that to amuse themselves or to sell hides—sometimes without consulting the livestock owners—they decimated the herds."[17] It

EARLY VAQUEROS USED THE DESJARRETADERA TO HAMSTRING CATTLE
they planned to slaughter for hides and tallow.
Drawing by an unidentified Spanish artist.

BEFORE VAQUEROS LEARNED TO THROW THEIR LAZO
over the head of a bull or cow, many placed the loop
over the horns using a long stick.
Drawing by an unidentified Spanish artist.

VAQUEROS SOMETIMES TIED THEIR LAZOS TO THEIR HORSES' TAILS
in sixteenth-century New Spain.
Drawing by an unidentified Spanish artist.

is a fact that vast numbers of cattle were killed in this manner during the 1560s and 1570s. Ranchers slaughtered thousands of cattle for their hides and tallow in a manner similar to the slaughter of American bison or buffalo for their hides more than three centuries later on the American Great Plains. Even heifers were killed in New Spain before they were two years old or mature enough to bear young. Still other cattle were lost in northern regions to raiding Chichimeca Indians. By 1573 there was fear that the cattle population of New Spain might be depleted. The Mesta, concerned about the killing, revised and strengthened their code in January 1574 in an effort to reduce the slaughter. The hamstringing of cattle was banned, as were *desjarretaderas*. Any person found to possess a "lance or hocking knife of any kind whatsoever" was required to pay a fine of twenty pesos or receive one hundred lashes in public.

Even though hamstringing was outlawed, it continued in general use for many years, especially along the northern frontier. There vaqueros sometimes wielded *desjarretaderas* against each other. Gradually, however, the lasso or *lazo*—a rope with a slipknot—replaced the hocking knife as the vaquero's primary working tool for cattle. Contrary to the belief of some, most sixteenth-century vaqueros did not circle their rope in the air above them and throw the loop over the horns of cows. That technique was developed later. In the sixteenth century a vaquero put the loop on the end of his lance and then, from atop his horse, raced after a cow. Nearing the animal, he would lower the end of the lance holding the loop and place the loop over the horns of the cow. Once it was in place, he would pull back on the lance and let the loop tighten naturally as the rope was pulled taut. The other end of the rope was either tied to the cinch on the vaquero's saddle or to his horse's tail.

Vaqueros soon saw that the lasso had advantages over the hocking knife. Although much slower, the lasso gave them a chance to check the brands on cattle before they were killed. Then too, the lasso could hold an animal during the branding process without causing serious injury. Most of the ropes used by the early vaqueros in New Spain appear to have been braided from strips of untanned cowhide. They stretched 15 to 20 yards and were as thick as a man's little finger.

Vaqueros also made good use of their lassos on the trail drives that became commonplace in New Spain by the late sixteenth century. Unlike the later trail drives from Texas northward to the Kansas railheads or northern ranges, sixteenth-century cattle drives posed some unique problems. Spaniards did not castrate their bulls. Thus they often faced the problem of having to move a large herd of cattle with many bulls. Vaqueros would harness the troublesome bulls to trained oxen. Using a hair rope or halter called a *cabresto*, the oxen would lead or drag the bulls until they were broken to the trail. These bulls would then lead the herd. Later, Texas ranchers would use a lead ox or steer on trail drives in a similar manner. A good lead steer might head two thousand longhorns up the trail from Texas.

By the 1560s there was regular movement of cattle from the area around Querétaro and northern ranches southward toward Mexico City. Within a decade San Juan del Rio became the center of much trail-driving activity. The town, centrally located about 160 miles northwest of Mexico City and conveniently situated at a ford on the San Juan River, became a point of registration where herds being moved south were counted and where brands were checked and certified by appointed justices. These agents of the viceroy had brand books containing all of the brands of the region; they guarded against any illegal transfer of stock and charged one peso for each one hundred head they checked. Ranchers had to obtain a permit from the viceroy's office to move cattle any distance. Each permit usually listed the number of cattle being moved, the ranch where the cattle came from, and where they were being taken.

Looking back to that period more than four centuries ago, one cannot help but be impressed by the effectiveness of the Mesta in New Spain. The Mesta formalized problem-solving among cattle ranchers in a manner unlike that which occurred in the American West, where most of the early ranchers had to establish their own justice because they arrived before government and law and order. But in New Spain these things generally accompanied the rancher to the northern frontier. One wonders how the history of the American West might have changed if such authority had arrived with the early cattlemen who, for the most part, had to struggle to survive. The American West of the nineteenth century might not be viewed as romantically today, and the circumstances of the period might not have created characters like Wild Bill Hickok, Wyatt Earp, Billy the Kid, and others on the fringes of the American cowboy culture.

In New Spain the Mesta code was revised in 1574. The revision was more detailed and much stricter than the code of 1537. It forbade mestizos, Indians, mulattoes, and Negro vaqueros to own horses. Ranchers had to provide mounts and could pay only in money, not in colts or other livestock. And the new code tightened controls over the sale of animals in an attempt to reduce cattle theft. No person was permitted to buy livestock except from the owner or his authorized representative. Under no circumstances could livestock be purchased from hired Indians, or sold to them, except in a public place. If a Spaniard broke this law, he was fined fifty pesos or given one hundred lashes if he could not pay. For a second offense the penalty was doubled and the offending Spaniard was banished for a distance of 20 leagues (about 50 miles) from the district where he committed the offense. If a mestizo, Negro, mulatto, or Indian violated the law, the penalty was more severe. The first time he received a hundred lashes. The penalty was doubled for a second offense, and mutilation was sanctioned—the cutting off of the offender's ears.

Many ordinances of the Mesta suggest that a large number of vaqueros may have been dishonest. Undoubtedly there were vaqueros who could not be trusted, just as there have been such human beings in all walks of life since the dawn of civilization. But not all vaqueros were dishonest or vagabonds. Many were honest and stable people, by the standards of the day, especially those who worked on the smaller ranches in Celaya, Silao, León, and Irapuato. Old Spanish records in Mexico City and Madrid contain passing references to bad vaqueros who banded together to roam the countryside, taking what they wanted—much like Jesse and Frank James, the Dalton boys, John Wesley Hardin, Sam Bass, and others in the nineteenth-century American West. The names of these vaqueros have not been preserved, perhaps because their activities did not seem very adventuresome or romantic or important to the Spaniards who kept the records. Such vaquero bands, however, may have been the forerunners of the *bandidos* of Mexico, who in the eyes of most poor Mexicans have been viewed as being more colorful and romantic than the common vaqueros.

Unlike Jesse James and other alleged "Robin Hoods" of American folklore, these roving bands of lawless vaqueros did not rob the rich and give to the poor. But then neither in fact did Jesse James and his counterparts in the American West. In his study *Land and Society in Colonial Mexico*, François Chevalier noted that the bad vaqueros robbed anyone who had anything they wanted and gave only to themselves. Another Spaniard wrote: "They strike terror to the heart of the population calling themselves vaqueros, they ride about armed with *desjarretaderas* or scythes; they collect in bands and no one dares withstand them." And still another said: "They are agile and hardy. Their breed grows apace, and trouble may well be brewing, for So-and-so is employing 300 of these mounted brigands as cowboys, and most of them are equipped with breastplates, harquebuses, scythes, desjarretaderas, and other weapons." Chevalier concluded by noting that "Because there simply was no other labor available, stockmen were forced to employ these seminomads, at least for a part of the year and during the big rodeos. If they regretted having hired them, they regretted it more if they did not."

Roaming vaqueros were sometimes hired to help move large herds of several thousand cattle from one location to another, sometimes to a market or new grazing area. For many ranchers, however, a trail herd of several thousand cattle represented only a small portion of the cattle they owned. Francisco de Ibarra, who had ranches in the borderlands of Zacatecas and Durango, reportedly owned about 130,000 head of cattle in 1578, and nine years later authorities certified that his vaqueros had branded 33,000 calves in one year, 1586. Another writer, who accompanied Father Alonso Ponce on an inspection of the Franciscan missions between 1585 and 1588, wrote that there were men "who brand yearly 30,000 calves, not counting those that wander off and go wild. There is hardly an Indian town that does not have a slaughter house for the natives themselves in which infinite numbers of animals are killed."[18]

It is not surprising that the continuing slaughter of cattle for their hides during the 1580s reduced the growth rate of the herds throughout New Spain. The attitude of many ranchers probably was similar to that of many American buffalo hunters who, centuries later, slaughtered the buffalo for its hide without much concern about depleting the supply until few buffalo were left. It may have been that the Spaniards, like the buffalo hunters, believed the supply of animals would never end. But, unlike the buffalo hunters in the American West, whose hide trade was facilitated by reliable transportation to the marketplace, namely the railroads, ranchers in New Spain had serious transportation problems. Their major marketplace was in Europe. Irregular fleet crossings by the dwindling Spanish merchant fleet and the general unreliability of ocean transportation late in the sixteenth century were responsible for the fluctuating hide trade. During 1591 and 1592, for instance, ranchers in New Spain had difficulty selling their cattle hides because there were no ships bound for Spain. But in 1594, partial figures indicate, nearly 75,000 hides were transported from New Spain to Seville, Spain, while a fleet bound for Europe in 1598 carried 150,000 cattle hides.

Viceroy Velasco had prohibited the slaughter of cows and had taken other measures to conserve livestock late in the 1500s. He had warned ranchers that the continued slaughter of cattle for their hides would deplete the supply, but this warning was not heeded. Many ranchers continued to kill cattle for their hides. One factor that may have influenced their behavior was the dearth of native labor: there was a shortage of responsible vaqueros. Soon after the conquest the Indian population of New Spain began to decline. One authority, Lesley Byrd Simpson, estimated that the native population dropped from about six million in 1540 to less than three million by 1590.[19] Certainly the lack of vaqueros and other native labor affected cattle ranching and the agricultural output of New Spain, as did rustling.

During the late 1500s, rustling continued on the increase. Abiqeos, or rustlers, especially those operating along the northern frontier, killed cattle solely for their hides. They would often leave the flesh to rot on the ground where the animals had been killed and skinned. These rustlers usually sold the hides for almost nothing to people at neighboring mines or traded them for supplies and weapons. Chichimecas and even Indians who had been on peaceful terms with the Spanish turned to rustling on the northern ranges. One large group of hostiles controlled the valley of San Francisco about 30 miles south of modern San Luis Potosí. The valley, surrounded by mountains, was like a fortress. The Indians would go out on raids, steal cattle, and drive them to the protection of their valley, where at times it is said several thousand head could be seen grazing. It was not uncommon for these Indians to drive large herds of cattle northward to native villages, where they were traded for supplies, weapons, and sometimes even women.

It was not until 1595 that the Spaniards succeeded in negotiating a workable peace with many of the hostile Indians, namely the Chichimecas, who for years had rustled cattle, raided, and burned ranches. The Indians agreed to permit a number of Christianized Indians to live among them and to teach the rudiments of the quiet pastoral life that the Spaniards had emphasized. In return the Spanish government agreed to provide annual donations of food, clothing, and cattle. Here again the Spanish were establishing a pattern—one that would surface time and again during the next few centuries—of seeking to break down the tribal structure, culture, and religion of the Indians. One of the most noteworthy examples of this in the American West was the Dawes General Allotment Act of 1887, which sought to make the Indians dependent upon whites for their survival. The Spanish-negotiated peace of the late sixteenth century did reduce some of the Indian rustling of cattle, but ranchers continued to slaughter their cattle primarily for hides.

By the 1590s the ranching frontier extended into what is today northern Zacatecas, Durango, south and eastern Coahuila, and along the Rio Grande. Perhaps the most significant settlement was that headed by Juan de Oñate, who established a temporary colony in the Rio Grande valley near where El Paso, Texas, stands today. The year was 1598. From there Oñate sent his lieutenants to explore the Great Plains to the northwest and the vast region between the Colorado River and the Gulf of California. Oñate, who was a wealthy silver mine owner from Zacatecas, received the contract from the crown to colonize the upper Rio Grande valley and introduce Franciscan missionaires to convert the Pueblo Indians. By late 1598, Oñate, who is often called the Father of New Mexico, had entered the region with perhaps as many as four hundred men—about 130 brought their families—to establish San Gabriel in the vicinity of the Tewa Pueblo of San Juan. It was the first Spanish settlement in what would become the American Southwest. He also furnished grain and some seven thousand head of cattle and other livestock for the colony.

The animals were driven by Oñate's vaqueros from the Santa Barbara–Parral region to New Mexico for food and breeding stock.

As the sixteenth century was ending, the ranching industry was firmly established in the New World. It had spread northward on two fronts, one up the western and one up the eastern slope of the majestic Sierra Madre. It had swept more than a thousand miles from where it began southwest of Mexico City less than a century before. And the vaquero had become an integral part of the spreading cattle-related culture that emphasized the mounted horseman.

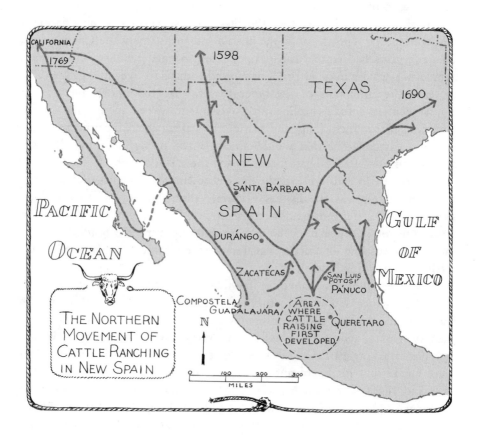

CHAPTER 2

·•·

Moving North

The ranching frontier was the "cutting-edge" of Spanish civilization as it pushed north. What the farming frontier was to Anglo-America, the ranching frontier was to Hispanic-America.

—RICHARD J. MORRISEY[1]

THE traditional home of the Mexican vaquero was the large Mexican hacienda that sprawled over thousands upon thousands of acres in the rugged country of Chihuahua, Coahuila, Nuevo León, or Durango in northern Mexico. There, until recent years, the vaquero worked cattle much like his father, grandfather, great-grandfather, and even his great-great-grandfather had. The vaquero's vocation was handed down from father to son. But today, modern ranching techniques have replaced the weathered vaquero, poor in material things but rich in skill and tradition, in many areas of Mexico. A few traditional vaqueros still remain in scattered regions of northern Mexico. They live and work on a few large haciendas, but even these ranches may soon be things of the past. Most such ranches have been reduced in size, the land redistributed by the Mexican government, and modern ranching methods and techniques have been introduced.

The word "hacienda," derived from the Spanish verb *hacer*, to do, primarily means an income-producing enterprise and not, as is commonly believed, a rich man's country home or estate surrounded by gardens. A hacienda could include a large home and gardens, but its main purpose was to produce a profit for the owner. It was a business. And the word "hacienda" does not mean cattle ranch. There can be lumbering haciendas, farming haciendas, mining haciendas, and even sheep haciendas, or combinations of these. It was once thought that the rise of the Mexican hacienda was a natural consequence of the Spaniards' conquest of Mexico. It seemed only logical that after the conquistadors took the land they would create huge

empires within an empire. Such was not the case. The hacienda system did
not develop until the early seventeenth century, well after the vaquero
had become a fixture in the ranching labor force of New Spain. And the
process that created the hacienda system was complex. To understand its
growth and its influence on the vaquero and the cattle industry, some background is necessary.

The seventeenth century was a time of depression in New Spain. By
the end of Philip II's reign in 1598, the crown was already faced with
retrenchment because of the depletion of its financial reserves. The cost
of conquering the New World had been great. While the rewards had
been many, the flow of silver and other precious metals from the mines
of New Spain had caused inflation in Old Spain. Philip II had discriminated
against the Moslems, who had been responsible for much of Spain's industrial wealth, driving many of them out of the country for the sake of
Spanish prestige and the protection of Catholicism. Consequently, manufacturing and commerce dwindled, and Spain's rigid commercial policy
drove trade into the hands of the English and Dutch. Thus, as the seventeenth century began, the once-great Spanish empire was declining and
decaying.

In New Spain the mining boom collapsed and the northward expansion slowed soon after Juan de Oñate, early in the seventeenth century,
settled what is today New Mexico. Although the crown continued to
control all political, social, and economic matters and, with the church,
continued to rule in strict accordance with divine and natural law, it could
generate little income in New Spain. Its encomienda system had failed, in
part, because of the decrease in the native population and a decline in
mining. As a result, land became the sole source of income to the crown.[2]

Land grants had been distributed by the crown soon after the conquest
as reward for military service. Other grants were given to influential citizens, widows, orphans, and destitute heirs of the conquistadors. This practice continued through the 1500s. In time, however, many such grants were
sold by people who could not or did not wish to work the land. Consequently, by the early seventeenth century, the wealthy Spaniards—government officials, encomenderos, miners, merchants, the church, including
individual clergymen and religious orders such as the Society of Jesus—
owned or claimed much of the land. As the crown's economic suffering
increased in the early seventeenth century, many of the wealthy landowners began to shoulder the responsibilities once handled by the crown.
Large landowners, especially cattle barons, became more powerful. These
men began to acquire additional land, not just to increase their wealth but
to eliminate competition from other wealthy landowners and to control
vast regions. At the same time something occurred that was to have a
striking effect on the cattle industry.

Until the seventeenth century, grazing rights were held in common—one rancher could not legally keep his neighbors and their cattle off his land grant—but such property rights became better defined in the 1600s. In an effort to raise needed capital, the crown offered to give wealthy ranchers and other landowners full title to the land they occupied—for a price. This included ranchers who had seized land years before without official sanction. The settlement tax, as it was called, added needed funds to the crown's treasury and made it possible for ranchers to define the boundaries of their growing ranches. These ranches or haciendas were strengthened and soon replaced the crown as the focal point of social, economic, and political life. As an entity, New Spain began to turn inward and each *hacendado*, or hacienda owner, became more powerful. The resulting decentralization of authority was a step backward into the days of feudalism in Europe. The *hacendado* ruled everyone within the boundaries of his hacienda. He was a lord and chief agent of local government. He created a world to his own liking.[3]

The vaquero was part of this world on the cattle-raising haciendas. The largest cattle haciendas were located in the northern regions of New Spain where the land was too poor for cultivation and best suited for grazing. But on such land many acres are required to support one cow. Although the cattle population began to increase again, the wealth produced by cattle for the seventeenth-century *hacendados* was limited, even on haciendas large enough to support thousands of cattle. Trade had declined, especially in hides and tallow exports. It was only natural that the *hacendados* searched for ways to cut their operating expenses, including the wages paid to vaqueros and other laborers. By giving these people credit at the hacienda store or lending them money, the *hacendado* was able to bind them to the hacienda.

Most vaqueros soon were in debt, and as the years passed it was not unusual for a vaquero to be born into debt, because children inherited their parents' obligations. The child's first clothes might be made from cloth obtained at the hacienda store on credit against his future wages once he could begin useful work. By the time he joined the work force the young man would be tied to the hacienda. Later the *hacendado* would lend him money to get married and to celebrate religious holidays. And when the vaquero died or was killed, he was buried with as much honor, drink, prayer, and festivity as borrowed money could provide. The vaquero's wages were undoubtedly low, forty to fifty pesos a year, at best. It was not uncommon for him to go through life without ever seeing his wages. They were simply credited to his account.

Many large haciendas became self-sufficient, and some gave the appearance of being small towns. As in so many of the smaller towns in the United States today, there was a square around which stood the main hacienda buildings. The largest was the *hacendado*'s house, often constructed of stone and built around several patios. Off each patio was an apartment. The *hacendado*, of course, had the largest apartment, furnished with canopied beds and large chests in which to store his personal effects. including jewelry and silver plate. By the eighteenth century, gargoyles and carved capitals decorated many a *hacendado*'s living quarters along with paintings on the walls. Flemish landscapes and religious subjects were very popular. It was not unusual for the *hacendado* to have a private chapel in his apartment.

The vaquero's living conditions, of course, were nothing like those of the *hacendado*. On most haciendas the vaqueros, when not on the range tending the herds, were provided with a place to sleep. It is possible that some *hacendado* set aside a large room, perhaps in the stable building, where unmarried vaqueros could curl up in their blankets. This could have been the beginning of what was later called the bunkhouse on ranches in the American West. If a vaquero was married, he might be permitted to build a crude shack on the outskirts of the main buildings. Some *hacendados* may have rented such shacks to vaqueros with families.

Most of the main hacienda buildings had thick walls and were one-storied with high, vaulted ceilings. Generally cool in the summer and warm in the winter, they were designed to conserve energy. Narrow windows, battlements, ledges, parapets, observation towers, and dovecotes were not just for show. They had a practical application in northern areas of New Spain where hostile Indians would often raid haciendas. Such features were even commonplace on hacienda buildings in areas of central Mexico where bandits sometimes were active.

Stables were generally the second-largest structure on cattle haciendas. Most *hacendados* were very good horsemen and kept many horses for their personal use. Stable buildings were often grouped around a second patio or courtyard. Rooms off the courtyard housed the horses plus the wooden or leather saddles, bridles, bits, spurs, and other riding gear. And since many haciendas were several days or weeks away by horseback or carriage from the nearest major city or town, riding apparel appropriate for the terrain to be crossed was often housed in the building.

Some haciendas had mills for grinding grain. The largest haciendas had a church and vicar, and there were workshops where nearly all tools and implements were made. Although some haciendas had blacksmiths who produced iron shares, others did not. Their plows, rakes, harrows, shovels, and other tools were made of wood. Rawhide was commonly used instead of nails. If mines were located within the boundaries of a hacienda, there would be machines for crushing minerals, stoves for smelting silver or other ore, and charcoal burners and carts to carry the ore from the mines. Like nearly everything else on the hacienda, the vaquero's saddle was handmade.

Initially most vaqueros probably made their own saddles, but gradually saddlemakers became commonplace on the haciendas, and saddlemaking became something of an art. By the early 1600s, saddlemakers were beginning to blend the more desirable features of the old Spanish saddles into a more practical saddle for the vaquero. The changes were slow. A modification made on saddles at one ranch might take months to be adopted and then later improved on at another ranch. The changes gradually spread across New Spain. By the late seventeenth century the rigging, exposed and suspended from the fork, carried a single cinch instead of two. The stirrup straps became longer and allowed the vaquero to get a better knee-grip while riding. Because of the scarcity of European metal stirrups, the foot supports of the saddle were carved out of wood. The best ones were made of oak. Saddlebags began to appear, sometimes built onto the saddle, and leather skirts were nailed to the underside of the tree. These changes plus the addition of a larger saddlehorn created a lower center of gravity for the vaquero and provided better support and comfort. The modern stock saddle has not changed greatly from the configuration of the early vaquero's saddle (in Spanish, *silla vaquera*).

The saddlehorns on the first Spanish saddles brought to New Spain were small and of little use to the vaquero, who often tied one end of his *reata*, or rope, to the cinch of his saddle or to his horse's tail. The vaquero had no place else to put it, and using his lance to guide the loop or slipknot end over the horns of a cow, he did his job. But this method was crude, brutal to the horse, and slow. Saddlemakers added a larger saddlehorn. The top—4 to 6 inches across—was much broader than the base. A *reata* tied around the base of the larger saddlehorn could not slip off. The larger saddlehorn gave the vaquero a sturdy tie or anchor for his rope, especially after saddletrees were constructed of harder woods than the light cactus wood first used. This saved many a horse's tail.

The roping technique used with the large saddlehorn was called *da la vuelta*, meaning "to turn around." After tossing the rope around an animal the vaquero quickly tied and then wrapped his end of the rope around his saddlehorn. Later American cowboys north of the Rio Grande learned the technique, and shortened and corrupted its Spanish name to "dally" roping. The technique required much speed. Without quickness a vaquero could injure a hand, sometimes losing one or more fingers, even a thumb. Injury would occur when the vaquero caught his fingers between the rope and saddlehorn as he was circling or snubbing the rope around the horn. If he did not complete the job by the time the cow pulled the rope taut, the vaquero chanced catching his fingers between the rope and the horn or in the rope. In spite of the danger, *da la vuelta* was better than tying the rope hard and fast to the saddlehorn, cinch, or horse's tail. A tied rope could not slip and therefore might cause injury to the vaquero's horse if

the animal became tangled in the rope or was charged by a mad bull firmly
attached to the other end. With the rope snubbed around the saddlehorn,
it could slip enough so that any abrupt stops by a caught cow would be
eased. Then too, the vaquero could release the rope quickly should the
need arise.

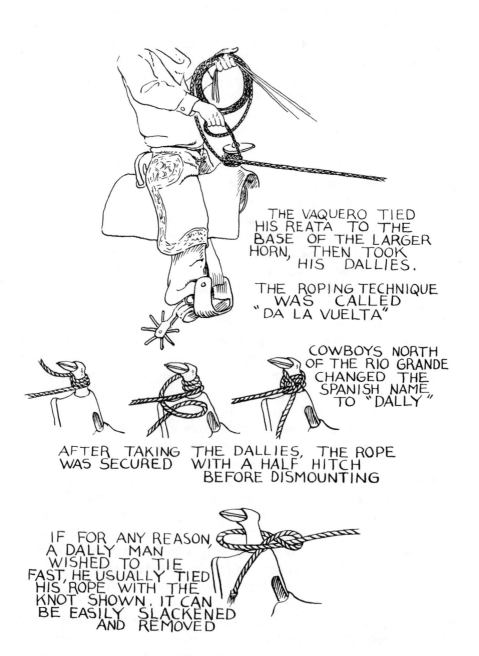

THE VAQUERO TIED
HIS REATA TO THE
BASE OF THE LARGER
HORN, THEN TOOK
HIS DALLIES.

THE ROPING TECHNIQUE
WAS CALLED
"DA LA VUELTA"

COWBOYS NORTH
OF THE RIO GRANDE
CHANGED THE
SPANISH NAME
TO "DALLY"

AFTER TAKING THE DALLIES, THE ROPE
WAS SECURED WITH A HALF HITCH
BEFORE DISMOUNTING

IF FOR ANY REASON,
A DALLY MAN
WISHED TO TIE
FAST, HE USUALLY TIED
HIS ROPE WITH THE
KNOT SHOWN. IT CAN
BE EASILY SLACKENED
AND REMOVED

The improved saddle enabled the vaquero to make more effective use of his *reata*. It appears that by the end of the seventeenth century most vaqueros had become so proficient with their ropes that they discarded their lances as regular tools with which to work cattle. Most vaqueros made their own ropes by braiding four to eight strands of rawhide together. The size of the finished product, of course, depended on the size of the strands and their number. In length, however, most *reatas* were about the same—60 feet long. But then there were *las reatas largas*—the long ropes. They ran from 65 to 110 feet or more in length. Jo Mora, who was born in Uruguay in 1876 and later lived the life of a cowboy in the American Southwest and California, wrote in 1949: "I have personally measured two of these incredibly long reatas largas, one was one hundred and five feet, the other one one hundred and nine feet. And I have seen descendants of those old-time vaqueros use eighty-five-foot reatas. Time and time again I have seen catches made at the full length which (allowing for a big loop, the wabble [sic] of the opening coils, and the loops for the dallies) would be, roughly speaking, about fifty-five or sixty feet."[4]

While 60 feet was and is about as far as a man can throw a lasso, 35 feet is considered good, with the average throw about 25 feet. Some accounts suggest that four-strand ropes were preferred by vaqueros because the strands on such ropes were generally wider and in turn stronger. When a vaquero wanted a new rope, he would get his knife, an awl, and a cowhide. Sticking the knife and the awl into a tree knot, and using the awl for a gauge, the vaquero slowly turned the cowhide into a single string by drawing the hide around and around against the edge of the knife. He then

SPANISH VAQUERO

trimmed off the hair. Trimming the hair last with a knife was apparently easier to do than stripping it from the full cowhide before it was cut. Next the strings were stretched and soaked. Further wetting allowed the braiding to be done while the strings were still damp and pliable. The completed rope was then stretched, oiled, and softened to the vaquero's liking. Rope-making, like saddlemaking, was and still is something of an art.

Originally the words *lazo* (lasso) and *lariat* meant different things. A lariat was a short rope used in picketing horses, especially when it was made of horsehair, while a *lazo* was a long rope with a slipknot, usually made of braided leather or rawhide. Today the words "lariat" and "lasso" are often used to identify the same thing: a cowboy's saddle rope. Both "lariat" and "lasso" are used as verbs, but the word *reata* has never been used as a verb, since it simply means "rope." California vaqueros, as late as the early twentieth century, preferred *lazo*, "lasso," or the words "lass rope," while cowboys in the American Southwest generally used the word "lariat" and later the English word "rope."

ONE MARVELS AT what the Spanish accomplished in cattle raising during their first century in New Spain, but then the land favored stock raising, especially in northern regions, and the people adapted to the land. Similar conditions favoring cattle raising were found in many areas of what is today the American Southwest—Arizona, New Mexico, and Texas. But once cattle raising was introduced into these areas, it did not grow at the same pace that it had to the south during the first hundred years following the conquest. The cattle did increase naturally, but New Spain lacked the population and resources necessary for the development of the northern frontier region. Thus the Spaniards turned to the mission system in an attempt to make Spanish colonists out of native Indians.

Missions were agencies of the crown as well as of the church. They were used to win converts and in turn secure the loyalty of the natives and the land for the crown. In frontier regions of New Spain, most missions were to be temporary. Once the missionaries firmly established the church, brought stability to the life of the converts, and ensured their loyalty to the church and crown, the missionaries were to turn over their mission to parish clergy and move on, repeating the process elsewhere. In the theory of church law, missionaries were given ten years at each mission. But along the northern frontier it soon became obvious that ten years was not sufficient. Many Indian tribes required a longer period of conversion. Unlike the more advanced Incas and Aztecs encountered far to the south, most Indians of the borderlands were primitive and even hostile. And by the time the Spanish introduced the mission system, many frontier Indians had already obtained horses. The Indian's possession of the horse not only occurred ahead of Spanish settlement in much of Texas, New Mexico, and Arizona, but the horse acted as a tonic for the Indians. It widened their horizons, much as a teen-ager's first automobile widens his. Exactly when and how the Indians of the northern borderlands obtained horses is still a matter of conjecture. Old documents contain numerous references as to when horses were *first reported* by the white man among the various tribes. Writers like Robert M. Denhardt, Francis Haines, Frank Gilbert Roe, J. Frank Dobie, and others have used such references in trying to explain the spread of the Spanish horse northward. Unfortunately, and most writers acknowledge the fact, the majority of first references are no more than first reports. They do not tell us when and how the various tribes obtained horses. Such questions may never be answered, although there is the possibility that additional documentation may be uncovered, perhaps in the provincial archives at Mexico City or Madrid.

There is little doubt, however, that the Apaches and Comanches were among the first tribes to obtain horses in what is now the American Southwest. Most authorities seem to agree with historian W. W. H. Davis's conclusion in his 1869 book *The Spanish Conquest of New Mexico* that horses were being used by Indians in conflicts with Spaniards by 1650. It appears that the Apaches and Comanches first obtained horses in trade or by stealing them from Spaniards or other Indian tribes. They preferred horses that were already broken for riding to the wild mustang that could be had for the catching. The importance of the horse to the Indian is obvious—it gave him mobility and style. And as Frank Gilbert Roe noted, Indians were quick to realize the combined potential of horse and rider and therefore were quick to master the equestrian arts.[5]

Some Indians in Texas undoubtedly had horses in 1659 when the Mission Nuestra Señora de la Guadalupe del Paso was founded south of present El Paso. The mission was located on the south bank of the Rio Grande in what is now Old Mexico. Yet because it helped to open the way for the establishment of missions in Texas, it is called the first mission *of* Texas. Father García de San Francisco founded the mission, and with the help of Indians, he built a church and a monastery of wood, mud, and clay mortar, the insides of which were plastered with lime whitewash. Most mission buildings on the frontier were constructed in this manner. Aside from Father García's association with Indians of the region, other Spaniards had little contact with the Indians in Texas until the 1680s. Although the crown had for decades claimed the area that is now Texas, the Spanish made no serious effort to occupy it until it was rumored that the French had established a settlement there. Captain Alonso de León, governor of Coahuila, and Father Damian Massanet were sent to investigate. They crossed and named the rivers Nueces, Sarco (Frio), Hondo, Medina, and

León (San Antonio) early in 1689, and soon learned that La Salle had established a French colony at Matagorda Bay. But they also learned that the colony had since been destroyed by hostile Indians. The first news of the destruction came from friendly Indians who greeted Captain de León and Father Massanet with the words "Thechas! Thechas!" Although the word meant "friends," Spaniards soon applied the name (they spelled it "Tejas") to all Indians in Texas. Later the early American colonizers corrupted the Spanish "Tejas" into "Texias" and called themselves "Texians." Still later the words became "Texas" and "Texans."[6]

Returning to Coahuila, Captain de León and Father Massanet reported that the French had been in the land of the Tejas. It was then decided that the two men should take another expedition into the region to see if other French settlements had been established, and at the same time to build a mission among the Tejas Indians. Early in 1690 the mission San Francisco de los Tejas was constructed on San Pedro Creek just northwest of present-day Weches in eastern Texas. Father Massanet and Captain de León brought supplies for the new mission and the first cattle of any consequence into what is today Texas.

Most accounts tell how Captain de León brought two hundred cattle and four hundred horses from Coahuila, but he reportedly left only twenty cows, two bulls, and nine horses at the new mission. On his return journey he took the remaining cattle and supposedly left "a bull and a cow, a stallion and a mare" at each of the various rivers crossed. This story appears in the diary of Fray Gaspar José de Solís, who heard it as he was inspecting Texas missions many years later, in 1767. He found "many Spanish cattle, unbranded and ownerless," and probably was told of Captain de León's efforts when he inquired about their origin.[7]

The story of Alonso de León's deliberately leaving seed stock along the streams between the Brazos and Trinity rivers to propagate reads much like a fairy tale. Yet some conjecture that it is probably true. Assuming it is, Alonso de León might be compared to John Chapman, who is better known today as Johnny Appleseed. But Captain de León's efforts—if the story is indeed accurate—were not solely responsible for the increase in Texas cattle during the late seventeenth and early eighteenth centuries. The expedition of Don Domingo Terán de los Ríos also brought cattle into Texas about a year later. How many head he brought is unknown, but numbers of them were lost through frequent stampedes as the troubled expedition pushed northeastward across Texas to reinforce missions. However they got there, Don Domingo's cattle, those brought by Alonso de León, and perhaps others brought into Texas before 1700 multiplied.

By the early eighteenth century large numbers of cattle could be found in Texas. Louis de Saint-Denis, a Frenchman sent ostensibly to open trade routes between Louisiana and Texas, saw many cattle as he crossed the region in 1714. That was two years before Texas was separated from Coahuila and made a separate province of New Spain. He saw five thousand head of cattle at the Mission Nuestra Señora del Rosario near Goliad and fifteen hundred yoke of oxen and five thousand head of sheep and goats at the Mission San Jose y San Miguel de Aguayo, where the city of San Antonio is located today. And Saint-Denis commented on the existence of private ranches along the banks of the Rio Grande between San Antonio and Bahía. The increase in cattle no doubt was due to natural propagation and the driving of more cattle into Texas from Coahuila and elsewhere to the south. The Marquis de Aguayo, for one, brought three hundred head of cattle to Texas in 1721.

Although I can find no documentary evidence, it appears the Franciscans in Texas began to teach their Indian neophytes how to work cattle around 1700. But the padres probably had only limited success. Indians in many areas of Texas shunned the fathers and their teachings. Some tribes in eastern Texas refused to submit to the discipline of Christianity and mission life, while to the west padres found missions among the Comanches and Apaches useless. The Mission San Saba, as an example, was established in April 1757 about 50 miles southeast of modern San Angelo, Texas. It was built in the heart of Comanche and Apache country. Nearby the Presidio San Saba was constructed, a strong and well-garrisoned fort. Weeks and months passed and no Indians came to live in the new mission. From time to time small bands of Indians would visit the mission and enjoy the liberal hospitality of the Franciscan padres, but they refused to stay.

The Franciscans heard rumors that Indians were gathering in great numbers in the north to attack the mission settlement, but nearly two years passed without any serious trouble. The rumors ceased to alarm the padres and the handful of soldiers at the nearby presidio. New rumors were heard in February 1759 of an impending attack, but the padres and soldiers passed them off as nothing. Then, in early March, many Indians were seen in the area and mission horses were stolen almost daily. On March 16, 1759, perhaps two thousand Indians led by several Apache chiefs stormed the mission. Armed with bows and arrows, lances, sabers, pikes, and old Spanish muskets, the Indians were dressed in war paint. Some of them fired their muskets into the air as they charged the mission.

The padres were quick to bar the doors to the mission stockade. The Indians stopped yelling and firing their rifles as they approached the barred gates. In broken Spanish some of them pretended friendship. One soldier inside the mission walls, recognizing some friendly Indians in the group, persuaded one of the padres to open the gates. That was a mistake. Before the day ended, the Indians had killed all except four Spaniards who fled to the nearby presidio, taken what plunder they could carry, and destroyed the mission. Even the mission cattle and five soldiers guarding them were slaughtered. The few soldiers at the presidio, no match for two thousand Indians, remained inside and prepared to do battle. But the Indians did not attack the presidio. They fled north.[8]

What success the padres had in converting the hostile Indians in Texas came from the hiring of Frenchmen, who were able to improve relations between the Spanish fathers and many of the Indians. Gradually the number of Indians submitting to mission life increased, and soon the fathers had selected a few of the more promising Indians to be vaqueros. In teaching them, the padres drew on their own experiences and perhaps those of seasoned vaqueros from missions far to the south. The fathers may have brought a few good stock saddles with them to their newly established missions, but more likely such saddles were constructed at the missions. Yet because of the scarcity of good Indian vaqueros in Texas, there is little doubt that many a Franciscan donned the spurs of the vaquero to work cattle on mission lands. This scarcity of competent vaqueros was to plague Texas missions and ranches into the early nineteenth century.

Records in the Béxar (San Antonio de Béxar) Archives at the University of Texas in Austin tell of cattle having been driven south from missions at Bahía and San Antonio to market in Coahuila in 1770. Francisco García of San Antonio apparently was the first Spaniard given official approval to export fifteen hundred to two thousand cattle to Louisiana in 1779. But it is almost certain that many Texas cattle, horses, and even mules were sold in Louisiana much earlier without official sanction. As early as 1768 the "English" were taking cattle out of East Texas and Louisiana in substantial numbers. It was much easier for Spaniards in East Texas to conduct trade with the French in early Louisiana than to go the much greater distance to San Antonio or into what is Old Mexico. Cattle and other livestock sold in Louisiana usually were driven to market in the autumn, when rivers were fordable and pastures good. The herds driven through the Indian-infested piny woods of East Texas and Louisiana generally were kept small for the purpose of control and to reduce pilfering by Indians. During 1761, a year before France ceded Louisiana to Spain to prevent it from falling into British hands, French records indicate the "interlope trade" with the Spanish amounted to $60,000 worth of goods taken from Louisiana.[9]

Even before Spain actually took over the administration of Louisiana in 1765, the crown had begun to follow the growth of Texas trade with much interest. With Louisiana under Spanish rule, trade restrictions were relaxed. And in what appears to have been an effort to gain a firm grip on Texas and the other northern provinces, the crown unified the territories of Texas, New Mexico, Arizona, and the northern provinces of Mexico under the name Las Provincias Internas. Theodore de Croix was put in

charge of the region, with orders to report directly to the king. He soon
set out to inspect the northern borderlands.

In Texas, Croix was impressed by the large herds of unbranded cattle.
Aware of the crown's hunger for increased revenue, he hit early in 1778
upon the idea of claiming all unbranded stock—even the offspring of animals owned and branded by ranches and missions—as crown property.
But he gave the stock owners four months to corral and brand their animals before the crown took title to all stock left unbranded. Thereafter,
Croix decreed, citizens who wished to round up and brand wild cattle
would pay a tax of four silver reals per head. The tax on wild horses was
six reals per animal, but later was lowered to two reals, since Croix believed wild horses were more difficult to capture than wild cattle.

At the same time Croix ordered each cattle raiser to have a different
brand and to register his brand with the governor. Croix said he would
use such information to compile a brand register which would be kept
up-to-date. The register would be used to show the number of animals
branded, killed, or sold. And he also included provisions relating to the
handling of lost animals, recovered property, and rustlers. Spanish criminal
law in Texas, based on royal ordinances, called for the death penalty for
anyone who stole twelve goats or sheep, five horses or hogs, or cattle of
comparable value.

Croix's decrees strongly suggest that before 1778 the crown had not
attempted to establish the Mesta in Texas. Of course, settlement had been
slow. By 1778 there were only three thousand colonists in all of Texas.
Some had settled in the area from San Antonio southward along the San
Antonio River to La Bahía. Others had settled in the Rio Grande–Nueces
valley and in the area around Nacogdoches in east Texas. Hubert H.
Bancroft, in his late-nineteenth-century book *North Mexican States*, indi-
cates that cattle on all mission lands totaled about 25,000 head by 1780, and
in all of Texas there may have been 100,000 head of cattle. Interestingly,
some ninety years later, Texans would drive in one year (1869) more
than three times that total number to the railhead market of Abilene,
Kansas.

The orders issued by Croix read much like the Mesta regulations
adopted at Mexico City in the sixteenth century. Croix apparently believed
that his orders—they were subject to the king's approval—would reduce
thefts by rustlers and Indians and would encourage settlers to make better
use of the wild cattle. At the same time he obviously hoped his orders
would bring additional revenue to the royal treasury. Croix was wrong
on several counts. While most cattle raisers probably were pleased with
the orders relating to the return of lost animals and the punishment of
rustlers (Spaniards and Indians alike), they no doubt grumbled at having

to corral and brand their cattle. And they strongly opposed the tax on unbranded cattle and horses. To pay a tax on colts and calves produced by their own animals was not right, they said. The padres complained openly while the ranchers sent petitions through the clumsy channels of communication to Spain protesting what they called the usurpation of private property.

In 1785, seven years after Croix issued his decrees, Fray José Franco López conducted an inspection tour of Texas missions. He reported that the missionaries and their charges were suffering from the tax, which forbade their eating what was "unquestionably theirs, that is, the cattle born of their own branded herds and in their pastures and ranches." Cattle, he added, constituted the principal wealth of Texas. And he pointed out that wild Indians, soldiers, and settlers paid little attention to the orders and had slaughtered cattle for meat, hides, and tallow. Fray López noted that revenue from the sale of unbranded cattle should have exceeded 25,000 pesos between 1778 and 1785, but the actual revenue totaled only six or seven thousand pesos. If the herds could be restored, he concluded, the missions would regain their former prosperity.[10]

Whether Fray López's report or the ranchers' petitions or both reached the king is unknown, but early in 1786 word reached Croix that the king had revoked his orders. A council was called in Mexico City to discuss the problem of wild cattle and horses in Texas and to settle the question of their ownership. It took the council nine years to reach a decision: in 1795, it decreed that Texas ranchers were free to do as they chose with the wild cattle and horses, and all Spaniards in Texas were free from debts owed to the crown for animals caught while Croix's orders were in force. But—and here the council was eyeing the royal treasury—it also issued a new code that was nothing more than a slight revision of Croix's 1778 orders. This new code read, in part: "No one is to catch cattle without a license, paying four reals per head for cattle and two reals per head for horses." And the council directed that anyone wishing to sell meat had to first obtain a permit to do so. If buyers were not shown the permit by the seller, they were expected to report the seller to authorities. This was an obvious attempt to encourage Texans to enforce the new code. And the council made it profitable to report violations. "Anyone denouncing a person selling meat in town without a permit or killing cattle in the fields without a license will receive half the fine levied against such malefactors," it declared.[11]

As the eighteenth century drew to a close, Texas cattle raisers were confronted with extensive government controls, the lack of competent vaqueros, numerous rustlers and hostile Indians, and a more primitive environment than that encountered by ranchers far to the south in Old

Mexico. Yet ranches, especially those in what is today south Texas, managed to flourish, and cattle continued to multiply in spite of rustlers and Indian raids. Some observers noted that if it had not been for the numerous thefts by Indians, cattle would have become so numerous as to be worthless. The Indians thus helped to keep the supply in balance with the demand—and the groundwork was thereby laid for what would become the nineteenth-century Texas cattle empire.

To the west of Texas province, the seventeenth-century Spanish advancement into what is today Arizona and New Mexico was just as sluggish as it first had been in Texas. By 1630 perhaps fifty padres were at work in twenty-five missions in New Mexico. Although Juan de Oñate brought cattle with him when he colonized the region, they did not increase extensively, as Texas cattle had. Apache raids, drought, and a violent struggle between civil and ecclesiastical officials weakened Spanish settlement of New Mexico during the seventeenth century. Although the Spanish regained control of the region later in the 1600s, cattle ranching grew at a slow pace until the nineteenth century. Even then, New Mexico proved to be better sheep than cattle country.

In Arizona cattle ranching had a better start. Father Eusebio Francisco Kino established cattle raising among the Indians in the valleys south of the Gila River in 1687. This area was part of what was then called Pimeria Alta (northern Sonora and southern Arizona). Here he established many missions among the Pima and Yuma Indians. It is said he baptized more than four thousand converts. Father Kino, an experienced rancher, had established a cattle-breeding ranch at his first mission in Old Mexico. From there he brought hundreds of cattle and sheep to his missions in Arizona. And just as missionaries in Texas were then seeking to do, Father Kino taught his converts how to breed and care for cattle. He introduced the tools of the vaquero: the rope, spurs, stock saddle, and branding iron. And he taught his Indian vaqueros how to use these tools effectively. In truth, Father Kino may have had more success with the Indians than the padres in Texas during the late seventeenth century. Of his contribution, historian Herbert E. Bolton has written: "He was easily the cattle king of his day and region. . . . Within fifteen years he established the beginnings of ranching in the valleys of the Santa Cruz, the San Pedro, and the Sonoita. The stock-raising industry of nearly twenty places on the modern map owes its beginnings on a considerable scale to this indefatigable man."[12]

Father Kino had much success in spite of hostile Apaches, who resented the white man's efforts to Christianize the region south of the

Gila. They stole cattle and horses and often raided missions and nearby ranches. Unfortunately, the actions of a few Spaniards caused serious problems among some of Father Kino's converts. Early in 1695, the Pima Indians in Altar Valley killed several persons and burned missions and ranches in the Altar and Magdalena valleys. The revolt was sparked by a Spanish official who had whipped the Indians for some minor offenses. The Pimas ran off many cattle and horses. Another time a Spanish military official killed three Indians and flogged others. The officer had found some meat in an Indian camp and thought it was stolen beef. It was venison.

Father Kino renewed his efforts and made considerable progress until his death in 1711. During the twenty years that followed, the Spanish did little to carry on his work. Mission Indians became more independent of and disrespectful toward Spanish authority and mission life. In 1731, two Jesuit missionaries entered Arizona and tried to take up where Father Kino had left off. But they had a difficult time, as did other Jesuits, who appear to have placed personal gain first in many instances. A Pima Indian revolt in 1751 brought greater problems to the Spanish, who in 1767 expelled the Jesuits from all of New Spain and confiscated their property. The viceroy of New Spain later wrote of the Jesuits: "There is no reason to doubt that they either wasted or embezzled the rich temporalities of all or most of the missions, and that these funds were lost, and decadence or ruin could not be prevented."[13]

Franciscan padres later replaced the Jesuits in northern Sonora (Arizona) and elsewhere in New Spain, but it was not until Spanish authorities aided the Franciscans with soldiers and money that conditions improved. Hostile Apaches were pacified by gifts and rations late in the eighteenth century. By 1790, the region was entering what has often been called the "golden age of Pimeria Alta." Mines were discovered, land grants were issued at the Sonoran capital at Arizpe, and cattle haciendas prospered. There was a demand for meat and hides among the miners and soldiers who quieted the troublesome Apaches. But following the Mexican revolution early in the nineteenth century, conditions in the region worsened. The money from Mexico City became inadequate to provide gifts and rations to the Indians. There was political turmoil, and taxes went uncollected. The Apaches again became hostile and drove miners, ranchers, and the Franciscan padres from the land. The cattle industry in what is now Arizona died soon after Mexican independence, and it was not revived until late in the nineteenth century.[14]

CHAPTER 3

The Californiano Culture

*Cattle ranching was the Californiano's preferred—his sole
—occupation for the first hundred years. . . . Indeed, from
1769 until the turn of the present century, cattle raising was
the most important industry in California.*

—ARNOLD R. ROJAS[1]

CALIFORNIA, like Texas, was far from the seat of authority in Mexico City. Although it was claimed by the Spanish, they made no serious effort to occupy California until, as had been the case with Texas, it appeared another nation was attracted to the area. Russians sailing down the coast from Alaska were looking with interest at California. Then, too, the British in western Canada were eyeing the region. The concerned Spanish crown ordered Captain Gaspar de Portolá, governor of Baja (Lower) California, to establish presidios and missions to the north along the coast of Upper California.[2]

Cattle, horses, and mules were in short supply in Lower California, but missions donated what stock they could spare. About two hundred cattle, "most of them cows with their calves," forty-five horses, 140 mules for saddle and pack stock, and two jennies were gathered from missions along the trail as an expedition pushed northward from Loreto, a settlement about 200 miles north of the southern tip of Lower California. Meanwhile, two ships set sail north early in 1769, one reportedly bringing the first cattle to California, perhaps six or seven head. The other cattle and livestock, including the first horses to reach California, were driven overland through 600 miles of deserts and rugged mountainous terrain. The overland expedition reached San Diego in May 1769 and linked up with those who had come by sea.

How many cattle survived the overland journey is not known, but many undoubtedly reached San Diego. They were pure descendants of Spanish cattle taken to Lower California from Sonora late in the seventeenth century. The horsemen who drove the cattle north may have been vaqueros who volunteered for the expedition or *soldados de cuero*— soldiers of leather—some of whom may once have been vaqueros. In Lower California and elsewhere in the hot land of New Spain, such soldiers had much earlier discarded their heavy metal armor and replaced it with sleeveless leather jackets. These jackets had several thicknesses and were quilted to cushion blows and lessen penetration of bullets or arrows. On their legs they wore *chaparreras*, chaps made of leather. And dangling down on either side from their saddlebows were two large slabs of cowhide, called *armas*, which served much the same purpose as the chaps, protecting the rider's thighs and lower legs from cactus and other thorny brush. They had been devised by seventeenth-century vaqueros in the thorny-scrub country from Guerrero and Michoacán to Sonora and Lower California. Later, in California and Sonora, vaqueros would modify the *armas* and create *armitas*, lightweight chaps, usually made of heavy buckskin. These would hang from a belt around the waist and extend down the vaquero's front legs to below his knees. Rawhide thongs would hold these chaps to the legs. Still later, variations would include *chaparejos*, leather breeches that fully encircled the vaquero's legs.

Soon after arriving in California the Spanish soldiers constructed a presidio, or fort, at San Diego. And the padres began to establish a mission under the direction of Father Junípero Serra, a Franciscan who later introduced agricultural methods and stock raising to the Indians. Before his death in 1784, Father Serra would personally establish a total of nine missions in California. Today he is as well known in California as Father Kino is in Arizona. (Statues of both men are in the National Statuary Hall at the U.S. Capitol in Washington, D.C.)

The Spanish were impressed with the richness of the California land. The fine grasslands along the coast were ideally suited for cattle grazing. The expedition of Captain Gaspar de Portolá, traveling about 1770 between San Diego and what is today San Francisco, left many records attesting to this. One account, written by Fray Juan Crespi on January 4, 1770, noted: "The country is delightful for it is covered with beautiful grass which affords excellent pasture for the animals."[3]

Three other Spanish missions were soon established—San Antonio and San Gabriel in 1771 and San Luis Obispo in 1772. By 1773 there were five missions in California, although each had less than fifty head of cattle. The presidios or forts—only four were built in California—probably had small herds of cattle to provide food for the soldiers and officers.[4] The cattle population in California was small, but it nearly doubled three years later when Juan Bautista de Anza's expedition of 240 people, many of them colonists recruited from Sonora and Sinaloa, brought about 350 head of

cattle and nearly seven hundred horses to California. The expedition came
overland from the presidio at Tubac, south of modern Tucson, Arizona.

The early presidios in California were nothing more than crude log
stockades that provided protection from Indian arrows. By about 1800,
walls of stone and adobe had replaced the early wooden exteriors, and each
presidio had at least one shore battery on a high point where it could fire
upon hostile ships in the harbors near which all presidios were located. The
presidio at San Diego, the first built in California, played an important role
in Father Serra's efforts in the 1770s to Christianize the Indians in the
vicinity of San Diego. When he found them unfriendly, armed soldiers·
from the presidio were called upon to stop the hostilities and convince the
Indians that they should listen to the padre.

Communication in the late eighteenth century was slow by modern
standards, but it was essential if Father Serra and the Spanish soldiers were
to maintain their foothold in California. Mexico City was a long way
away. By 1776, Father Serra was arguing the need for a monthly courier
from California to the Mexican capital. He also proposed a plan to improve
communications within California while at the same time helping to spread
the gospel. He expressed his thoughts on both matters in a little-known
letter, dated July 27, 1776, to Captain Don Fernando de Rivera y Moncada,
a Spanish commandant:

For the time being, it seems to me advisable that the Most Excellent
Lord might content himself with sending a courier from the Presidio
at San Diego on the first of every month, for the frontiers of Old
California. This should be done, whether or not there are letters to be
forwarded from Monterey and San Francisco. In this way they will
be able to hear with some sort of regularity from these parts, and
letters from farther north will reach them whenever the opportunity
makes it possible. In this I can see no major obstacle, especially for
those who have had experience; the journey, for a mail carrier, is one
of three or four days. But to have to make the trip every month from
the Port of San Francisco—then I grant you that all the difficulties
you mention in your letter, and put before me, are to be faced. Most
assuredly it would be of the greatest assistance in making less difficult—
or had I not better say in totally removing—the most serious obstacle,
if there were put into effect one of my favorite old desires.

These desires, which were great and are now even greater, have
been and are that the Presidio here at San Diego, and the one at Monterey should be joined together by completing a chain of missions,
twenty-five leagues distant one from the other, both for the propagation of the Faith, as the chief purpose, and also for the convenience of

travellers, as well as to strengthen the peaceful dispositions of the peoples along the way. . . . By taking this simple line of action, couriers from Monterey to San Diego could sleep, every night, in Christian pueblos, and in places that are well defended. In this way, it would not be necessary to expose their tired animals to the whims of the gentiles [Indians], with every chance of losing them, nor would they be constantly exposed to an outbreak on the part of the said gentiles during their repeated journeyings. On the other hand, there would be the advantages that spring readily to the mind. But, without such precautions, I feel very much afraid in regard to the constant passing to and fro of our men through that ill-omened, yet fascinating, Santa Barbara Channel.[5]

The missions proposed by Father Serra were built. He personally established nine of the twenty-one Franciscan missions, which ran from San Diego to Sonoma. These missions, about 30 miles apart, were separated by about a day's travel on horseback. Serra, however, died in 1784 before all of the missions were completed.

FORTUNATELY FOR THE SPANIARDS during the latter half of the eighteenth century, the Indians in California did not have horses. In all probability, these California Indians never saw a horse until the Spanish arrived with their steeds. The Indians' reaction on first seeing such creatures probably was similar to that of Indians decades earlier when Cortés and his followers brought the first horses to New Spain. It is not surprising that the Spanish in California adhered to the law that no Indian should be allowed to own or ride a horse. By the late eighteenth century they knew from experience that unfriendly mounted Indians could cause serious trouble.

Initially, the few vaqueros who arrived in California with cattle could handle the animals with ease. These cattle were quite tame, having been in nearly constant contact with humans since they were first headed north. The vaqueros found it easy to corral the cattle at night and to herd them near the missions during the day. But as the cattle population increased, and missions had to loose their cattle on open ranges to provide sufficient grass, there were not enough vaqueros to handle them. Many of the animals born on the open ranges became wild. By the eighteenth century the padres had no choice but to train some of their Indian converts to be vaqueros. In turn the Spanish authorities, realizing the need, ignored the law forbidding Indians to ride horses.

The Franciscan padres were experienced in dealing with Indians. Their method of Christianizing friendly Indians had been tested elsewhere in

New Spain: They began by selecting the most promising Indians and giving each a blanket. If it was lost, torn, or worn out within a year, the Indian would be given a new blanket. Each Indian male also was given a new *taparrabo* (breechcloth) and a twilled cloth blouse. While the padres taught the Spanish language to the new recruits (often they first had to learn the Indians' language) they would look for Indians who might make good vaqueros. Strength and endurance were important, but since the work of the vaquero would take him many miles from the mission and the watchful eyes of the padres, they sought men who could be trusted with the cattle and, especially, the horses. By the time the padres began to train converts as vaqueros in California, the Indians had developed a fondness for beefsteak and a greater love of horsemeat. To them the steak of a horse was a delicacy. Needless to say, the padres wanted to avoid selecting Indians for vaquero training who might prefer their horseflesh inside of them instead of underneath. Once Indians were tested and selected, they were taught the art of roping, how to hobble, throw, and saddle a horse, and how to use a hackamore.

The word "hackamore" is a corruption of the Spanish word *jáquima* (*hah*-ke-mah), meaning a halter. The early hackamores were made of a braided rawhide noseband or *bosal* with two leather strips, one on each side of the horse's head, that acted as cheek plates. The cheek plates were very close to the horse's eyes. They ran down from the top of the head where they were attached to a light leather headstall and a braided rope running around the horse's neck. The cheek plates were attached high on the noseband at the two extremes of the nose button, the extra braiding on the top of the noseband. The ends of the noseband came together under the horse's chin. At that point the reins were tied. The reins were made of a horsehair rope, called *mecate* in Spanish. (American cowboys later corrupted this word and called the *mecate* a "McCarty.") Many early Indian vaqueros in California used hackamores until Spanish bits became plentiful, but even then some of them preferred hackamores to bits.

Most early vaqueros in California made no effort to tame horses until the animals were three or older. Although horses born to rancho herds were captured and branded early, no attempt was made to break the animals at that time. When the time did come, vaqueros usually roped the horse by the front feet and threw it to the ground. Next the hackamore was put on the horse's head. A 1-inch cotton rope was then tied around the neck and run through the base of the hackamore under the horse's chin. The other end was tied to a tree or stout post. The horse, not liking the restraint, was then allowed to fight it out. There was usually about 20 feet of rope. "Generally it was a real fight," recalled H. T. Lilliencrantz, an early California ranchero, who broke countless wild horses. He wrote that the horse "would pull back, sometimes until he fell; jump forward,

A HACKAMORE (*jáquima*)

get a front foot over the rope, squeal with rage, trying to get free. He would be sure, before a great while, to straddle until he fell. The harder he fought the more complete was his final submission."[6]

A horse might struggle for two days before giving up. All of the time someone would keep a watch on the animal. By then his neck was sore and nothing would induce him to pull back on the rope. The horse's hind legs would be sore too, and a vaquero could tie a hind foot to the shoulder with ease. This is known as "side lining" a horse. When a horse accepted this without protest, he was broken and ready for the first saddle. Most horses broken in this manner offered little resistance and would respond readily to the hackamore. The rider's control in turning and stopping the horse was quickly established.

Using a hackamore to break a horse for riding created, in the eyes of most California vaqueros, a soft-mouthed horse. By about 1800 it was a standard practice in California to use a hackamore until a horse was well trained. Then, and only then, would vaqueros consider using a bit in the horse's mouth. The opposite was true to the east on the Great Plains, where bits were and still are used in breaking horses. Cowboys on the plains used the hackamore only on experienced horses, if at all. There was also another difference: Vaqueros in California, and later in Oregon and Nevada, believed a low noseband could shut off a horse's wind and thereby cause the animal to get in the habit of throwing his head. Cowboys on the plains, however, set the noseband low, almost to the horse's nostrils, because their animals were broken with bits and not hackamores.

The hackamore probably was developed in the New World by

Spaniards who needed to control wild horses but did not want to use bits that would tear up the horses' mouths. Bits, of course, were brought to New Spain by the Spaniards. The bit—a metal bar that fits into a horse's mouth—functions as a lever. With the reins attached to the bit, the rider can control and direct the horse.

Who created the first bit and when is unknown, but bits have been around for centuries. The Moors took them to Spain in the eighth century, and three hundred years later the Crusaders met the Saracens riding horses with curb bits in Palestine. A curb bit, as the name implies, has an upward curve in the center of the mouthpiece. It is just one of many kinds of bits that have been used by horsemen through the years.

The Indian vaqueros in California, as elsewhere in New Spain, also were taught how to build a branding fire, how to keep the branding irons hot and apply a brand, and how to earmark a calf. By the eighteenth century, brands and earmarks were used on horses as well, although the earlier Mesta regulations had outlawed earmarks for a time. A brand might be a single letter, insignia, figure, or combination of any or all three. They were applied in one of five positions: "either naturally, upside down, at a forty-five degree angle known as 'tumbling,' horizontally and termed 'lazy,' or, finally, reversed. Brands are always read from top to bottom and from left to right. When letters are joined, they are called 'connected.' "[7]

These brand positions, applied to horses and cattle more than a century ago, are still used today in most regions of the American West. The early mission brands in California used either letters of the mission name or some figure with religious significance. Presidios all used the same type of brands: each chose a combination of one numeral and one letter of the alphabet such as "2a" or "3c" or "4b." The brand "2a," for instance, was used by the San Diego presidio.

By the middle 1830s, some vaqueros who had proved their skills in horsemanship, branding, and roping were taken from the mission ranges and apprenticed, by consent of the local military authorities, to the blacksmiths at one of the four California presidios. There they learned the art of horseshoeing and working with iron, including the making of branding irons. In time some vaqueros became saddlemakers. By the 1830s saddlemaking was well under way in California, although the first saddles were crude. They were simple affairs constructed of rawhide-covered skeleton trees with open seats. Vaqueros at missions in Texas and northern Mexico used similar saddles late in the eighteenth century. They were lashed together with rawhide thongs, had no skirts or other trappings, and were held on the horse's back by a surcingle or bellyband that ran over the seat of the saddle. The stirrups were carved wood blocks. Sometimes Indian vaqueros would place a blanket, animal skin, or piece of leather over the seat to provide a little comfort. Only after California craftsmen received instruction from expert *talabarteros* (saddlemakers) brought from what is now Mexico did the quality of saddles improve. By the middle nineteenth century they had created what became known as the "California saddle."

One nineteenth-century writer observed that the merits of this saddle "consist in its being light, strong, and compact, and conforming well to the shape of the horse." He added:

> When strapped on, it rests so firmly in position that the strongest pull of a horse upon a lariat attached to the pommel can not displace it. Its shape is such that the rider is compelled to sit nearly erect, with his legs on the continuation of the line of the body, which makes his seat more secure, and, at the same time, gives him a better control over his arms and horse. The position is attained by setting the stirrup-leathers farther back than on the old-fashioned saddle. The pommel is high, like the Mexican saddle, and prevents the rider from being thrown forward. The tree is covered with raw hide, put on green, and sewed; when this dries and contracts it gives it great strength. It has no iron in its composition, but is kept together by buckskin strings, and can easily be taken to pieces for mending or cleaning. It has a hair girth about five inches wide. The whole saddle is covered with a large and thick sheet of sole-leather, having a hole to lay over the pommel; it extends back over the horse's hips, and protects them from rain, and when taken off in camp it furnishes a good security against dampness when placed under the traveler's bed. The California saddle-tree is regarded by many as the best of all others for the horse's back, and as having an easier seat than the Mexican.[8]

The saddle-covering described was called a *mochila* and was used later by the Pony Express riders of the mid-nineteenth century. They could easily remove the *mochila* from one horse and toss it on a fresh mount fitted with another saddletree. It took only seconds. Two pouches on each side of the *mochila* held the mail.

WHEN THE MISSION HERDS began to increase in the 1770s, the crown began providing enormous tracts of grazing land for the cattle. By 1800 the padres had a monopoly on cattle ranching in California. Since cattle raising was the only industry in the region, the mission padres controlled the economy. But this was not to last. In 1786 the crown gave Juan José Domínquez, Manuel Nieto, and the sons of "the widow Ignacio Carrillo" individual grants of land for cattle grazing. They became the first private cattle ranchers in California.

History tells us very little about the sons of Ignacio Carrillo, but Manuel Nieto was a soldier. He established and built his cattle herds while soldiering. When he retired from the army in 1795, Nieto spent his remaining years on the land grant known as Rancho Santa Gertrudes. His original grant included nearly 300,000 acres stretching from near Long Beach harbor 25 miles down the coast, but because it overlapped with the lands of the Mission San Gabriel, his actual holdings by 1800 amounted to only 150,000 acres. Still, that was a sizable chunk of California. On his ranch he raised "great numbers of horses and cattle, fifteen or twenty thousand or more." Nieto died in 1804, the wealthiest man in the province.

The grant of land given to Juan José Domínquez was not as large as Nieto's, only about 75,000 acres. It was known as the Rancho de Domínquez, or the Rancho of San Pedro of the Cove. His ranch house on the San Pedro River was constructed of adobe with an earthen floor, but Juan José himself did not live there until late in his life. He spent his days at the Presidio in San Diego and had a *mayordomo*, or manager, run his ranch. Even after he did move there, he neglected the ranch and let the cattle go unbranded. He also failed to "properly herd his brood mares, and they became wild and many horses of the San Gabriel joined them so that . . . there were thousands of wild horses on the plains, to the great detriment of the Mission and other owners of stock.⁹ In 1809, at the age of ninety, Juan José died at the Mission San Juan Capistrano.

Between 1786 and the early 1820s, the crown made about twenty private land grants for cattle raising. The authorities said the grants could not encroach upon the water, pastures, wood, and timber allotted to pueblos or towns. And from the beginning, those people receiving grants were expected to build a stone house upon the land, stock the land with at least two thousand head of cattle, and provide enough vaqueros to prevent the stock from wandering. Not all people receiving grants did these things. Many grants were not developed for cattle raising.

Until the early 1820s, these private ranchos grew slowly and made no substantial dent in an economy that was still controlled by the mission padres and their very large cattle herds. Then something happened that eventually changed the ranching industry of California. Agustín de Iturbide, a Mexican army officer working for the Spaniards, was sent on an expedition to crush rebels who were revolting against Spanish rule in New Spain. Instead of fighting the rebels, Iturbide made himself their leader and freed all of Mexico. On February 21, 1821, Mexico proclaimed independence from Spain.¹⁰

Changes were slow in coming to far-off California, but they came. In 1826 a group of influential Californians demanded that the new government in Mexico City restore to the public domain the land held by the twenty-one missions. The government, going through many changes in

Mexico City, eventually agreed, and the era of wealthy missions along El Camino Real—"The King's Highway"—came to an end. The Secularization Act of 1833, actively pressed beginning in 1836, saw the government generously distribute land to private petitioners. But by then the padres had already begun to save what they could from their condemned missions with their flourishing herds of cattle and other livestock. As one writer noted in the early 1880s: "With nothing to hope for, and but a limited time in which to act, a general slaughter of cattle for the hides took place. The slaughter was conducted in the most expeditious manner possible."[11]

Figures from two sources indicate that California's twenty-one missions owned at least 535,000 cattle about 1830; 423,000 cattle by 1834; but only 28,220 cattle by 1842. These figures suggest that more than 394,000 cattle were slaughtered for their hides and tallow. The mission-by-mission breakdown is:

Numbers of Cattle[12]

Mission	Incomplete figures for about 1830	Complete figures 1834	1842
San Diego	15,000	12,000	20
San Luis Rey	60,000	80,000	2,000
San Juan Capistrano	20,000	70,000	500
San Gabriel	80,000	105,000	700
San Fernando	50,000	14,000	1,500
San Buenaventura	25,000	4,000	200
Santa Barbara	20,000	5,000	1,800
Santa Inez	20,000	14,000	10,000
La Purisima Concepcion	20,000	15,000	800
San Luis Obispo	?	9,000	300
San Miguel	35,000	4,000	40
San Antonio	10,000	12,000	800
Soledad	25,000	6,000	none
Carmelo	?	3,000	none
San Juan Bautista	60,000	9,000	none
Santa Cruz	?	8,000	none
Santa Clara	65,000	13,000	1,500
San José	?	24,000	8,000
Dolores de San Francisco	30,000 (Sonoma)	5,000	60
San Rafael	?	3,000	none
San Francisco Solano	?	8,000	none
	535,000	423,000	28,220

While it is likely that some mission cattle may have been sold to private ranchos, most cattle probably were slaughtered for their hides and tallow. The large numbers of cattle recorded at a few missions in 1834 suggest that these missions (San Luis Rey, San Juan Capistrano, San Gabriel, San Fernando, Santa Inez, Santa Clara, and San José) may have had more vaqueros than the others. Vaqueros did the slaughtering and the missions profited from the sale of hides and tallow. One estimate of the amount of this trade was made by William H. Davis, an American who married a Spanish woman and made California his home between 1838 and his death in 1909. Davis wrote in his book *Seventy-Five Years in California*, published in 1889, that between the years 1831 and 1848, perhaps 1,250,000 hides and more than 62,500,000 pounds of tallow were exported from California. Nearly all of the hides and tallow were shipped to Boston and other New England ports. Assuming Davis's figures are correct, and assuming each hide was valued at $2, the hide trade alone amounted to $2,500,000 during the eighteen-year period mentioned by Davis. Much of that profit went to the missions while their lands were being taken by the government and distributed to private citizens.

The California hide-and-tallow trade is vividly portrayed by Richard Henry Dana in his classic *Two Years Before the Mast*, first published in 1840. Dana, who left Harvard College for reasons of health, became a sailor and sailed around Cape Horn to California in 1834. He wrote of the Californians: "The truth is, they have no credit system, no banks, and no way of investing money but in cattle. Besides silver, they have no circulating medium but hides, which the sailors call 'California bank-notes.' Everything that they buy they must pay for by one or the other of these means."

Dana and a few other early writers have described how cattle were slaughtered for their hides and tallow beginning each year in early July. The process, called *matanza*, lasted until October. William H. Davis described how during the spring rodeo, or roundup, the vaqueros would drive the cattle to be killed to a spot on a ranch "near a brook or forest. It was usual to slaughter from fifty to one hundred at a time, generally steers three years old and upward, the cows being kept for breeding purposes." (The general rule on private ranchos was to preserve one bull for every twenty-three cows, but at mission ranchos the Indian vaqueros were often more careless in the management of stock and allowed large numbers of bulls to grow up without castration. This naturally increased the cattle population.)

A vaquero would rope a steer in the corral and lead or drag the animal outside, where another vaquero would lasso "one or both hind legs" and thereby throw the animal to the ground. With two ropes holding the steer, each from opposite directions, a vaquero would tie "the forelegs of the animal together with an extra piece of rope, and the hind legs also, drawing all the feet together in a bunch and tying them." Once the downed animal was securely tied, the *reatas* that first caught the creature would be taken off and the man on foot would stick a knife in the animal's neck. When the animal had bled to death, two vaqueros on foot removed the skin or hide in a short time, "not over half an hour, so expert were they at the business," wrote Davis.

Davis added that the killing of cattle lying flat on the ground "preserved a great deal more of the blood in the meat" than the method used during the late nineteenth century and even today in the United States. "The meat was therefore sweeter and more nutritious than if the blood had been drained as much as possible."

Once the hide was removed, holes were cut in the ends and it was staked out to dry in the sun. Meanwhile, the tallow or fat lying nearest to the bullock's hide was removed; this usually amounted to seventy-five or a hundred pounds. After the fat was cooked in huge metal vats (obtained from the Yankee traders) and liquefied, it was placed in bags made of hides and used in trade. The interior fat, perhaps forty or fifty pounds, was saved for domestic cooking use. Californians preferred the fat of cattle to that of hogs. Later, much of this tallow would be sold and made into soap. Two hundred pounds of the best meat was next removed from the carcass of each animal and made into *carne seca*, jerky. The meat was cut into strips about an inch thick, perhaps 6 inches wide, and from 12 to 36 inches long. It was then dipped in brine and hung on a *reata* to dry in the hot sun. Every twenty-four hours it was turned. In four or five days the meat—hard, black, and dry—was made into fifty-pound bales, bound together with rawhide, and stored in a cool, dry place until needed. The balance of each animal was left on the killing grounds to be devoured by the buzzards, grizzly bears, and other wild animals. These places of killing were known as *calaveras*, "(places of) skulls." They were littered with the bleached bones and skulls of cattle for years afterward.

Once the hides were dry, they were doubled once, lengthwise, usually with the hair inside. Then they were sent to the coast on the backs of mules or in carts and placed in piles above the high-water mark. When a Yankee trading vessel arrived and the captain and Californians had come to a business agreement, sailors would, as Richard Dana wrote, "take them upon our heads, one at a time, or two, if they were small, and wade out with them and throw them into the boat, which, as there are no wharves, we usually keep anchored by a small kedge . . . just outside the surf."

Ships would spend many months going up and down the coast trading for hides and tallow at San Pedro, Santa Barbara, San Luis Obispo, San Simeon, Monterey, Santa Cruz, and Yerba Buena (San Francisco). The Yankee traders would exchange goods for the hides. When their vessels were full, they sailed back down the coast to San Diego and deposited their collection of green hides and tallow in a company warehouse. There the hides were soaked up to forty-eight hours in large vats of brine to preserve them against moths and other insects. Sailors from the ships assigned to warehouse duty then spread the hides on the sandy beaches to dry. Later the hides were hung on ropes and beaten by the sailors, using wooden sticks perhaps 3 or 4 feet long with strips of hide attached to the ends, to remove the dust and sand. Afterward the hides were folded and stored in the warehouses until ships were ready to leave for Boston or other ports.

As the mission system was decaying in California, the padres may have encouraged some of their mission vaqueros and other mission Indians to work for private rancho owners. Other Indians may have sought such work on their own. The Secularization Act of 1833 gave mission Indians their freedom, but by 1840 many were becoming entrapped on the increasing number of private ranchos. The new government had distributed more than six hundred private land grants by 1840, and California had entered upon its era of private ranchos.

These California ranchos were, in many ways, like the haciendas that still flourished in northern regions of Old Mexico. The homage paid the rancho owners—they were called rancheros—was similar to that accorded the hacendado in Mexico or a feudal lord in Europe much earlier. Even family and friends paid him much honor. As their ranchos grew, the rancheros recruited large numbers of Indians from the rapidly decaying mission settlements. In exchange for their labors they were provided with food, simple clothing, and crude shelter, usually primitive huts clustered near the adobe *casa*, or main ranchhouse, or in small villages called rancherias scattered over the rancho. And, as in the case of the hacienda system, the rancho system soon trapped many Indians, especially many of the vaqueros, in a peonage very close to slavery. The California dons—or *gente de razón*, "people of reason," as they referred to themselves—ruled their ranchos and most of California, since there was little central authority. The government of Mexico was far away and had little influence over what was happening in California.

Not all of these early private ranchos were large. Many, at least at first, were modest in size, about 6½ square miles, with the labor handled by the men of the family and a few Indian vaqueros. But under the new law, citizens could obtain as much as 71½ square miles if they could convince the Mexican governor of their ability to raise cattle successfully. Once a person became a landowner, there was nothing to stop him from acquiring additional acreage by purchase or trade.

Life on these early ranchos was rather primitive. Like the haciendas

VAQUEROS DRIVING CATTLE PAST THE MISSION OF SAN GABRIEL.
Etching by Friedrich Salomon Wyttenbach.

THE VAQUEROS OF NEW SPAIN BECAME EXPERT ROPERS
during the latter half of the seventeenth century.

in what is now northern Mexico, each ranch was generally self-sufficient. Whenever meat was needed, a steer was slaughtered. George W. B. Evans, an American who arrived in California much later, witnessed the process. He had stopped at the rancho of Isaac Williams, a native of Pennsylvania, who had come to California with Ewing Young in 1832. The process, which changed little over the years, was described by Evans:

> The Indians who do this work are well acquainted with the manner of catching cattle, but they are poor butchers. When he wants a beef, orders are given, and in a few moments you will see an Indian galloping swift as the wind across the plains, and in a short time he has one singled out from the herd before him and the lasso thrown over his horns. The horse well understands his part of the tragedy. The moment he sees the well-directed rope fall over the head of the victim, he suddenly stops, and the next moment the beef is brought to his knees; as soon as he rises, he is led off to the place of slaughter, his feet there entangled in ropes, and then thrown, and his throat cut. As soon as he is dead, his skin is stripped off of one side, the leg and shoulder blade cut off and the meat taken from the side of the backbone, and then the same process is gone through with on the other side, and the hindquarters are removed. This done, nothing remains but the head, backbone, and entrails. These are food for the buzzards, which are here found in great numbers, and we saw sailing over our camp this morning a very large bird pronounced a vulture by all. I have seen some very good riders in Mexico, but these Californians are much better, and it is said that they will throw the lasso better with their feet than Mexicans can with the hand.[13]

The cool, dry climate kept the meat fresh for a long time. The tallow was used for candles and the fat for cooking. Meat, corn, and beans, with plenty of fruit and wine, constituted the list of domestic luxuries by the early 1840s. Wine grapes had been introduced by the padres at Mission San Gabriel in 1771 and were soon planted at every mission to provide both sacramental and drinking wine. But the wine was heavy and bitter. California wine did not improve until Americans planted vineyards using mission cuttings grafted with more palatable varieties from Europe.

One peculiarity in the ranchero's life was the bed. A visitor to one rancho in 1844 later wrote:

> The beds which were furnished us to sleep in were exquisitely neat, with coverlids of satin, the sheets and pillowcases trimmed with lace

and highly ornamented, as with the Californians. It was one of the striking peculiarities of Californians that the chief expense of the household of the poorer families was lavished upon the bed; and though the other furniture may have been meager and other useful articles, such as knives and forks, scanty in supply, the bed was always excellent, and handsomely decorated; sumptuously often, with those of more means. I never knew an exception in any household.[14]

The Californian obsession with beds was probably related to the women's fondness for the finer things, a fondness that was excessive. More generally, it was tied to what can only be described as the carefree life style of the California rancheros. They labored only for as long as it took to ensure time for socializing or other pleasures. The Puritan ethic of work for work's sake was of little concern to them, since they delighted in everyday living. They often seemed to live by impulse, which was viewed as shocking and perhaps even sinful by some visiting Americans and Europeans. Edward Vischer, a thrifty and industrious German businessman who made his first visit to California in 1842, noted the strange effect of the horse on the California rancheros. In a letter to his family in Bavaria, Vischer wrote:

The quickness and agility of a Californian on horseback are a strange contrast to his usual languor. With utmost nonchalance he will saddle and harness his horse in the morning, chatting and smoking, using more time than is necessary. But after he has mounted his steed, often without using the stirrup, he is a different person. He never stops until he reaches his destination, no matter how far distant it may be. If the horse gets tired, the rider lassoes another at the next pasture, changes saddle, and continues his journey. Outside of notifying the owner of the borrowed horse, and releasing it to find its way back home, there are no formalities necessary. Traveling is nowhere easier and quicker than in California. A Californian will tear along the road as if it be a matter of life and death, yet he may only want to light a cigar at the house of a friend. He can talk for hours in front of a door, slumped in his saddle, until a sudden idea pulls him out of his indolence and causes a new outbreak of energy. Many spend days in this manner, going home only when they get hungry and are not invited to stay anywhere. If it happens that a man comes upon a gambling or drinking party, the ride is over for the day. Such a party often lasts twice twenty-four hours, until the last drop is consumed or the last coin gambled away. The poor animal remains saddled and tied to a post without fodder or water. When a ranchero comes to town to attend some festivity, the

horse is treated in like manner. In spite of the long ride, it is left standing until the party is over, and then it has to carry its master home.

Vischer observed that the "brutal treatment" was due to the large number
of horses in California. "An animal must take care of itself, for stables are
unknown. . . . The barbarous Californians look upon a horse as a useful
commodity which is of little value and easily replaced. There is a pro-
verbial saying among the common people of Spanish America: 'Who told
him to be a horse? Had he been born a bishop, he would have no other
work to do but to give his blessing,' " wrote Vischer.[15]

Another story about California horses was told by William H. Davis
in his *Seventy-five Years in California.* One day he and an associate were
about to leave a rancho. When their hostess learned that they had to cross
the nearby Santa Ana River, which was very high due to recent rains, she
ordered her *mayordomo* "to group four or five *manadas,* which was done.
Having the horses together, the vaqueros drove them into the river, across
to the other shore, and then immediately back to the same place." Davis
explained that the movement of so many horses trampled down and
hardened the soft sediment or river quicksand at the bottom so that the
party could cross the river with ease and safety. He noted that as they
prepared to cross, "the band of horses was driven over the river again at
the same place and we followed immediately in their wake."[16]

Whether a ranchero lived on his rancho or not, it became the custom
to leave its management in the hands of a *mayordomo.* The *mayordomo*
made certain that the cattle were cared for by the vaqueros and that
other labors were performed, and he supervised the *matanza,* the slaughter
of cattle for their hides and tallow. When arrangements were made to
sell cattle to another rancho, the *mayordomo* made certain they were delivered to the buyer. Such drives were generally done in the spring, when
new grass was plentiful. An adequate number of vaqueros would herd the
cattle to their new home. If the cattle were not to be slaughtered, the
vaqueros would remain with them until they became accustomed to their
new surroundings. The vaqueros would then return home and report to
the *mayordomo.*

The *mayordomo*'s chief assistant was called a corporal, and under him
were ten or twenty or more vaqueros, each receiving $12 to $15 a month
plus crude living quarters, simple but abundant food, horses, saddles, ropes,
and other tools as required. Some vaqueros, of course, owned their own
saddles. They obtained their riding horses from a *caballada* (herd of saddle
horses) or *remonta* (remounts), as the herd was sometimes called. Most
such horses were trained by experienced vaqueros for use in roping, cutting out cattle from a large herd, and rounding up stock. Edward Vischer

saw such a herd being driven into a corral at one rancho. He described the scene as "lively" when the "thirty or forty horses, led by a mare with a bell," were driven inside. "The desired saddle horses are then caught with a lasso. In vain did the animals try to escape the dreaded noose. Unfailingly the lasso caught its victim, and, submitting to fate, the animal was pulled out of the throng until the necessary number was reached. The unsaddled horses which had served the riders till now either joined the rest of the drove or else found their way to the home pasture."[17]

When a rancho needed more saddle horses, he would hold a *recogida*, or horse roundup. Wild and unbroken horses became so numerous on some ranchos during the early nineteenth century that hundreds were slaughtered to save pastures for cattle. Such killings often occurred during drought years.

While horse roundups were held whenever ranchos needed new riding stock, cattle roundups were held in the spring and fall. During these roundups calves were branded, stray cattle were separated from the herds, and animals to be sold on the hoof or slaughtered for their meat, hides, and tallow were cut from the herds. During the fall roundups, sometimes earlier, California vaqueros often were involved in a practice unique to their region called "runs through the mustard." Wild mustard grew in many areas of southern California in tall, thick stalks with yellow blooms. It might cover whole valleys, plains, and even portions of the rolling foothills of the Sierras. The stalks were 5 or 6 feet tall. When the bloom and the leaves died in late summer and the stalks dried and became brittle, the mustard plants formed small forests. Here cattle would hide. It was then that vaqueros would "run through the mustard." It was not uncommon for vaqueros from several neighboring ranchos to come together for two or three days to clear cattle from large mustard forests. The cattle were driven from hiding, many with their calves, and the mustard stalks were trampled to the ground by the vaquero's horses.

Each California rancho was virtually self-sustaining, except for the luxuries obtained from Yankee trading vessels stopping along the coast. The first such ship arrived at Monterey in 1817, although trading with foreign vessels was banned by the Spaniards. After Mexico's independence from Spain, such trading was legalized by the Mexican government and customs houses were opened in Monterey and San Diego. Missions with their vast herds of cattle were then at the zenith of their power. The only market for them was among the Indians and some of the three thousand colonists then living in California, most of whom did not raise cattle. The padres and the small number of private ranchers may have wished they could transport their cattle by the Yankee trading vessels to New England, but they realized this was impractical. A ship could carry only a few head of cattle, and the chances were almost nonexistent that the animals would survive the long voyage around Cape Horn. Cattle hides and tallow, however, could be shipped with ease by the hungry Yankee traders, and there was a good market for them in New England. A brisk trade developed and grew. Later it strengthened the rancho system as the mission system decayed.

Soon after the first Yankee traders arrived by sea they gained considerable knowledge of the character, dress, language, and wants of the California rancheros and their families. Richard Dana wrote in *Two Years Before the Mast* that the traders brought spirits of all kinds, teas, coffee, sugars, spices, raisins, molasses, hardware, crockery, tinware, cutlery, clothing of all kinds, boots and shoes, calicoes, cotton, crepes, silks, shawls, scarves, necklaces, jewelry, and combs. Dana noted that the Yankee traders even brought furniture, Chinese fireworks, and English-built wheels with iron tires for small carts.

But Dana, who was a good observer, described Californians as "idle, thriftless people." He could not understand why they would buy at great prices bad wine made in Boston when California abounded in grapes. "Their hides, too, which they valued at two dollars in money, they barter for something which costs seventy-five cents in Boston; and buy shoes (as like as not made of their own hides; which have been carried twice around Cape Horn) at three and four dollars, and 'chickenskin boots' at fifteen dollars a pair. Things sell, on an average, at an advance of nearly three hundred per cent upon the Boston prices," wrote Dana.

It is easy to understand why the Yankee traders sought the California trade. At the same time, it is doubtful whether the carefree rancheros cared about the profits being made by the Yankee traders. After all, the traders were providing them with their only regular contact with the world outside of Mexico. And their lives were enriched by the luxuries brought thousands of miles and exchanged for cattle hides and tallow. Cattle were plentiful. Even during years of drought, the hides could still be taken from the dead cattle. During the bad drought of 1828 more than forty thousand cattle and horses died. There was a hint, however, that change was coming to California when, in 1837, Ewing Young, an American fur trader and mountain man, purchased a small herd of cattle and drove it north to Oregon.

Young, a native of eastern Tennessee, had headed west in the 1820s and soon became a fur trader in the Rocky Mountains. Kit Carson served his apprenticeship as a mountain man under Young, who arrived in California in 1832. By 1834 he had gone to Oregon with a herd of two hundred horses from California. That same year the first American immigrants arrived in Oregon, which was then in British hands. Cattle were scarce in Oregon. The American settlers could borrow milk cows from the British

Hudson's Bay Company, but the British refused to sell any cattle. It was then that the Americans formed a company to buy California cattle.

Ewing Young, who had experience trading in California, was given the job of obtaining the cattle. He took ten men, including Philip Leget Edwards (who may have been told to keep an eye on Young), and sailed south to San Francisco. Edwards is important because his diary of the journey has preserved the event for history. Young secured a license from the Mexican governor and purchased about eight hundred head of cattle for the company. In late July of 1837, Young, Edwards, and the other men started to drive the cattle north on what was apparently the first cattle drive north out of California. They trailed the cattle across the San Joaquin and Sacramento rivers and followed the Hudson's Bay Company fur brigade's old trail over the Siskiyou Mountains. The trail later became the route followed by the Oregon and California railroad between Sacramento and Portland. Young and the others had many difficulties, but they reached the settlements on the Willamette 120 days later, early in October. The cattle that had cost $3 a head in California were worth $7.67 a head in Oregon. Young and his party arrived with 630 cattle.[18]

Ewing Young retained 135 head as his own and became a pioneer stock raiser, wheat farmer, and grist mill owner in Oregon in the four years that followed. He died a wealthy man in 1841. He was then about fifty years old.

Back in California, life on the ranchos continued to be sweet. The climate was favorable, and during most years there were good pastures and an abundant supply of water. In contrast to today, when many Californians struggle to survive in smog, with frequent water shortages, too many people, and too many automobiles, with other evils of modern civilization, ranch life was attractive, especially as painted by Walter A. Hawley:

The *rancho* lay beyond the mountain range and extended over rolling hills and little valleys. A creek flowed through it, and on the banks were many sycamores. Shaded by oaks was the long, low adobe house, with its red tiled roof and wide veranda. Behind the fence of chaparral was the orchard and the melon patch, and beyond the orchard was the meadow, golden with buttercups in the early spring. In the open fields, dotted with oaks, the rich alfilerilla grew, and on the hillsides were the wild grasses which waved like billows as the breezes from the distant ocean blew across them. The sameness of recurring events of each succeeding year never seemed monotonous, but brought repose, contentment and peace. When the dew was still on the grass, we would mount our horses and herd the cattle if any had strayed beyond the pasture. In the wooded cañons where the cool brooks flowed, and where the wild blackberries grew, we ate our noon day meal and rested. And as the hills began to glow with the light of the setting sun we journeyed homeward. When the long days of summer came, we ate our evening meal beneath the oaks, and in the twilight we listened to the guitar and the songs of our people. In the autumn we harvested the corn and gathered the olives and the grapes.[19]

Rancho life in Mexican California was good even for the Indian vaqueros, most of whom found contented happiness in the saddle, where they felt they were boss. Horses were plentiful and the vaqueros, like the rancheros, rarely walked if they could ride. In the Spanish tradition, only stallions were ridden, not mares. "It was not considered a proper or becoming thing," William H. Davis observed, "for a lady or gentleman to ride a mare; it would, in fact, have been regarded as humiliating."

But mares were, of course, essential in breeding. Each ranch had one or more *manada*—a Spanish feminine noun meaning a herd of brood mares—with a stallion for each. The mares were usually wild and unbroken. Their only training was that provided by vaqueros to form the *manada*. The tails and manes of these mares were closely cut. Vaqueros made ropes from the hair for use as reins and halters. Many vaqueros became skillful in making horsehair ropes. Some worked colored hair together into beautiful ropes that were very strong. But the hair of the stallions kept with the mares in the *manada* was rarely cut. When one old rancher was asked why, he replied: "The mares would take a dislike to them, would lose their respect and affection for them, and would not recognize them as their stallions."

When vaqueros tired of braiding horsehair ropes or of catching horses and cattle and even elk and deer, they would seek out grizzly bears to have some fun. Grizzly bears were plentiful. During the first decade of the nineteenth century, vaqueros complained that grizzlies were killing and eating cattle. In one instance a vaquero, apparently helpless to prevent the slaughter, watched a grizzly feast on five mules and seven cows.[20] By the middle of the nineteenth century there were five grizzlies to every 20 square miles of California, or ten thousand grizzlies concentrated in and around the fertile valleys near the coast. Andy Russell, a Canadian who may know more about grizzlies than any man alive, wrote that they thrived and increased in California after the arrival of the Spaniards because "nowhere else did the settlers, by their way of life, so completely train the grizzlies to join them in easy living off their livestock."[21] The Californians probably did not realize they were contributing to the increase by slaughtering cattle for their hides and tallow. The grizzlies prospered on the meat left over from the *matanza*.

On a grizzly hunt one night in the early 1830s, Don José Joaquin

LASSOING CATTLE ON A CALIFORNIA RANCH.

CALIFORNIA VAQUEROS CAPTURING A GRIZZLY WITH THEIR ROPES.

Estudillo and ten soldiers, who had been vaqueros, "lassoed and killed forty bears in the woods at San Francisquito," one of the many ranchos of the Mission Santa Clara. They used a relay of horses trained to catch bears. William H. Davis, who heard the story from José Joaquin, wrote that the horses were quite at home in the sport. He added: "The animals were lassoed by throat and the hind legs with a horseman on each end, the two pulling in opposite directions until the poor brute succumbed. The fun was kept up till daylight. When they were through they were completely exhausted, and then it was they discovered how much work they had done."[22]

Another American, William R. Garner, watched vaqueros hunting grizzlies with *reatas* in 1846 and later wrote that their horses seem to delight in the sport as much as the vaqueros. Sometimes a lone vaquero would lasso and kill a grizzly, but Garner, Davis, and other nineteenth-century writers relate that generally four or five riders worked together. It was not unusual for a captured grizzly to be paired in a fight with a bull. Many such struggles took place on the killing grounds where the bears had come to eat, only to be captured. There are stories of such fights being staged at missions, presidios, and towns during fiestas and on feast days and Sundays. The earliest formal fight between a bear and a bull appears to have been held at Monterey in 1816 to honor a new governor. There, as elsewhere, an arena was built for the event. The one at Monterey was constructed of adobe and stone. Raised platforms outside the arena provided spectators with good and safe vantage points, especially the ladies, most of whom enjoyed such fighting. But accidents did occur. In the early 1840s at Mission San Gabriel, a man accidentally fell into a pen during a bear-and-bull fight. The grizzly, seeing the man, ignored the bull and ran "straight at the man, striking one paw at his head. The man was literally scalped, and in a second more the grizzly had torn the man into a horrible mass."[23]

California vaqueros, mounted on their best horses, also enjoyed fighting bulls in the arenas. And horse racing was another sport enjoyed by the carefree Californians. The large ranchos bred horses just for racing, and rivalry at times was great. Cattle, silver, and even land might be wagered on one horse or another. This Spanish sporting heritage and temperament, which existed throughout most of Mexico, was particularly prevalent in sunny California, where such outside activities could take place twelve months of the year. But events occurring in the United States and in Mexican Texas were destined to change the carefree life of the California ranchero and vaquero, and the rancho system in which they existed.

CHAPTER 4

⬩•⬩

The Texian Culture

The Texas cowboy, along with the Texas cowman, was an evolvement from and a blend of the riding, shooting, frontier-formed southerner, the Mexican-Indian horseback worker with livestock (the vaquero), and the Spanish open-range rancher. The blend was not in blood, but in occupational techniques.

—J. FRANK DOBIE[2]

AFTER Mexico declared its independence from Spain in 1821, the new government in Mexico City demanded that all government and church officials take an anti-Spanish oath. The few Franciscan padres remaining in Texas refused. Most abandoned their missions and left the country, giving their mission cattle herds to Indian converts or leaving the animals to fend for themselves as many wild cattle were already doing. The padres' departure resulted in the collapse of the Spanish mission system in Texas.

More than fifty missions had been established in Texas during the Spanish reign. In fact, there were 20 active missions in Texas even before the first California mission was established at San Diego in 1769.[3] After Spain acquired Louisiana in 1761, thus ending a possible foreign threat from the east, the Spanish withdrew much of their support from Texas. As a result they failed to induce large numbers of Spaniards to settle in Texas and made only a token settlement, just enough to secure their claim. At the same time they cut their support of missions. The result was a failure to convert most of the Indians in Texas to Christianity. The few Spanish soldiers stationed in Texas were unable to conquer the hostile Apaches, Comanches, and other tribes. It is not surprising that by the late 1700s many Texas missions had been abandoned, some destroyed by Indians.

Things might have gone differently had the Spanish found gold and silver in Texas. Settlement probably would have been rapid, and the crown would have provided more soldiers and money for more padres to control the Indians. But precious metals were not found in Texas by the Spanish, only more land, much of it good only for grazing livestock. The Spaniards already had plenty of good grazing land south of the Rio Grande. The additional land in Texas did little to excite them.

In spite of the difficulties the Franciscan padres managed to make important contributions to Texas. They helped to explore, map, and settle a few small areas of Texas, leaving their imprint on the architecture, place names, and customs. And if you believe the legends, the padres were responsible for bringing to Texas the honeybee, and even the bluebonnet, which, it is said, they gathered from the hillsides of Jerusalem. Far more important, the padres introduced cattle ranching to support their struggling missions. Ranching would be the only Spanish institution to survive in Texas and the American West.

Just before the Mexican revolution, an American from Connecticut by the name of Moses Austin, then about sixty, secured approval from Spanish authorities to bring American colonists to settle in Texas. As the Americans began to arrive, Mexico declared its independence from Spain. Before Austin could renegotiate an agreement with the new government, however, he died. His twenty-seven-year-old son Stephen, who had studied law in New Orleans, took over his father's work. After much time and effort, young Austin succeeded in helping to get the Mexican government to pass an immigration law in 1825.

Americans by the thousands came to Texas. Some were farmers, but many followed other occupations. A few were from the North, but most came from the South and had names like Green, Johnston, Fanin, Houston, Smith, Crockett, Bowie, White, Ward, and Kuykendall. Most of them had fallen on hard times in the States. The Panic of 1819, following the War of 1812, had caused serious hardships for many Americans. The Land Law of 1820 did not help those wanting a fresh start in the expanding America that was pushing westward. It required cash payment of $1.25 an acre on a minimum of 80 acres in the States. Many Americans did not have that kind of money, but in Texas land was almost a gift. The colonists who declared themselves farmers received up to 277 acres. If they said they planned to raise stock as well, they could receive up to 4,338 additional acres. Most colonists professed farming and stock raising in order to receive as much land as possible, about 4,615 acres.

Some colonists came to Texas by ship, arriving along the Gulf Coast, most arriving at Galveston Bay. Others traveled up the Red River to Natchitoches and then west to Nacogdoches. Some came overland through southwest Louisiana on the Opelousas Road, originally an east–west Indian trail.[4]

Some of these early colonists, especially those from Alabama, Mississippi, and Louisiana, may have been cattle raisers. Cattle raising dominated the South as a means of livelihood from the end of the eighteenth century until King Cotton achieved primacy just before the Civil War. It was not unusual for a plantation owner in the South to have slaves on horseback herding and hunting down lost cattle. Descendants of these southern cowhunters were probably among the first black Texas cowboys.

As for the early Texas colonists, apparently few of them gave thought to the possibilities of stock raising until after their arrival. Most colonists wanted land and a fresh start, and they began as farmers. Even Austin did not consider the potential cattle had for his colonists. It was the Mexican authorities, not Austin, who insisted that two articles dealing with stock raising be added to his code of civil and criminal regulations drawn up to govern the colonists. One article pertained to the disposition of stray stock and the other provided for the registration of brands.

Ranching, as it was then practiced on the haciendas of south and southwest Texas, across the Rio Grande to the south, and far to the west in California, was not part of the culture from which these predominantly American colonists came. Even the word "ranching" was foreign to their language: it came from the word "ranch," which in turn was derived from the Spanish word *rancho*, meaning "farm," particularly one devoted to the breeding and raising of livestock. In the States, stock raising was usually conducted along with farming, and not on a large scale except in a few southern states. And only in the South was stock normally herded on horseback. In the North, men and boys herded cattle on foot. Contrary to the impression given by some writers, these colonists did not hurry to Texas, break wild mustangs, round up wild Spanish cattle, and become cattle kings overnight. Their involvement in ranching as practiced by the Mexicans was gradual, and their initial purpose in raising cattle on their farms was to provide food for themselves. But the building of their homes came first.

Unhewn logs were snaked out of the woods by ox teams to build cabins on their newly acquired land. The floors of these early houses were either dirt or split logs chinked with mud. Most of the earliest cabins had only one room, although some settlers added a second room later. One style of cabin, already popular in the South and to become popular in Texas, was known as the "dogtrot." It had two rooms with a connecting roofed-in breezeway, or "dogtrot." Each room had a stick-and-dirt fireplace with a rock back that served for both heating and cooking. Most colonists built their own furniture. The bedsteads were held between the logs of the walls on one side and by legs on the other. Rawhide ropes held the mattresses in place. A table and stools and benches, all made of split trees, usually stood in the center of these early one-story cabins. An iron pot, a Dutch oven, a three-legged skillet, and a teakettle could be found in or around most fireplaces, where a kettle usually hung from a pothook.

Matches were scarce. The hot coals from the day's fire were banked each night and saved until morning, or a new fire was started at dawn by flint on punk. If no flint was available, and the old fire gave out, a settler would walk to a neighbor's cabin to obtain a few hot coals with which to start a new one. Most settlers made their own soap by dripping lye from their ash hoppers. They poured water over the ashes in the hopper, usually kept just outside the cabin, until lye began to drip into a trough below. They used the liquid lye not only to make soap but to clean their cabins, to loosen the hair of hogs during the butchering process, and to produce hominy. Hominy was made by putting clean corn kernels into an iron kettle with enough lye water to cover, then cooking until the husk was loosened. The corn was then washed in hot water to remove the husk or skins and the lye. After the corn was washed several times, it was boiled again and rewashed until it was tender enough to be eaten.

Light from fireplaces and candles illumined the cabins at night or on cloudy days. The settlers made their own candles in molds with tallow and string. While candles and lye were essential, these early Texians soon learned that guns were more important. They were used to kill deer and other wild game, and they also were needed for defense. Many men and women, especially those involved in cattle raising and living away from the settlements, lived in fear of hostile Indian attacks. By 1821, 3,500 colonists had arrived in Texas, but there were perhaps twenty thousand Indians. Many were hostile, and since the Mexican government did not provide any protection, the Texians organized their own militia, consisting of all able-bodied men between the ages of sixteen and fifty. As early as 1823, Stephen Austin employed ten men to serve as "rangers," the first of the Texas Rangers.

Nearly all of the men had brought their American long or "Kentucky" rifles, with percussion firing caps, made famous by Andy Jackson's ragtag army in the Battle of New Orleans (1815). Some also brought their percussion pistols and perhaps a few of the older flintlock models made before 1825. Each man used what weapons he had, but each had to be loaded after each shot (except for a small number of double-barrel percussion rifles). The long rifles had been developed for use on foot in the woodlands of the East. While these weapons could be effective in defending cabins, they were difficult to use when chasing Indians on horseback or atop a sturdy mule. They required careful aiming, something that was often difficult to achieve while in motion.

When in pursuit of Indians, some Texians carried two pistols and a rifle—three ready shots at best—plus a knife; but the weapons were bulky, difficult to manage, and awkward to reload on the move. The Indians often had the advantage, since they preferred spears and bows and arrows to guns. A skillful Indian brave could shoot a dozen or more arrows during the time it took a Texian to fire one shot from a rifle and reload, and at close range the bow and arrow could be just as accurate as a pistol. The Texian's firepower would improve after the invention of the six-shooter, but that weapon came later.

The importance of guns was stressed by two colonists, Jemima and Mary Toll, who settled in Texas in the early 1830s. They wrote a letter to friends in the States and advised them to bring "good guns, and powder and shot of every kind." They told their friends to bring many other things as well. Although the Toll letter suffers from poor punctuation, bad spelling, and improper usage, it conveys the flavor of the life led by early Texas colonists, especially their needs and wants. The letter reads in part:

> Bring some boxes of glass, bars soap, plenty wick, bring seeds of every kind, shallots; bring cross cut, whip, and frame saws. . . . Bring as many cart wheels and cart mountings as you can, Chains for oxen; no timber, as this is the country for timber of every kind. Bring a supply of sugar coffee and tea and flour for 8 or 9 months; if you have any to spare, you get your price. Gun locks and every thing belonging to locks, screws of every kind, plates for screws Your goods both small and large and every little article you can pack. Pots, pans with covers, oven &c, white muslin both white and brown in pieces. Bring tin cups. Porringers. Any man working 2 days in the week may take his gun and fishing rod the remainder and his horse. Bring your clean english blankets both second hand and new. . . . Bring a candle mould. . . . Bring your beds. you'll have no work, your daughters can milk 50 cows for you, and make butter which is 25 cents a lb here. . . . A cow has 2 calfes in 10 months. . . . The healthiest country in the world. P.S. Bring corn mills, do not bring such a mill as I brought, as it is only a pepper mill.[5]

Jemima and Mary Toll's reference to milking "50 cows" was a strong hint that cattle were plentiful in Texas. Indeed they were. No one is certain just how many cattle there were, but one estimate suggests there were 100,000 in Texas about 1830. Probably 20 percent were "native American" with a sprinkling of French cattle included. The remaining 80 percent were Spanish cattle, most of them wild, ranging from the Rio Grande to the Red River over about four-fifths of what is now Texas.[6] These wild cattle usually ran in small bunches, hiding by day in the thickets and running by night. They could go for days without water and outwalk any of the "native American" cattle. These Spanish cattle had descended from mission herds and their strays and those stolen by Indians. Their environment had made them a hardy breed. They had long horns and were lanky, flat-sided, thin-flanked, and sway-backed in appearance, with big ears and long tails. In early Texas they were called either Spanish or Mexican cattle. But in time there was interbreeding between these cattle and the "native American" cattle. By the 1840s there was a noticeable difference between the cattle along the border and those in central Texas. The fusion of the Spanish and the "native American" stock created what many Texans believed was a better breed that became known as "Texas cattle." By about the time of the Civil War these cattle would become known as longhorns, sometimes spelled with a capital *L*, and usually as "Texas Longhorns."

Evidence of the interbreeding is provided in descriptions of the cattle with their wide range of color patterns—red, black, black-and-white, red-and-white, and various shades of brindle stock. As one historian of Spanish cattle wrote: "Old photographs confirm patched color patterns and the brindles." He added that modern blood-typing work of the best representatives of these longhorn cattle today show a basic Spanish genetic development.[7]

The cows of the mixed breed cared for their calves better than Spanish cattle, but they could be just as wild as their Spanish cousins. Left in the wild, both types reverted to the wild and were dangerous. Their sense of smell was keener than a deer's. Several wild cows and their calves might be found bunched together for mutual protection, but the bulls were usually alone. Should two wild bulls meet, there was often immediate combat, sometimes ending in death for the loser. Nature apparently provided these cattle with their long horns for self-protection. They were set forward to kill like those of buffalo. One can imagine a new colonist seeing his first bunch of wild cattle on the edge of a thicket. Advancing toward them on foot, perhaps believing them to be docile like many cattle back in the States, he is suddenly surprised by the appearance of a wild bull, pawing the earth and tossing his head in anger at the man's appearance. In a flash the bull charges. The colonist turns and runs to safety as the wild-eyed bull gives chase. Colonists learned quickly that wild Spanish cattle were dangerous and should be approached only on horseback. Even then wild cattle often charged man and horse. For that reason many newcomers to Texas let Mexicans or Indians capture and tame these sharp-horned beasts.

Some colonists in southeast Texas may have traded for or bought their first Spanish cattle from James Taylor White, a pioneer rancher in the area. White, who was originally named LeBlanc and usually called Taylor White, came to Texas as early as 1819, even before land was opened to settlement by the Spanish. One account, however, says White arrived in 1823 with three cows and calves, two small ponies, and a wife and three children. He introduced cattle ranching in southeast Texas and undoubtedly set the example for many American colonists. His cattle, carrying the JTW brand, roamed on both sides of the Trinity River and south to the Gulf of Mexico. Exactly when White first started using his brand is not known, but Mexican authorities first recorded it about 1830. Between the 1820s and 1850, White made frequent cattle drives to New Orleans, where he sold his cattle and banked his money. He may have been the first white man to drive cattle from Texas to New Orleans. By 1842, when Joseph Eve, United States chargé d'affaires to Texas, visited his ranch, White owned about forty thousand acres of land, "upwards of 90 negroes," thirty thousand head of cattle, and $60,000 in specie deposited in New Orleans. In the fall of 1841, White had "marked and branded thirty-seven hundred calves" and sold 1,100 steers weighing about a thousand pounds each which "cost him not more than 75 cents a head to drive them to market. . . ." What was extraordinary about White, wrote Eve, is that he "cannot read or write and has made his fortune raising stock alone."[8]

During the early 1830s most Texians had little to use for business transactions but cattle. There was almost no money. The only silver coin generally in circulation was the provincial and thin sand dollar, a coin of the Mexican Revolution made by Mexican patriots before they obtained possession of the mints. Cattle, however, especially cows and calves, were often more valuable than money. And gradually many a person's wealth came to be estimated in terms of how many cattle he branded. Nearly all Texians branded their cattle with "dotting irons." These were the forerunners of the modern stamp irons which place the entire brand on a cow in one application. With dotting irons, it might take three or four applications to complete the brand. Three irons were used. One iron would have a large half-circle at the end. Another would have a small half-circle. The third iron would have a bar or straight-edge 3 or 4 inches long. Many letters and characters were possible with these irons. For example, the half-circle iron and the straight-edge iron could make the letter *D* when combined. Four applications of the small half-circle could create the numeral 8.

While most cattle raisers branded their animals, not all brands were registered. From Mexican independence through the years of the Republic of Texas, the recording of brands seems to have been provided for but not enforced. Because most Texians were unable to interpret the Spanish brands, which were generally pictographs, the settlers branded letters onto the sides of their cattle, often the owner's initials.

David Woodman, who compiled a 192-page promotional book titled *Guide to Texas Emigrants* (1835), made cattle raising sound so easy that his book may have drawn settlers to Texas just for that purpose. Woodman wrote that the only cost to cattle owners was "that of herding them once or twice a week, to prevent their straying too far from home, and becoming wild." Woodman, who may never have visited Texas before he wrote the guide, added: "It is believed that no country in the world presents so great temptations to the grazier as the prairies and cane-brakes of Texas afford. Fat cattle fetch a fair price at New Orleans; mules find a ready market in the West Indies, and other crops which are not sold to the new emigrants, command prices far above any which are demanded with us."[9]

Woodman's *Guide*, published in Boston, included letters from colonists already in Texas. One was written by William Wilson, who with his wife Amelia had settled at Clowper's Point on Galveston Bay (San Jacinto). Wilson described how Amelia was trading goods "for what is considered the best property in Texas—cows and calves." He noted that she already had "twenty head," and was trading for more each day. "The price in Texas for a cow and a calf is ten dollars . . . paying in goods, they cost her about five dollars. . . . With one hundred head of cows in Texas, a man is considered independent . . . for, if you sit down and calculate the increase, you will find it enormous."

Wilson then described how the colonists sold their cattle:

The steers they dispose of either to the merchants in the country, or, if they have large stock, so that they drive them through to New Orleans, which is 300 miles from here. The price of a yearling here is five dollars. . . . A five-year-old, in New Orleans, generally brings about thirty-five dollars. Takes twenty-one days to drive through, at an expense of four dollars twelve and a half cents a head, including all expenses for man and horses, if you have in your drove sixty head; if less, the expense is more in proportion; if a greater number, less. The calculation is, in Texas, that, allowing for loss of cattle by disease and other things, the increase is sixty per cent, a year; so that you can easily imagine what kind of property it is. All you have to do is to keep the calves up, and the cows come nightly to them; thus the cattle are kept perfectly gentle, and you have nothing to do. It is also better property for the reason, you have no trouble with them, not even to salt them; I mean to give them salt to eat, which has to be done in the States. But not so here, as the atmosphere is salt.

Wilson probably was referring to the salt air blowing up from the Gulf, or perhaps the salt stocks or domes of the Gulf Coast region, intrusions from unknown depths that almost reach the surface in some places. Salt for cattle was certainly not a problem. Wilson concluded by writing that it was his wife's intention to have one hundred cows before the year ended. "She will kill none, dispose of the male cattle when she has sufficient number to drive them to New Orleans, and the heifers will so increase her stock, so that, in five years, she will have more stock than she will know what to do with."[10]

Amelia Wilson was not the only woman in Mexican Texas involved in stock raising, since the hardships of frontier life required that all members of each family work to make ends meet. Mary Austin Holley, a cousin of Stephen F. Austin, wrote in 1836 that living in the "wild country of Texas forms the character of great and daring enterprise." She observed that in Texas some women performed "exploits, which the effeminate men of populous cities might tremble at. . . . It is not uncommon for ladies to mount their mustangs and hunt with their husbands, and with them to camp out for days. . . . All visiting is done on horseback, and they will go fifty miles to a ball with their silk dresses, made perhaps in Philadelphia or New Orleans, in their saddle-bags."[11]

There were more than thirty thousand people in Texas by the middle 1830s. Nearly two-thirds of them were American colonists living in the wooded areas of east and southeast Texas. Many were raising cattle. The principal Mexican settlements were San Antonio and Goliad, formerly La Bahía. San Antonio had about 2,500 inhabitants, Goliad perhaps eight hundred. A smaller Mexican settlement was Victoria on the Guadalupe River southeast of San Antonio. There were perhaps five hundred Mexicans at Nacogdoches in east Texas. The remainder of the Mexican population in Texas were scattered in Texian settlements "employed by the settlers mostly as herdsmen." One observer wrote: "They are universally acknowledged to be the best hands that can be procured, for the management of cattle, horses and other live stock. The occupation of the Mexicans in Texas generally, is raising live stock, and agriculture on a limited scale."[12]

A few Mexicans were involved in slaughtering cattle for their hides and tallow during this period. They did their work along the coast near where ships could transport the hides and tallow. Nearly all of this work was done by Mexicans, and most of the cattle killed were of poor quality. The profit from this trade was not sufficient to induce many Americans to engage in it before the Civil War. And during the 1830s and 1840s some American settlers thought the killing of cattle for their hides and tallow was wasteful.

Mexican vaqueros, soon after the colonists arrived, began catching and taming mustangs, or wild horses, which they then sold or traded to the settlers. These vaqueros rode their best horses onto the plains until they found a band of wild horses. Some of the men watched the horses while others built a large corral nearby. The enclosure had a gate leading to a small corral. From the entrance to the large pen they constructed wings onto the plains. The vaqueros would then mount their horses and drive the herd into the large corral. These Mexicans always tried to get a "small drove, not a large one." If there were too many mustangs in the large corral, according to one Texian, they might "burst the walls of the pen or some horses might trample others to death, and then run over them and escape; in which case the party is obligated to leave the place, as the stench arising from the putrid carcasses would be insupportable; and, in addition to this, the pen would not receive others." Should the Mexicans succeed in driving in a few horses, perhaps two or three hundred, they would select the "handsomest and youngest, noose them, and take them into the small enclosure, then turn out the remainder; after which, by starving, preventing them taking any repose, and continually keeping them in motion, they make them gentle by degrees, and finally break them to submit to the saddle and bridle."[13]

Later many Texians would become proficient at catching their own wild mustangs, especially in south and southwest Texas. In the area north-west of modern Corpus Christi, they would tie a dummy of a man on the back of a wild mustang and turn him loose. "Of course, he would make for the herd, which would try to outrun him. This would start every mustang for miles around to running and the noise from these running horses, which sometimes numbered thousands, often sounded like the terrific roar of a passing cyclone. After they had run themselves down we could guide them into the pens with long wings which we had built for capturing them," remembered Patrick Burke.[14] By the late 1830s there were hundreds of mustang pens on the Texas frontier between the Nueces River and the Rio Grande.

But not all Texians preferred horses. Some of the settlers who came from the South rode mules. They preferred them. Mules are more intelli-gent, surer-footed, and tougher than most horses. And their life span—thirty to thirty-five years—is ten to fifteen years longer than that of horses. Southerners found that mules can stand heat better than horses, and they have the ability to do a third more work on a third less food on a hot day. A horse starts to get bothered when it gets hot and then only gets hotter and more bothered. Although the Spanish had introduced mules in the New World, those ridden by the settlers were not of Spanish heritage. They were from the East, where George Washington began raising the first mules in the United States after Lafayette gave him a gift of a jack and two jennies. Both male and female mules, of course, are sterile and will not reproduce. A mule is out of a mare (female horse) and a jack (male ass). If a female ass (jenny) is mated with a male horse (stallion), the offspring is called a hinny, usually an inferior animal. It often takes an expert to distinguish a hinny from a mule; the only significant difference in appearance is that hinnies are slightly narrower at the heel. Being a hybrid animal, mules were not as plentiful as horses in early Texas, but they were more valuable.

Most of the southerners who settled in Texas during the early 1820s were experienced horsemen or mule riders, but such was not the case for many of the settlers from the North. Many of them had to learn to ride after coming to Texas, sometimes being taught by southerners who had ridden overland to Texas from Mississippi or Kentucky or elsewhere in the South. Most of these settlers had, of course, brought what saddles they owned. They were constructed on a plain wooden tree, often with a metal fork. Some were covered with leather. They usually had single cinches of leather or webbing and plain stirrup straps without fenders. Most stirrups were plain and narrow and made of iron. There were few saddlehorns of prominence. These eastern saddles were made for riding and not for working cattle.

As the Texians observed the Mexican vaqueros at work, it became evident that eastern saddles were unsuited for such labors. The Texians soon adopted the vaquero's saddle, either trading for or buying them from vaqueros. Or the Texians would make their own by constructing a plain wooden tree, usually covering it with rawhide, and attaching large inner skirts to the underside of the tree. Saddlebags were often attached to the skirts. Large stirrups covered with tapaderos (a wedge-shaped piece of leather over the stirrup's front and sides) were added, along with a single cinch. The fork, with a large saddlehorn styled after the Mexican vaquero's, was cut from either a willow or a cottonwood jackknife. In time, these Texians covered the seats with leather and added fenders to the stirrups to improve the saddle's riding comfort. And they lined the large skirts with sheepskins to prevent saddle blankets from slipping off the horse. The sheepskin also made the ride more comfortable. Such saddles were made the basic stock saddles used by Texians from the late 1820s until about 1850.[15]

As late as 1850, however, some open-tree saddles covered only with a blanket were still being used by vaqueros. One traveler crossing Texas saw several of them and wrote that the tree had no rawhide coverings whatever. The writer described the open-tree saddles as "well-fitting" and noted that they did not gall the horse's back provided the rider un-covered, washed, and rubbed the horse's back dry "at every opportu-nity."[16]

While many of the early Texians learned much from the vaqueros and other Mexicans and gained respect for them, some of the later arrivals from the States did not like the Mexicans, or the Mexican government that ruled their new homeland. Their culture was not that of the Mexicans, nor was it that of the Indians. As might have been expected, the conflicts were many. These Texians brought their language, their ways, their beliefs, and their dreams and ambitions, and in all these respects they differed from the Mexicans and the Indians. The newcomers, sharing the racial and cultural beliefs held by other American frontiersmen of the day, considered whites superior to people of other colors, including brown Mexicans.

When the government in Mexico City stopped nearly all American immigration in 1830, Texians objected. They believed they should have more say in their government, and soon sought to make Texas a separate state of Mexico. Stephen F. Austin, who was not altogether in favor of these moves, agreed to go to Mexico City in July 1833 to present the colonists' views and petitions to the Mexican government, namely Santa Anna, then dictator of Mexico. After many weeks he met with Santa Anna, and finally was able to get the ban on American immigration to Texas lifted. The Mexican government also agreed to give Texians more say in their government and to establish trial by jury and appellate courts. But Santa Anna opposed separate statehood for Texas, then in union with Coahuila.

Austin started home to Texas only to be arrested, supposedly for trying to incite insurrection through a letter sent to friends in Texas. The Mexicans had intercepted his letter. Austin was held without charges until early in 1835, when he was released. He hurried back to Texas a changed man, and before 1835 had ended, the Texas revolution began. The events that followed are well-known; there was the bloody Texian defeat at the Alamo and at Goliad, but victory came in eighteen minutes at San Jacinto, when General Sam Houston and a force of Texians surprised Santa Anna and his soldiers during an early afternoon siesta. On that day, April 21, 1836, the Texians won their independence and the Republic of Texas was born.

The new nation, however, was nothing more than a loud baby. Its treasury had no funds. Its army was paid with borrowed money. Aside from the people and the land, about the only thing of value in the new nation was cattle, but the herds had been scattered. Some had been slaughtered to feed both Mexican and Texian soldiers. When the war ended, it appeared that cattle were in short supply. Sam Houston, acting in his capacity as commander-in-chief, issued an order prohibiting the driving of cattle across the Sabine River. Houston apparently wanted to keep Texas cattle in Texas to feed his army, and he ordered soldiers to turn back cattle drives at the Sabine. Meantime, Houston was forced to reduce the size of the Texas army from about 3,500 to six hundred because he had no money to pay them. These discharged soldiers returned to their homes, and those who had been raising cattle before they went off to fight soon found their scattered herds and rounded them up. There were more cattle than Sam Houston had believed.

Members of the Texas House of Representatives appear to have realized this, because on May 26, 1836, a little more than a month after the San Jacinto victory, they passed a resolution. It read: "Resolved that the President be requested to state to this house upon what authority he has stationed Soldiers upon the Sabine to prevent citizens of this Country from taking their cattle out of the Country." Houston apparently canceled his order. The matter was dropped, and stock raisers resumed their drives of small herds to markets in Louisiana.

About three years after the Texas revolution, percussion rifles and revolvers appeared in the hands of some Texians. They had been purchased by the Texas government from Samuel Colt, who was manufacturing them in Paterson, New Jersey. In 1839, Colt was producing both a .44-caliber ring-lever rifle with eight- or ten-shot cylinders and a .525 smoothbore-caliber six-shot carbine. The revolving breech pistol, first patented in England by Colt in 1835, was known as a No. 5 pistol. It was a five-shot, .36-caliber revolver with a 9-inch barrel. Just how many revolvers and rifles were procured by the Texas government is unknown, but the weapons apparently went first to the Texas navy. Later some of the revolvers, and perhaps some of the rifles as well, fell into the hands of Texas Rangers. These weapons were to revolutionize warfare on the Texas frontier. In 1844, Colonel Jack Hays and fifteen Rangers took on a force of about eighty Comanches. The Rangers, armed with their five-shot Colts, defeated the charging Indians. One of the Rangers was Samuel Walker, who later wrote to Colt and praised his pistols. Walker noted: "The Texans who have learned their value by practical experience, their confidence in them is so unbounded, so much so that they are willing to engage four times their numbers."[17]

Early in 1846, Walker became a lieutenant colonel in the Texas Rangers and later a captain in a newly formed Regiment of Mounted Rifles, organized to fight in the Mexican war. Many accounts credit Walker with having influenced Samuel Colt to improve his earlier five-shot model revolver. The traditional story is that Walker visited Colt in the East, and suggested that he produce a heavier revolver. The five-shot weapon, said Walker, was too light, and he argued that it should be heavy enough that it could be used as a club when empty. He also pointed out another problem: since the gun had to be taken apart to load, there was a good chance a mounted horseman might drop one of the pieces. Walker suggested that the construction be changed to eliminate the problem and that a trigger guard be added. Although his New Jersey factory had since failed, Colt soon resumed gunmaking and produced about 240 new revolvers more to the liking of the Texas Rangers. They adopted the revolver late in 1847 and called it a "six-shooter" since it shot six bullets. In time other Texians, including cattle raisers, would acquire the revolvers along with carbines. These weapons eventually enabled Texians to defeat the mounted Indians on the Texas frontier.

BY THE TIME TEXAS joined the Union, stock-raising methods were changing in the new state. In the 1820s cattle raising and farming had been combined. The early colonists found that both were essential for survival. But gradually, along the Texas frontier, cattle became a separate operation. Texans, undoubtedly influenced by the methods of Mexican ranchos, were adopting the open-range approach to cattle raising. Although it is impossible to say in what year the range-herding technique was first used by Anglo-Texans, it was in evidence in most regions bordering on the Texas plains by the late 1840s.

Raising cattle on the open range had been practiced by Mexican rancheros in Texas for many decades, especially to the south and west of San Antonio. In that region, between the Nueces River and the Rio Grande, many large Mexican ranchos had existed for years. The Mexican government had made at least two hundred grants for ranching in the region. The ranchos were located in the *brazada*, or brush country, a land that even today seems hostile to man. A large chunk of this region east of the Rio Grande—from near present Starr County northward beyond Laredo—was called by the Mexicans El Desierto Muerto, "The Dead Desert." This region did provide fairly good grazing for cattle and was sprinkled with live oaks, mesquite, and thick shrubs, but it was far to the southwest of the American settlements in Texas. After Mexico became independent in the early 1820s, hostile Comanches stepped up their raiding there, and several Mexican ranchers abandoned their cattle and fled. Many of the cattle became wild. During the Texas revolution some Texians made raids into this area, driving off cattle from Mexican ranches at Viego, north of Matamoros, at Las Animas, Santa Rosa, and elsewhere along the upper Rio Grande. Colonel John S. "Rip" Ford recalled in his memoirs, now in the University of Texas archives, that these Texians became known as "cow-boys." Ford said the name "was not meant as a term of reproach. War existed between Mexico and Texas, and the operations of the 'Cow-boys' were considered legitimate."

When the Texians won their independence, many Mexican ranchers

TEXAS CATTLE RAISERS GUARDING THEIR HERDS.
Harper's Weekly, 1874.

TEXAS CATTLE STAMPEDE.
Drawing by J. Andre Castaigne.

on the Texas side of the Rio Grande fled across the river into what is now
Old Mexico, leaving their cattle behind to fend for themselves. Most of
these cattle also became wild. It was to this region that the new government of Texas sent a company of one hundred men soon after the Texian
victory at San Jacinto. The men were ordered to secure beef for the
Texas army. The company rounded up many wild cattle and drove them
to Goliad, where they were placed in newly constructed cattle pens built
of cedar posts and rawhide, then the most common materials used in constructing such pens on the frontier. But the Texas army was soon reduced
in size. Many of the soldiers were discharged, although some of them
stayed on the frontier and began rounding up wild cattle with personal
profit in mind. These four-legged prizes could be had for the taking.

One of these men was Ewen Cameron, a native of Scotland, who
came to the United States in the early 1830s. He later enlisted in the
Kentucky Volunteers for service in the Texas revolution. From what is
known, Cameron may have been one of the Texians who made raids on
Mexican ranches along the Rio Grande during the fighting. Discharged
from the army, Cameron remained in the area and organized a group of
former soldiers to round up wild cattle roaming the region between
the Nueces and the Rio Grande. J. Frank Dobie, writing for a Texas Folklore Society publication called *Tone the Bell Easy* in 1932, said these
men too, were called "cow-boys." They employed the same technique that
Mexican vaqueros had used for decades to catch wild cattle. They would
first find the cattle, usually by the light of the moon at night, when the
animals were most active, and stampede them. Cameron and his men
would run the cattle east, away from Mexico, until the animals slowed to
a trot or walk. This was sometimes twenty-four hours after the stampede
began: longhorns were noted for their endurance. Once they slowed their
pace the cow-boys would keep them moving. A day or two later the tired
cattle—the cow-boys would also be tired—would act much like domestic
stock and could be handled with ease.

The cow-boys often continued their drives until they reached Goliad
or some other settlement east of the Nueces that had cattle pens. There the
cattle either were sold or, after a few days' rest, were trailed to settlements in central Texas where they could be sold for meat, hides, and seed
stock. Still other cattle were driven across Texas to be sold in Louisiana.
Texians saw nothing wrong with capturing these cattle. They viewed such
activity as legitimate—either as recovering property abandoned by Mexicans who had left Texas (such cattle were viewed as public property under
Mexican law) or as compensation for property destroyed or carried off
without compensation by the Mexican army in its retreat from Texas.[18]

The word "cowboy"—the natural combination of the words "cow" and "boy"—was not coined by Ewen Cameron, nor did it originate in Texas. It seems to have first appeared in Ireland about A.D. 1000, where horsemen and cattle wranglers became known as cow-boys. In the seventeenth century, when England was scrambling to populate the American colonies, some Irish cow-boys fell into disfavor with their British rulers, and were given a choice between jail and America. Many chose America, where they were indentured to farmers for work and keep. It is no wonder that stock raisers in the colonies shunned the "cow-boy" label and adopted the English "drover" as their occupational title when driving cattle to market. Colonists sometimes referred to cattle raisers as "cow-keepers." The word "cow-boy" was not held in high regard during the American Revolution, when Loyalist guerrillas calling themselves "cow-boys" stole cattle from American farmers and sold them to Redcoats.

It is possible that Ewen Cameron, with his Scottish background, or perhaps some other Texian who may have been from Ireland (some Texas colonists were Irish), knew the term and what it suggested. It may have been adopted, since the earlier activities of the Irish and British cow-boys were similar to what the Texians were doing along the Mexican border late in the Texas revolution. Regardless, the term was first used in Texas in the late 1830s, but it was not quickly adopted by other Texans to identify someone working with cattle. In fact, from the late 1830s until the late 1860s, Texans, even those who later settled in the brush country of South Texas, generally used the Mexican word *vaquero* "without reference to race" when referring to someone handling cattle.[19] It was not until after the Civil War, when Texans began to drive their cattle north to the railroads in Kansas, that the term was used to identify a man working with cattle. Even then, it sometimes designated, instead, a cattle rustler. Joseph McCoy, who established Abilene as the first railroad cattle town in Kansas in 1867, acknowledged the newness of the term in the North in his 1874 classic *Historic Sketches of the Cattle Trade of the West and Southwest.* McCoy wrote: "We will here say for the benefit of our northern readers that . . . the ordinary laborer is termed a 'cow-boy.' "[20] It was not until around 1900 that the hyphen was dropped by most writers and the accepted spelling became one word—"cowboy."

The region where the early Texas "cow-boys" operated was something of a no-man's-land. Mexico claimed that the Nueces River was the international boundary, but Texas said the boundary was the Rio Grande. The very nature of the region attracted other adventuresome men, some of whom were nothing more than outlaws and freebooters who had fled the States in search of their fortune. These men were rough characters. They began raiding ranches and settlements on both sides of the Rio Grande, driving off cattle, horses, and even mules. Texans and Mexicans alike were the victims of these "cow-boys." According to one account, some of these men made Victoria their headquarters. In a report to the adjutant general of the Texas army, a U.S. army officer wrote from Victoria: "They are all in the cow stealing business, and are scattered all over this frontier. They pretend . . . they steal only from the enemy; but I am convinced, to the contrary, that they steal from Texans as well as Mexicans. . . . I am convinced that there are no less than three or four hundred men engaged in this business."[21]

The names of some of the leaders of these murdering and thieving bands are known. One was Mabry "Mustang" Gray, who came to Texas in 1835 from South Carolina. According to legend, he earned his nickname when he lost his horse during a buffalo hunt with friends. Left stranded miles from any settlement, he managed to kill a wounded buffalo, skin the shaggy, and make a *reata* from it. He then climbed a tree near a water hole and waited for wild horses to come to drink. He roped a mustang stallion, broke the animal, and soon rode him back to where his friends were camped. Later his band of cow-boys was called "Mustangers." In 1842, Gray was involved in killing seven Mexicans who had obtained permission from the mayor of Victoria to visit a nearby ranch.[22]

Another cutthroat was known as "Big" Brown. His real first name is unknown. He supposedly came to Texas from Missouri and was later shot to death in Texas.[23] But little else is known about Brown or his men or the men who rode with "Mustang" Gray. History suggests that other "cow-boy" bands engaged in rounding up cattle had little to do with Gray and Brown and their bands.

Raids by the outlaw bands of Gray, Brown, and at least two other outlaw groups did not help relations between Texas and Mexico, but then Mexico had not concluded a definitive peace treaty with the new republic and so did not recognize its independence. Texians along the southwestern frontier lived in almost constant fear of a Mexican invasion. To the east beyond San Antonio, however, things were not as tense. Many cattle raisers were more concerned with Indian raids, especially those men who had to leave their wives and children at home when they drove their cattle overland to market in Louisiana or elsewhere in Texas.

When such drives occurred, other men in the neighborhood often helped one another. Sometimes three or four settlers would combine their cattle into one herd and drive them to market after gathering their families at one home and leaving the old men and young boys to guard the women and children. Often the stock raisers would be gone for several weeks, during which time the families remained together. When the men returned from New Orleans or Shreveport or elsewhere, there would be a celebration, sometimes lasting a couple of days.

LIVING CONDITIONS for cattle raisers by the early 1840s had not changed greatly since the early colonists first arrived. Most houses were constructed of logs. But for settlers on the western edge of the wooded country near the open prairie and plains, experience with the Indians had taught them much. Indian raids by Comanches living on the plains were common. William Banta, who came to Texas as a boy of thirteen in 1839, recalled:

> The houses were from fourteen to sixteen feet square; the first six logs were fourteen feet in length, the next four rounds sixteen feet long; thus the house had the appearance of a big house set on a smaller one, forming what was then called a block house. . . . The doors were made of split and hewed puncheons pinned together with an auger, and hung to the log wall with wooden hinges. On the inside of the house they were fastened by heavy wooden bars in such a manner that it was impossible for any one to get into the house from the outside. The cracks of the house were stopped with pieces of timber split for the purpose and driven in with an axe, then pinned fast with wooden pins, leaving two or three holes in each side and end between the chinking, called port holes, used for the purpose of shooting outside in case of an attack. . . . The object of the projecting wall above was to be able to shoot straight down from the upper floor; and in fact this position commanded any approach from the outside.

Banta remembered that the men and boys of the early 1840s were dressed in buckskin pants, hunting shirts, and moccasins. Home-tanned leather was common. Hats or caps were made of fur skins, "and these, with a home spun shirt, composed the everyday wear," he added. The only difference on Sunday, Banta wrote, was that "they put on a clean shirt, provided they had two, which was sometimes the case." As for store-bought clothes, few settlers could afford them: "Women and children wore homespun clothing. The finest cotton cloth I saw made, the cotton seed was picked out by hand, the cotton carded by hand, and spun on a spinning wheel, and then woven on a hand loom. It was coarse, but lasted well."

On Sundays, according to Banta, the man of the family

> would hitch up the team, belt on his knife and pistols, and shoulder his gun; now all aboard were off to church. On arriving the guns were stacked in the corner of the house, and the side arms retained on the person of the owner. After preaching was over they returned home in the same manner. At parties men went armed the same as at other places, dancing in moccasins and buckskin pants with hunting shirts

made of the same material; the girls wore homespun dresses, and sometimes shoes and sometimes moccasins, and looked well at that.[24]

For some Texian stock raisers, perhaps as early as 1839, the amount of
overland travel to market was reduced by the introduction of water transportation. Before the Texas revolution some attempts had been made to
navigate Texas rivers, especially the Red. River. But the channel of the
Red River was blocked by what came to be known as the "Great Raft,"
a floating but stationary island of tightly woven logs, brush, and other
debris. There were even cottonwood trees growing on the raft, some with
trunks 8 inches in diameter. In 1833, U.S. engineers estimated that the raft
was 130 miles long, running from Loggy Bayou, about 100 miles above
Alexandria, to Hurricane Bluffs some 50 miles above modern Shreveport,
Louisiana. The federal government appropriated money to clear the
"Great Raft" and gave the job to Henry Shreve, a steamboat builder and
river captain of some prominence. He cleared part of the channel with
four steamboats and more than half a hundred men. The following year,
1834, the settlement of Shreveport was founded and named for the captain.
He finished the job in 1838, making the Red River navigable for more than
a thousand miles upstream from where it joins the Mississippi, but a few
months later new drifts closed it. Later, other problems developed, making
the river navigable only as far as Natchitoches, but that was far enough
north to help Texian stock raisers. Perhaps as early as 1839, some Texians
were driving small herds of cattle to Shreveport and probably to a few
other river towns in Louisiana, where their bawling and somewhat nervous
cattle were loaded on flatboats and sent down the Red to the Mississippi
and on to the New Orleans market. From there Texas cattle may have
been shipped by steamboat to Mobile, then the only other major market
along the central Gulf Coast.

Most historians who have mentioned the early Texas cattle trade
through the Gulf to New Orleans and Mobile have written that it began in
the late 1840s or in 1848. It seems that most of them relied on one sentence
contained in the *Tenth Census Report* of 1880 published in 1883. The
writer, Clarence W. Gordon, a special agricultural agent, wrote: "The
first shipment [of cattle] from Texas was by a Morgan steamer in
1848. . . ."[25] But an examination of the history of Texas steamboating
suggests that cattle may have been shipped from Texas Gulf Coast ports
much earlier. The Morgan Lines, established by Charles Morgan about
1836, had three steamers plying Texas waters by 1837. And eight years
later, in 1845, when Galveston and Velasco were the most important
Texas ports, 250 vessels alone arrived at Galveston, fifty-two of them
being steamboats going between Texas and New Orleans. Nearly all of the

steamboat trade during the very late 1830s and 1840s was of the common-carrier type, as opposed to the merchant-trader sort which existed in the early part of the nineteenth century.

Thus it seems highly probable that some Texas cattle were shipped to New Orleans through the Gulf from Texas well before 1848, perhaps as early as 1839. And it seems to this writer that the flow of cattle from Texas ports and down the Red River to New Orleans may have been much greater than most writers have suggested. Yet the total number of cattle exported in this manner was no doubt only a small fraction of the total cattle population of Mexican Texas, about 240,000 head in 1845.[26]

Aside from New Orleans and Mobile—and these markets could absorb only so many Texas cattle—there were really no readily accessible markets for Texian beef by early 1845. The southern states to the east were well supplied by their own cattle. To the southwest and west of the Republic of Texas, the region was sparsely settled. To the south in Mexico, there were more cattle than the Mexican population needed, and to the far west California had sufficient cattle for its people. To the north was Indian country and what some people were still calling the "Great American Desert." There was no market there. Only to the northeast, perhaps a thousand miles beyond the border of the Republic, were there large numbers of people and a demand for cattle. That direction offered the only real hope for new and better markets, and the day would come when Texians would drive their longhorns north and northeast in great numbers.

But political change and another war not only delayed such drives to the northeast but created a new market to the west and caused many a Texian to drive his cattle toward the Pacific Ocean. The sudden change that occurred would firmly establish a basic element of the evolving and adapting Texian cattle culture, the necessity for mobility. Tied to the independence, self-reliance, and individualism already evident in the Texian breed of cattle raiser, the unrestricted trail-driving way of life was soon to play a major role in spreading the Texian cattle culture.

CHAPTER 5

⚫

The Mixing of Cultures

The Texans had much beef to sell, but few places to sell it.
But now California needed the beef that Texas had, and
Texas cowmen ventured upon the long trail of some fifteen
hundred hazardous miles.

—J. EVETTS HALEY[1]

AMERICANS think nothing of traveling thousands of miles in a few hours. Modern air travel has enabled us to breach great distances in hours instead of weeks or months. Modern communication also has changed the face of the nation. Together, modern transportation and communication have eliminated many cultural differences that once existed in widely separated areas of the country. Unfortunately, these things have contributed to a growing sameness about most areas of America. Today one finds the same franchise restaurants and eating establishments from Maine to Oregon. Highway signs on the modern interstates look alike from Wisconsin to New Mexico, and people in Miami view the same canned entertainment in their living rooms as do people in Seattle. The sameness found today in California and Texas did not, of course, exist in the early 1830s. Communication between the two regions was limited. Hundreds of miles separated them. About the only similarities were the Spanish influences that had been planted in both areas. These influences were stronger in California than in Texas, where Americans from states like Alabama, Georgia, Mississippi, and Tennessee had settled and had introduced aspects of their own cultures. This fusion created the Texian culture, and it was quite different from the Spanish-dominated California culture. But the California culture of the 1830s and early 1840s was to change. Gold would be the catalyst. This precious metal would bring the Texian and Californian cultures together, and each would influence the other. To understand how, a thumbnail sketch of history is in order.

Sam Houston was elected president of the Republic of Texas in 1836, with voters indicating a desire for annexation to the United States. But there were insufficient votes in Congress to approve Texan statehood. Abolitionists charged that the Texas revolution had been a "slaveocracy conspiracy" by southerners. Thus it was nearly ten years before Texas succeeded in joining the Union as the twenty-eighth state on December 29, 1845. When Texas became part of the Union, Mexico refused to accept the Rio Grande as an international boundary and soon severed its relations with the United States. President James K. Polk, anticipating trouble with Mexico, ordered Brigadier General Zachary Taylor to move a force from Louisiana to the Nueces River in Texas. In the meantime, Polk sent John Slidell to Mexico in hopes of settling differences peacefully. Slidell's mission failed, and General Taylor started south with his forces toward the Rio Grande across territory then claimed by Mexico. The expected happened. Mexican soldiers attacked the American forces. When word of the conflict reached Washington, Congress declared war, voted $10 million for an invasion of Mexico, and authorized the President to call up fifty thousand volunteers.

Within days General Taylor crossed the Rio Grande and occupied Matamoros. Within a month Brigadier General Stephen Watts Kearny was ordered to occupy the Mexican provinces of New Mexico and California. He marched from Fort Leavenworth on the Missouri River with about 1,600 men for New Mexico and by mid-August entered Santa Fe without opposition. He claimed New Mexico for the United States and then divided his forces. Kearny sent Colonel Alexander W. Doniphan south into Chihuahua, and Captain Philip St. George Cooke to open a wagon road through northern Sonora to California. Kearny then took one hundred dragoons and headed west to join the American forces already struggling to conquer California.

The Americans won in California, as did those who fought their way to Mexico City, where the American flag was raised over a foreign capital for the first time on September 14, 1847. A little more than four months later, on February 2, 1848, Mexico and the United States signed the Treaty of Guadalupe Hidalgo. The treaty established the Rio Grande as the international boundary in Texas and ceded California and New Mexico (then including much of modern Arizona) to the United States. Communications still being very slow, particularly in the West, the signers of the treaty were unaware that gold had been discovered in California nine days earlier near Coloma, at a sawmill owned by John Augustus Sutter. The discovery of gold in northern California was to have great impact on the carefree life of California rancheros and on the life of Texas stock raisers searching for new cattle markets.

For centuries gold had been sought, cherished, lusted after, and fought over by men and women dreaming of instant wealth. When word of the discovery finally raced across the mountains and deserts and plains to the prairies of Texas and the rolling country of Missouri and eastward, the rush was on. Within a year California's population of fourteen thousand whites grew by more than sixty thousand people. California, a new territory of the United States, was not prepared for the unparalleled migration. The swarms of people entering the state created problems that were not even dreamed of a year earlier. Perhaps the most complex problem concerned land grants. The treaty with Mexico had bound the United States government to recognize "legitimate titles to every description of property, personal and real, existing in the ceded territories." This included the Spanish and Mexican land grants for California ranchos. But the influx of immigrants demanded immediate action on the part of congressmen and senators working at their desks more than 2,000 miles to the east, on the other side of the "Great American Desert," and the lawmakers in Washington, D.C., were busy. Southern states were threatening secession over sectional differences. After long and bitter debate, Congress accepted a free-state constitution for California. This was part of the Compromise of 1850, and California was admitted to the Union as the thirty-first state on September 9. Congress then turned its attention to California's internal problems, and it passed into law an act providing for the appointment by the President of three commissioners to settle private land claims.

Had gold not been discovered in California, the rancho system might have continued unchanged for perhaps fifty years or more, but the act establishing a land commission placed the burden on proving land grant claims upon Spaniards and Mexicans. American immigrants needed only to obtain two signatures to their petitions to establish rights to vacant lands. Thus began the dissolution of the rancho system in northern California, where, although many rancheros struggled to hold them, they eventually lost large portions of their ranchos. The ways of the eastern United States were taking hold. To the south, however, the rancho system remained intact, and the sudden influx of people into the gold region of the north created an immediate market for beef, with prices jumping as high as $75 a head in San Francisco and small calves bringing $20 to $25. Even on the ranchos far to the south, full-grown steers were selling for $30 to $40 a head. Since the cattle were worth more in the north, rancheros in southern California began driving their herds to San Francisco, Stockton, and Sacramento. The old custom of slaughtering cattle for their hides and tallow gave way to a much more profitable business.

The culture of the rancheros in southern California began to change. Mobility became an important feature as the herds were driven north. Most herds numbered about a thousand or less and were driven either along the coast or through the almost uninhabited San Joaquin Valley, although one of the first trail herds to use the San Joaquin route did not make it. The cattle belonged to Henry Dalton, an Englishman, who came to California in 1843. Early in October of 1848, Dalton made arrangements to send a thousand head from his Azusa and Santa Anita ranchos to Stockton. He envisioned a $20,000 profit from the drive. Dalton contracted the trail driving to Pedro Lopez, furnished the necessary provisions, and then went ahead to arrange for the sale of the cattle. Lopez and his vaqueros began the drive north, herding the cattle over Tejon Pass and through the Tehachapi Mountains in what is modern Kern County. The cattle averaged about 10 miles a day, but by the time they reached Four Creeks near modern Visalia, the animals were tired. So were the vaqueros and Lopez. And their horses were worn out. Lopez and his vaqueros were resting at Four Creeks, and the cattle were grazing nearby, when Dalton found them late in December. He decided to take charge, but first he headed for Los Angeles to obtain fresh horses and more vaqueros. Before he returned, three hundred Tulare Indians went on the rampage and attacked Lopez and his men. All of the vaqueros were killed, and the cattle were stampeded over the nearby hills. Dalton never delivered his herd to Stockton and never restored his rancho. He quit the cattle business.[2]

Other ranchers in southern California did succeed in getting their cattle to the markets in the north, but for at least two years after the massacre at Four Creeks, most ranchers followed the safer coastal route through Ventura and Santa Barbara and then northward, bypassing the Indian-infested San Joaquin Valley. The Indians continued to cause problems, often making forays to the coast. With every new moon ranchers, especially those north of Los Angeles, could expect raids on their horse herds by small bands of Indians. The Indians often drove off cattle as well.

The northern drives in California during the early 1850s were important economically, but they were also as colorful as a twentieth-century Hollywood western—the vaqueros with their red sashes blowing in the breeze as they drove the cattle northward; the sound of the rawhide on their saddles, creaking with the movement of their horses; stampedes; severe thunderstorms; raids by hostile Indians; and bands of outlaws who rustled cattle. Unfortunately most historians of the cattle trade and even writers of western cowboy adventure books and films have generally ignored the importance and color of these California drives. Instead they have favored the later Texas cattle drives to Kansas and the uproarious cattle towns, or, still later, the great drives over the Bozeman Trail in Wyoming and Montana. Robert Glass Cleland, in *The Cattle on a Thousand Hills,* is one of the few historians and writers to examine the early California drives.

Just as the region between the Nueces and Rio Grande in Texas had attracted many unsavory characters in the late 1830s, so did California after the discovery of gold in 1848. In both instances there was a noticeable lack of law and order, but in California it was gold and not wild cattle that first attracted so many men of questionable character. In California, however, some of these men soon sought to cash in on the high value of cattle by rustling, and on the ranchos the vaqueros became the first line of defense in protecting cattle from outlaws and hostile Indians. Ranchers soon built large adobe walls around small pastures or corrals and moved their prize cattle and horses inside. In some instances rows of bleached cattle skulls were attached to the tops of the walls with the horns pointing outward. Other ranchers dug trenches 5 feet wide and equally deep around pastures where they kept their best animals. In a few cases ranchers planted willow trees close together around the pastures, creating an almost impenetrable hedge.

In spite of these physical obstacles and the watchful vaqueros, many ranchos in southern California lost cattle and large numbers of horses to rustlers and especially to bands of Ute and Mojave Indians who came from the desert via Cajon Pass or other trails to the south. Even emigrant trains were not immune from such attacks, since many California-bound emigrants brought cattle with them. They had followed the Oregon Trail from the Missouri River westward to about Fort Hall in present Idaho and then turned southwest toward the Humboldt River and on across the mountains to California.

As early as the spring of 1850, enterprising men began trailing cattle from Missouri over this route to take advantage of the high prices being paid for beef in the California gold region. Perhaps the first man to take a large herd of more than five hundred cattle to California from Missouri was Walter Crow, who first went to California in 1849, and decided to settle in the rich San Joaquin Valley. But first he returned to Missouri to obtain a herd of Durham cattle, a better grade of stock than the Spanish cattle. The Durham is an English breed of shorthorn cattle brought to America about 1817. By 1850, a few herds could be found west of the Mississippi, most in Cooper County around Boonville, in central Missouri.

Late in February of 1850 Walter Crow and his four sons—Ben, Alfred, James, and Martin—along with Cyrus Clark Loveland, bought Durhams in Cooper County. Like Crow, Cyrus Loveland had been to California. He had gone there in 1848 and with two friends spent seven months in the gold region. They took out $18,000 worth of the precious metal. Loveland returned east and later joined Walter Crow's party in Missouri. Everything was ready early in May 1850, and with 721 cattle and 64 head of work steers, they crossed the western border of Missouri south of modern Kansas City and made for the Oregon and Santa Fe trails.

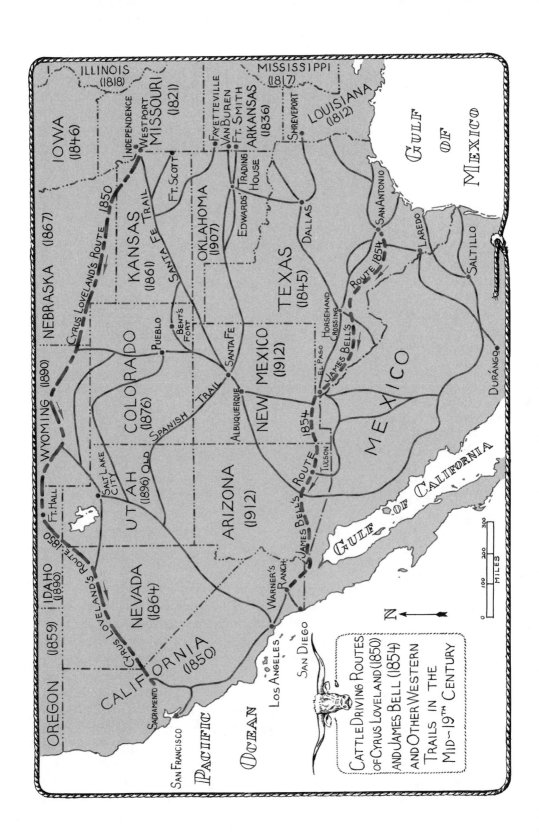

CATTLE DRIVING ROUTES of CYRUS LOVELAND (1850) AND JAMES BELL (1854) AND OTHER WESTERN TRAILS IN THE MID~19TH CENTURY

Near today's Gardner, Kansas, the Oregon and Santa Fe trails split. There they turned their cattle toward the northeast and followed the Oregon or California trail, as it was then being called. South of modern Lawrence, Kansas, within a mile of where this narrative is being written, they herded the cattle across the shallow Wakarusa River and struck a northwesterly direction. They crossed the Kansas River near present-day Rossville, which in 1850 consisted of a handful of log cabins on the north side of the river, and was then called Union Village. Gentle inclines on both banks made the crossing easy for the cattle, since the river was not high. A short distance upstream a ferry took their wagons across.

Details of this cattle drive from Missouri to California are preserved in the diary of Cyrus C. Loveland, which is now in the California State Library at Sacramento. By May 23, 1850, Crow, Loveland, and the other men had herded the cattle across the Big Blue River southeast of modern Waterville, Kansas. Loveland noted in his diary: "Last night we lost no cattle but have nearly every other night." Once across the Big Blue, Loveland recorded that a member of the party "found a human skeleton with a pair of shoes on it." Three days later he wrote: "Began to see signs of buffalo." These California-bound cattle herders were soon using buffalo chips to fuel their evening campfires. By May 29 they reached the South Platte in what is now south central Nebraska. They passed Fort Kearny and learned that 4,500 teams and 21,287 emigrants were ahead of them on the trail. They pushed their herd by Devil's Gate in early July. On July 4 they rested and quietly celebrated Independence Day. "We killed a beef and had a fine spot of soup, which was the best of anything that we have had on the trip. We also had a desert [sic] of peach pie which really reminded me of home," wrote Loveland.

On the last day of July, Crow, Loveland, and the others reached Fort Hall on the Snake River. "It consists of four or five small buildings built of adobe, surrounded with a wall of the same material built by the Hudson Bay Fur Company. At this time there are but five or six men at this fort. This is a pretty country and I think it would produce some things very well. Grass plenty," noted Loveland. Crossing the Port Neuf and Bannock rivers, they drove their herd past American Falls on the Snake River, where a boatload of American trappers had been lost several years earlier. Travel was often difficult and grass was not always plentiful for the cattle. The men drove the herd past Thousand Springs and on August 13 reached the North Fork of the Humboldt River in what is now north central Nevada. Eighteen days later they reached the area of the Humboldt Sink and killed two beeves for emigrants who had run out of provisions. The same day Loveland wrote in his diary: "Provisions are very scarce. Our mess has just ate the last of our breadstuff and fruit. We have one mess of beans and then beef is our only show." Travel during the next three days was difficult, since they passed through what was mostly desert, herding the cattle day and night.

On September 5, 1850, they moved the cattle up along the Truckee River and stopped. Loveland wrote:

> Never was this party so completely used up as when we came in from the desert. We were so wore out with fatigue and for want of sleep that like many of the old crows it might have been said of us that we were give out, for we had been without sleep two days and nearly all of two nights and on the go constantly. The last night on the desert we were so overcome with sleep that we were obliged to get off our horses and walk for fear of falling off. As we were walking along after the cattle it certainly would have been very amusing to anyone who could see us a staggering along against each other, first on one side of the road, then the other, like a company of drunken men, but no human eye was there to see, for all alike were sleeping while walking. Thanks to the Almighty Ruler above, we overcame all difficulty thus far on our long journey.

Three days later found the herd nearing the site of modern Reno, Nevada, and five days later they had climbed more than 9,200 feet above sea level and were crossing Donner Pass. It was there four years earlier that the late-crossing Donner party had been trapped by winter weather, but Walter Crow's party was crossing in good time. They made it safely over the mountains by late summer and reached California, where the last entry in Loveland's diary is dated September 30. On that day the herd was driven across the Sacramento River and set to graze, while Loveland and some of the other men made camp. It had taken Crow's party about five months to travel from western Missouri to California, and their cattle losses were not great.[3]

Other herds of cattle were driven to California from Missouri that summer of 1850, but little is known about them or the men who drove them. Sometimes the long journey had exciting moments, although seldom of the magnitude shown in Hollywood westerns. Indians trying to steal a few horses or a few head of cattle on a dark night or someone getting bitten by a rattlesnake or kicked by a horse was the usual "exciting" fare. Most of the time the drives were rather routine. They were not romantic in the eyes of most drovers, nor were they filled with adventure, unless one viewed the ever-changing countryside as romantic. Few did. Weak cattle would die. The carcasses found along the trail left proof of this. And men on the trail drives would sometimes get sick. Those who did not recover were buried beside the trail.

The spring of 1851 saw more cattle pointed west toward California from Missouri and the Mississippi Valley. And in 1852, more than ninety thousand head reportedly passed Fort Kearny, most en route to California, some to Oregon.[4] That year Ansel Martin of the firm of Martin, Pomeroy and Co. of Lexington, Missouri, drove 2,500 cattle toward California, but whether they followed the Oregon or California trail is unknown. From what is known, Martin's herd may have taken the Santa Fe Trail to New Mexico and then followed a southern route into California.[5] This southern route was used by other California-bound herds in 1852. Jotham Meeker wrote in his diary on May 15, 1852, that "about 800 wagons and 10,000 cattle" had already gone over the trail, which passed close to the Ottawa Baptist Mission east of modern Ottawa in east central Kansas, many miles south of the Santa Fe Trail.[6]

At about the same time Meeker made the notation in his diary, an army officer met a drover about fifty miles northwest of the Ottawa Baptist Mission. The officer, probably Lieutenant William D. Whipple of Major Enoch Steen's Santa Fe–bound command, had crossed the Kansas River west of modern Topeka, Kansas. In a letter later published by a New York newspaper, he wrote: "Beyond the Kansas some of our party met a drover who stated that he was driving ten thousand head of cattle before him to California. Whether he was able to drive such a number in one drove or divided into several droves I cannot say. Such is the statement given to me, and it illustrates, better than anything else could, the amount of travel and trade in the direction of the Pacific shore. . . ."[7]

The following year, 1853, the post register at Fort Kearny on the South Platte recorded 105,792 cattle having passed the spot by August 15. But estimates of cattle reaching California that year total only about 62,000 head, and many of them arrived by other routes. A lot of the cattle driven west over the Oregon or California trail may have ended up in Oregon. Others probably died en route. Most cattle lost weight, becoming lean and weary well before they reached the California border. The stock raisers who drove large herds across the plains and through the deserts and mountains knew that animals surviving the journey would fatten on grass and regain their strength once in California, but many emigrants who drove small groups of cattle ahead of their wagons apparently did not realize this. When people met them on the trail and offered to trade one fresh beef with meat on its bones for half a dozen jaded cattle, many emigrants did not hesitate to do so.

One man who made his fortune in this manner was Colonel Oliver Wheeler of Connecticut. Wheeler went to California for his health in 1851. He worked briefly as a store clerk in Sacramento and then began trading for worn-out cattle on the border of the desert. He placed the tired cattle on good grass along the mountains and rivers, and soon had fat, highly salable animals. Gradually Wheeler became wealthy, acquired several ranches, and opened a wholesale meat market in San Francisco.

Enterprising Mormon traders did the same thing along the California trail from the Sweetwater to the Humboldt. But they often traded Indian ponies for the exhausted and footsore cattle. Most emigrants were glad to have another horse to ride. In 1853 the Mormons drove 23,000 work steers described as "fine, heavily fattened animals" to the Sacramento market; there they reportedly sold them for $200 to $250 per yoke.[8]

Not all cattle from east of the Rocky Mountains were driven to California over the Oregon Trail route via Fort Hall to Sacramento. Many drovers followed the already mentioned southern route. In June of 1850, a Captain Forrest, probably from Arkansas, collected a herd of 744 cows and 231 calves in southwest Missouri. With twelve Americans, four Mexicans, and two Delaware Indians, "all heavily armed," Forrest drove the herd southwest. They crossed the Arkansas River northwest of present Muskogee, Oklahoma, and then continued southwest into Texas. Forrest appears to have followed a route already in use by many Texas drovers.[9]

Many Texans headed west to California in search of their fortune soon after word of the gold strike reached their new state early in 1848. But other Texans saw the discovery of gold as a solution to the problem of countless cattle. The goldseekers in California had created a new and growing market for the multiplying Texas herds. Early in the spring of 1848, several Texans started west with herds of longhorns. It was a gamble, but most had little to lose. Cattle prices in Texas were very low, about a dollar or two per head. Even if they lost half the herd on the trail, they could still make a profit. One of the early Texans to drive cattle toward California was T. J. Trimmier, from Washington County. He supposedly drove five hundred head to the Pacific and sold them for $100 each. When Trimmier returned to Texas the following spring, he met herd after herd of cattle, most of them from Texas, bound for the California markets over the southern route.[10]

It took five or six months to drive a herd from Texas to California. San Antonio and Fredericksburg were among the starting points for the long drives, which struck west from San Antonio, crossing West Texas to Franklin or Coons' Rancho, as it was sometimes called, in the area of modern El Paso. It was named for Franklin Coons (sometimes spelled Coontz), a Santa Fe trader, who established a general merchandise store there about 1847. From his store the trail headed west across what is now southern New Mexico toward the Gila and Colorado rivers in present-day Arizona. There, near the villages of Tubac and Tucson, the trail generally followed the wagon road opened by Captain Philip St. George Cooke a few years earlier. Once across the Colorado Desert into California, the cattle were trailed to Warner's Ranch, owned by John Trumbull Warner, an American from Connecticut who had emigrated to California in 1831. By 1844, Warner had obtained the Rancho Valle de San Jose on the trail near San Diego. He turned the rancho into a trading post that became a well-known rest stop for thousands of forty-niners coming to California over the southern route. From Warner's Rancho, which marked for many travelers their arrival in California, cattle herds could be driven to San Diego, Los Angeles, or northward to the profitable markets of San Francisco, Stockton, or Sacramento.

The southern route probably carried more cattle to California than the northern route that followed the Platte, South Pass, and the Humboldt River. But the northern route carried most of the goldseekers, in spite of the efforts of businessmen in the frontier states of Arkansas and Texas who had hopes of establishing the main travelway from the Atlantic to the Pacific over the southern route for the sake of trade.

From Fort Smith and Van Buren in Arkansas, the trails headed west, coming together at a point on the north bank of the Canadian River near modern Holdenville, in Hughes County, Oklahoma. There a man named Edwards ran a "trading house" and maintained a stock of merchandise plus corn, horses, and cattle. The route followed the Canadian River west from Edwards's store into New Mexico and Albuquerque. West of there, goldseekers could either continue due west and then southwest across New Mexico and Arizona, or turn south at Albuquerque to the Mexican border and move west along the border into California.

Still another route that was considered southern left either Fayetteville, Arkansas, or Fort Scott in what is now eastern Kansas. Each trail led to the Santa Fe Trail, which was then used mostly by emigrants. At Santa Fe, goldseekers could go west or south. Still others followed the Santa Fe Trail to Fort Mann and Bent's Fort on the Arkansas River, and then to where Pueblo, Colorado, stands today. From there they turned north, following either a route north to Fort Laramie and the Platte River or a trail over the Rockies, one blazed by John C. Frémont in 1844. It went north to just inside the modern boundary of Wyoming and then west toward Salt Lake City. From there emigrants could either go southwest across what is now Utah and southeast Nevada, striking the Mohave River in California and continuing to Los Angeles, or move west across Utah and northern Nevada until they hit the Humboldt River route. Many trails led west to California in the late 1840s and early 1850s.

The southern routes traversed rugged and mostly unsettled country. Grass and water were not always plentiful, although Texas cattle could go for days without water. There was always the possibility of hostile Indians, especially the fierce Apaches and Comanches. But the hardships, dangers, and drawbacks of such a lengthy journey were more than outweighed by the promise or dream of huge profits at the end of the trail. And, as the Texans learned, should prices not be to their liking once they reached California, it cost little to pasture their cattle, let them get fat, and, when the demand for beef increased, sell their herds.

It seems likely that cattle losses may have been greater over the southern route than on the northern trails. The grass was not always plentiful to the south, but was generally adequate to the north. Indian problems were also greater on the southern route. John Hackett, who had traveled to California in 1849 in search of gold, returned to Arkansas in the early 1850s. By 1853 he had gathered a herd of 937 cattle and crossed Texas, following the most traveled southern route to California. Three-quarters of his cattle died on the way, and Hackett "arrived in Stanislaus county, California, with only 182 survivors." He had lost 755 head, but he still made a profit.[11]

Frederick Law Olmsted, who traveled through Texas early in 1854, saw one "California cattle-train," as he called the herd, preparing to leave San Antonio. Olmsted wrote that it consisted of "four hundred head of oxen, generally in fine moderately fat condition." He noted there were twenty-five men to guard and drive the cattle, and he added: "Only a few of these, old frontier men and drovers, who had before been over the road, and could act as guides, were paid wages. The remainder were young men who wished to emigrate to California, and who were glad to have their expenses paid for their services by the proprietors of the drove. They were all mounted on mules, and supplied with a short government rifle and Colt's repeaters. Two large wagons and a cart, loaded with stores, cooking utensils, and ammunition, followed the herd."[12]

About two months after Olmsted observed the California-bound herd, a young Texan named James G. Bell decided to work his way to California with another herd then being formed in San Antonio. Bell, twenty-two years old, had been living in San Antonio, where his father had opened the first jewelry store. Young Bell wanted to join his brother, who was in California. So he signed on with John James, a stock raiser from Seguin, Texas. Bell agreed to work for his keep and the protection offered by the drovers in crossing the southern route to California. On June 3, 1854, he left San Antonio with the herd.

James Bell probably was typical of many young men who worked their way west with a cattle herd during this period, but he is particularly noteworthy because he left what is one of the earliest accounts of a Texas trail drive to the Pacific. How experienced Bell was in handling cattle is not known. He could, however, ride a horse or mule, although this was not unusual on the frontier. The experience of driving cattle seems to have been new to him, however, and the people, animals, and even the terrain crossed during the journey fascinated him. Because of this his log of the drive is delightful and interesting. His writing style is honest and straightforward, although his spelling, punctuation, and grammar leave something to be desired.

The following excerpts from his trail log convey the flavor of life while herding cattle from Texas to California in 1854:

June 6: Heavy fog last night, cloudy this morning. Travelled about 9 miles, came up in front and found an hombre skinning 3 rattlesnakes. When I enquired the use he would put the skins to, he told me that by stretching the skin on the cantle of the saddle no harm would come to my posteriors IE no Gall or sore; also by putting a piece of the skin between the lining and hat, that I never could have the headache. The hombre took the fat out of the snakes and divided with those who had faith in its virtures; it is good for wounds of various kinds. The Mexican gave me a very large snake skin when we arrived in camp, which was early, only nine miles to the next water hole; having time I stretched it tigtly on the cantle covering it entirely, and used the end for covering the horn. Evening, Killed a beef being in want of fresh meat—it would astonish a regular bred butcher to see with what dispatch 3 Mexicans can rope, kill, and have a beef cut into *ropes*. The beef is first thrown down by means of rope then stuck, not struck on the head. The head is turned to one side which holds the beef in the proper position, one side is skined, the skined side is allowed to turn up—half of the beef is dissected, the entrails then taken out, the ribs are left whole and roasted before the fire, the other half and head is made into ropes and exposed on a line in the sun until jerked. There is an old Comanche Indian in the train. . . . When the beef was being made into ropes he drew a 12 inch butcher knife and pitched in with an energy which told me plainly that the sight of blood was rather to his habit than otherwise.

June 18: There are three men in camp 1 Mexican, 1 American and 1 German who are perfectly worthless and it would be a God send if the Indians would kill them. Some of the men have verry little thrift, and take no care whatever of their health, have no thought for the next hour, and are content to let others do what they should do themselves. We have one poor fellow (German, or Pole) who immagins every one trying to insult him. He will probably be sent back, when we meet the San Antonio mail.

June 25: Reach Live Oak Creek at 2 O'clock and are encamped for the night. Made 17 miles. By the by, this *is* Sunday. No matter, it is all the same to us, we work as much on Sabbath as one week days. Not one half the men know how long we have been out. There is a fall of six feet in Live Oak Creek, several of us are going bathing now—returning I found an oblong pile of stones. At one end found the inscription Amanda Lewis, 1852. I read . . . it aloud when one of the young men present spoke with astonishment. He was acquainted with the persons in Missippi. She was a mother of a large family; How desolate must have been the husband and children when they performed the last sad rights over their loved mother, —when, with mournfull feelings they turned away knowing that *then,* thay beheld the last of her whom thay had ever looked up to with love and veneration. . . . Night is now approaching and the serious business of the trip is about to comence—that of standing guard, and a posability of an attack from the Indians.

July 3: I find the blue coat to be perfectly superfluous and generally carry it tied behind the saddle, pants in my boots, both boots and pants begin to have rather a shocking bad appearance for after eating (having left my handercheifs at home—I use the pants for wiping my knife & hands on; in riding the bosom of my check shirt works open, and along down the center of my breast is a brown stripe like the stripe on a black Dutchman back. My nose and ears and neck are undergoing the scaling prosses until I look as scaly about the face and gills as a buffalow fish. My riding outfit consists of—on either side of the horn is a *rope* and canteen, behind the cantle is my tin cup and iron spoon, while occasionally there is to be found a dead rabbit hung by the neck waiting to be devoured. And when we expect to travel over dinner time, a slab of jerked beef finds itself flaping against the side of the mule. My bed is made with the over and Indian rubber coat next the ground, saddle at the head, horse blanket on the saddle to make it soft, bed blanket over all, and myself on top of that; sometimes to luxuriate a little I pull off my boots and hat. When it rains I roll up into a ball like a porcupine, and spread the gum coat over me. I like to sleep in the open air, for when I get up in the morning my sleep has been refreshing and comfortable.

July 5: Smith reports a fight some 40 miles ahead—Mr. Erskin had with the Indians—they stole 3 head oxen. Erskin retaliated by killing 6 Indians and taking 10 horses. he was foolish to follow them into a cannon where with additional forces the Indians turned on him and compelled him to retreat. If the Yellow bellies should attack us doubtless they would have a warm reception. All the men are well armed. The only thing lacking is more horses.

July 7: None but a poet could appreciate this evening; the rising moon, the setting sun, the calm sensation, the clear sky and smooth verdant prairie gives, all combine to make it the most pleasant and delightful camp we have had during the trip.

The low mountains which surround us are just far enough to keep the eye from waring with the desert wast, while the rich coloring of the sky, combined with the whole landscape make any one who has 'music in the soul' wish to be a Painter, and any Painter wish for the power to coppy it.

July 20: Left camp early, made six or eight miles to camp, passed a portion of the day in lounging about, eat some—what the mexicans call—Mexican strawberry, these are nothing more than a species of *Prickly Pear;* the inside of the pear resembels the strawberry, it is the most delicious of the species I have tasted. Last night I was kept from sleep by the Musquito, thay annoyed and bit me beyond all patience.

July 23: At noon we encamped opposite a Mexican town or *rancho.* About one dozen men came over, bringing new onions, as large as my fist, eggs, chickens, and Muscal liquor; we bought everything except the liquor which they would not sell, but gave to us. This liquor has a tast between whiskey and brandy, and considerable intoxicating power. Not one of these men have on pantaloons; but a few have white cotton drawers about I yard wide at the bottom, some have on a cotton shirt, just long enough to be decent, some have simply a cloth around the wast.

August 4: The features of James Company are considerably changed, some men have been discharged and some new ones received; I can hardly tell whether the change has made any improvement; it is verry difficult to collect any body of men together, without having some black sheep in the flock.

August 7: Camp life brings out all the utility men have—for instance I took an old worn out pair of pants, and threw them up in a tree. Shortly I saw one of the men cutting them into sections of a circle, to make a scull cap of—who would have thought that the pants I started from San Antonio with would have been used on a mans head the ballance of the trip.

August 27: Sunday. Cloudy and damp. Left camp half past six. Saw a new method for driving fractious steers, this morning; the cartmen yoked in a new one; when ready to start, he would not move, so the men verry deliberately put a chunk of fire on his rump. After it burnt through the skin he travelled verry well.

September 1: Now encamped near—some three miles—the 'Old Rancho of San Bernardino' [early settlement in Northeast Sonora]. About four o'clock in the afternoon a severe rain and Thunderstorm came up. The cattle were feeding in the hollow, a vivid flash of lightning which made a report like the explosion of thousand cannon, struck a *white* steer, glancing along the belly, and scorching the hair off, thence to another *white* steer— he showed no marks—about fifty yards distant and killed them both, nocking down all—some twenty—intervening and on the line of the stroke; several men felt the effects, although the camp was about one hundred and fifty yards from the herd.

September 21: Still in camp. South of Teuson [Tucson] about two miles. Went up in the ambulance this morning to have some repairing done to the woodwork. A mule pack train came in from *Guymos* and brought intelligence from Mexico of the ratification of the Treaty re-running the line of the Treaty of Hidalgo [this was the Gadsden Purchase, in which the United States purchased a wedge of territory between Texas and California from Mexico]; we now consider ourselves in American territory; what the people of this place think of U.S. as their master I can't tell.

October 3: Sitting quietly down, after supper, a few nights ago, several of us made a calculation of the amount of property lost during the present year, on this route. At reasonable calculations we make out that, three thousand head of cattle at $25 each, $75,000, and enough Mules, Horses and other property destroyed to make $25,000 more, making it all $100,000, not very far from the true amount. The Indians are in possession of ¾ of it.

November 11: Saturday. Encamped within sight of Warner's Rancho a fine spring; two or three straw houses situated in a beautiful little valley compose the celebrated place of Warner's Rancho.[13]

From Warner's Rancho young James Bell went to Los Angeles and later to the gold region in the north. Few details of his life in California are known, but thirteen years later, at the age of thirty-five, he died in California.

Other Texans who, like Bell, drove cattle to California undoubtedly learned much about long trail drives, and in California they saw, heard, and learned much more about cattle and ranching along the Pacific. While there was undoubtedly contact between the Texans and the California rancheros and vaqueros, it is impossible to say to what extent one influenced the culture of the other. Some may have bought or traded for a lariat or bridle or saddle or learned a new rope throw. Unfortunately, neither people left much of a record of their meetings. One may only guess at whether the men of the Texian culture were influenced by the Californianos or vice versa.

Until the middle 1850s the California markets easily absorbed the many California cattle driven to market plus the thousands that arrived from Texas, Missouri, and elsewhere. Times were good, especially for the California rancheros, who almost overnight had more money in their pockets than most had ever imagined possible. And they hurriedly tried to spend their money, buying "saddles trimmed with solid silver, spurs of gold, bridles with silver chains," and anything else that caught their fancy. Even the ladies covered their earthen floors with costly rugs and purchased four-post bedsteads with expensive lace curtains. The wives and daughters of ranchers were soon "dragging trains of massive silk and satin" over their dirt floors. It was "an odd mixture of squalor and splendor," as one observer noted.[14]

Many California ranchers, anxious to sell as many cattle as they could, failed to keep their breeding stock. They sold their bulls along with their cows and steers. The normal increase of the cattle herds in southern California began to fall off, from about fifteen thousand head annually to less than half that figure by 1855. The decline of the cowboy culture in California had begun, and by the end of 1856 what Robert Glass Cleland had called "the golden age of the cattle industry in California" was over.[15]

The combination of so many California cattle, plus the immense numbers of cattle from Texas, Missouri, and elsewhere to the east, glutted the California markets almost completely in 1856. Prices dropped to $16–$18 a head, with young stock bringing only $7–$8. Before the summer of 1856 ended, a severe drought struck portions of California, forcing many ranchers to sell even more cattle at low prices. The markets were completely glutted with cattle as 1857 began, much to the dismay of those herders who had driven cattle to California during the summer of 1856.

The editor of a Los Angeles newspaper summed up the situation in 1856 when he wrote: "The teeth of the cattle have this year, been so dull that they have been able scarcely to save themselves from starvation; but buyers are nearly as plenty as cattle, and sharp in proportion to the prospect of starvation. . . . Neither pistol shots nor dying groans have any effect; earthquakes hardly turn men in their beds. It is no use talking—business has stepped out and the people is [sic] asleep."[16]

As word of the collapse of the California market spread east, the flow of California-bound cattle slowed and by 1859 was nothing more than a trickle. By then stock raisers in Missouri and the Mississippi Valley were looking eastward and watching the railroads push beyond the Allegheny Mountains toward the west. And in Texas, stock raisers were not just looking northeast toward the approaching railroads; some of them had already driven their longhorns north toward the Missouri River and that dreamed-of market for Texas cattle.

CHAPTER 6

•◆•

Texas Trails North

By the middle of the decade [1850s] the range-cattle business had attained so great a development in Texas ... it had become commonly regarded by the public as the characteristic industry of Texas....

—JAMES W. FREEMAN[1]

BY 1850 more and more Americans were coming to settle in the new state of Texas. Many came to raise cattle, attracted by stories they had heard about how easy it was to raise cattle and become wealthy in Texas. For some, this "cattle fever" may have been as strong as the "gold fever" was for those who chose California. Like many of the forty-niners, who started west on the strength of unconfirmed stories, settlers headed for Texas on the strength of rumors. They dreamed their own dreams of a promised land. Certainly, some people did make a fortune raising cattle in Texas, but there were many people who did not. Yet the promise was always there that today would be better than yesterday and tomorrow even better than today. Even when tomorrow was not better, the warm sunshine and gentle breezes made frontier life in Texas bearable.

There were those who sought to learn more about Texas before deciding to settle there. One such person was Philips Fitzpatrick of Ellmore's Mills, Autauga County, Alabama. He wrote to his uncle Alva Fitzpatrick, who had moved from Alabama to Texas in 1843 and settled in Victoria County on Arenoso Creek. Alva Fitzpatrick replied to his nephew, encouraging him to come to Texas and get a piece of good land with plenty of timber and water and grass "that will hardly ever give out." He wrote that the land should be near the Gulf, where boats would come and carry off what was produced. "Stick down upon it with some good woman for your wife for with out a good wife it is hard to get along," he wrote, adding: "Get as many cows as you can. Get say one hundred Brude Mairs & about two good Jacks to go with them." He noted that mares could be delivered to his door for $5 a head, that a cow and a calf cost $8, $4 for a cow alone, and that three-year-old beeves could be sold for $10 cash "by from one to five hundred at a dash." And he reported that every steamship that left nearby Port Lavaca each Thursday carried fifty to seventy-five beeves and that the trade was increasing.[2]

Whether Philips Fitzpatrick took his uncle's advice and settled in Texas is not known, but plenty of others did. Many settled along the coast near the ports of Galveston, Brazos Santiago (Port Isabel), Corpus Christi, and Indianola. Cattle were shipped from most of these ports, but by 1850 Indianola had most of the trade. Located on the west shore of Matagorda Bay, and originally called Powderhorn and later Karlshaven by German immigrants, Indianola was chosen in 1849 by Charles Morgan as the principal port for ships of his Morgan Lines. He had been using Port Lavaca but found the port charges excessive. When he changed to Indianola a man named James Foster began buying Texas cattle and shipping them to New Orleans on Morgan Line ships. By 1851, Foster was making a handsome profit by buying only the best grade of Texas cattle at low prices and selling them high in New Orleans. He rapidly acquired control of the entire stock-carrying capacity of nearly all steamboats in the New Orleans–Texas trade. Foster is described as "a very shrewd and prompt business man."[3]

Few Texans profited from Foster's enterprise, and by late 1853 most cattle raisers, especially those along the Gulf Coast, seem to have given up much hope that Gulf shipping would be the solution to the problem of finding good markets for their ever-increasing herds. Foster almost monopolized the Gulf cattle trade by the mid-1850s, and a man named William B. Grimes, who liked neither the high rates charged by the Morgan Lines nor the monopoly Foster had created, decided to send a herd of cattle overland to New Orleans. He ordered a young hired hand named Abel Head "Shanghai" Pierce to drive the herd. Pierce, a 6-foot 4-inch native of Rhode Island, was twenty years old. He earned his nickname soon after arriving in Texas because people thought he looked like a Shanghai rooster. Pierce, who would later become a well-known Texas cattleman, took the herd through. When he returned to Texas, he gave the following account of the journey:

The mud and water of the Louisiana swamps compelled us to pick every step. Why the public roads—where there were any—would bog a saddleblanket. My steers were nice, fat slick critters that knew how to swim, but they were used to a carpet of prairie grass. They were mighty choosey as to where they put their feet. They had a bushel of sense; and purty soon over there in Louisiana they got to balancing theirselves on logs in order to keep out of the slimy mud. Yes, they got so expert that one of them would walk a cypress knee to the stump, jump over it, land on a root, and walk it out for another jump. If there was a bad bog-hole between cypresses you'd see a steer hang his orns into a mustang-grapevine, or maybe a wistaria, and swing across like a monkey. The way they balanced and jumped and swung actually made my horse laugh.[4]

Pierce, of course, liked to stretch the truth. Still, driving cattle to New Orleans was a difficult task. Grimes made a profit off his cattle and probably thumbed his nose at the Morgan Lines and James Foster.

"Shanghai" Pierce was just one of thousands of people who had settled in Texas by the early 1850s. Most settlers preferred to live in the wooded areas of east and central Texas, but many spilled over onto the prairie lands that began west of the ninety-eighth meridian, on a line near present Fort Worth and Dallas south to west of Austin and then southwest to a point west of San Antonio. East Texas was similar to the country most of them came from, whether it was Tennessee or Georgia or elsewhere to the east. The Texas prairie was different. To many it seemed alien. It was drier than the wooded regions, and trees were not as plentiful. The land was rolling. Then, too, the Texas prairie and plains were the home of the Comanche Indians. Together, the new environment and the threat of hostile Indians made the prairie uncomfortable for many settlers. Years later a Texas rancher would sum up his feelings about the region with these words: "The cowboy of the west worked in a land that seemed to be grieving over something—a kind of sadness, loneliness in a deathly quiet. One not acquainted with the plains could not understand what effect it had on the mind. It produced a heartache and a sense of exile."[5]

By the early 1850s some Texans had established ranching operations tailored after the Mexican rancho. A few Texans even called themselves ranchers, although they continued to raise crops like farmers. Life was still primitive, and most Texans were involved in stock raising and farming to survive. Gardens were common, with lettuces, tomatoes, onions, carrots, corn, potatoes, radishes, black-eyed peas, beets, okra, cucumbers, squash, cabbages, and cauliflower. Wild grapes were found in some areas. But flour was often scarce, as was coffee. When a Texan ran out of coffee, it was not unusual for him to use parched okra or corn, or parched meal bran and sweet potato peelings. At a dollar a pound or more, real coffee was often a luxury.

For the ranchers' wives, there was little female companionship. Few hired hands had wives. Most ranches were many miles apart. Unless a rancher and his wife had one or more daughters, there was little "woman's talk" except on infrequent visits to other ranches or to town. The towns were only county-seat villages with a few hundred people, but they provided a meeting place for ranch women. A few towns had constructed "Sunday houses." These were very small cabins that were used only during weekends by families that came in from the neighboring countryside.

Some Texans during this period chose not to gamble with the distant California markets. They also gave up trying to ship cattle by the Gulf, either because James Foster had refused their asking price for cattle or because they were simply too far from the Gulf to care. These ranchers began to look intently toward the northeast, beyond the Smoky Mountains of Tennessee and the Blue Ridge Mountains of Virginia to the population centers along the Atlantic seaboard. Surely, they said, the people in the East would buy Texas beef.

Some Texas cattlemen may have wondered whether it was possible to drive their cattle to eastern markets by overland routes. Others probably suspected it was possible, since they had heard stories about small numbers of Texas cattle driven north during the 1840s. One unidentified Texan supposedly drove a herd of 1,500 longhorns to Missouri in 1842. Who he was is not known, nor are there any details of his drive. Even the route followed is a matter of speculation, but most historians suspect that he followed a trail that led north from Texas through the Indian Nation or

TEXAS CATTLE BEING DRIVEN ACROSS THE RED RIVER,
or some other stream, on a trail drive north from Texas.
Drawing by J. Andre Castaigne.

what is now eastern Oklahoma to Fort Gibson and then a military trail into southwest Missouri. Many settlers had followed a similar route to come to Texas. From southwest Missouri the Texan could follow an established trail to St. Louis, then the only cattle market west of the Allegheny Mountains. The trail across the Indian Nation was later called the Osage Trace by some, the Shawnee Trail and Kansas Trail by others. The earliest documented Texas cattle drive to Missouri over this route occurred in 1846 when a herd of longhorns was driven to southwest Missouri. There Edward Piper, a cattle buyer, was reported with the herd. Whether he drove them north from Texas or purchased the cattle in Missouri is not known, but he drove them from Missouri to Ohio, fattened them during the winter, and took them east to market in the spring of 1847.[6]

By the early 1850s the trail northeast was pretty well established. There is no doubt that other herds of Texas longhorns were taken north over this route. After crossing the Red River at Rock Bluff crossing, near Preston in present-day Grayson County, Texas, the trail entered the Choctaw Indian Nation and veered a bit to the northeast. At a fork in the trail the drovers could cut over and pass near Fort Washita, established in 1842 to protect the Chickasaw Indians from hostile Indians on the plains to the west. Or the drovers could follow a more direct route to the east. Both trails came together again south of Boggy Depot, about 50 miles north of the Red River. Boggy Depot was located on Clear Boggy Creek and had been a distribution point for the rations given to the Chickasaw Indians being resettled in the region. From there the trail continued northeast, crossing the Canadian River below the joining of the North and South forks. The trail next crossed the Arkansas River just above the mouth of the Grand or Neosho river and just below the mouth of the Verdigris River, where the trail continued north along the west bank of the Grand River past Fort Gibson, established in 1824. From there the trail followed a military road northeast along the west bank of the Grand River until it was within a few miles of the southern border of what is now southeast Kansas. There the trail crossed to the east bank of the Grand River and passed near what is now Baxter Springs, Kansas, then only springs on the Spring River. From that point the trail turned northeast into Missouri, entering the state south of the modern-day city of Joplin.

Another branch of the Shawnee Trail, used earlier by settlers going to Texas, became known as the Sedalia Trail by drovers heading north. It crossed at Preston on the Red River but then veered northeast across the Indian Nation, entering Arkansas south of Fort Smith. From that point the trail crossed the Arkansas River near Fort Smith and continued through the Ozarks north, passing through the then Cherokee Nation just west

of the Arkansas line. The trail crossed into southern Missouri near Mays-
ville, Arkansas, and continued north to Sedalia, Missouri.

The first drive of Texas cattle to Missouri of which very much is
known was made not by a Texan but a young man from Illinois, who
eventually took some of the cattle on to New York City. He was Thomas
Candy Ponting, the son of an English stock farmer. Ponting was born in
1824. He came to America and settled on the prairies of Illinois when he
was twenty-three years old. Ponting was already experienced in driving
cattle overland when he arrived in America. As a teen-ager in England, he
and an older man had driven a herd of cattle from Somerset to London, a
distance of 110 miles. By the early 1850s, Ponting and his partner, Washington Malone, were driving cattle from Illinois to Wisconsin, where the
cattle were sold to newly arriving settlers. But by the summer of 1852,
many settlers were bringing their own cattle with them to Wisconsin and
selling their surplus animals to people already there. By early in 1853, as
the Wisconsin market for Illinois cattle declined, gold from California
began to get into circulation in Illinois. Ponting and Malone traded off all
of their paper money for gold and decided to go to Texas to buy cattle.
Like other people in Illinois and in the East, they had heard stories about
how plentiful and cheap cattle were in Texas.

Ponting and Malone traveled by horseback and wagon from central
Illinois to St. Louis, where they crossed the Mississippi by ferry and then
headed southwest to Springfield, Missouri. From there they turned south
and traveled through Arkansas until they crossed into Louisiana. There
they headed west into northeast Texas. Soon after they arrived in Texas
they met an old man who wanted to return to Illinois. They agreed to
take him if he would drive their ox team and wagon. He agreed, and the
three men traveled into Hopkins County, just east of modern Greenville,
Texas. There Ponting met Merida Hart, a native of Kentucky, who had
been raised in Arkansas. Hart had moved to Texas in 1827 and later became a lawmaker in Austin. With Hart's help, Ponting and his partner
bought seven hundred longhorns and probably branded the animals; it was
common in those years to impose a "sale brand" over the existing one to
indicate that the cattle had changed hands. The three men then prepared
to drive the herd of cattle to Illinois.

They crossed the Red River many miles east of the Preston crossing
mentioned earlier, southwest of the Armstrong Academy, a Choctaw
Indian mission established in 1845 and named for William Armstrong, then
the Indian agent in the region. Once in Indian territory, Ponting decided
to buy more cattle. He left Malone with the seven hundred head and
eventually found eighty head that he was able to purchase from a man
named Pussly, an Englishman who had settled in the area some years

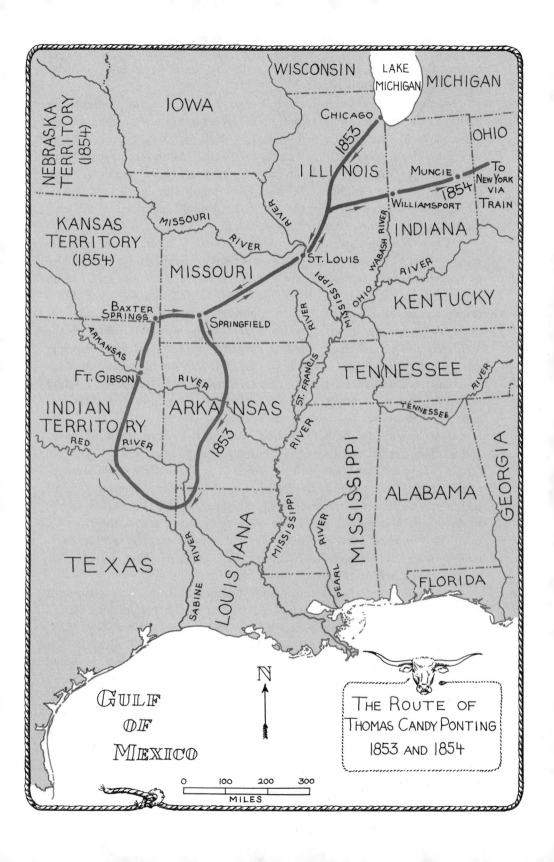

WISCONSIN
LAKE MICHIGAN
MICHIGAN
IOWA
CHICAGO
1853
ILLINOIS
OHIO
MUNCIE
WILLIAMSPORT
1854
To NEW YORK VIA TRAIN
NEBRASKA TERRITORY (1854)
KANSAS TERRITORY (1854)
MISSOURI
MISSOURI RIVER
RIVER
ST. LOUIS
WABASH RIVER
INDIANA
OHIO RIVER
KENTUCKY
BAXTER SPRINGS
SPRINGFIELD
ARKANSAS
FT. GIBSON
RIVER
ST. FRANCIS RIVER
MISSISSIPPI RIVER
RIVER
TENNESSEE
TENNESSEE RIVER
INDIAN TERRITORY
RED RIVER
ARKANSAS
1853
MISSISSIPPI
ALABAMA
GEORGIA
TEXAS
SABINE RIVER
LOUISIANA
MISSISSIPPI RIVER
PEARL RIVER
FLORIDA

GULF OF MEXICO

N

THE ROUTE OF
THOMAS CANDY PONTING
1853 AND 1854

0   100   200   300
MILES

earlier. Ponting drove the eighty cattle east until he caught up with Malone and the main herd.

Herding the cattle across the Indian Nation was not difficult for Ponting and Malone. Their wagon, pulled by an ox team and driven by the old man, had an ox, with a bell around its neck, tied to the back. The ox served as a lead steer: the other cattle followed it wherever it went. Ponting, however, was nervous about traveling through Indian country. "I sat on my horse every night while we were coming through . . . I was so afraid something would scare the cattle that I could not sleep in the tent; but we had no stampede," he later recalled.

When Ponting's party reached the Arkansas River, about 15 miles west of Fort Gibson, they asked some Indians to help build a raft of logs to float the wagon across the river. Ponting could not swim and had an Indian ride across with him to rescue him if he fell into the river. But a rescue was never called for. The men got across the stream safely and the cattle swam to the other side. From that point the trail followed the Verdigris and Grand rivers. "It was beautiful country," recalled Ponting, who noted that they drove the herd out of Indian country and into Missouri near where Baxter Springs, Kansas, stands today. But when Ponting passed the spot in 1854, there was no settlement at the Springs and the territory of Kansas was only a few weeks old.

Ponting and Malone herded their cattle to near Springfield, Missouri, and as they headed northeast they bought butter, eggs, and bacon from farmers along the route. Once they arrived in St. Louis they made arrangements to put their cattle in the Pacific Stock Yard for the night, pitched their tents nearby, and the following morning herded their cattle to the banks of the Mississippi. The cattle were transported across the river by boat. The journey northeast from there was as uneventful as the four-month drive from Texas to Missouri. In Illinois, Ponting and Malone wintered the cattle and fed them shock corn.

In the spring of 1854, Ponting and Malone sold most of the longhorns in central Illinois, but they kept 150 of the fattest beeves and started driving them east. Ponting wanted to take the cattle to New York City. Using a lead steer, they crossed the Wabash River at Williamsport, just below Attica, Indiana. Ponting put the ox with the bell on a ferry boat and started across. The other cattle—without urging from Malone—entered the river and swam to the other side, following the lead steer and the sound of the bell. From Williamsport they continued east until they reached Muncie in eastern Indiana. There Ponting learned they could get railroad cars to ship their cattle the remainder of the way east to New York. In 1854, however, railroads did not ship much livestock, especially not cattle. Ponting and Malone had to put together a makeshift ramp to load the cattle into railroad cars that were not designed to carry them. The cattle's long horns undoubtedly caused problems in loading, and in later years horns were often trimmed, but there is no indication in Ponting's recollections that anything was done about them.

"We unloaded them at Cleveland, letting them jump out on the sand banks. They did not have shipping yards to feed them in . . . we had to let them go out on grass. We unloaded them next at Dunrick, then at Harnesville, and then at Bergen Hill," wrote Ponting. Bergen Hill is in Bergen County, New Jersey, just across the Hudson River from New York City. Ponting, Malone, and the longhorns arrived at Bergen Hill on Saturday afternoon, July 1, 1854. The cattle were put on pasture until after midnight on Sunday and then ferried across the Hudson to New York and taken to the Hundred Street Market.

Early on the morning of Monday, July 3, 1854, as Ponting recalled, he located James Gilcris, a native of Ohio who was a cattle salesman. Ponting told Gilcris "not to turn a bullock out of the yard until they were all sold and not to tell where the cattle were from." Ponting wrote that the New York butchers thought the long-horned cattle were from Iowa. Apparently no one imagined that the longhorns came all the way from Texas. The cattle were sold in small bunches of ten to twenty, and after each sale a man painted a buyer's mark on every head sold.

As soon as the sale ended, a well-dressed man walked up to Ponting and started to ask questions about the cattle. Ponting talked freely, and the man took everything down in shorthand. When the conversation ended, the man told Ponting he was a market reporter and that a story would be published in the New York *Daily Tribune* the following day.[7]

The newspaper reporter was Solon Robinson, who later became a well-known agricultural historian. He was then reporting the New York markets for the newspaper, and the following day, Tuesday, July 4, 1854, Robinson's story describing the arrival and sale of Texas cattle in New York City appeared on page eight of the *Daily Tribune*. Robinson reported the arrival of 130 head from Texas (Ponting and Malone apparently lost twenty head on the journey east from Illinois), and he added: "Another thing is demonstrated in the yards to-day, which proves that cattle can be brought two thousand miles with profit to the drovers, and sold at such prices as prevail to-day. We have a drove of Texas cattle— one step beyond those reported last summer from the Cherokee nation; and as soon as the California tide ebbs, we shall have plenty from Texas, Arkansas, Missouri, and the two Territories where Senator Douglas desires to rear another kind of stock."

This last comment of Robinson's, of course, was in reference to the new territories of Kansas and Nebraska. He continued:

From Illinois here the expense is $17 a head. . . . The top of the drove
are good quality of beef, and all are fair. A lot of twenty-one, short 8
cwt., sold to Weeks at $80, and a good many others sold at 10¢ [per
pound]. These cattle are generally 5, 6, and 7 years old, rather long-
legged, though fine horned, with long taper horns, and something of
a wild look. Some of them are the descendants of a most excellent
breed of cattle from the South, originally imported by the Spaniards,
and generally known in all the south-western States as Spanish cattle.
It is said that the meat of this description of stock is fine-grained and
close, somewhat like venison, and apt to be a little tough cooked in the
ordinary way, and therefore not as good to eat fresh as that of cattle
of a more domestic character. This will be somewhat changed by
purchasing them young and feeding them two years as well as this
drove has been fed one year.[8]

Ponting bought several copies of the newspaper containing the article and
sent them to his parents in England and one copy to Merida Hart in
Texas. Hart wrote back telling Ponting that he had done a great deal for
Texas. Hart no doubt showed the newspaper story to other Texans, and
there is a good likelihood that still others received copies from friends
and relatives in the East. But it is doubtful whether the article had much
impact on Texas trail drives that year. Even before the article reached
Texas early in the fall of 1854, other Texans were already driving herds
of longhorns northward. The *Texas State Gazette* in Austin reported on
August 5, 1854, that fifty thousand longhorns had crossed the Red River at
Preston during the summer, most headed for Missouri and points east, and
that most of these northbound cattle were from the valleys of the
Colorado and Brazos.

    Five hundred head of these cattle may have belonged to George
Squires, who like Ponting made his home in Illinois. In February of 1854,
Squires, his wife Emeline, and her father and brother left Illinois and
traveled by train and steamboat to New Orleans. George Squires went
ahead to Texas, where he arranged to buy five hundred longhorns near
Houston. Mrs. Squires and her brother soon joined George Squires at
Austin while her father, who was ill, returned north by steamboat via
New Orleans. When the cattle arrived in Austin, the trio began driving
them north. The route they followed is not known, but they crossed the
Indian Nation, Kansas Territory, and Missouri. The drive followed a route
to Hannibal, Missouri, where the cattle supposedly were "driven across the
Mississippi." The cattle were then herded on to Illinois, where they were
put on grass southwest of DeKalb. Later they were driven to Chicago and
sold to the slaughterhouses.

    The Squireses' trail drive is noteworthy if for no other reason than for the distance covered. But the fact that a woman went along makes it even more significant. It is possible that Emeline Bent Squires was the first woman to make such a long trail drive north from Texas. She rode in a covered wagon most of the time, but she often walked beside the wagon picking up unusual rocks and placing them in a carpetbag. (What she did with the rocks is not recorded, but they were certainly more reasonable in cost than most souvenirs one finds today in the tourist traps along the same general route.) While crossing what is today Oklahoma, Indians "would peak at Mrs. Squires as she lay propped up in the wagon. Their interest in her was attributed to the fact that a white woman, especially one with light hair, was something of an oddity."[9]

Many Texas drovers received demands from a Choctaw Indian who was charging 10¢ a head for longhorns passing over his land. The Texas drovers protested, but they paid it. Soon the Choctaw tribal council took over the toll business and raised it to 50¢ a head. Later the Cherokee and Creek Indians would do the same, with the Cherokees charging 75¢ a head. But sometimes drovers made it across Indian land without being stopped. Thomas Candy Ponting may have been one of these drovers. He makes no mention in his recollections of having paid a toll.

The careful observer of the Texas drovers driving cattle toward Missouri or California in the early 1850s would have noticed some changes in the Texan's saddles. Initially they were like those of vaqueros in northeast Mexico, but on long cattle drives the Texans soon learned that riding comfort, serviceability, and security were more important than style or tradition in saddles. They began modifying the old vaquero rigs to suit themselves. Although lacking in refinement, these modified Texas saddles later inspired saddlemakers throughout the West. In 1850, however, there were only a few saddlemakers in Texas, and they were located in isolated areas of the state. In addition, not all Texans had access to their work, nor could all afford to buy saddles.

Most Texans probably made their own saddles in the early 1850s. These Texas saddles did not include the large rigging rings that were still seen on the Mexican vaquero's saddle; they had smaller rings but did continue to use the narrow latigos or straps that held the saddle on the horse. The Texans also cut down the size of the Mexican saddlehorn, making it slimmer, but maintaining the strength of the larger Mexican saddlehorn by running the front rigging on their saddles around the saddlehorn.

Another style of saddle made its appearance in Texas during the early 1850s. It seems to have been a Texas creation. The saddle was light—only twelve or thirteen pounds—and it had sidebars lined with square leather inner skirts, and short outer skirts back of the cantle. The seat of rawhide was stitched on the tree, and leather often covered the fork. The cantle was better-fitting. The stirrups were wide, of the "boxcar" variety, as they were later called. But this saddle does not appear to have been as popular in Texas as the older and heavier Mexican-style saddle with *mochila* with Texas modifications. Certainly, Texans were exposed to other kinds of saddles on their long drives to California or to Missouri, where a wide variety of commercial saddles were then being offered by saddlemakers in St. Louis.[10]

The oldest saddlery firm west of the Mississippi was that of J. B. Sickles on North Main Street in St. Louis. He opened for business in the summer of 1834. At first Sickles made saddletrees of hardwood, but when he learned that hardwood was prone to warp and split, he changed to softwood and covered the more expensive trees with good rawhide. The less expensive saddles were covered with goatskin or sheepskin. By the late 1840s Sickles was building many saddles after the hybrid rigs developed by the early Texans who had started with the basic Mexican vaquero saddle.[11] Few Texans, however, could afford high-priced St. Louis saddles during the early 1850s. They continued to make their own saddle trees and *mochila* coverings. This heavier Mexican-style saddle would remain the most popular Texas saddle until after the Civil War.

AS DROVERS WERE RETURNING HOME to Texas in the fall of 1854, some of them were calling the route north the "Kansas Trail." Kansas Territory had been created by Congress with the Kansas-Nebraska Act of May 30, 1854. Instead of entering southwest Missouri, some Texans had turned north and driven their cattle just inside the eastern edge of the newly established territory. They generally followed a military road that ran from Fort Gibson to Fort Scott and northward to Fort Leavenworth. Over this road from the Indian Nation, Jesse Chisholm, born of a Scottish father and a Cherokee mother in Tennessee, had supplied Indian cattle to the military at Fort Scott close to the Missouri border. Thus it could be said that some Texans in 1854 were following Chisholm's trail. It was not, however, the same Chisholm Trail that would carry thousands upon thousands of Texas longhorns to Kansas following the Civil War. The military road along the border of eastern Kansas used by Chisholm between about 1843 and 1853, the year Fort Scott was abandoned, carried the Texas longhorns from near present-day Baxter Springs, Kansas, north to Westport and Kansas City. The cattle market in those towns was growing in the early 1850s.

Westport and Kansas City had become outfitting centers for freighters preparing to travel the Santa Fe Trail and emigrants making ready to follow the Oregon or California trails. The demand for cattle was great. But there was another reason why many Texas drovers had turned north in 1854 to travel through eastern Kansas Territory: they were avoiding Missouri.

About a year earlier, in June 1853, indignant farmers and stockmen in southern Bates County, Missouri, had turned back drovers herding three thousand head of longhorns along the western edge of Missouri to Westport and Kansas City, because they feared the longhorns would infect their cattle with what the Missourians were calling "Texas fever." The disease was a splenetic fever caused by ticks carried by the longhorns. While the disease sometimes made longhorns sick, these hardy animals did not die from the fever, as northern cattle did. Despite the name bestowed on it, it did not originate in Texas, and its cause was then unknown. It was noticed in Pennsylvania as early as 1796, following the introduction of cattle from South Carolina. By 1812, Virginia prohibited the entry of cattle from South Carolina and Georgia during the warm months between April and November when the disease seemed to spread. (The ticks could not survive the cold months farther north.) In 1837, North Carolina instituted similar restrictions. The disease gradually attracted attention in Missouri after Texas drovers began crossing that state with their longhorns. As early as 1851 it was reported in two of Missouri's far western counties, Jackson and Cass, just south of Westport and Kansas City. Of that outbreak, a Savannah, Missouri, newspaper reported that "great numbers" of Missouri cattle had been destroyed by "Texas fever."[12]

Most Texas drovers resented efforts to blame their longhorns for the disease. Their cattle remained healthy and unaffected, although soon after Missouri cattle came into contact with the Texas longhorns during the summer or early fall, or were put on land that had been occupied by the longhorns, the Missouri cattle contracted the disease. Their backs arched or roached, their heads hung low with ears drooping; their eyes became dull and glassy; and they wavered as they walked, sometimes staggering in the hindquarters. Many cattle thus affected eventually died. Those that recovered remained in generally poor health.[13]

The first Texas drovers who were met and turned back by Missouri farmers were probably angry. They had traveled several hundred miles with their cattle, most had submitted to the Indian toll shakedown as they crossed the Indian Nation, and now they were being met by angry Missourians. One can imagine the discouragement they must have felt. But Texans were a strong-willed lot, inured to hardship and disappointment. They simply retraced their steps out of Missouri, and just below the southeast border of Kansas Territory turned north and followed the military trail. They passed Fort Scott and continued north along the sparsely populated eastern border of Kansas Territory. This shifting of the Texas cattle trails farther west beyond farming settlements occurred time and again as most Texans tried to avoid conflicts with farmers. It would continue until the 1880s.

During the mid-1850s some drovers of Texas cattle apparently skirted

farming settlements in Missouri. Thomas Candy Ponting's recollections
contain no reference to such trouble on his trail drive across Missouri in
1853, and there is a newspaper account reporting the safe arrival and sale
of longhorns in St. Louis late in October of 1854. The cattle brought $15
to $30 a head, but the newspaper reporter who covered the sale did not
think much of the Texas cattle. He wrote:

> They were driven nearly or not quite five hundred miles, and it may
> be a matter of astonishment how they could be sold for so small a
> price. The thing is explained when we say that they subsisted all the
> way on grass and kept in tolerable order. They never ate an ear of
> corn in their lives. An attempt was made to feed them corn and prov-
> ender in the stockyards, but they ran away from it. Texas cattle are
> about the nearest to wild animals of any now driven to market. We
> have seen some buffalos that were more civilized.[14]

Of an estimated fifty thousand longhorns that headed north from Texas
in 1854, six hundred were driven through to Chicago. Whether they
traveled through Missouri or north through the territories of Kansas and
Nebraska and then northeast through Iowa is not known. But in Chicago
another newspaper reporter viewed the longhorns with some reservations.
He did describe them as "fine looking cattle, remarkable for their sleek
appearance and long horns," but he added that they were not superior "to
those raised upon our own prairies."[15]

Although the St. Louis and Chicago newspaper articles made no mention of "Texas fever," it was certainly on the minds of stockmen in Illinois, Ohio, Missouri, and elsewhere in the North where many cattle had
been infected by the disease. Missouri stockmen and farmers were becoming concerned about their pastures as well. The trailing herds of longhorns
were eating grass that Missourians wanted to preserve for their own cattle.
Angry farmers in Missouri formed armed "vigilance committees" to watch
for and stop herds of Texas cattle. In some instances, they reportedly
threatened to kill the longhorns if the drovers did not turn back. The
summer of 1855 also found Missouri stock raisers holding meetings in
several county seats in western and southwestern areas. They demanded
action by the Missouri state legislature. The action soon came, with lawmakers passing legislation to keep diseased cattle from being brought into
Missouri. The measure became law on December 15, 1855, making it
illegal for drovers of other states to drive into or through Missouri with
diseased cattle, especially those afflicted with Texas fever. The penalty was
a fine of $20 for each offending beef. (A beef was any bovine over three
years old.) The legislature gave the enforcement responsibilities to local
justices of the peace.[16]

In a way the law worked in favor of the Texas drovers. Their cattle were immune to Texas fever and showed no symptoms of the disease. There is no record of any longhorns having been stopped because they were afflicted with Texas fever. Unfortunately for all concerned, no one knew that it was the ticks on the longhorns that transmitted the disease, although Missouri stockmen knew for a fact that their cattle caught the fever after Texas cattle passed through. To cattle raisers everywhere, the real cause of Texas fever remained a mystery for about three decades, and the belief that Texas cattle were the guilty party would haunt Texas drovers even after 1889, when scientists determined that the carrier was a tick called *Margaropus annulatus.*

The law passed by the Missouri legislature in 1855 caused an increase in the use of the trail along the eastern border inside Kansas Territory. By the summer of 1856 some drovers simply tried to avoid Missouri and possible trouble, although those drovers intent on reaching Sedalia or St. Louis markets stopped and let the Missouri stockmen inspect their cattle. Since the cattle showed no symptoms of Texas fever, they were permitted to continue. How many cattle were driven north from Texas that year is not recorded, but thousands probably completed the journey. It is known that 52,000 cattle were sold in the Kansas City market alone in 1857, and 48,000 in 1858. Two-thirds of these were from Texas.[17] By then Kansas City had rapidly become the largest cattle market on the western frontier.

In 1855 a man named John J. Baxter settled close to some springs on the Spring River about a mile north of the present Oklahoma border in southeast Kansas. The settlement would become known as Baxter Springs after the Civil War, and it would be the first cattle town in Kansas. In its first years, however, the settlement did not fit the mold of the later Kansas cattle towns. At first, John Baxter had little to offer the tired Texans and the Mexican vaqueros who came up the trail with herds of longhorns: there was only cool spring water, shade, and a small stock of goods kept for sale in Baxter's cabin. But these things were a start, and Texans were probably appreciative of the tobacco, flour, and other items they could purchase from Baxter and his wife. By the late 1850s, Baxter had built corrals to accommodate cattle and had enlarged his cabin, which he now called a tavern. Nearby he built and operated a tannery.

Baxter was a huge man. He stood 6 feet 7½ inches tall and had a massive frame. His hair was dark, and he wore a well-trimmed beard and mustache. His wife and their four daughters kept him neatly dressed in homespun clothes; stores, if there had been any in the neighborhood, could not have fitted him. Baxter always went fully armed, usually with two Navy Colts in open sight. It was unethical to carry concealed weapons on the border. Although Baxter was a northerner and an abolitionist, and many feared him for his size, he got along well with the Texans. Unfortunately, Baxter did not live to see the town of Baxter Springs develop. On January 26, 1859, he was shot to death in a claims dispute near his cabin.[18]

To the northeast in Missouri the often exaggerated Texas fever scare was really more anxiety about the unknown than anything else. The uncertainty of what to expect in Missouri and even Kansas Territory undoubtedly tested the character of many a Texas drover preparing for the long drive north. It was not until the late 1850s that the government established a mail service through Texas to California, and poor communication kept most from learning about the problems they might encounter near the end of the trail. For the wives of Texas drovers who had heard of the troubles, life must have been hard. It is not difficult to visualize a drover's wife, standing in front of the family cabin, watching her husband and perhaps her sons leaving on a trail drive north and wondering whether they would survive not only the natural hardships of the journey but the anger and the rifles of the northern stockmen and farmers.

The year 1858 was particularly difficult for Texas drovers, since a new outbreak of Texas fever had occurred in western Missouri and in eastern portions of Kansas Territory. Thousands of local cattle died. The 1855 Missouri law did not seem to be doing any good: all of the Texas cattle entering the state were in good health; so were the cattle entering Kansas Territory near Baxter's cabin. By June of 1858, stockmen in Henry County southeast of Kansas City became so angered by their cattle losses from Texas fever that they took matters into their own hands. They began stopping herds of longhorns as they approached the bridge over the Grand River 5 miles west of Clinton. Although these longhorns appeared healthy, and therefore under the law should have been permitted to pass, the stockmen ordered the drovers to turn back. If they did not, warned the stockmen, they would use force. Within a few days about two thousand longhorns were turned back. "No one can for a moment blame the citizens of Missouri for adopting summary measures to protect their stock from the fearful ravages of Spanish fever," declared one Missouri newspaper.[19]

Farmers and stockmen in eastern Kansas Territory, already troubled by free-state and pro-slavery problems, were also beginning to complain about their cattle losses to Texas fever. The summer of 1858 was particularly bad. The following February, the territorial legislature of Kansas passed a law similar to that of Missouri. It barred all Texas, Arkansas, and Indian cattle coming from what is now Oklahoma from entering the four organized counties along the southeastern border of Kansas between June first and November first.[20] A few Texas drovers, some apparently unaware of the new law, tried to enter Kansas Territory in June of 1859, only to be met by farmers and stockmen who had formed rifle companies.

Before the summer ended, some longhorns had been shot and killed by the angry Kansans, who in a couple of instances narrowly avoided what probably would have been bloody fights with the armed Texans. The Texans were also becoming angry.

The result of the Kansas law was a return by the Texas drovers to the trails in western Missouri. The cattle, appearing in good health, were permitted to travel north. But some groups, arriving along the border of southeast Kansas in October, put their cattle on grass and waited for November. On the first day of the month they started north toward Kansas City along the eastern border of Kansas Territory. A few other Texas herds probably entered Kansas west of the four prohibited counties in June, July, and August and followed a northerly course, remaining west. After fording the Kansas River they headed east, crossing the Missouri at St. Joseph, north of Kansas City. Once on the other side, they found the western end of the recently completed Hannibal and St. Joseph Railroad, and a growing market for cattle that could be shipped east by rail.

Late in 1859 Abraham Lincoln came to Kansas Territory, crossing the Missouri River at St. Joseph near the spot where some of the longhorns had probably crossed earlier in the year going in the opposite direction. There is no record that Lincoln and the longhorns met on his visit, but the journey by the Illinois lawyer, who was then becoming prominent in politics, brought to the troubled territory of Kansas another reminder of the growing controversy over sectional differences in the North and the South. Earlier in the year, as two thousand longhorns passed through Dallas, Texas, a newspaper there noted that the cattle were going north, "to feed our abolition neighbors. We hope that southern diet may agree with them."[21]

Something else was happening, however, that would create still another market for Texas cattle. Early in 1858, when the free-state legislature met at Lawrence, Kansas Territory, rumors abounded that a Delaware Indian named Fall Leaf, a burly fellow who lived on a reservation north of Lawrence, had brought some fine specimens of gold from the Rocky Mountains. Almost overnight, gold fever replaced politics. By the spring of 1858 parties of goldseekers were leaving eastern Kansas Territory bound for the eastern slopes of the Rockies, then part of Kansas Territory. By summer, news had spread across the nation telling of a fresh gold strike. The rush was on.

When the news reached Texas, some cattle raisers were skeptical about the "Kansas gold fields," as they were called. There was doubt that the rush would produce a cattle market like that of California nearly a decade earlier, although some thought a good market might develop. They realized that the Rocky Mountains were half as far away from Texas as California and that there were no angry farmers or stockmen between Texas and the Kansas gold fields. They also knew the most direct route from central Texas ran northwest across the unsettled plains through the Texas panhandle, across the neutral strip that is now the Oklahoma panhandle into what was then far western Kansas Territory (now Colorado). Unfortunately, water and grass were not always plentiful on the Texas plains. In addition, much of the region, crisscrossed by the warlike Comanche Indians, was unexplored. Oliver Loving knew this when he started a herd of about a thousand cattle toward the new gold fields on August 29, 1860. With the help of John B. Dawson, Sylvester Reed, Jowell W. Curtis, and Charles Goodnight, Loving moved north from Palo Pinto County. Goodnight helped drive the herd through northern Texas and then turned back, but the others remained with Loving as he continued on through what is now central Oklahoma, entering Kansas Territory near modern Arkansas City. From there the cattle were driven across Walnut Creek about 35 miles above its confluence with the Arkansas, then across the Little Arkansas River near modern Wichita, Kansas. From that point the herd followed the Arkansas River past the Big Bend and on west to present Pueblo, Colorado. There the herd was turned north and followed the east bank of the Fountain Qui Bouille Creek near Little Buttes, east to the head of Squirrel Creek and then northwest across the divide and down to the mouth of Cherry Creek near the present site of Denver.

The herd was put on grass during the winter of 1860–61. Early in the spring of 1861 Loving sold the herd. As J. Evetts Haley relates in his superb biography *Charles Goodnight*, Loving was still in Denver when the Civil War began in the spring of 1861 and "the authorities refused to let him return to Texas." Loving, however, had made friends with Lucien Maxwell, Kit Carson, and other prominent mountain men. They were able to get the authorities to release Loving, who took a stage east across Kansas (Kansas had become a state on January 29, 1861) to St. Joseph, Missouri. From there Loving made his way south to his Texas home.

So far as is known, no other herd of Texas cattle was driven to the gold fields before the Civil War, but there are at least two other accounts of drives from Texas to Kansas and Missouri during the spring of 1860. Captain F. M. Harris took a herd of work oxen to Leavenworth, Kansas Territory, and made a profit. And Jesse Day and his two sons set out from Hays County, Texas, with a large herd of longhorns bound for Kansas City. Unfortunately, Day drowned in the Brazos River at Waco, Texas, on April 22, 1860, as he and his sons were swimming the herd across the swollen stream. After the sons buried their father at Belton, Texas, they continued on with the herd toward Kansas City. Just inside the southeast border of Kansas Territory, near Baxter's cabin, they were met by armed settlers. The sons of Jesse Day turned the cattle around, entered the Indian Nation, then turned northeast, drove the herd through Missouri, and sold the cattle in St. Louis.[22]

Aside from Thomas Candy Ponting's account of driving cattle north behind a lead steer in the early 1850s, little is known about the techniques of these early trail drivers. Wagons and carts were used to haul supplies, including food, but the "chuck wagon" had not yet been invented. The drovers often slept in tents and bought some food from Indians and settlers, or lived off the land and a few beeves taken from their herds. It seems safe to assume that other drovers similarly made use of lead steers. These Missouri and Kansas Territory–bound drovers of the 1850s probably tried to solve problems as they developed on their first drives north. Through experience they learned what to expect and how to handle it, and on later drives they were able to anticipate many problems and solve them before they occurred. It might be said that the 1850s gave a few Texas cattlemen the opportunity to learn how to drive herds of cattle over long distances.

There are few details of how these men lived on the trails. Most had little time for or interest in recording their recollections. They probably viewed trail driving as hard work, not the exciting life some eastern writers portrayed after they discovered the "romance" of the cattle drive and the "cow-boy." By then, many of the drovers who had followed the trails to Missouri and Kansas in the 1850s would have forgotten them, or were dead. Some Texans who came along during the late 1860s and early 1870s apparently were influenced by articles of eastern writers. These drovers—some may have been convinced late in life that their occupation had been romantic—did leave their recollections, although they are sometimes hazy. Far more is known today about the later trail drives than those of the 1850s and very early 1860s.

The trailing of Texas cattle north, especially to Missouri and eastern Kansas Territory, was slowed by the summer of 1860 by the problems of Texas fever and rumbles of impending war. Early in 1861, the Missouri legislature strengthened its law on Texas fever by authorizing each county court to appoint a board of cattle inspectors. Each board was empowered to inspect all incoming herds of Texas cattle and, if necessary, turn back any stock afflicted with Texas fever or suspected of carrying it. If the Texas drovers refused, the cattle could be driven back or killed by the Missourians.[23] But before any Texans could test this new law, the Civil War began. And for the already troubled Texas cattleman, who may have believed the world was against him, the Civil War was to become still another obstacle to survive and overcome.

CHAPTER 7

❖

The Civil War
and Change

*Perhaps in no other occupation of men was the theory of
the "survival of the fittest" more plainly demonstrated . . .
than in the quick weeding out of the weaklings, of the
visionary, and of the inherently depraved, among those
who understood the cowboy life.*

—ANONYMOUS[1]

FOR at least three decades before the Civil War, the evolving culture
of the Texans who raised cattle had been shaped by their longhorns, the
land, the Spanish tools and techniques used to handle the cattle, and the
search for markets where the cattle could be sold. But the emerging culture was shaken at its very roots when the Civil War began in the spring
of 1861. No longer did cattle or cattle-related activities shape the lives of
Texas ranchers and their families. The war and its demands dictated
change, and cattle, like people, became pawns in a political struggle.

From the outbreak of the war, Texans faced the twofold problem of
having to protect their frontier from hostile Indians and outlaws while at
the same time providing not only material resources but fighting men for
the Confederacy. Texans, like southerners elsewhere, were poorly
equipped to fight an all-out war against the industrial North. They lived in
a frontier society with an economy based on agriculture, especially cattle
raising. There was little industry. But there were more than 600,000 people
in Texas when the war began. Many were patriotic, and here was their
strength. The tradition of rallying instead of running in any crisis had
existed in Texas since before the Texas revolution. It was part of the unwritten code of living on the western frontier; everyone had to help
everyone else. There were exceptions, of course, but when the Confeder-

acy called for volunteers soon after the war began, many Texans, including men involved in cattle raising, volunteered for service in the Confederate army or to help fight Indians and outlaws along the frontier.

Within a few months, however, it became apparent throughout the
South that the volunteer system alone would not be sufficient, nor would
it provide the uniformity needed for a strong military force. Therefore,
in April of 1862, the Confederate Congress passed a conscription law draft-
ing all men from eighteen to thirty-five years old. Five months later the
age limit was raised to forty-five years, although conscripted men could
hire substitutes to fight for them, and numerous occupations and professions were exempt from military service. Government officials and their
clerks were exempt, as were printers, mail carriers, ferrymen, ministers of
religion, railroad and transportation employees, presidents and professors
in colleges, and schoolteachers having twenty pupils or more. Nurses were
exempt, along with one druggist to each store and superintendents and
operatives in wool and cotton factories. Exemptions were designed to
protect the government of the Confederacy, state governments, and certain
industries.

Initially, cattle raisers, farmers, shoemakers, newspaper editors, tan-
ners, blacksmiths, millers, wheelwrights, and industrial workers, including munitions makers and others, were not exempt. But people in many of
these occupations raised such a clamor that in October of 1862 a new
conscription law greatly increased the number of exemptions. It even
touched ranching. The law exempted one person for every five hundred
head of cattle or sheep or 250 head of horses or mules. Although many
Texas cattle ranchers qualified for exemption under the law, and perhaps
for other reasons, no self-respecting rancher took advantage of it. They
either joined the Confederate army to fight east of Texas or they joined the
Texas forces to protect the frontier from Indians. The frontier military
posts had been abandoned by Union forces at the beginning of the war,
leaving no armed force to check the hostile Indians.

Soon after the war began, John A. Wilcox, a Texas congressman
representing the first Texas district in the Confederate Congress, declared
that his state had so many cattle that it could furnish the whole Confederate
army with beef during the war and charge nothing for it. All he asked was
that the Confederacy pay the expense of driving the cattle east from
Texas. The Confederate Congress did not do exactly what Wilcox
wanted, but it did designate a large number of prominent Texas ranchers
as "Government stock raisers, whose duty it was to furnish the Commissary
Department of the army with all the beef possible, for which they paid
forty dollars per head in Confederate States money."[2] These government
stock raisers apparently were exempt from military service.

One of these ranchers was John Simpson Chisum, who is sometimes confused with Jesse Chisholm. Chisum was born in Madison County, Tennessee, on August 15, 1824. By the late 1830s his family had moved to northeast Texas near the present community of Paris. As a young man John Chisum became a farmer and was elected county clerk. But the office work was too confining. Chisum believed it would ruin his health. So during the mid-1850s he entered the cattle business. Chisum soon became prominent, and after the Civil War began, he was appointed a government stock raiser and began driving Texas cattle east.[3]

Another supplier of beef was Terrel Jackson, a wealthy Texas planter and landowner at Chappell Hill in Washington County. He received a government contract to deliver several thousand head of beef cattle to the Confederate Commissary Department. Jackson hired Dudley H. Snyder, a Texas horse trader, to make the deliveries, most of which were in Mississippi. On his first drive east in 1862, Snyder had problems getting the cattle to cross the numerous rivers, especially the Mississippi. Before he set out on his second drive, Snyder obtained two lead steers that were trained swimmers. When they reached a river they "would plunge right in and the herd would follow without trouble."[4]

Still another Confederate contractor was Oliver Loving, who had driven the herd to the Kansas gold fields in 1860. Born about 1812 in Hopkins County, Kentucky, Loving settled in Lamar County, Texas, in 1845 and the next year moved to Collin County. There he farmed, dealt in livestock, and freighted between Houston and Shreveport. By 1855 he moved his herds to Palo Pinto County and soon adopted the open-range approach to ranching. He drove a herd of longhorns to Chicago in 1858, two years before his drive to what is now Colorado. After he succeeded in returning to Texas following the outbreak of the war, Loving, like Chisum and Snyder and others, began to supply Confederate troops with beef. He made several drives east of the Mississippi.[5]

At the start of the war, cattle were plentiful throughout the South. Georgia had perhaps the largest number of cattle of any southern state outside of Texas, but in Georgia and elsewhere to the east, farming, cattle raising, and cotton growing were generally practiced together, especially on the larger plantations, which functioned as very large farms. In Texas, however, most ranching had become separate from farming and the raising of cotton. More and more ranches were being established on the unfenced prairies and plains west of the older settlements. On the frontier the cattle grazed on the open range and increased in number.

The imperfect census of 1860 had reported 3,500,000 head of cattle in Texas, or one-eighth of *all* the cattle in the United States. The actual cattle population of Texas in 1860 was probably closer to 4,500,000, since, according to government accounts, census takers did not adequately cover the region between the Nueces River and the Rio Grande and along the state's western frontier.

Exactly how many of these cattle were driven across the Mississippi River by Snyder, Chisum, Loving, and other Texans is unknown, but conservative estimates range as high as 100,000 head during the very early 1860s. Still other cattle were shipped by steamboats to New Orleans until the summer of 1861, when the Union blockade of the Texas coast suddenly cut off such shipments. At the same time, overland drives to Louisiana, unaffected by the blockade, continued. The main cattle trail to Louisiana crossed the Trinity River at Liberty in southeast Texas and the Calcasieu River above Lake Charles, Louisiana, up to Opelousas, and on to Atchafalaya, where the cattle were put aboard steamboats and shipped down to New Orleans. Another trail ran from central Texas to Shreveport, with branches to Natchitoches and Alexandria. Most of the cattle driven to Alexandria ended up in a slaughterhouse, where their meat was packed with salt. The slaughterhouse had a contract to provide 100,000 barrels of salt beef for the Confederate army.[6]

Few details of these trail drives are known. Most herds seem to have been under a thousand head, small enough to be handled by a few men. Although some Texans had gained experience in driving cattle long distances during the 1850s and earlier, there does not appear to have been any uniformity of procedures in the drives from the 1840s through the Civil War. Some drovers used lead steers and others did not. The number of mounted men required to drive a herd varied, depending upon the manpower available. One drive with five hundred head of cattle might have three men while another with the same number of cattle might have seven or eight men. At the same time there was no uniformity in saddles and riggings. Although a lightweight, purely Texan saddle had appeared during the 1850s, most drovers still used the heavier Mexican-style saddle. Undoubtedly there was an exchange of ideas and experiences by the drovers when they met each other and talked about their work, but most men relied on their own experiences when it came to trail-driving techniques.

Confederate records tell us very little about the Texas drives east; but scattered newspaper accounts suggest that most crossed the Mississippi River south of Vicksburg. A newspaper at Raymond, Mississippi, about 35 miles east-southeast of Vicksburg, reported in the fall of 1862 that a herd of six hundred longhorns had passed through the town. The newspaper editor added: "Texas Beeves in great numbers continue to pass through this place."[7]

One Texan who left a written account of a trail drive to Mississippi was W. D. H. Saunders. At the age of seventeen, he helped two Texas cattlemen, Jim Borroum and Monroe Choate, drive eight hundred beeves to Mississippi in October of 1862. Many years later he wrote of the experience and the problems encountered on the trail:

> We crossed the Guadalupe River at Clinton, and went to Sweet Home in Lavaca county, where we rented a field in which to pen our cattle. In this field was a large haystack. The cattle became frightened at this haystack and stampeded. Next morning we were eight miles from camp and lost three hundred of the beeves. We remained there several days to round up our cattle, and then started on our trip, crossing the Colorado at Columbus, the Brazos at Richmond, the Trinity at Liberty, the Natchez at Beaumont, the Sabine near Orange, and then passed into Louisiana, after which we crossed the Culeshoe [Calcasieu] River and passed through Operluches [Opelousas], where we met Crump and Fleming who bought half interest in our herd, and put in three hundred more, making eleven hundred in all.
>
> When we were near the Mississippi River the Confederate soldiers arrested all of our crowd, thinking we were trying to get the beeves to the Yankees. They took the owners of the herd to Alexandria and held the rest of us four or five days, but as they could not prove anything, we were all released and permitted to pursue our journey. When we reached the Mississippi a thousand of the beeves took the water and easily swam across, but we had to sell one hundred on this side of the river as we would not get them across. We had an old negro with us who was very excitable, and was always uneasy for fear the Yankees would get him, and we had a great deal of difficulty in keeping him with us.
>
> We found sugar mills at all of the large plantations and whenever we stopped at a mill our boys were told to "help themselves," which they usually did with the result that they often ate too much and were sick from the effects of it.
>
> After we crossed the Mississippi the Confederate soldiers arrested us again, and took our men to Fort Hudson, where they kept them several days, but as in the former case, they found nothing against us and turned us loose. At Woodville, Mississippi, the cattle were divided, and Borroum and Choate sold theirs to parties there. Crum and Fleming went on to Mobile, Alabama, where they sold their cattle.[8]

Young Saunders made his way back to Texas. In February of 1863, a few days before his eighteenth birthday, he enlisted in the Confederate army. He was of age to fight in the war.

It was not uncommon to see Confederate soldiers driving Texas steers east of the Mississippi River during the early years of the war. Branch Isbell, who moved to Texas after the war, recalled seeing a squad of Confederate soldiers driving a herd of about "300 big Texas steers" near his home in Sumter County, Alabama, in 1863. The soldiers "pastured them over night in my mother's fields from which the corn had been harvested. The next day when the herd was started to cross the Tom Bigbee River at Gainesville, four miles distant, I persuaded Mother to let me accompany the outfit that far on my pony," wrote Isbell. He added: "On the way the soldiers sang over and over a song which one of their number had composed. The song had many stanzas, but two of them so impressed my boyish fancy that I recall them still." From memory, early in this century, Isbell wrote them out:

> *Driving cattle's our promotion,*
> *Which just exactly suits my notion,*
> *And we perform with great devotion,*
> *There's work enough for all.*
>
> *I'd like to be a Virginia picket,*
> *But I'd rather be in the cattle thicket*
> *Where the hooting owl and screaming cricket*
> *Make noise enough for all.*

When Isbell returned home that night, he told his mother that when he grew up he wanted to go to Texas and herd cattle. He did go to Texas in 1871, and became a prominent Texas cattleman.[9]

In addition to the cattle drives east during the early years of the Civil War, there are a few accounts of Texas cattle having been driven to Arkansas. A Mississippi-born Texas rancher, Pleasant Burnell Butler, recalled how his older brother was sent home to Texas in 1862 from his Confederate military post in Arkansas to gather "a bunch of cattle." Butler recalled: "I was then a youth of fourteen and went along to the Hickok pens, near Oakville, where the cattle men had assembled 500 head which were headed at once for Arkansas. I helped to drive them as far as Pecan Springs, near the present town of San Marcos, where I bade my brother good-bye and returned home.[10]

Life in Texas was not easy before the Civil War, and it was even more difficult during the war. The Union blockade caused an economic revolution that was to have far-reaching effects on the lives of Texans, especially the women. As the men left to join the fighting, the responsibility of raising crops fell upon their wives, children, and slaves. Many cattlemen, however, owned no slaves and did no farming; life was even more difficult for their wives. Many of the women moved to settlements, but some stayed to ranch. A rancher named Drewry L. Middleton left his wife and family on Ruckers Creek in Hood County, Texas, and enlisted in the Confederate army, fifth regiment, under Tom Green. That was in the spring of 1861. Middleton was then twenty-four years old. As he later wrote, he had to leave his wife "unaided, and buffeting the dangers and hazards of frontier life." She stuck it out and supported herself and their two children and eight other dependents until her husband returned.[11]

Another Texan, L. B. Anderson, who spent most of his life near Seguin in Guadalupe County, was only a young boy when the war began, but he remembered what happened:

> We lived care-free and happy until the outbreak of the Civil War, when father and my older brother went into the service to fight for the South, leaving me, a lad of only 11 years, the only protection for my mother and younger brothers and sisters, but mother was a fearless woman and the best marksman with a rifle I ever saw, so we felt able to take care of ourselves. My duties during the war were many and varied. I was mail carrier and general errand boy for all of the women in the neighborhood. Among other things it was my duty to look after the cattle. During this trying time the cattle accumulated on the range. . . .[12]

Gardens appeared on ranches where none had existed before. Much acreage in eastern and central portions of Texas was put to corn and other food crops, and the planting of cotton gradually declined. Texas women spent long hours in the fields with plow and hoe producing food during the war. If there were boys and old men in the ranchers' families, they took care of the cattle as best they could, but they often found it impossible to keep up with the branding of new calves. It was not uncommon for them to leave the cattle to fend for themselves. Texans lived on beef, which of course was plentiful, bacon, sweet potatoes, beets, okra, and other vegetables. Corn was the main staple through much of the war. But many other things were in short supply. Ashes from pipe tobacco were sometimes used for soda and Texans experimented with coffee substitutes. One was the burnt okra used occasionally before the war. Another was a combination of parched peas and corn ground together. Others included such ingredients as bran, toasted rye and wheat, chicory, parched garden beets, okra seeds, yams, pumpkin seeds, and even acorns. Trying to create the perfect coffee substitute became something of a popular pastime. People from different areas frequently exchanged their recipes. One southern wit, apparently tired of hearing about substitutes, offered his own: "Take tan bark, three parts, three old cigar stumps and a quantity of water, mix well, and boil fifteen minutes in a dirty coffee pot, and the best judges cannot tell it from the best Mocha."[13]

The Union blockade forced Texans to make do with what they had. Unlike the Mexican haciendas across the Rio Grande, Texan farms, ranches, and even cotton plantations were not self-sufficient. Texans had come to depend on the North for various tools before the war. By the mid-1850s many had turned to store-bought clothes made in Northern factories. The war forced them to improvise, much as they had done during the days of the Republic and early years of statehood. The women began to weave cloth for clothing, including Confederate uniforms. Many plantations in east Texas established small factories to make such things as hoes, plows, and knives. A cap-and-ball factory was started at Austin. Its output was not great, although it did produce a few cannon.

Cotton, like cattle, could not be exported because of the coastal blockade and the closing of the Mississippi River in the summer of 1863. But cotton growers began freighting their bales across the Rio Grande to Matamoros, where English and French merchants maintained a brisk market for the scarce raw material. Some cotton was shipped to the Texas penitentiary at Huntsville, where convicts produced several million yards of cloth during the war years. The cloth was then made into clothing, especially military uniforms, in Confederate Quartermaster's department shops in Houston, Austin, Tyler, and San Antonio.

DRY WEATHER CONDITIONS made things even worse for cattle ranchers in southwest Texas. The summer of 1861 marked the beginning of what was to become a "disastrous drouth." By 1863, it was at its worst. "The Nueces and San Antonio rivers became mere trickling threads of water with here and there a small pool. The grass was soon gone and no cattle survived except those that had previously drifted across the Nueces river on to a range that was not so severely affected by the drouth," wrote one rancher.[14] William Kuykendall, another Texas rancher, recalled that the death rate of cattle in some localities "was estimated as high as seventy-five per cent." But as he noted, the drought was "a virtue in disguise, as it offered the only available means of recuperation to the overstocked ranges at the time."[15]

During the winter of 1863–64, the weather dealt still another blow to Texas. A series of northers—sudden cold winter storms from the north— swept across the prairies and coastal plains of Texas. Northers sometimes are accompanied by freezing drizzle or snow, but these were dry. It was so cold that portions of Galveston Bay froze over. More cattle died, and many a rancher suffered from the bone-chilling winds. The vicious weather caused what ranchers came to call "The Big Drift." As the storm swept south across Texas, thousands upon thousands of cattle from the unfenced ranges of north and central Texas drifted with the storms. Many

cattle had been deserted when their owners went off to war. Huge numbers were even reported along the beaches of the Gulf of Mexico, and
ranchers found countless cattle with strange brands competing for the
sparse grass in the drought areas. More died. It was the winter, ranchers
would later say, when all Texas cattle made their home in south Texas.

Fortunately, with the arrival of spring of 1864, the drought broke.
The rains came. The rivers filled. The grass grew and became plentiful.
Pleasant Burnell Butler recalled in his recollections how a search was organized to look for the cattle that had drifted south. Butler wrote: "All the
young able bodied men were in the army, so a party of forty-five young
boys and old men, headed by Uncle Billy Ricks, of Oakville, went to San
Diego to the ranch of Benito Lopez, from which point they worked for a
month rounding up cattle and cutting out those of their own brands.
Every week a herd was taken across the river and headed for home and in
this way 500 head were put back on the ranges of Karnes county where
thousands had grazed before the drouth."[16]

The owners of many of the drifted cattle had no idea what had happened. They had gone off to war. Many had been unable to find anyone
to watch their cattle. Unclaimed, these cattle mingled with others that had
survived the drought and winter storms and were "acquired" by ranchers
in the region. It has been said that the surviving cattle were the strongest
of the longhorn breed. The weaker ones had died.

Cattle were not the only ones to suffer from the elements. People
suffered, especially the families of soldiers. By the fall of 1863 the resources
of many families had been exhausted. Poverty reigned. And when the
winter storms struck Texas there was more suffering. The government of
Texas appropriated $600,000 for direct relief in 1863, and some Texans
drove small herds of cattle to Mexico and traded the beeves for goods.
William Carroll McAdams drove a small herd from Palo Pinto County
across the Rio Grande and traded them for sugar and other articles.

George W. Saunders was only ten years old in 1864, but he remembered
helping to gather a Mexico-bound herd of longhorns. What happened is
best told in his own words:

George Bell, who was exempt from military service on account of
one eye being blind, agreed to take a herd of beeves to Mexico and exchange for supplies for the war widows. The neighbors got together
about two hundred of these beeves, my mother putting in twenty
head. We delivered the herd to Mr. Bell at the Pettus ranch where
Pettus Station now stands. This was in 1864, when I was ten years old.
We put our cattle in the herd and brother Jack and I agreed to help
hold them. That night shortly after dark something scared the beeves

and they made a run. I had never heard anything like the rumbling noise they made, but I put spurs to my horse and followed the noise. We ran those cattle all night and at daybreak we found we had not lost a beef, but we had five or six bunches four or five miles apart, and two or three men or boys with each bunch. We soon had them all together and Mr. Bell started them on the trip. When he returned from Mexico he brought us one sack of coffee, two sets of knives and forks, two pairs of spurs, two bridle bits, and two fancy 'hackamores' or bridle headstalls, for which we had traded our twenty beeves, and we were well pleased with our deal, for in those days such things were considered luxuries, and we were glad to get them, particularly the knives and forks, for we had been drinking bran coffee, and were using wooden knives and forks we had made ourselves.[17]

ALTHOUGH A SMALL NUMBER OF CATTLE were driven to Mexico from Texas during the war, the market was not good. And drovers during some periods had to avoid Union forces along the coast and in far-south Texas.

When Union forces gained control of New Orleans in the summer of 1862, most Texans stopped driving their cattle to that market; but a few Texans continued to drive small herds of cattle to Crescent City and sell them for Union gold. Who these Texans were is not recorded, and whether they were simply desperate for funds or whether profit was more important than ideological differences is anyone's guess. Confederate officials made some futile efforts to end this trading with the Yankees.

Texas cattle drives across the Mississippi River came to a halt during the summer of 1863. Union forces had gained control of the river by then, although a few herds of longhorns reportedly were spirited across the Mississippi below Vicksburg, some in the dark of night. But cattle losses were high. Union gunboats soon made the practice too hazardous. By the fall of 1863 there was no way to get Texas cattle to Confederate troops east of the Mississippi.

The Confederacy turned to the only available supply of cattle, which was in Florida. Soon Confederate agents were buying up cattle in northern Florida near the railheads and larger towns. When this supply was exhausted, the Confederate Commissary turned toward central and south Florida. One government stock raiser, Jacob Summerlin, was awarded a two-year contract to supply the Confederates with cattle on the hoof at $8 to $10 per head delivered. Accounts suggest that he supplied about 25,000 head to the Confederacy, but since there were no connecting railroads in central and south Florida linking those areas with northern Florida, the cattle had to be driven overland.

Joe A. Akerman, Jr., in his excellent book *Florida Cowman: A History of Florida Cattle Raising*, recounts how Union raiding parties and Confederate deserters hampered cattle drives from Florida northward. "Drovers and cattle alike were often bushwhacked on the trail. Some drives took as long as six weeks, some cattle losing as much as 150 pounds along the way. . . . At one time as many as 2,000 head each week were coming to the Confederate army off the Florida ranges," wrote Akerman.

Florida drovers seem to have experienced many of the same problems with cattle as Texas drovers during the Civil War. One Confederate who participated in many of the Florida drives gave the following account:

A detail of six men, under the command of Mr. James P. McMullen, was ordered to the cattle pens at Fort Meade to take charge of a herd of 365 beef cattle bound for Savannah. Early one morning the drive was commenced. The course was a northerly one, and in line with Orange Lake in Marion County. The cattle were driven along at a "grazing rate" of speed, usually averaging around 8½ miles a day. At night, if we were fortunate, we would reach a cattle pen, and there the beeves would be corraled until morning. With the coming of day, the drive was started again, the cattle slowly grazing over the countryside at a pace set by the animals themselves.

When we reached Orange Lake, the cattle were driven into one of the regular stopping pens. It was a good place to bed down, covering about 4 acres and hemmed up by a rail fence 10 to 12 rails high. The "cowboy-soldiers," feeling that their herd was safe for the night, made camp about fifty feet in front of the gate and there lay down to sleep. But late that night, the cattle became frightened and stampeded right out of those pens onto the prairie. But fortunate for us, the milling of the beeves before they actually busted out woke us up giving us all a chance to saddle up. We followed them about a mile, and before long they held up in a large swamp about a hundred yards from an old plantation house. A fence around the area had helped to direct them into the swamp. When the cattle seemed ready to bed down again, we decided the pen was too far away to move them, so we built some large bonfires about 50 feet apart, hoping that would keep the restless beeves there for the night. But the next morning when we got up, there wasn't a cow in sight. Sometime during the early morning one of the leaders had evidently scented water and had led the rest of 'em through a space little more than 30 feet wide. All were found a mile or two away, placidly chewing their cuds at a bend in Orange Creek. Such was the perversity of the beast.

From Orange Lake we continued our drive to the state line crossing the St. Marys River near the ferry at Traiders Hill. All was un-eventful until the herd came to the fording of the Altamaha River some miles northwest of Brunswick, Georgia. Here a crowd of several hundred people had gathered to see us cross at a point where the river was less than a fourth of a mile wide. All went well until two steers swam too far downstream and found themselves on the far side of the old flat, below the landing. They drowned. They were pulled ashore by ropes, and enough meat was butchered from one to supply the drovers for two or three days. The crowd collected by the river was then told that they could have the rest. Within the hour not one horn, hoof or tail remained of the beasts. It shows you how hungry folks were then. From there we drove the cattle on to Savannah where they were delivered. Three hundred and sixty-two head out of the original herd of 365 had made it. Besides the two that were drowned, one was also lost somewhere between Fort Meade and Savannah. The herd was actually in far better condition than when they left their prairie home in Florida five weeks earlier.[18]

This account points up some of the differences between Florida and Texas cattle-driving techniques during the early 1860s. While Florida drovers moved their cattle at a "grazing pace," Texans on long drives kept their cattle moving at a faster pace because of the vast distances that normally had to be covered in the West. Florida drovers, unlike those in Texas, had the benefit of "stopping pens" located at regular intervals along the trail. Texans may have found these on their drives through Mississippi and Alabama, but such pens were rare in Texas and Louisiana. In open country Texans simply posted a guard around their herds as the cattle bedded down for the night.

Whether Florida drovers made use of trained lead steers is not known. The account of the drive from Florida to Georgia makes no mention of lead steers having been used to get cattle across rivers and streams. Such steers were, of course, used by many Texas drovers even before the war.

Such differences in trail-driving techniques were common during the Civil War not only between Florida and Texas drovers but among drovers in each state. Texas cattlemen were still learning to adapt to the terrain being crossed, the weather, and other conditions, including the mood of the cattle. The cattle, of course, were most important. They were the moving force behind the developing cowboy culture, a culture that would soon burst forth from Texas and eventually spread throughout the Great Plains and beyond.

CHAPTER 8

◆•◆

On the Open Range

The cattle industry is, of necessity, a frontier industry.
When the population increases the herder must move to a
new frontier or change his occupation; at the same time
there is a stronger demand for his products.

—CLARA M. LOVE[1]

IT was about two months after Lee surrendered to Grant at Appomattox Courthouse in Virginia on April 9, 1865, before the last Confederate forces in Texas surrendered. Long before then the war had demoralized Texans. One can only imagine the humiliation felt by these proud people—before the war they had conquered Mexicans and hostile Indians, but now they were the conquered, and by an army that fought few battles on Texas soil. Many Texans were bitter, especially those who came home from the battlefields of Tennessee, Georgia, Virginia, and elsewhere. They returned by the thousands, only to find their state's economy in ruins. The Confederate dollars in their pockets had little value. Texas banks were closed and the deposits gone. Yet most of these returning Texans considered themselves lucky. They knew that many would never return. About a fourth of the state's productive white male population either had died or was crippled.

For cattle raisers during the months immediately following the war, the most pressing problem was the condition of their herds. The winter storms of 1863–64 had scattered cattle. Others had been neglected by the old men or young boys left to watch them during the war. Few bulls had been castrated, and herds had increased. The neglect had been particularly bad during the last two years of the war, when the value of cattle dropped to $1 or $2 a head, and that price was dependent upon finding a buyer.

It is not difficult to imagine a Texas rancher returning to his former home along the Texas prairie, perhaps on the Brazos River near Crossed

Timbers with its dwarfed post oaks, or in the brush country south of San Antonio. The rancher probably had entered the cattle-raising business during the 1850s. Perhaps he had taken a herd of cattle north to Missouri or west to California during that period, but when the war came he volunteered. Before leaving to serve on the Texas frontier or in the states to the east, the rancher took his wife and children to stay with friends in east Texas. He knew they would at least be safe from the hostile Comanches that roamed the Texas prairie and plains. When the war ended, he made his way back to a tearful reunion with his family and friends. He undoubtedly thanked his Maker in his own way for his safe return and savored playing with his children and holding his wife in his arms. As the hot summer days passed, he gathered his family and their meager belongings, along with what few supplies they could afford or were given, and headed back to their ranch, where the cattle had been left to fend for themselves perhaps two or three years earlier.

The slow wagon journey across Texas that summer of 1865 was hot and dry. When they reached the ranch house they found it in disrepair. The rancher had to go 20 miles to obtain wood to make repairs, but they were soon made and the family settled. The rancher then set out to find his stock.

Some men were lucky and found most of their cattle plus their unbranded offspring, but others found none. In southwest Texas, men pooled their efforts and organized "cow-hunts" to locate their cattle. One rancher, Lee Moore, remembered what they were like:

We didn't call it roundup in those days. We called it cow-hunts and every man on this cow-hunt was a cattle owner just home from the war and went out to see what they had left and to brand up. . . . I was the only boy on this cow-hunt and was looking out for cattle that belonged to my father before the war. We had no wagon [chuck wagon]. Every man carried his grub in a wallet on behind his saddle and his bed under his saddle. I was put on herd and kept on herd when we had one and I don't think there was ever a day on this hunt when we didn't have a herd, and I carried a lot of extra wallets on behind my saddle and a string of tin cups on a hobble around my pony's neck. A wallet is a sack with both ends sewed up with the mouth of the sack in the middle. . . . Whenever the boss herder couldn't hear those cups jingling, he would come around and wake me up. We would corral the cattle every night at some one of the owners' homes and stand guard around the corral. I didn't stand any guard but I carried brush and corn-stalks and anything I could get to make a light for those who were on guard to play poker by. They played for unbranded cattle, yearlings at fifty cents a head and the top price for any class was $5 a head, so if anyone run out of cattle and had a little money, he could get a stack of yearlings. My compensation for light was twenty-five cents per night or as long as the game lasted. Every few days they would divide up and brand and each man take his cattle home, as we now call it—throw back. . . . This cow-hunt continued all summer.[2]

Another Texan who went on cow-hunts just after the war was L. B. Anderson of Seguin, Texas. He came from Mississippi with his parents in 1853. When the war ended he joined hunts in Guadalupe County. Anderson was in his seventies when he recalled:

Each man would take an extra pony along, a lengthy stake rope made of rawhide or hair, a wallet of cornbread, some fat bacon and coffee, and plenty of salt to do him on the round-up. Whenever we got hungry for fresh meat we would kill a fat yearling, eat all we wanted and leave the remainder. On these trips I acquired my first experience at cow-punching. Our route usually would be down the Cibolo by Panamorea and old Helena to the San Antonio River, and up Clate Creek gathering all the cattle that belonged to our crowd and some mavericks besides. The drives would generally wind up at old man [Gus] Kenda's, from where we had started, and here division was made, each man taking his cattle home where they would be branded and turned out on the range again.[3]

Anderson was sixteen years old at the time.

James G. Shaw was still another Texan who went on cow-hunts in 1865. He was only thirteen years old as the soldiers returned home. Late in life he remembered clearly the "poor soldiers" who came home "barefooted, with little clothing and very much discouraged." Some, he recalled, had contracted "chronic diarrhea, which followed them to their graves." Most of these men were too weak to go on cow-hunts or to perform hard ranch work. But he remembered that those who did return in good health spent much of the summer of 1865 searching for their cattle, and they "branded anything that was not branded." Shaw added: "When the cattle would come on the creek for water I have seen as many as five head of mavericks in one bunch. Those conditions did not last long after the old soldiers got home."[4]

There are several versions of the story relating how unbranded cattle came to be known as "mavericks." J. Frank Dobie gives a few versions in his book *The Longhorns*, and other writers have told still other variations, nearly all involving Samuel A. Maverick, a native of South Carolina who moved to Texas in 1835. He joined the volunteer army and later was one of the signers of the Texas Declaration of Independence. Maverick farmed and ranched in Matagorda County on the Gulf Coast near Decrows Point between 1844 and 1847. During this time, in what seems to be the most probable version of the story, Maverick reluctantly accepted a herd of four hundred cattle from a neighbor in payment of a debt of $1,200. Maverick was not very interested in cattle raising at the time. He placed the cattle under the care of a Negro and his family with instructions to "brand up" and care for the stock.

Many of Maverick's cattle were not branded, especially the calves. As the months passed, the cattle were neglected more and more. Within a year or two the residents of the coastal region began referring to every unbranded head as "one of Maverick's." Early in 1854 someone reportedly sent Maverick a note warning that if he did not do something about his wandering cattle, he would not have any. Within a few weeks Maverick, his two sons, and some hired men moved what cattle they could find to Maverick's ranch on the San Antonio River about 40 miles south of San Antonio. The Negro and his family were brought along to care for the cattle. Some of the unbranded stock were then branded, but others were not. Maverick's cattle were again neglected and allowed to roam unchecked over a wide area.

In 1856, Maverick sold his cattle and brand to another rancher, A. Toutant Beauregard, a brother of the well-known Confederate general. Beauregard and his men accepted the cattle for range delivery, which meant they had to hunt for the cattle themselves on the open range. The men roamed over several counties looking for strays from Maverick's herd. Whenever they found unbranded cattle, they claimed them as "Maverick's" and branded them. By 1857, people in a wide area south of San Antonio were referring to all unbranded cattle as "Mavericks." But the term did not come into general use throughout Texas until after the Civil War, when there were countless unbranded cattle, especially in southwest Texas and on the coastal plains southeast of San Antonio.[5]

Much of the area bounded by San Antonio, Corpus Christi, and Laredo was settled by cattle ranchers immediately after the war. Some had not planned it that way. They were Texans who had been unable to find jobs in the towns; others were southerners who had come to Texas from the war-torn states to the east. Many had been farmers in Georgia, Alabama, or elsewhere. They came to Texas to get a fresh start. When they could find no good land to farm or jobs in towns, they went where the cattle were, in the sparsely settled regions of south and southwest Texas, and entered ranching. Free land was plentiful in that region.

Land was perhaps easier to obtain in Texas following the Civil War than in any other state. Texas, unlike other states, had been able to retain its public land when it joined the Union. As a Republic, Texas had claimed a public domain of 225,299,800 acres, including parts of the present states of New Mexico, Oklahoma, Kansas, Colorado, and Wyoming. But Texas gave up its claim to much of the land outside its present boundaries in exchange for $10,000,000 in bonds in 1850 and an additional $2,750,000 in cash in 1855 from the federal government. It managed to continue its land policies established after the Texas Revolution. The first homestead legislation was passed in Texas in 1838. The first preemption act was passed in 1845, and Texas gave people who had previously settled or would settle upon and improve public lands the preference right to purchase up to 320 acres. In 1854, however, a new homestead act was passed, reducing homestead grants to 160 acres and requiring residence of three years. Still, the land policies of Texas favored the individual, even after the Civil War. As one looks back, it appears that from Texas's earliest days as a republic its lawmakers were trying to create a state where every white family could own land.

This background on land policy is important, since land was and still is essential for cattle ranching. Millions of acres of prairie and plains land, most of it unsuitable for farming because of limited water, could be used for livestock grazing. As an area with a mild climate, much of south, southwest, and west Texas was ideally suited for cattle raising. A few men owned thousands of acres of this land before the Civil War began. They had arrived in Texas during the 1840s or 1850s. Undoubtedly the man who owned the most land in Texas following the Civil War was Richard King. He had title to about 84,000 acres located along the Gulf Coast of south Texas. On this grass-covered plain he grazed more than 65,000 cattle and ten thousand horses. King employed about three hundred Mexicans, most of them vaqueros, to work his ranch. Before the nineteenth century ended, King owned 1,270,000 acres, one of the largest parcels of land under one owner anywhere in the world.[6]

The King Ranch, however, did not have the distinction of being the largest ranch in the United States during the late nineteenth century. Texan John Chisum probably controlled the largest piece of country ever held by one cattleman for ranching purposes: it covered southeastern New Mexico and portions of west Texas. Chisum trailed his first cattle herd into the area in 1867. Within a few years he controlled the region, although he actually owned very little of the land and the boundaries of his range were never definitely marked. His ranch did cover an area equal to three or four New England states. Many stories tell how Chisum's El Rancho Grande ranch house was always open and how his dining table was ready at all times, seven days a week, to seat forty guests at a moment's notice. Before Chisum's death in 1884, his cowboys branded eighteen thousand calves in one season, certainly something of a record.[7]

Another large ranch in northeastern New Mexico and southeastern

Colorado belonged to Lucien Bonaparte Maxwell. Born in Kaskaskia, Illinois, in 1818 of Irish and French ancestry, Maxwell came west to join the American Fur Company on a two-year trapping expedition. He worked for John C. Frémont in 1842 and two years later married Maria de la Luz Beaubien and settled in Taos, New Mexico. Through his wife's father, Maxwell acquired an interest in the huge Beaubien-Miranda land grant east of Taos. In time, he bought up the rights of other heirs and was sole owner by 1865. Unlike John Chisum, who controlled much land that he did not own, Maxwell owned about 97,000 acres extending from modern Springer, New Mexico, north into Colorado. Maxwell built a large mansion at Cimarron, New Mexico, and made it his ranch headquarters. In addition to ranching, he had extensive farming and mercantile interests. His wealth increased in 1867 when gold was discovered on his land near what became Elizabethtown, New Mexico. Maxwell sold out to a group of capitalists in 1870 for the sum of $1,350,000. He died in 1875.

A few men who entered ranching in Texas just after the Civil War were able to purchase large parcels of land, but many others simply took over an unclaimed area or settled for a 160-acre homestead on the plains. Such a homestead of generally sparse grassland was hardly enough to support a dozen head of cattle. Even in years of average rainfall—3 or 4 inches was "average" in some areas—it took 15 to 25 acres to support one cow. By necessity the ranchers let their cattle graze on surrounding public land, and several might use the same public land, although this depended upon who controlled the water supply.

Ranchers sought homesteads on land through which rivers or streams or even good springs flowed. If a rancher was fortunate enough to acquire one or two miles of land on both sides of a river, he might enjoy exclusive use of the nearby public land, or open range, as it became known. Controlling the water in a region meant controlling the surrounding grazing land. Without water for cattle, the best grassland was of little value. Often, after ranchers secured water rights in an area, they did not trouble themselves about the legal ownership of land beyond that containing the water source. This practice was repeated time and again as the business of cattle ranching spread northward across the plains and prairie lands of the West.

Under such circumstances it did not require a large outlay of money to enter ranching in Texas by the summer of 1865. The returning soldiers and other newcomers first located a homestead with water. The rancher-to-be then decided on the spot to build his "ranch" headquarters. The word "ranch" had several meanings in the late 1860s. Philip Ashton Rollins, writing in 1922, observed:

Whether it appeared as "ranch" or in its earlier American form of "rancho" . . . it denoted interchangeably either an entire ranching establishment inclusive of its buildings, lands, and live stock, or else the principal building, which usually was the owner's dwelling-house, or else that building together with the other structures adjacent to it. . . . The principal building, however, was more commonly specifically designated as the "ranch house," or, on the Mexican border, as the "rancheria."[8]

The ranch house of an unmarried Texas rancher was most likely nothing more than a small one-room shack. If he was married and had a family, he might construct a two-room house or something more elaborate. In areas where wood was plentiful, the rancher might cut down trees and use logs to construct his ranch house or freight lumber for the purpose from a nearby town. If his funds were limited, and they usually were, he used what material he found on his land: stone or earth. If the terrain was rolling, he might start by digging into the side of a rise. On the exposed side he would construct three walls of stone or earth, leaving room for a door and perhaps two small windows.

While the new house was being built, the rancher and his family might sleep in a lean-to or a tent constructed from the cover of the wagon that had brought them and their worldly possessions to the ranch site. If stone was not available and the ranch house was being built on the treeless prairie, the rancher might arrange to borrow a plow or would otherwise cut pieces of sod from the ground. They would be 8 to 10 inches wide and about 18 inches long. These sod blocks were stacked much as a bricklayer lays bricks. Frames for the door and windows were set into the walls, and sod was laid around them. A fireplace usually was constructed at one end with the chimney also built of hard earth. Inside, the floor was earth, beaten hard and smooth. Once the walls were completed, the rancher would construct the roof. It generally was supported by heavy ridgepoles, perhaps freighted to the site by wagon. The ridgepoles generally ran the entire length of the home. Sod or perhaps wood and tar paper would then cover the roof. The poorer the rancher, the cruder his roof. The thick walls, however, made a sod house remarkably cool in summer and warm in winter.

In areas of southwest Texas and along the Mexican border, many ranch houses were constructed of adobe. In some instances ranchers hired Mexicans to build their houses. Adobe is clay and sand mixed with water and suitable bonding materials such as straw, plant roots, or burned grasses. Adobe bricks are molded in wooden frames and dried in the warm sun. Each brick is about 10 by 18 by 5 inches in size. The bricks were stacked to form the walls of the ranch house. Because of Indians and outlaws in southwest Texas, many adobe ranch houses had only small windows with

WACO, TEXAS, IN 1865.

BRANDING AND CUTTING CALVES ON A ROUNDUP IN TEXAS.
By Texas photographer Erwin Smith.

A TEXAS COWBOY.
Photograph by Erwin Smith.

"STRETCHING ONE OUT."
In this early photograph, two cowboys bring a steer to the ground.
Photograph by Erwin Smith.

wooden grilles set deeply into the walls. The fireplace was usually in a corner of one room. It was not unusual for a rancher to mix animal blood and wood ashes into the dirt floor to harden the earth. If properly mixed, the combination made the floor water-resistant.

Once the ranch house was constructed, the rancher might turn his attention to constructing one or more corrals for his saddle horses and small bunches of cattle. Some ranchers built their corrals before their ranch houses in order to control their saddle horses. Corrals might be built of wood poles about 6 feet in length tied with rawhide strings, but should wood not be available, the walls were constructed of sod or adobe blocks stacked 5 or 6 feet high and perhaps 2 feet thick. Because sod or adobe walls took three or four times as long to build, most ranchers chose wood poles and rawhide strings, even if they had to go some distance to obtain the poles.

By this time the rancher probably would have decided on a brand to use for his cattle. Selecting a brand required not only some imagination but knowledge of other brands in the area. Each brand had to be different. The new rancher might travel to the county seat and study the brands that had been recorded by the county clerk. The Texas legislature in 1848 had provided for the recording of all brands with the county clerk in the county where cattle were kept. Under the legislation, an unrecorded brand did not constitute legal evidence of ownership. It was not until 1913 that this provision was modified because thefts were going unpunished where unrecorded brands were involved. Checking the recorded brands in a rancher's county would indicate whether the brand he had created was unique enough to be registered.

In addition to the brand, the new rancher had to record a distinctive earmark or a "wattle" cut elsewhere on the bovine. A wattle is a mark of ownership made on the neck or the jaw of an animal by pinching up a quantity of skin and cutting it. However, the skin is not cut entirely off, and when the cut is healed, a hanging flap of skin is left. Earmarks, as the name suggests, are marks on the animal's ears. They are made by cutting a design into one or both ears of an animal. Sometimes a portion of the ear might be removed. The same mark on both ears became known as a "flickerbob." A "double over-bit" was the mark created by cutting two triangular pieces in the upper part of the animal's ear. One of the better-known earmarks in Texas was the "jinglebob," a deep slit that left the lower half of the ear flapping down. It was considered by most cattlemen as one of the most hideous ever devised. It was the mark of John Chisum, whose great ranch lay in southeastern New Mexico and west Texas.[9]

CATTLE WERE NUMEROUS in southwest Texas when the war ended, but the region was sparsely populated with humans. Cattle did not need man to multiply in the mild climate, only grass and water. Most counties had barely enough people for a county organization. In most instances these counties had only one village or town, the county seat. Luther A. Lawhon, an early cattleman in southwest Texas, recalled with fondness that the typical county seat had

> its rock or lumber court house, which was rarely two stories, and near by, as an adjunct, a one-cell rock or lumber jail. Around the public square were built the few unpretentious store houses, that flaunted the proverbial signs, "Dry Goods and Groceries" or "Dry Goods, Boots and Shoes," as the case might be. That the weaknesses as well as the social predelictions [sic] of the sturdy citizenship might be readily and conveniently catered to, a saloon or perhaps several, could always be found on or near the public square. Clustered about the commercial center, and growing further apart as the distance increased, were private residences which went to make up the hamlet. After the court house and jail, the hotel—generally a two-story building—was considered the most important, as it was frequently the most imposing structure in the village. In addition to the official and business edifices, there was always a well-constructed school house (there were no free schools in those days) and a commodious, comfortable church house . . . in which these pioneer men and women with their families, irrespective of denomination, met together with good and honest hearts, and worshipped God in spirit and in truth.

Lawhon, like most ranchers, was close to the land. Looking beyond the village square and the frame homes on the edge of the small community, he wrote of the vast expanse of unfenced and uncontrolled range:

> Luxuriant grasses and fragrant wild flowers covered prairie, hill and valley for two-thirds of the year. Herds of cattle and horses grazed in every direction, and each ranchman, by his mark and brand, was enabled to identify his stock and secure its increase. Trained to the range and keen of eye as they were, the old time ranchmen and their cowboys would necessarily fail to find some of the year's increase when they worked this vast territory. As a result, there was a small percentage yearly, of unmarked and unbranded calves. These animals, after being weaned from the mother cows, would thenceforth be abroad on the prairies, the property of whomsoever found and branded them.[10]

Such was the custom. From the days of the Republic of Texas, unbranded cattle had been considered public property. Unbranded could be appropriated by anyone with the ability to capture and brand them. By the fall of 1866, many of these wild mavericks had been branded by one man or another. Only in remote areas, particularly the brush country of south Texas, were there many wild cattle left. Some men then began to brand other men's calves before the owners could brand them. The Texas legislature moved to stop this practice on November 12, 1866, by passing a law prohibiting anyone from driving another person's live-stock from its accustomed range. But the law was difficult to enforce, and the practice continued in most areas of Texas until the late 1880s, when mavericking became stealing under Texas law.

The cow-hunts that Luther Lawhon, Lee Moore, L. B. Anderson, James Shaw, and others participated in just after the war were not always well organized. The men would sometimes run short on the prepared foods which they carried with them from their homes. Lawhon remembered that when he and some others ran out of biscuits they relied on an

unwritten law, recognized by the good women of the towns as well as of the country, that whenever a party of cowhunters rode up and asked to have bread baked, it mattered not the time of day, the request was to be cheerfully complied with. . . . I remember the many times that cowhunters rode up to my father's house, and telling my mother they were out of bread, asked that she would kindly bake their flour for them. Everything was at once made ready. The sack was lifted from the pack horse and brought in, and in due time the bread wallets were once more filled with freshly cooked biscuits, and the cowboys rode away with graceful appreciation. These acts of consideration on the part of my mother were entirely gratuitous, but the generous-hearted cowboys would always leave either a half sack of flour or a money donation as a freewill offering.[11]

Cow-hunts existed in Texas during the 1840s and 1850s, but they became more numerous following the Civil War. Some details of these hunts are known, as recorded here, but unfortunately for history old-time cattlemen left little record of the techniques they used to gather up the cattle. It appears that the stock were driven into small herds or "bunches" and then driven to where the branding fires were waiting. When it came time to begin the branding, these Texans undoubtedly used *reatas* or ropes to catch unbranded calves. Most Texas ranchers in the late 1860s, especially those who had raised cattle before the war, had some practice with the rope. But very little is known about their roping techniques.

…s in New Spain learned to make excellent use …venteenth century and that their techniques im-…ears. But although we have numerous descriptions …re no firsthand accounts of the roping techniques by … could read or write, and their techniques were simply … generation to another in the oral or practical tradition. …tered accounts telling how early Texians learned the va-…ques, but so far as is known no educated Texian took the time … …cribe these techniques in writing during the nineteenth century.

OVERHANDED HEAD CATCH

UNDERHANDED HEAD CATCH

It was not until early in the present century that anyone attempted to
explain in words how to use the rope. Perhaps the earliest published book
on the subject is Charles H. Coe's *Juggling a Rope* (Pendleton, Oregon,
1927). Unfortunately, Coe's book, and another published a year later—
Chester Byer's *Roping: Trick and Fancy Rope Spinning* (New York,
1928)—concentrate on roping as an entertainment, in the spirit of Will
Rogers's act with Texas Jack's Wild West Show in South Africa and later
with the Ziegfeld Follies.

One may surmise that basic roping techniques did not change greatly
between the eighteenth century in New Spain and the early nineteenth
century when Texians first learned them from Mexican vaqueros. It appears that at least five basic catches were used by most Texas cowboys in
the period immediately after the war. The catches were the *pitch*, *slip*,

AL MARTIN
NAPOLETANO

HEELING CATCH

heeling, backhand slip, and *forefooting,* a type of catch sometimes combined with the slip or pitch catch. These catches are still used today. The *pitch catch* is generally used by a roper on foot in catching horses in a corral. The loop is spread out behind the roper, who moves forward and pitches the loop on the head of a horse. The loop travels in a horizontal position. The *slip catch* is similar to a pitch except that the loop travels in a vertical position. A *heeling catch* is designed to catch horses and cattle by their hind legs. It is used to catch calves and drag them to the branding fire, usually by a roper on horseback. It is also used in catching an animal that has been roped around the head by another roper. The heeling catch was used by vaqueros in early California to rope grizzly bears. The roper takes the loop in his throwing hand, makes one revolution in the air with the loop, and throws it so that the loop falls under the animal's body just in front of its back legs. The animal being roped literally walks into the loop and it is quickly pulled tight.

A *backhand slip catch* is more difficult than the others. It takes much

BACKHAND SLIP CATCH

skill. Mexican vaqueros developed this catch to rope a calf when the animal runs behind the mounted roper's horse. The roper reverses the revolution of his rope from that in a heeling catch and lets the loop fall in front of the calf. This is difficult, since the calf is behind the roper's horse and the roper must turn in his saddle to throw the loop. In this catch it is im-

FOREFOOTING SLIP CATCH

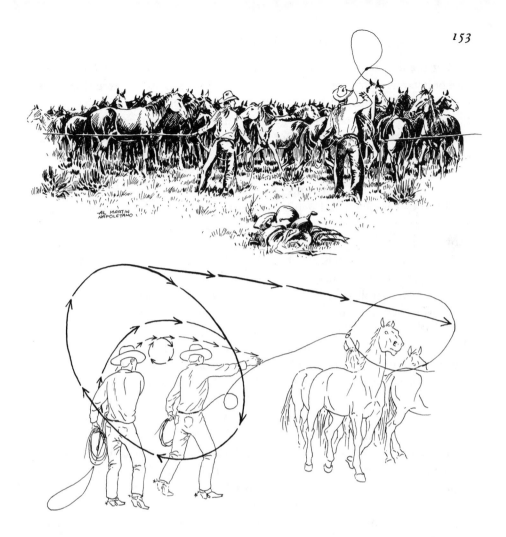

HOOLIHAN CATCH

portant for the roper to let the calf get into position before throwing the loop. A roper, depending upon his skill, might use a backhand slip in a *forefooting catch*. As the name suggests, forefooting is catching a horse or bovine by its forefeet. Some Texans during the late 1860s probably used the Mexican vaquero's *backhand forefooting catch*. It is sometimes called a *mangana*. The roper, standing on the ground, makes a large loop and swings the loop above his head in backhand motion until a running horse is almost directly opposite him. At that moment the roper turns toward the horse and rolls the loop in front of the animal. The horse runs into the loop. The roper then pulls the loop tight around the animal's fore-feet and the catch is made.[12]

There is one other catch that appears to have been common in Texas

during the late 1860s. It was and still is known as the *hoolihan* (or hoolian
or hooleyann) *catch,* and is similar to the overhead swing except that the
cowboy swings the loop in the air for only one revolution before throwing
it. A fast loop designed for a head catch, it is used to catch horses in a
corral. It is thrown with a rather small loop and has the additional virtue
of landing with the honda (the eye through which the rope is run to form
a loop) sliding down the rope, taking up the slack as it goes. Half a dozen
men using this catch can rope mounts at the same time without exciting
the horses. It is quick and generally quiet. The origin of its name is something of a mystery. Although today the art of bulldogging steers in rodeos
is often called hoolihanning, the name appears to have been used first for
the rope catch. It is possible that Hoolihan was some early Texan who
either invented or popularized the catch.

Another catch was either perfected or made famous by John R.
Blocker, a well-known Texas cattleman. The catch is called the "Blocker"
or the "Johnnie Blocker." It has been described by old-timers as "perhaps
the most versatile loop of them all," but then all ropers may say the same
about their favorite catches. The "Blocker" can be thrown from horseback
or by a man standing on the ground, and it can be used for a head catch,
forefooting, and for heeling from either position. One description of the
"Blocker" was written down in 1940 by W. F. French, who noted that the
roper starts by whirling the loop over his right shoulder. When he is
ready to throw the loop—he is using his right arm to whirl the rope—
he whips his right arm straight forward under the whirling loop. At the
same time he throws the loop he twists his hand toward the left. As the
loop moves toward the left, the roper continues to hold the rope in his
right hand, letting it pass through his fingers and playing it out as necessary. In this throw the loop goes out in front of the thrower, stops, stands
up, rolls to the left, and turns over. French observed that the throw is
"deadly" because the loop has a "bigger opening at the right place and at
the right angle."[13] Such large loops were, of course, necessary to get over
the horns of a full-grown longhorn. Sometimes the loop was thrown over
one horn and the nose, making almost as good a catch as one around the
neck or over both horns. A big flat loop was sometimes called a "Mother
Hubbard" or a "Washer Woman."

The earliest kind of lariat used by vaqueros was constructed of
braided rawhide strips 30 to 35 feet in length. The rawhide held a good
loop when thrown, and handled nicely. Some rawhide lariats used during
the nineteenth century were as small as ⅜ inch in diameter, but most were
about ½ inch. A rawhide lariat, however, can be slow in running through
the honda. And if a rawhide lariat has even one broken strand—most had
three or four strands—it is utterly worthless to the roper.

Not as common as the rawhide lariat was the kind made of horsehair. It was never as popular as the rawhide lariat, because it was very light and not as strong. Some vaqueros and cowboys preferred to use a horsehair rope for picketing their horses, either by fastening the rope around the animals' necks or by tying the front legs together. (Old-timers' stories claiming that rattlesnakes would not cross the scratchy surface of a horsehair rope laid around a cowboy's bed on the ground were pure fiction.)

Still another kind of lariat came north with Mexican vaqueros. It was constructed with fiber from the maguey plant (from which the popular Mexican drink mescal is also produced). The Mexican maguey rope, as it is sometimes called, was quite popular in southwest Texas and northern Mexico. Vaqueros made these lariats one at a time and at any length from 35 to 75 feet or more. The maguey fiber is extra hard. It holds a big wide loop and throws very fast. But maguey becomes stiff as a poker in damp weather and breaks easily if tied hard and fast. Vaqueros and cowboys used maguey lariats only in dry climates and for light work, where many believed it was the best rope available.

The maguey rope's Mexican cousin is sisal, produced from the leaves of an Agave cactus plant which has a hard fiber like maguey. But sisal ropes, like cotton rope (much too soft), never became as popular as ropes made of Manila hemp. Even the popularity of maguey and rawhide lariats declined with the introduction of Manila hemp rope. Lieutenant John White of the U.S. Navy brought a sample of a fiber grown in the Philippines back to this country in about 1820. Although it was not true hemp—the fiber was produced by a variety of the wild banana plant, *Musa textilis*—ropemakers in America recognized that the Manila hemp, as it was called, was superior to the dark-gray American hemp produced in Kentucky and the upper Mississippi Valley, and even to the smooth, creamy-tan Russian hemp imported from the Baltic. Even before the Civil War the popularity of Manila hemp rope was growing in the West. The nation's oldest and largest rope manufacturer, the Plymouth Cordage Company in Plymouth, Massachusetts, became a primary supplier of a strong three-strand Manila hemp rope that became a favorite among many cowboys by the late nineteenth century. It was not uncommon for big ranches to buy large rolls of the rope manufactured in Plymouth. When a cowboy's rope became limp and lifeless from hard use, it was discarded, another lariat was cut from the roll, and a honda was formed at one end. A honda may be tied in the rope itself, or it may be made of metal, horn, or rawhide. Most cowboys stretch a new lariat between two trees to remove the kinks and render it pliable. They then condition it with tallow or petrolatum to which an equal part of melted paraffin has been added. The conditioning also helps to make the rope pliable and waterproof.

Another tool of the old-time cowboy was the quirt. It was a flexible, woven-leather whip made with a short stock about a foot long. Two to four heavy loose thongs hung from its end. The word "quirt" was derived from the Spanish *cuarta de cordón*, meaning "whip of cord." Like many other tools of the American cowboy, the quirt was brought north from Mexico. The handles of most quirts were filled with lead or shot to provide weight. Cowboys sometimes used quirts as blackjacks, but most often they were employed to strike down rearing horses that threatened to fall backwards, or to make a horse increase its speed.

If there was one moment that stood out in the mind of the early Texas cowboy, it may have been the memory of putting the first hot iron to the flank of a calf. Some men hesitated the first time. The thought of placing a red-hot stamping iron against the flesh of a living creature probably bothered these young men. Others were unconcerned. Details of the branding process in Texas during the late 1860s are sketchy, perhaps because the practice was then commonplace. Branding occurred during cow-hunts when the cattle in one area were driven to a central point. One can imagine perhaps half-a-dozen cowboys herding a few hundred head of cattle, including many calves, to an open area near a spot marked by a narrow band of white smoke gently moving skyward from burning mesquite or live-oak logs. The smoke is caught in the midday breeze and is quickly dissipated, vanishing in the blue sky dotted perhaps by a few puffy white clouds. As the herd nears the branding fire, the cowboys and vaqueros begin to circle the cattle to slow and stop the moving mass, which they do perhaps 50 yards from the waiting fire. The fire is hot, and a closer look shows many coals glowing bright red. The men who built the fire have already placed the brand ends of the irons on the coals to absorb the heat.

Presently the boss or leader yells a command. Two cowboys who are good ropers mount their horses and ride toward the nearby herd. With their *reatas* in readiness, they cut out a calf and catch the animal with their loop. Slowly the roper drags the calf toward the branding fire. As the calf nears the spot, another cowboy on foot grabs the rope and pulls himself to the struggling animal. Depending upon the position of the calf, the cowboy might grab it around its center and toss it to the ground or grab its tail and pull to one side. This throws the calf off balance, and over it goes, onto its head and shoulder. The cowboy then holds the little bovine on the ground and yells for a "hot iron." Another man picks up one of the hot irons from the fire, moves to the downed calf, and in a moment places the red hot brand on the calf's flank. The calf bawls. The smell of burning hair and flesh drifts skyward in a puff of white smoke.

Seconds later the branding is over. Meantime, another cowboy takes out his pocket knife—probably sharpened for the occasion—and begins to mark the calf's ear. This cowboy has his foot on the calf's nose to help hold the struggling animal to the ground. Finishing the chore, the cowboy moves to the rear of the calf—assuming it is a male—places his foot on the lower hind leg, bends down, and cuts the testicles from the calf's body. The cowboy then dabs some creosote dip on the cut to keep flies away. Moments later the calf is released, scrambles to its feet, and runs off looking for its mother. By then another calf has been roped and dragged to the branding fire and the process is repeated. The use of one mounted roper and a man on foot is called the Texas method, although its use became widespread on the Great Plains, where many ranchers still use it today.

What is called the Mexican or California method involves two mounted riders using rawhide *reatas* perhaps 80 feet long. One mounted roper slowly moves into a herd and loops a calf by the neck. He takes his dallies (half-hitches with his rope around the saddlehorn) quickly before the rope is pulled taut by the calf. He then drags the calf near the branding fire, where a second roper loops the hind legs, pulls in the slack, dallies his rope, and backs away. The calf flops to the ground, and other cowboys and vaqueros on foot complete the branding and other chores. When they are finished, the mounted riders move toward the calf, shake open their loops, and let the calf get to its feet and scamper off. Should a full-grown animal be in need of branding, the mounted ropers usually rope both front and hind legs.[14]

No law dictated the exact spot on a cow's hide for the branding, yet through the years the left side of the animal, especially the hip area, became the traditional spot for branding. Nowhere in old documents or recollections does anyone say why the left side was chosen, but perhaps the guess of Colonel Jack Potter of Clayton, New Mexico, is as good as any. Colonel Potter, who made a trail drive from Texas to Montana in 1882 at the age of seventeen, once observed that cattle have a peculiar habit of milling more to the left than to the right; hence brands on their left sides would be more visible to cowboys inside the roundup herds.[15] Another writer explained that cattle were branded on their left hips "because persons read from left to right" and thus read "from the head toward the tail." He added: "A right-handed roper would ride slightly to the left of the animal and could see the brand better if it were on that side."[16] It is likely that both reasons and perhaps others were responsible for the branding of cattle on their left sides.

IT WAS PERHAPS ONLY NATURAL that the cow-hunts of the late 1860s became better organized as cattle ranching became a more profitable business in Texas. Cow-hunts became more than a search for wild cattle. Such cattle were scarce. Cow-hunts were held to select already-branded cattle to be sold, and to brand new calves. The opening of railhead markets in Kansas brought further change to Texas cattle ranching and the people involved. About 1870, three years after the market opened at Abilene, the label "cow-hunt" was replaced by the word "roundup." But unlike most ranching terms in Texas, which can be traced to a Spanish-Mexican origin, the word "roundup" first appeared in the mountain country where North Carolina, Kentucky, Tennessee, and the two Virginias meet. In that region Americans let their cattle run at large. Once a year they would "round up" their cattle, brand the calves, and remove any cattle to be sold or slaughtered for meat. The remainder were released to wander through the mountains.[17]

The climate of Texas, unlike that of the Appalachians to the east, was mild, and cattle multiplied rapidly. The generally treeless terrain made it easy for the long-legged longhorns to drift as far as 150 miles. Aside from small corrals for horses close to the ranch house, fences were uncommon. Each rancher had a line rider who rode the line or limits of his ranch to turn back drifting stock, but it was impossible to keep all cattle on their own range. It became necessary on the open Texas prairies to hold two roundups a year to return cattle to their rightful owners. One roundup was held in the spring to separate stock, brand new calves, and remove the cattle to be driven to market. Another roundup was held in the fall to brand up the calves missed in the spring or born since the last roundup, and to return wandering cattle to their rightful owners.

Many people have written about the open-range roundup, but one of the best descriptions was left by Hiram G. Craig, who was born at Sandtown, Texas, in 1855. Craig became a cowboy at an early age and spent more than half a century in cattle ranching. At the age of sixty-five, Craig wrote down his recollections of an early Texas roundup:

> Word was sent to stockmen for many miles around when the round up was to take place at a certain ranch. Then eight or ten neighboring stockmen would rig up a "chuck wagon" and place a cook in charge. One of the men would furnish the wagon one time, and the next time some one else—turn about. These stockmen going with the "chuck wagon" would meet at the appointed time with their saddle horses. Each man having his bedding lashed to a horse, when they met the chuck wagon, would put all their bedding in the wagon. This "chuck wagon" was drawn by two, and sometimes four horses. Next, they would turn all their saddle horses in a bunch, detail one of their number as "horse wrangler," and start off for the round up. At the round up there

would be a number of these chuck wagons or outfits—possibly six, eight or ten such wagons, according to the notices sent out, or the size of the round up. In the Slaughter round up [C. C. Slaughter in 1881] there were ten "chuck wagons," and each wagon would receive a number from the round up boss, making ten numbers—in this case representing some ninety men, or stock owners.

On the evening before the round up, Billy Stanefor, the round up boss, went to all the wagons and called for two or three men from each wagon to go out from ten to fifteen miles and make what is called a "dry camp." Each man was to stake his horse so that when daylight came every man was ready to follow out instructions to bring all the cattle towards the grounds. The men, so sent out, all going in different directions, formed a veritable spider's web, with the round up grounds in the center. As soon as the boys would "whoop-em up," the cattle were on the run, and would make for the grounds. There was little danger or chance for any cattle escaping, as when they would leave the path of one man they would drift into the path of the next man, and the nearer they came to the grounds, the more men would come in sight—finally forming one big herd, and then the fun would start. We found on bringing in these cattle in this manner, that five buffalo and some twenty or more antelope had drifted in with the cattle. Several of the boys, I for one, were sure we were going to rope an antelope. We got our loops ready, and started after them. Our horses were too short, and also a little too slow. We did not rope any antelope. Some of the other boys fired into the buffalo but did not bring in any meat either. The herd was now ready for cutting. The round up being on Slaughter's ranch, the foreman, Gus O. Keith, and his men, including old man Slaughter, cut the beef cattle, cows and calves first, and drove them back on the range to avoid "chousing" them. [The word "chousing" meant to handle cattle roughly and stir them up unnecessarily.] As soon as Slaughter was through with his part, the herd was ready for general work.

Now Billy Stanefor calls out "No. 1, cut, and No. 2 Hold;" meaning that the men from wagon No. 1, were to go into the herd and cut all of their cattle, while the men of wagon No. 2 would hold the herd. When No. 1 finished the round up boss would call "No. 2, cut and No. 3 Hold;" when No. 2 would go into the herd and cut, while the men from wagon No. 3 were holding the herd, and so in this manner until the cutting was finished. Then, to the branding of the cattle. This was also all done on the open prairie. We made our fires to heat the branding irons, would rope the calves or cattle as the case may be on horse back, drag them to the fire and put the brand on them. It was also the duty of the round up boss to see that no large calf was cut out of the round-up herd unless it was accompanied by its mother. The round-up boss had to act somewhat in the capacity of a judge. He had to see that all disputes were satisfactorily settled. If trouble arose regarding ownership of an animal the round-up boss would find out what brand each one of the disputing parties were claiming the animal under, and if they could come to no agreement, the animal was roped, the brand moistened with water to make it plainer, or he would shear the hair off where the brand was located, and in that way determine the ownership. All this was done immediately, and then the work would proceed. In those early days the ear-mark would not always be proof of ownership and an animal without brand was called a "sleeper." A sleeper was nominally everybody's property, and was so called because some one had overlooked branding this animal in a previous round-up—had slept on his rights. Naturally, all hands had a leaning towards these sleepers; and I have seen a sleeper cut out of the round-up by one man and during the day changed several times to other bunches. The man that was lucky to get away with a sleeper would put his brand on him. However, if such an animal had an ear-mark and any of the parties claimed the mark he would then hold the best title.

The round-up boss would let no one ride through the herd and "chouse," or unnecessarily disturb them; these fellows found guilty of such misconduct were called "loco'ed." Ofttimes it was known for the round-up boss to put him out of the herd and cut his cattle for him. The whole round-up was conducted in a strictly business way, and such a thing as "red tape" was unknown.

The work being finished, each wagon with its little herd would start for the next round-up. Possibly night would overtake them and pens being unknown, it would be up to the boys to herd them and 'sing' to them as it was usually called. Each man would rope his night horse and they would herd in shifts.

This night herding is nice and novel in fair weather, and on a nice moonlit night; but when it comes to one of those dark nights of thunder, lightning and the rain pouring down on you, your life is in the hands of God and your faithful night horse. There is to my mind no nobler animal in God's creation than a faithful horse. We would always pick out the clearest-footed, best-sighted horses for this work. All horses can see in the night, and better than a man, but there are some horses that can see better than others.[18]

During the years immediately after the Civil War, most cattlemen did not actually count the number of cattle carrying their brand in a roundup.

CHARLES GOODNIGHT,
the first cattleman to settle
in the Texas Panhandle,
and the first rancher to have
a wagon (later known as a
"chuck" wagon) built especially
to carry food and bedding
on roundups and trail drives.

A TEXAS RANGE BOSS.
Photograph by Erwin Smith.

"COOKIE" MAKING SOURDOUGH FOR SUPPER.
Dutch ovens were important in every chuck wagon outfit.
Photograph by Erwin Smith.

CHUCK WAGON LUNCH BREAK ON THE SHOE BAR RANCH
in Texas in the early 1900s.
Photograph by Erwin Smith.

Instead, they figured their herd size and their potential wealth by counting five head for every calf branded.[19] The man selected to count the calves as they were being branded was called a "tally hand" or "tally man." His selection was especially important when several ranchers would combine or pool their forces to hold a roundup on the open range. The "tally man" was chosen because of his honesty and clerical ability. He was usually appointed by the elected roundup captain. And since the tally man was in the position to falsify the count, his selection was of considerable importance to the participating cattlemen.

The chuck wagon, like the organized roundup, was another innovation that occurred in ranching between 1865 and 1870. On cow-hunts lasting only a few days, cowboys and vaqueros had carried their own rations. On longer hunts, pack mules or horses might carry the supplies of roasted coffee, bacon, and hard biscuits. But Texans involved in long drives to California or to Missouri and Kansas Territory during the 1850s carried their supplies in ox-drawn carts or in wagons. As ranching pushed onto the Texas plains following the Civil War, mess wagons, or "chuck wagons" as they became known, appeared. Most historians agree that Charles Goodnight, the first rancher to settle in the Texas panhandle, was the man responsible for the first customized chuck wagon. J. Evetts Haley, in his fine biography of Goodnight, wrote that in the spring of 1866 Goodnight "bought the gear of a government wagon, pulled it over to a wood-worker in Parker County, and had it entirely rebuilt with the toughest wood available, seasoned bois d'arc. Its axles were of iron instead of the usual wood, and in the place of a tar bucket he put in a can of tallow to use in greasing. . . . For the back end of the wagon he built the first chuck-box he had ever seen. . . ."[20]

A swinging leg attached to the hinged lid on the chuck box held the lid at tabletop height when lowered and provided the cook—he was often nicknamed "cookie," "beanmaster," "doughbelly," or "sourdough"—with a work table. Shelves and drawers in the box held containers of staples such as coffee, flour, salt, soda, baking powder, sugar, beans, lard, rice, dried fruit, and a jar or crock of sourdough from which the cook made flapjacks and bread. The box held tin plates, cups, spoons, knives and forks, and the smaller cast-iron cooking utensils. Most cooks kept a drawer for medicines or simple remedies such as horse liniment—for man and beast—quinine, calomel (a purgative), and perhaps some pills of one kind or another. Another drawer might contain a bottle of "snake bite medicine"—whiskey—although some cattlemen forbade their cooks and cowhands to carry a bottle.

Gradually, as ranchers added chuck wagons to their operations, the cowboy's bedrolls were carried in the wagon bed behind the spring seat. Under that seat most cooks kept a bag or two of grain for the mules or horses that pulled the chuck wagons. On one side of the wagon was fastened a water barrel. Most were fitted with a wooden spigot. On hot days it was not uncommon to see the water barrel wrapped with wet gunnysacks to keep the contents cool. Most chuck wagons had a tool box, and some carried a "jockey box" containing horseshoeing equipment, hobbles, and perhaps spare ropes. Underneath the wagon bed were additional compartments for the heavier cooking utensils such as large pots, skillets, and especially Dutch ovens. Some cooks, however, simply hung these larger utensils from the side of the wagon. By the late 1870s most chuck wagons, especially those used on the trail drives north from Texas, contained a large canvas sheet, or "fly," that could be stretched over the chuck-box end of the wagon to provide shade and shelter for the cook. By then, also, most chuck wagons carried a shovel or spade for digging fire trenches, an ax for chopping wood, and large pans or tubs for the deposit of dirty dishes after each meal.

With the addition of a chuck wagon and the services of a cook, one would imagine that most cowboys ate well during roundups and on trail drives. Most did, but it depended on the cook's culinary skills and the rancher's concern for his men. Most cattlemen realized that if the cowboys considered the "chuck" (food) inferior or scanty, they would be discontented and their work would suffer. A good cook and a well-supplied chuck wagon were signs of good management and often attracted more prospective cowboys than a cattleman needed or could hire.

Texan Ramon Adams, in his delightful book *Come an' Get It*, wrote: "There was no one particular type in wagon cooks, except that very few were young men. . . . One might be a Negro, a Mexican, or a white man from the dregs of the city, whose only knowledge of cow was that it was 'dished up in a stew.' Many were broken-down punchers whose riding days were over, but who could not endure life away from cattle and horses, and thus took up cooking to follow the chuck wagon. . . . Foreign-born cooks, such as Germans and Swedes, did not exercise the common 'horse sense' with which the cowmen were endowed."[21]

The "horse sense" referred to by Ramon Adams was only one of several traits that distinguished the character of early Texas cowmen from that of men in other walks of life. Cowmen were practical. They were strong and direct. Their work and their environment demanded these traits for survival. The treeless and generally flat Texas plains with vague and receding horizons and vast distances to overcome left an unmistakable feeling that man was rather insignificant. There was and is the feeling of an ever-present supreme being or force not always found in the woodlands and certainly not in the cities, where man was and still is considered by some to be a supreme being. The plains environment, which probably had

A ROUNDUP CAMP DURING THE 1880s
in Clark County, Kansas. The tent and "chuck box" removed from a wagon
suggest a semi-permanent arrangement. The two young boys
in front were helping with the roundup.

A TEXAS ROUNDUP CAMP,
with two OR Ranch chuck wagons together.

a greater impact on men who had their roots in the woodlands to the east than on those who were born there, required adjustment and perhaps for some a little soul-searching. The vastness of the plains from Texas to Canada could not help but affect most men in one way or another, just as the mountains or the woodlands had, but few put their feelings into words. Even today men ponder the question: Why does the vastness, silence, and solitude of the plains affect man as it does? It is a question that may never be answered.

Early Texas cowmen seem to have accepted their situation. They were well aware that Nature provided the grass and water and the natural increase in their herds. They had little control over these things. It is easy to understand why many a cowman appeared to be at peace with himself and the world and why he felt there was a dignity in his calling. Certainly, he was isolated from what then passed for civilization. Perhaps that is why nearly all cattlemen in Texas were honest. They respected the rights and property of others. If one cattleman found a neighbor's cow and unbranded calf in his herd, he would return them to their owner or at least brand the calf with the owner's brand. And when it came to hospitality, the cowman rarely turned away anyone, even a stranger. Luther A. Lawhon recalled that should illness overtake a visitor, "the watchful vigils and tender hands of the ranchman's wife and daughters ministered to his sufferings as though he was one of the family, until health was restored, and he was sent on his way rejoicing."[22]

There was much trust among cowmen, as is evident by the fact that they paid 50¢ a head to other ranchers who branded their stray calves. If one rancher told another he had branded ten of the other cowmen's calves, the second rancher paid the first. And it was a custom that when a rancher sold his cattle, should the herd contain any strays belonging to other ranchers, the selling rancher acted as an agent for the others and collected a dollar from the selling price of each stray for his efforts. As J. Frank Dobie wrote: "It was fifty times easier to bring home the money for a steer that had strayed fifty miles away than it was to bring the steer home."[23]

Since there were no banks, ranchers kept their money at home. They used gold and silver, not paper money. And when they bought stock, they carried the gold and silver to where the animals were to be received "and paid it out, dollar for dollar." Luther A. Lawhon, one of the few old-time Texas cowmen to leave more than just his record books for historians to review, wrote in his recollections that cattlemen "generally carried the money in leather belts buckled around their waists, but the silver being more bulky, was placed in duckin' sacks, and was loaded on a pack horse or mule. It was necessary in those days to know the weight as well as the value of money, and therefore it was a matter of current knowledge that one thousand dollars in silver weighed sixty-two and one-half pounds. Robbery was a crime unknown among those rugged and honest old pioneers," wrote Lawhon, who added that at home the gold and silver, "if of considerable amount, was put in saddle bags, morrals, etc., and secreted in remote corners of the house or up under the roof, or buried on or near the premises, and was brought forth from its hiding places as occasion demanded."

Lawhon recalled the story of one early cowman whose ranch was about on the line between Karnes and Goliad counties in Texas. Finding himself with a great deal of money on hand and no immediate need to spend it, he waited for a dark night. Carrying his money in a bag, he made his way to his cowpen, removed one of the fence posts, dropped the money in the post hole, replaced the post, and returned to his ranch house. After many weeks or months the rancher needed some of the money. He returned to the cowpen but could not remember under which post he had hidden the money. He had to dig up half his fence posts before he found it.[24]

For the cowmen who moved out onto the Texas plains following the Civil War, life was full of adjustment and change. The business of cattle raising was beginning to take on the proportions of a full-fledged industry. The Texas cowmen's search for good markets for their increasing herds of longhorns would end with success, but before then other changes and adjustments would begin to influence the revived cattle culture of the post–Civil War era.

CHAPTER 9

•◉•

Trail Herds to Railheads

*The cattle-trails were in a measure educative. They brought
the north and south of the Mississippi Valley into close
business relations, a condition which was to the advantage
of both. But the life that surrounded them could not endure.*

—CHARLES MOREAU HARGER[1]

IN this expensive world of the late twentieth century, it seems almost
unbelievable that sirloin steaks once sold for 25¢ to 35¢ a pound. Yet in
the spring of 1865 that was the then exorbitantly high price being paid
in New York City. The demand for beef was simply greater than the
supply. The Civil War had drained the North of its cattle. When Texans
read month-old copies of the New York *Tribune* and learned of the high
prices being paid for beef, they realized the value of their countless longhorns. It was then the cow-hunts resumed. However, most cattlemen did
not complete the gathering of cattle until late summer of 1865; and by
then it was too late to drive their herds north to Missouri or Kansas.
Winter weather was likely to set in before they could reach the buyers.
So ranchers looked for markets in Texas and elsewhere in the South and
Southwest.

Some cattlemen took their herds to New Mexico. Others drove their
cattle from central Texas to markets in Louisiana. Still other cowmen
sought to ship their cattle to New Orleans from Indianola and Galveston
when the Morgan Steamship Company resumed operations along the coast.
However, Morgan resumed its prewar practice of charging high rates to
discourage ranchers from shipping, and Morgan representatives renewed
the practice of buying good Texas cattle at cheap prices, shipping them to
New Orleans and Cuba, and selling them for a handsome profit.

New Orleans was normally a two-day journey by steamer from Texas, while it took about four days to reach Cuba. One account of Gulf shipping paints a vivid picture of what it was like:

Cattle shipped to New Orleans are not usually provided with feed during the trip, but an ample supply of bedding is furnished, which litters down their pens 5 or 6 inches deep. Owing to their wild nature, Texas cattle rarely eat heartily during a short voyage like that to New Orleans; hence no regular allowance of feed is carried for them. The voyage to Cuba, being of longer duration, requires the provision of from 15 to 20 pounds of hay per day for each bullock, which, after the second day, when subdued by hunger and accustomed somewhat to their unusual situation, they consume greedily. Cattle are carried by the Morgan steamers both between decks and on deck, elevators being in use to lower them into the vessel, where pens are fitted for confining them. During the passage the crew of the vessel, or special attendants, feed and water the animals. The average loss from natural causes is not over 1 per cent., but accidents incident to loading and unloading the wild and terrified beeves sometimes swell this average greatly, while the shrinkage on steers of 900 pounds live weight during the Cuban voyage has been found by frequent tests to range from 100 to 125 pounds under the most favorable treatment.[2]

There is no mention of problems relating to the length of the animal's horns. Some measured 5 feet from tip to tip or longer. They were sharp. It seems likely their horns were trimmed back to fit as many cattle as possible in the pens belowdeck and to eliminate the goring of other longhorns. Each steamer carried between two hundred and three hundred animals. An 1880 government report published in Washington suggests that between 1,200 and 1,500 head of cattle were shipped from Texas ports each month during the late 1860s and early 1870s. At that rate perhaps eighteen thousand were transported from Texas by steamer between the end of the Civil War and the early 1870s.[3] But another source, the *Texas Almanac*, notes that in 1868 alone, 38,568 head of cattle were shipped to New Orleans and Havana, suggesting that the number of cattle shipped by steamers was considerably more.[4] Even if the higher figure is correct, the total number of cattle shipped through the Gulf was small when compared to the total number of cattle in Texas. The census of 1870 reported 3,990,158 cattle in Texas, although Walter Prescott Webb in his classic *The Great Plains* observed that "the actual figures probably ran a million more, making approximately 5,000,000 head."

In some ways the period beginning in 1865 was similar to the earlier years in California when the hides and tallow of cattle were more valuable than their meat. The demand for hides, bones, tallow, and even horns grew rapidly after the war ended. Sold separately, the parts of a bovine were more valuable in Texas than the live kicking and breathing animal. Most of the hide and tallow industry in Texas had been operated by Mexicans before the Civil War, but beginning in 1865 it was rebuilt by enterprising Texans who saw a profit to be made. Many Texas cowmen built hide and tallow plants to process not only their own cattle but also those of smaller ranchers who could not afford plants of their own. Nearly all of these "factories," as they became known, were located on the coast. The towns of Fulton and Rockford became major hide and tallow centers. It was a common sight during the late 1860s to see stacks of hides and horns, barrels of tallow and pickled beef, being loaded aboard steamers bound for New Orleans and then the East Coast or elsewhere.

Texan John Young, whose reminiscences are recorded by J. Frank Dobie in *A Vaquero of the Brush Country*, recalled that "thieves" in the region between Corpus Christi Bay and Galveston Island would shoot cattle found in the thickets, skin them on the spot, and carry the hides to the coast on pack horses or in ox carts. Young said two factors were responsible for the Texas hide trade. One was that it had long been a custom in Texas for any man to take the hide off a dead animal, no matter what brand the animal bore; such skinning on the part of the finder was, in fact, almost expected. The other factor was the open range: During the winter months it was not uncommon for cattle to drift south with the storms. The colder and wetter the weather, the more they drifted. The more cattle that drifted into south Texas, the greater the number killed for their hides. Young recalled that people came to speak of the "skinning season" as they would speak of the "branding season," both of which occurred in the spring. Ranchers within a reasonable distance of the coast took advantage of the hide market, particularly during dry years when many cattle died for lack of water and grass. Young remembered that during the winters of 1872 and 1873, one rancher named Jim Miller along the Nueces River skinned four thousand dead cattle lost in a "die-up," as ranchers came to call cattle deaths caused by drought and winter storms.[5]

The slaughter of cattle for their hides and tallow reached its peak in Texas during the early 1870s. The severe winters of 1872 and 1873 were in part responsible. Many cattle died of starvation. Ranchers drove their surviving cattle to the hide and tallow factories. By 1875, however, the business began to decline. During the five years that followed, many hide and tallow factories were abandoned, and by 1880 the business had all but died in Texas.

Not all Texas cowmen sought the hide and tallow markets for their cattle after the war. Many cattlemen gave much thought to the northern markets. As noted, they were well aware of the high prices cattle were bringing in the North. Joseph McCoy, writing in 1874, recalled that at the end of the Civil War the bullock, "a select, matured animal," was worth $5 or $6 in Texas. But in the North the animal was worth "ten times that amount. This vast difference constituted a wide and tempting field to the cattle speculator—a field that he was not slow to attempt to occupy. During the winter and spring of 1865 and 1866 large herds of beeves were gathered in Texas preparatory to driving North the following summer."[6]

By middle February of 1866 the warm breezes from the south foretold of the hot summer days ahead. When March arrived, the herds were started toward Kansas and Missouri and the markets developed before the Civil War. But the problem of Texas fever still existed. In Missouri, Texans had not yet tested the law enacted early in 1861 authorizing each county court to appoint a board of cattle inspectors who could turn back any stock afflicted with Texas fever or suspected of carrying it. And in Kansas the legislature, apparently fearing Texas fever, approved a new act on February 11, 1865, prohibiting the bringing of stock into Kansas from Texas or any territory south of Kansas. On February 16, 1866, however, a short time before the Texans began driving their herds north, the legislature in Topeka repealed the law, leaving only part of an earlier anti-Texas-fever law in effect.

Some Texas drovers may have been aware of the legal ramifications of driving longhorns into Kansas or Missouri; others probably were not. But almost all were aware of the westward push of railroads. Construction had progressed rapidly following the Civil War. By early 1866 the probability that the iron horse would link them to eastern markets appeared promising to the Texans, even though the railroad had not yet pushed onto the plains. But the drovers couldn't wait, and in the spring of 1866 they began driving their cattle north in search of what markets they could find. One of these drovers was James M. Daugherty. He was sixteen years old in 1866 when he took his first herd of more than a thousand head up the trail. Born in Texas County, Missouri, February 27, 1850, Daugherty grew up in the state of Texas. There, a few weeks following his sixteenth birthday, he obtained his first herd of cattle. With five cowboys, Daugherty set out to drive the longhorns to Missouri. They crossed the Red River near Rock Bluffs and then started northeast across what is now Oklahoma. Several days later they were met by Cherokee Indians who demanded a tax for crossing their land. Daugherty refused to pay and turned his herd east. Crossing into Arkansas near Fort Smith, he and his men drove the cattle north. They may have stopped at Elkhorn Tavern in northwest Arkansas near the summit of Elkhorn Hill. The hill is also known as Pea Ridge, the scene of a bloody Civil War battle. The tavern de-

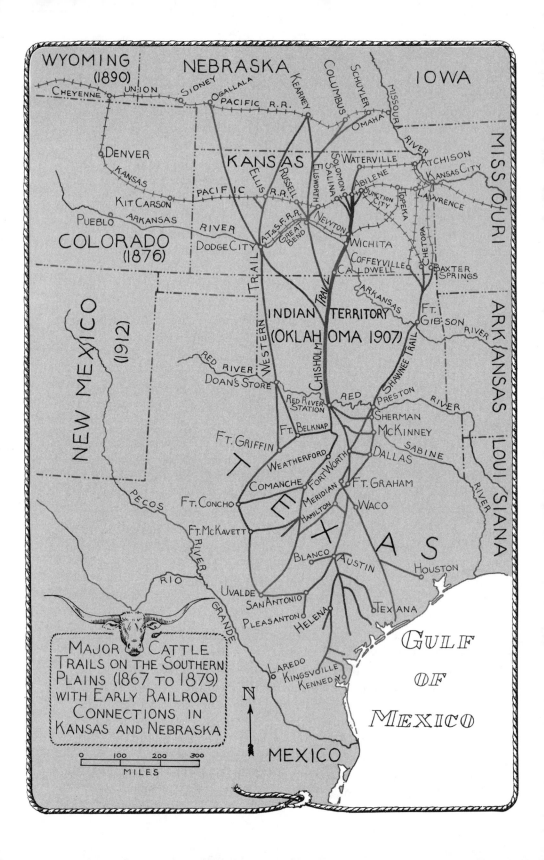

MAJOR CATTLE TRAILS ON THE SOUTHERN PLAINS (1867 TO 1879) WITH EARLY RAILROAD CONNECTIONS IN KANSAS AND NEBRASKA

veloped as a rest stop for cattlemen driving their herds north. From there Daugherty and his men turned their herd northwest, returning to Indian Territory and what was then known as the Neutral Strip, a piece of land about 20 miles wide running across the northern edge of Indian Territory and the southern border of Kansas. South of Baxter Springs, Kansas, Daugherty told his cowboys to watch the herd. He headed north into Kansas to "investigate conditions."

What happened next is told in Jim Daugherty's own words:

On arriving at Baxter Springs I found that there had been several herds ahead of me that had been disturbed by what we called . . . Kansas Jayhawkers, and in one instance the Jayhawkers had killed the owner, taken the herd, and ran the rest of the cowboys off. This herd belonged to Kaynaird and was gathered in the southern part of the Chocktaw National in Indian Territory. . . .

I rode as far as Ft. Scott, Kansas, and there I met a man by the name of Ben Keys, whom I told I had a herd on the Neutral Strip I would like to sell. He agreed to buy them if I would make deliverance at Ft. Scott, Kansas. I returned to the Neutral Strip and we started driving the herd north along the Kansas-Missouri line, sometimes in the state of Kansas and sometimes in Missouri. From the information that I had received regarding the big risk we were taking by trying to drive through, we were always on the lookout for trouble. Some twenty miles south of Ft. Scott, Kansas, and about four o'clock one afternoon a bunch of fifteen or twenty Jayhawkers came upon us. One of my cowboys, John Dobbins by name was leading the herd and I was riding close to the leader. Upon approach of the Jayhawkers John attempted to draw his gun and the Jayhawkers shot him dead in the saddle. This caused the cattle to stampede and at the same time they covered me with their guns and I was forced to surrender. The rest of the cowboys stayed with the herd, losing part of them [cattle] in the stampede. The Jayhawkers took me to Cow Creek which was near by, and there tried me for driving cattle into their country, which they claimed were infested with ticks which would kill their cattle. I was found guilty without any evidence, they not even having one of my cattle for evidence. Then they began to argue among themselves what to do with me. Some wanted to hang me while others wanted to whip me to death. I being a young man in my teens and my sympathetic talk about being ignorant to ticky cattle of the south deseasing any of the cattle in their country caused one of the big Jayhawkers to take my part. The balance were strong for hanging me on the spot but through his arguments they finally let me go. After I was freed and had joined the herd, two of my cowboys and I slipped back and buried John Dobbins where he fell. After we had buried him we cut down a small tree and hewed out a head and foot board and marked his grave. Then we slipped back to the herd. This being soon after the close of the Civil War, the Jayhawkers were said to be soldiers mustered out of the Yankee army. They were nothing more than a bunch of cattle rustlers and were not interested about fever ticks coming into their country but used this just as a pretense to kill the men with the herds and steal the cattle or stampede the herds. After rejoining the herd I found that during the stampede I had lost about one hundred and fifty head of cattle, which was a total loss to me.

I drove the balance of the herd back to the Neutral Strip, and after resting a day or two, went back to Ft. Scott, and reported to Mr. Keys what had happened. Mr. Keys sent a man back to the herd with me to guide us to Ft. Scott. On my return to the herd with the guide we started the drive to Ft. Scott the second time. The guide knew the country well, which was very thinly settled. We would drive the herd at night and would lay up at some secluded spot during the day. After driving in this manner for five days and five nights we reached Ft. Scott about day-break of the fifth night and penned the cattle in a high board corral adjoining a livery stable, which completely hid them from the public view. . . . As soon as the cattle were penned Mr. Keys paid me for them. Then we ate our breakfast and slept all day. When darkness fell we saddled our horses and started back over the trail to Texas.[7]

James Daugherty made many other trips up the trail to Kansas during the years that followed, but none was filled with as much excitement. He became a well-known Texas cowman. In 1923, at the time he put his experiences on paper, Daugherty owned a large ranch in Culberson and Hudspeth counties of Texas and was known as "Uncle Jim" Daugherty.

The cattle driven north by Daugherty in 1866 were part of more than 260,000 head of Texas longhorns trailed north toward Kansas and Missouri that spring and summer. But less than half of them reached their intended destinations. Bands of armed men calling themselves jayhawkers, red-legs, bushwhackers, guerrillas, or some other name waylaid many. Before and during the Civil War these men had fought each other along the Kansas-Missouri border, and although the war was over, many of them were still bitter. Most were outside the law. One unidentified reporter for a St. Louis newspaper wrote that these men

combined against the cattlemen, whom they called invaders. They would have followed their lawless course without pretext if necessary,

JAMES M. DAUGHERTY BEING WHIPPED BY THE "JAYHAWKERS,"
or border ruffians, south of Baxter Springs, Kansas,
in 1866. The artist makes Daugherty appear older
than the sixteen he was, and Daugherty's recollections make no
mention of being whipped. Drawing by Henry Worrall for
Joseph McCoy's classic *Historic Sketches of the Cattle
Trade of the West and Southwest.*

TEXAS CATTLE ON A DRIVE NORTH.
Drawing by J. Andre Castaigne.

but one was afforded them in this case by the opposition to Texas
cattle, which began to manifest itself among the small growers of other
States. The bushwhackers and red-legs at once became vigilant health
officers to establish and maintain a cattle quarantine against the
pleuro-pneumonia, or customs officers to keep the cheaply fed pauper
steers of Texas from competing with those of the North.

The newspaperman went on to describe the tactics of these armed outlaws:
They would go in force, surround a drover's camp, and provoke a quarrel;
they would kill the drover and then drive off his herd. "It was idle to talk
about the protection of the law. Such a protection was, at that time and
under the circumstances of the case not to be relied upon. The Texas men
were compelled to take their lives in their own hands and defend themselves as they could," wrote the reporter. He noted that many Texans
were killed, but not before they killed or wounded many of the outlaws.
Yet the murders and robberies continued. If the outlaws could not frighten
the drover into abandoning his herd or if they failed to find a pretext for
killing the drover, they would leave. Then after darkness some of the
mob would creep close to the herd, make loud noises, and stampede the
herd. The cattle would rush pell-mell in every direction. Many head might
be killed or injured. By morning the drover might recover some of his
stock, but the greatest part of the herd would fall into the hands of the
outlaws. Then, as the drover and his men were exhausted and their horses
worn out, some member of the outlaw gang would come into camp and
offer to "hunt up the lost cattle for a snug price, $5 a head perhaps. If a
bargain was struck, and one was in almost every such case, the outlaw
would mount, ride away and return in less than a day with nearly all the
lost cattle, expatiating upon the difficulties he had experienced in finding
them."
    The newspaperman added:

The mobs knew and understood the drover's condition and helpless-
ness so far as legal methods of prosecution were concerned. If the
drover had ready money and could obtain an interview with the
leader of the mob it was not difficult to secure safe transit for his herd,
but such a privilege was always expensive and few drovers were dis-
posed to buy a recognition of their legal rights. Many of them had not
the money necessary for such a purchase, having invested all their
available cash in cattle before leaving Texas.[8]

Not all of the Texas longhorns driven north during the spring and summer of 1866 were bound for markets in eastern Kansas or Missouri. In

Iowa, two men had heard of the plentiful supply and low prices of cattle in Texas. Harvey Ray and George C. Duffield had been in business at Burlington, Iowa, on the Mississippi. But the panic of 1857 and the Civil War had hurt their businesses. When they learned that Texas steers could be purchased at $8 to $10 a head, they formed a partnership early in 1866 to go to Texas and buy cattle. They reached the Colorado River country west of Austin, Texas, by March of that year, having traveled down the Mississippi to New Orleans and then through the Gulf to Texas. They purchased one thousand head of Texas cattle at $12 a head. While Harvey Ray started north for Iowa by Mississippi steamer, Duffield hired some men and began to gather and brand the longhorns and make preparations for the drive north. By early April he had obtained provisions and cooking utensils, bought two wagons and oxen to pull them, and with seven cowboys started north from the area west of Austin.

An account of the drive may be found in George Duffield's diary. His record is not in beautiful prose, nor does it contain much detail, yet it creates in the reader's mind a realistic picture of the hardships on the trail from Texas northward to Iowa in 1866. The following are excerpts:

April 5th: Started for Sansaba with two wagons & 5 yoke oxen and seven hands. Travelled 12 miles & camped. Rained hard during the night.

April 6th: Everything wet. Morning cold & stormy & rainy. Travelled 12 miles. Hard wind & rain. Cold. Put up at Mr. A. Branch.

April 7th: Wet cold morning. Travel 8 miles & camped for the night.

May 1st: Travelled 10 miles to Corryell co. Big stampede. Lost 200 head of cattle.

May 2nd: Spent the day hunting & found but 25 head. It has been raining for three days. These are dark days for me.

May 3rd: Day spent in hunting cattle. Found 23. Hard rain and wind. Lots of trouble.

May 13th: Big thunder storm last night. Stampede. Lost 100 beeves. Hunted all day. Found 50. All tired. Everything discouraging.

May 14th: Concluded to cross Brazos. Swam our cattle & horses & built raft and rafted our provisions & blankets &c. over. Swam river with rope & then hauled wagon over. Lost most of our kitchen furniture such as camp kittles, coffee pots, cups, plates, canteens, &c., &c.

May 16th: Hunt beeves is the word—all hands discouraged & are determined to go. 200 beeves out & nothing to eat.

May 20th: Rain poured down for two hours. Ground in a flood. Creeks up—Hands leaving. Gloomey times as ever I saw. Drove 8 miles with 5 hands (359 head). Passed the night 6 miles S.W. from Fort Worth in Parker Co.

May 28: Cold morning. Wind blowing & all hands shivering. Are within 12 miles of Red River. Moved up 6 miles.

May 29th: Moved up to river & after many difficulties got all my drove over but 100.

May 30th: Worked in river all day & 50 beeves on this side of river yet—am still in Texas.

May 31st: Swimming cattle is the order. We worked all day in the river & at dusk got the last beefe over—& am now out of Texas—This day will long be remembered by me—There was one of our party drowned today (Mr. Carr) & several narrow escapes & I among the no.

By this time, Duffield had merged his herd with those of other drovers heading north. According to his account, the combined herds totaled more than five thousand cattle. The drovers combined their herds for protection against Indians.

June [1]st: Stampede last night among 6 droves & a general mix up and loss of beeves. Hunt cattle again. Men all tired & want to leave. Am in the Indian country. Am annoyed by them. Believe they scare the cattle to get pay to collect them—Spent the day in separating beeves & hunting —Two men & bunch beeves lost—Many men in trouble. Horses *all* give out & men refused to do anything.

June 20nd: Hard rain & wind storm. Beeves ran & had to be on horse back all night. Awful night. Wet all night. Clear bright morning. Men still lost. Quit the beeves & go to hunting men is the word—4 P.M. Found our men with Indian guide & 195 beeves 14 miles from camp. Almost starved not having had a bite to eat for 60 hours. Got to camp about 12 P.M. *Tired.*

June 14th: Last night there was a terrible storm. Rain poured in torrents *all* night & up to 12 M today. Our beeves left us in the night but for *once* on the whole trip we found them *all* together near camp at day break. *All* the other droves as far as I can hear are scattered to the four winds. Our other herd was all gone. We are now 25 miles from Ark [Arkansas] River & it is very high. We are water bound by two creeks & but beef & flour to eat. Am not homesick but heart sick.

June 19th: Good day. 15 Indians come to herd & tried to take some beeves. Would not let them. Had a big muss. One drew his knife & I my revolver. Made them leave but fear they have gone for others. They are the Seminoles.

June 20th: All quiet last night. Have called on the military from Ft. Gibson & have the promise of help. River falling slow & weather cloudy. All quiet last night.

June 22: Off for the river early to try to cross. Worked all day hard. Got 200 head across. Indians killed one steer & we took it from them.

June 23rd: Worked all day hard in the river trying to make the beeves swim & did not get one over. Had to go back to prairie sick & discouraged. Have *not* got the *Blues* but am in *Hel of a fix*. Indians held high festival over stolen beef all night. Lost 2 beeves mired & maybe more.

June 25th: We hired 20 Indians to help us cross. We worked from morning until 2 o'clock & finally got them over with a loss of 5 & camped near the *old* mission between the Ark River & the Verdigris.

July 10th: The boys are hunting cattle & at noon they claim they have them all—We moved up 12 miles & camped 2 miles from Baxter Springs. We are now on the Quaw Paws land & have moved off the Shawnees land (were ordered off). Hard rain today.

July 11th: Are camped near Spring River. Wharton got back from Ft. Scott with the information that *all* our letters have been sent to the dead letter office. Very warm. Herded all day.

July 20th: Last night we had another of those miserable nights. Rain poured down. Beeves ran. Wind blew. Was on my horse the whole night. Are out 100. At 10 o'clock Mr. Davis commenced work today. Found all our beeves & are now ready to go to settling up with the other party to get ready to take my share & go around Kansas.

July 21st: Spent the day settling.

July 22: Tried to hire a new outfit of hands & continued the settlement. Sold our company property at auction.

July 24: All arrangements completed. We started & recrossed the Neosho & camped for the night.

July 25th: We left the beefe road & started due west across the wide prairie in the Indian Nation to try to go around Kansas & strike Iowa. I have 499 beeves. Travelled about 11 miles.

July 26th: Was notified that I could not go farther on that direction & we turn southwest. The day was warm & the flies was worse than I ever saw them. Our animals were almost ungovernable. Travelled about 12 miles over a grand & picturesque prairie. Camped far out in the open prairie. We are in the Shawnee Nation.

August 5th: Sunday. Travelled about 6 miles & are laying over washing & resting ourselves & stock. Saw a fine drove of antelope today. Splendid spring. We have been traveling a little south of west & are now near the Arkansas River but we don't know how far nor where we are now going to turn north & trust to luck.

August 6th: Travelled 10 miles N.W. over a high mountainous prairie. The grass was dried by the sun that it would have burned. Killed a fine lot of chickens [prairie chickens] & had a pot pie. (good water) Beefe died last night.

August 7th: Cool & windy. Travelled 10 M to little Walnut Creek. Two white men visited us—are within 10 miles of a settlement.

August 8th: Come to Big Walnut. Cattle stampeded & ran by 2 farms & the people were very angry but we made it all right. Was visited by many men. Was threatened with the law but think we are all right now. (Plenty of vegetables)

A day or two later, Duffield crossed from what are today called the Osage Hills, in northern Oklahoma, into the Flint Hills in southernmost Kansas. He probably did not realize he was entering Kansas as the herd moved northward—there was and is a sameness about the land. There were no roads or trails of any consequence for Duffield and his men to follow, but the terrain was not rugged. The summer had been wet, and the creeks winding through the generally treeless Flint Hills had plenty of water.

For about ten days Duffield and his men pushed northward through the Flint Hills. On August 20, 1866, they sighted the tree-shaded town of Council Grove in the Neosho river valley. After obtaining supplies from merchants in that long-established stopping point on the Santa Fe Trail, Duffield's party trailed their herd in a more northeasterly direction. A few days later they crossed the Kansas River at St. Marys Mission. By August 26 they were within 28 miles of the Nebraska border. Since entering Kansas the drive had gone well. Their route up through the Flint Hills had been west of most settlements. They had not been bothered by outlaws or Indians or settlers or bad weather. But two days after entering Nebraska, Duffield, on August 31, 1866, wrote in his diary:

Last night was one of those old fashioned rainy stormey thundering nights just such as we used to have in Texas. Was up with the cattle all night. They travelled where they pleased but we stuck too them until morning. Today we crossed Big Muddy & camped on North Fork of Nimehah [Nemaha]. It commenced raining at dark & rained all night. Was up with cattle until midnight & then went to bed. Found them all in the morning.

September 1st: Moved the herd up to within 5 miles of Nebraska City —& went to town. Took a good look over into Iowa. Got my dinner & no tidings from Ray & returned to camp. Prospects of more rain. This is a fine country without timber.

Duffield had more problems getting the cattle across the Missouri River at Nebraska City. Many were lost and several days were spent in hunting them. It was not until early November that the remaining cattle reached Burlington, Iowa, eight months after leaving Texas. Duffield's last few entries describe his journey's end:

November 1st: Shipped cattle from Burlington [to] Chicago.

November 2nd: Spent day at Union Stock Yard & in evening drove cattle to slaughter house to have them packed.

November 3rd: Viewed city & attended to packing.

November 4th: Busy all day at work & looking at the wonders of a fast city.

November 5th: Returned to Ottumwa [Iowa].

November 6th: Got home sick & tired & glad to get to rest.

November 7th: Spent most of the day in bed & feel badly.[9]

George Duffield was one of the lucky drovers in 1866. Although he reached Iowa with less than half of the thousand longhorns purchased in Texas, the drive was considered a success. It was an exception to the fate of Texas trail herds driven north that year. Obstruction, embarrassment, losses of stock—sometimes whole herds—money paid as tribute, and outlawry made the year disastrous for most Texas drovers. Some tried to avoid trouble by following a route similar to the one taken by Duffield. Once they crossed the Kansas River at St. Mary's Mission, they turned northeast and crossed the Missouri River at St. Joseph, where they sold their cattle. But other drovers turned their herds east near Baxter Springs and trailed their cattle along or near the northern border of Arkansas until they were able to flank the hostile regions in Missouri and turn north to the railroad and a shipping point east of Sedalia, Missouri. This route along the southern border of Missouri was mountainous and rocky. There was a lot of timber. The cattle became footsore and weary. Many lost weight and, by the time they were driven to market, were a sorry lot. Often long-horns driven over this route were sold at a loss.

But the largest number of drovers appear to have remained in and around Baxter Springs, Kansas, during the summer of 1866. They were hoping for conditions to change. Conditions did not change. The first frost of the fall came early and killed the grass, which after a few drying days "was set afire and the whole country burned over. This was a great calamity to the cattlemen," wrote one newspaperman, who added:

> All along the border a host of sharpers and thieves—men with good address and plausible pretensions—were anxious to obtain cattle, but owing to the unsettled condition of affairs were afraid to bring the cash with them, but had what purported to be New York Exchange [checks], with which they bought cattle of such as they could induce to accept their draft. Of course their drafts were worthless, but before the drover could find it out the rascal would have turned the stock into some secret confederate's hand and left for parts unknown. . . . Never, perhaps, in the history of Texas was the business of cattle ranching at so low an estate as about the close of the year 1866. . . ."[10]

Stories of the troubled cattle drives to Kansas and Missouri spread rapidly across Texas by late in the year. The news was discouraging, especially since the herds continued to multiply. An increasing number of cattlemen —even more Texas farmers turned to ranching when their crops failed in the summer of 1866—realized the need for better access to the northern markets. As 1867 began, many cattlemen, especially those who had experienced failures on northern drives the summer before, decided not to make new drives north. Some sold their cattle for hides and tallow along the coast; a few cattlemen decided to try again. The higher prices paid for longhorns in the North was sufficient inducement. To the north, however, new legal barriers were being readied to stop the drovers with their long-horns and Texas fever. Missouri strengthened its law against the fever, and the states of Colorado, Nebraska, Illinois, and even Kentucky passed laws barring or restricting the trailing of cattle from Texas or Indian Territory. Texas fever losses in those states had been heavy the year before.

The losses had also been heavy in Kansas, where Governor Samuel J. Crawford signed into law on February 26, 1867, an act to protect livestock in Kansas from what was labeled "Spanish fever." The law prohibited the driving of Texas or Indian cattle into Kansas between March and December *except* west of the sixth meridian and south of a line running from northeast of modern McPherson, Kansas, west to the Colorado line. While protecting Kansas stock raisers, most of whom were then in the region east of the sixth meridian, the law opened a large piece of unsettled land in south central and southwest Kansas to Texas cattle traffic twelve months a year. The law said any person, association, or company could select a route through this region to some point on the Union Pacific Railroad, Eastern Division. There such cattle could be shipped out of the state. The law also required a $10,000 bond by the drover to ensure payment of any damages caused by Texas cattle.[11]

Some lawmakers in the state legislature at Topeka changed the wording in the final bill to favor the settlement of Ellsworth, Kansas, about 60 miles west southwest of Abilene. They apparently represented interests wanting to capture the Texas cattle trade. But by late February, when the legislation was signed into law, the tracks of the Union Pacific Railroad, Eastern Division, the first line to build across Kansas, had not yet reached Ellsworth. Bad weather and floods had caused delays; the tracks were only approaching the tiny settlement of Abilene, the county seat of Dickinson County. The sixth principal meridian formed the western boundary of the county; but the fact that Abilene was east and north of the "deadline," or the restricted portion of Kansas where Texas cattle were pro-hibited from March to December, didn't bother a young man from Illinois who decided to establish the Texas cattle trade there. His name was Joseph McCoy, and with his two brothers he had been involved in stock raising in Illinois.

McCoy, a rather slender man sporting a goatee—perhaps to hide his weak chin—looked older than his twenty-nine years. He would later describe the Abilene of early 1867 as "a very small, dead place, consisting of about one dozen log huts, low, small, rude affairs, four-fifths of which were covered with dirt for roofing; indeed, but one shingle roof could be seen in the whole city. The business of the burg was conducted in two small rooms, mere log huts, and of course the inevitable saloon also in a log hut, was to be found."[12]

Writing in 1874, McCoy observed that he picked Abilene "because the country was entirely unsettled, well watered, excellent grass, and nearly the entire area of country was adapted to holding cattle. And it was the farthest point east at which a good depot for cattle business could have been made."[13] The key, of course, was the railroad. It provided transportation to the east. Since it was already early March and some Texans were beginning to move their herds north, McCoy moved rapidly. He bought 250 acres adjoining the town for a cattle yard and made plans to construct a barn, small office building, livestock scales, a bank, and an elegant three-story hotel with livery stable. By July workmen were changing the face of not-so-sleepy Abilene. Lumber was arriving by railroad, and the buildings were being constructed along with a shipping yard next to the railroad tracks. The yard could accommodate three thousand cattle. A large pair of Fairbank's scales were installed nearby.

McCoy in the meantime hired a stockman friend from Illinois, W. W. Sugg, to ride south and "hunt up every straggling drove" of longhorns and tell the drovers about Abilene. McCoy later recalled: "Mounting his pony at Junction City [about 20 miles east of Abilene], a lonely ride of almost two hundred miles was taken in a southwesterly direction, crossing the Arkansas River at the site of the present city of Wichita, thence far down into the Indian country; then turning east until trails of herds were found, which were followed until the drover was overtaken. . . ." McCoy's man informed each drover he met that Abilene was "a good, safe place to drive to, where he could sell or ship his cattle unmolested" to eastern markets.[14]

During the summer, McCoy had traveled east to Topeka and visited with Governor Crawford. McCoy outlined his plan and told the governor what he was doing. Crawford appears to have acknowledged that Abilene was east and north of the "deadline" established earlier in the year by the legislature, but McCoy explained that the Texas cattle trail to Abilene would lie west of the settlements and that the longhorns would not damage any farms or infect Kansas cattle. Governor Crawford liked the plan. Many years later Crawford remembered: "I wrote a plain, vigorous letter commending Mr. McCoy's scheme and the location he had selected. I approved of the undertaking in a semi-official manner."[15] Pleased, McCoy returned to Abilene with what seemed to be assurances that the "deadline" law signed by Crawford would not be enforced.

The first shipment of Texas longhorns left Abilene on September 5, 1867, in twenty railroad stock cars. The cattle probably attracted attention as the train traveled east to Junction City, crossed the Kansas

TEXAS LONGHORNS HEADING FOR ABILENE.
Drawing by Henry Worrall.

"ABILENE IN ITS GLORY."
Abilene residents welcome a train in this 1868 view
of the Kansas cattle town.
Drawing by Henry Worrall, from McCoy's *Historic Sketches*.

CATTLE LOADING PENS,
probably near Ellsworth or Great Bend, Kansas,
in the 1870s.
Drawing by Henry Worrall.

"LOADING TEXAS CATTLE AT ABILENE."
Drawing by Henry Worrall
in *Leslie's Magazine*, August 1871.

River, and entered Fort Riley. The tracks paralleled the Kansas River through the military reservation and continued along the river valley until it reached Manhattan, Kansas. There the engine probably took on fuel and water while the townspeople viewed the longhorn cattle. From Manhattan the train with its historic cargo continued east along the north side of the Kansas River through rolling countryside dotted with jack oaks and cottonwood trees. Another stop for fuel and water may have been made at St. Marys, and then on to Topeka. From there it was another 50 miles to Kansas City.

About 35,000 cattle arrived at Abilene before winter in 1867. Perhaps twenty thousand head were shipped east by rail. The remainder were wintered on the prairies in the area west and north of Abilene because the sudden influx of Texas cattle had, in part, caused a depression in beef prices at Abilene, Kansas City, and other markets to the east. Yet the sales that did occur were sufficient to please many Texas drovers. When they returned south the news spread rapidly that Texas cattle could be sold at Abilene. For some Texans the news sounded too good to be true. They "could hardly believe that there was not some swindle in it somewhere," wrote Joseph McCoy, who added:

They are all mindful of individual, selfish undertakings, but are indifferent to public ones. For instance, advertise the Texas cattle as being for sale upon the prairie, adjacent to their villages, and how seldom a Texan will pay a dollar willingly to advertise up a given point as being a good market for his cattle. They do not hesitate to squander tens, fifties and hundreds for the gratification of their appetites or passions, yet to pay a few dollars to help some legitimate enterprise for the benefit of the whole, is generally esteemed a great hardship, and often they refuse entirely. This is not because they are penurious, for they are not, but because they lack that public spirit so necessary for the accomplishment of any great public good.[16]

McCoy was determined to convince the Texans that Abilene offered a good and safe market with no strings attached. In preparation for the season of 1868, he had printed a circular letter describing the new market and how drovers could reach Abilene. Copies were sent to leading Texas cattle raisers, newspapers, and other publications read by Texas cowmen. To attract buyers, McCoy's brothers in Illinois placed advertisements in newspapers, including the *Missouri Republican* at St. Louis. An advertisement in that paper on March 27, 1868, read: "Cattle—the best grazing cattle in the United States can be had in any number, on and after the 15th of May, 1868, at Abilene, Kansas, weighing from 1,000 to 1,200 pounds, live weight. They reach Abilene from the Southwest and will take

on from 50 to 150 pounds more than native cattle, and cost less than half as
much. Until the 1st of May we may be conferred with personally at
Springfield, Illinois, and thereafter at Abilene, Kansas. W. K. McCoy and
Brothers."

About April 1, 1868, Joseph McCoy hired some men to go south from
Abilene to survey and shorten the cattle trail running from the Arkansas
River, near where modern Wichita, Kansas, stands today, to Abilene 90
miles to the north. McCoy put Timothy F. Hersey, a surveyor and farmer
near Abilene, in charge of the party. After straightening the trail, Hersey
and his men marked it with blocks of sod cut from the earth and piles of
dirt. Near the mouth of the Little Arkansas River, they met the season's
first northbound herd of Texas longhorns and guided the drovers and
their cattle to Abilene. There workmen had completed the Drovers Cottage,
and McCoy had hired James W. Gore, a steward from the St. Nicholas
Hotel in St. Louis, to operate it.

The trail from Texas to Abilene is often referred to as the Chisholm
Trail, but Jesse Chisholm, for whom it was named, was responsible for
blazing only a portion of the actual trail. Chisholm, a pioneer trader on the
southern plains, had helped to lay out a wagon road from Fort Smith,
Arkansas, to Fort Towson in Indian Territory as early as 1832. In 1836, he
guided a party of men up the Arkansas River to the mouth of the Little
Arkansas at the site of modern Wichita, Kansas, in search of a legendary
gold mine. The mine did not exist, but Chisholm liked the area and later
made his headquarters there. After the Civil War, he blazed a wagon trail
south to near the Red River, on the northern border of Texas. It was
this wagon trail from what would later be Wichita, Kansas, south to near
the northern border of Texas, that was truly Chisholm's trail. It did not
become common usage to call by that name the longer trail from southern
Texas to Abilene, Kansas, until about 1870, two years after Chisholm
died in Indian Territory.[17]

About 75,000 cattle were trailed from Texas to Abilene in 1868, and
by the following year increasing numbers of drovers gathered their herds
and took them north. The Texans finally realized that Abilene was not a
swindle, and by the fall of 1869 more than 350,000 head had reached the
Abilene area. Not all of them were shipped east by railroad. Some were
trailed farther north and west to stock new ranches in Colorado,
Wyoming, Nebraska, and elsewhere. Other drovers were attracted to
alternate shipping points on what was then called the Kansas Pacific. (The
Union Pacific Railroad, Eastern Division, had changed its name to Kansas
Pacific on May 31, 1868.) Still other drovers trailed their cattle north of
Abilene to Waterville, Kansas, the western terminus of the Central Branch
Railroad. In 1870 the same number of longhorns was trailed from Texas

TWO DIFFERENT KINDS OF MEN
whose names are connected with trail-driving days.
Left: Jesse Chisholm. *Right:* Joseph McCoy,
several years after he helped establish Abilene
as a railhead cattle town.

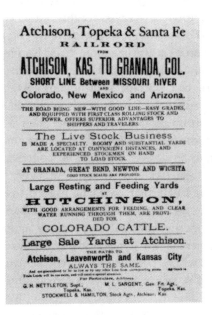

TWO 1874 ADVERTISEMENTS.
The Kansas Pacific Railway ad was on the back cover
of a map packet published by the railroad, showing Texas drovers
the trails to Ellis, Russell, Ellsworth, Brookville, Salina, and Solomon.
In 1874 most of the cattle reaching their line
were shipped from Ellsworth.

to Abilene as in 1869, but 1871 found twice as many cattle, more than 700,000 head, driven north to Kansas. That was Abilene's biggest year as a cattle trading center. It was also the last.

The townspeople of Abilene realized that the ever-increasing number of farmers around their town provided year-round business and a stable economy, but that the Texas trade was seasonal and the unsavory characters attracted by the cattle trade often carried off much of the money spent or lost by the cattlemen, drovers, cowboys, and vaqueros. Early in February 1872, Theodore C. Henry, who had been Abilene's first mayor from 1869 to 1871, wrote copy for a circular to which four-fifths of the citizens of Abilene signed their names. The circular asked that Texas cattle be driven elsewhere because the residents of Abilene and surrounding Dickinson County would no longer submit "to the evils of the trade." Copies of the circular were distributed south from Abilene into Indian Territory and Texas. Texas cattle did not return to Abilene, but the circular was not the cause. A few weeks after it had been printed, the Kansas legislature in March 1872 pushed the quarantine line farther west, making it illegal to drive longhorns to Abilene. By then towns like Wichita and Ellsworth sought to capture the cattle trade. And Baxter Springs, the first cattle town in Kansas, recaptured its share with the coming of the railroad.

There is no question that by 1871 Texas cowmen viewed the Kansas markets as a dream come true. Kansas provided the long-sought-after accessible markets for Texas longhorns, and by then the trailing of cattle north had become routine business. Although many Texas ranchers accompanied their own herds north, an increasing number of cowmen were entrusting their cattle to other men who became known as trail drivers or professional "drovers." The drover would make a contract with a buyer in Kansas to deliver stock. The contract usually specified how many cattle, their age, sex, condition, and type. For instance, some buyers wanted young cattle that could be grazed to maturity, or young cows for breeding, or steers and dry cows for Indian agencies, packing houses, and other slaughtering places. The drover would then contact ranchers and take their cattle on consignment. The drover's aim was to "put on the trail what will answer profitably the demands he believes will arise."

The organization of a drover's trail herd was described as follows:

Early in the year, the drover goes to that region of the state [Texas] where he expects to find suitable stock and visits the various ranches. Having bought the cattle and arranged with the sellers to deliver his purchases on a fixed day at a certain point, he goes to some horse ranch and buys such a lot of horses as shall carry his drove through, say 40 horses for each average drove of 2,300 to 2,500 cattle. He also engages about a dozen cowboys for each such drove, at the rate of $25 to $30 per month, and a "boss" drover as captain and field manager of the stock, equipment, and men, at $90 per month. Having made these engagements, and purchased a camp-wagon [chuck wagon], team (four mules or four oxen), cooking utensils, and other necessaries of an outfit, he is ready to receive his purchases, only enough coming in at a time to make one drove, which is road-branded,[18] and is then started out on the trail. So the deliveries go on until all his droves are under way. When first put on the road the cattle are closely guarded and driven briskly for several days, until the danger of their breaking away

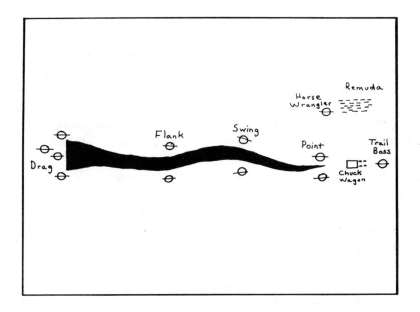

AFTER THE MIDDAY BREAK, A BIRD'S-EYE VIEW OF A TRAIL DRIVE
to Kansas would look something like this. The trail boss rode ahead
of the herd unless he chose to ride back to talk to his men.
The chuck wagon came next, usually pulled by four mules or oxen.
Off to one side were the horse wrangler and the *remuda*, or
remounts. Behind the chuck wagon came the point riders, whose
job it was to lead the cattle; they often used a lead steer. Next,
where the cattle began to swell, came the swing riders, and farther
back, the flank riders. Where the remaining cattle bunched together
toward the end were three or more drag riders, usually young men
new to cowboying. They ate dust in dry weather and kept the
cattle moving. By mid-afternoon it was not unusual for the cook
driving the chuck wagon to push ahead to the night's campsite.
The horse wrangler usually moved the *remuda* along behind
the wagon.
Drawing by the author.

for home is passed. For the first few days at sunset the drove is "rounded up" compactly, and half of the men, relieved by the other half at midnight, ride round and round the bed-ground. This labor decreases as the cattle become tractable, and two men at each watch are then sufficient to guard them through the night. The ordinary order of march is the foreman ahead, searching for camping place with grass and water; the drove drifting onward in the shape of a wedge, the strong few stretching out to a sharp point in front, then the line growing thicker and wider, until in the butt end is crowded the mass. On each side of the lead rides a man on "point", that is, to direct the column. Back where the line begins to swell ride two more at "swing", further back ride two at "flank", and the remainder are on "drag", (i.e., about the rear,) to push on the march. These positions give *cowboy rank*. The "greenhorns" or "tender-feet" serve at "drag", while the cowboys experienced in driving hold the places at "point", the post of honor. These distinctions are observed at mess and bed. One man drives the horse herd apart from the line of cattle, or, with large bands, two men are employed. The distance traveled each day is 12 or 15 miles, according to grass and water. At daybreak the cattle are moved off the "bed-ground" to graze, and while the two men who were last on guard remain with them all other hands breakfast. The first to finish breakfast relieve the guards on duty and allow them to come in for their morning meal. Then, the horses being caught and saddled, and the cook having cleaned up, the drive is started and continued until about eleven, when the cattle are allowed to graze again, and lunch or dinner is eaten. Immediately after that the men who are to stand first guard at night, and who also act as horse-herders, go on ahead with the mess-wagon and the horses to the next camp, where they get supper, so that when the herd comes up they are ready to "graze", and hold it until the first relief of the night. The bed-ground is, when possible, on elevation, with space sufficient for all the stock to sleep. The men off guard roll themselves in their blankets without removing their clothing and lie down on the ground near the camp-fire to sleep.

This description by an unidentified writer in the late 1870s was labeled as "the ordinary details of a drive from Texas." The writer noted, however, that departures from these practices were made "according to circumstances and the different degrees of skill of drovers." He added:

A herd traveling with calves cannot make 12 miles per day. A "mixed" herd—that is, one made up of various ages and of both sexes—is the easiest to control; a beef-herd of four-year-olds is the most difficult.

The slightest disturbance at night may stampede them. The first symptom of alarm is snorting. Then, if the guards are numerous and alert, so that the cattle cannot easily break away, they will begin "milling", i.e., crowding together with their heads toward a common center, their horns clashing, and the whole body in confused rotary motion, which increases, and, unless controlled, ends in a concentrated outbreak and stampede. The most effectual way of quieting the cattle is by the cowboys circling around and around the terrified herd, singing loudly and steadily, while too, the guards strive to disorder the "milling" by breaking up the common movement, separating a bunch here and there from the mass and turning them off, so that the sympathy of panic shall be dispersed and their attention distracted, as it is in part, no doubt, by the singing. The somber surroundings of a wild country at night, with the accompanying strange sounds—the tramp, the clashing of horns, the bellowings of alarm, and the shouted song of the cowboys—are very weird.[19]

The image of a cowboy singing to cattle on the late-nineteenth-century Texas trail drives became the model for the singing cowboys in many Hollywood westerns years later. However, beautiful women were substituted for cattle, and the Hollywood cowboy often played the guitar. The real singing cowboy never accompanied himself on a guitar atop his horse. Few cowboys, if they even owned and played a Spanish guitar, took their instruments on trail drives. And their songs were not romantic love songs. The real songs were simple. They reflected the cowboys' work, their likes and dislikes, their experiences and their dreams. Andy Adams, who wrote the classic *Log of a Cowboy*, described real cowboy music as "a hybrid between the weirdness of an Indian cry and the croon of a darky mammy. It expresses the open, the prairie, the immutable desert." John A. Lomax, who spent many years early in this century collecting cowboy songs and other frontier ballads from the lips of men who had sung them, remembered first hearing cowboys sing to cattle when he was a young boy. Lomax wrote:

Herds of cattle, bound, were often bedded down only a few hundred yards from my father's Texas home. On rainy nights I listened to the cowboys softly singing and calling to the cattle to keep them quiet. Long afterwards I wrote of these calls as yodels. "You are entirely wrong," a cattleman complained to me. "No cowboy that I ever heard yodeled." "But," I protested, "I heard them many times. I can repeat the tones." And I did. "Oh," the old trail driver agreed. "Is that what you call a yodel? We called it humming."[20]

"IN CAMP, THE TEXAS CATTLE TRADE."
This supposedly depicts Texas cowboys
camped on the trail en route to Kansas.
Drawing by Frenzeny & Tavernier, *Harper's Weekly*, May 1874.

THE ONLY MUSIC FOR THESE "OR" RANCH COWBOYS
after a day on the range was a fiddle player.
One cowboy, right, danced.
Photograph by Erwin Smith.

Lomax wrote that cowboy songs

> sprang up naturally, some of them tender and familiar lays of child-
> hood, other original compositions, all genuine, however crude and
> unpolished. Whatever the most gifted man could produce must bear
> the criticism of the entire camp, and agree with the ideas of a group
> of men. In this sense, therefore, any song that came from such a group
> would be the joint product of a number of them, telling perhaps the
> story of some stampede they had all fought to turn, some crime in
> which they had all shared equally, some comrade's tragic death which
> they had all witnessed.[21]

One cowboy song collected and preserved by Lomax that probably was
the creation of several cowboys is "The Kansas Line." Its words read:

Come all you jolly cowmen, don't you want to go
Way up on the Kansas line?
Where you whoop up the cattle from morning till night
All out in the midnight rain.

> *The cowboy's life is a dreadful life,*
> *He's driven through heat and cold;*
> *I'm almost froze with the water on my clothes,*
> *A-ridin' through heat and cold.*

I've been where the lightnin', the lightnin' tangled in my eyes,
The cattle I could scarcely hold;
Think I heard my boss man say:
"I want all brave-hearted men who ain't afraid to die
To whoop up the cattle from morning till night,
Way up on the Kansas Line."

Speaking of your farms and your shanty charms,
Speaking of your silver and gold,—
Take a cowman's advice, go and marry you a true and lovely little wife,
Never to roam, always stay at home;
That's a cowman's, a cowman's advice,
Way up on the Kansas line.

Think I heard the noisy cook say,
"Wake up, boys, it's near the break of day,"—
Way up on the Kansas line,
And slowly we will rise with the sleepy feeling eyes,
Way up on the Kansas line.

The cowboy's life is a dreary, dreary life,
All out in the midnight rain;
I'm almost froze with the water on my clothes,
Way up on the Kansas line.[22]

Whether the cowboy composers of this song created an original melody for the words is unknown. Only the words have survived. They may have sung the words to an established melody in the way that another cowboy song, "The Cowboy's Dream," was sung to the air "My Bonnie Lies Over the Ocean." The first four stanzas read:

> *Last night as I lay on the prairie,*
> *And looked at the stars in the sky,*
> *I wondered if ever a cowboy*
> *Would drift to that sweet by and by.*
>
> *Roll on, roll on;*
> *Roll on, little dogies, roll on, roll on,*
> *Roll on, roll on;*
> *Roll on, little dogies, roll on.*
>
> *The road to that bright, happy region*
> *Is a dim, narrow trail, so they say;*
> *But the broad one that leads to perdition*
> *Is posted and blazed all the way.*
>
> *They say there will be a great round-up,*
> *And cowboys, like dogies, will stand,*
> *To be marked by the Riders of Judgment*
> *Who are posted and know every brand.*[23]

Such songs are a good gauge of the mood and thoughts of the nineteenth-century Texas cowboys who made the long trail drives to Abilene and and other railheads in Kansas and elsewhere. But the songs do not reflect the relief that must have been felt by their bosses, the ranchers, who finally had good and safe markets for their longhorns. Nor do the songs reflect the fact that the trail drives created jobs for the cowboys. The only interest most cowboys had in such economic matters related to whether or not they got paid off in cash at the end of the trail. Some songs, however, suggest that their composers may have sensed the change that was occurring in the cattle business. By the early 1870s the growth of the cattle trade had firmly established the cowboy as a hired man on horseback, although no self-respecting cowhand would ever permit anyone to call him that or to call a ranch a cattle farm. Yet that is what they were and still are today. What made the cowboy different from hired help in other vocations was the horse. The cowboy felt independent on the trail or on the open range. It has been said that he was in a position to look down on the rest of the world. Many a cowboy had contempt for any labor that could not be performed from what Charles A. Siringo described as "the hurricane deck of a Spanish pony."

The Northern cattle markets had created a demand for this unique man on horseback, but those markets had been created by the coming of the railroads. As the iron horse conquered the problem of covering vast distances on the plains, it also brought civilization and all of the things associated with the East that most cowboys regarded with scorn. The railroads saved the Texas rancher from ruin and brought change. Rancher and cowboy alike would be affected by the change, which marked the beginning of the end of the cattle culture and the cowmen's way of life.

CHAPTER 10

Where the Trails Ended

*There were a score of shipping points in Kansas for Texas
cattle. Of these, only four or five have gained a national
reputation as wild and woolly cow towns.*

—FLOYD B. STREETER[1]

THE best-known Kansas cattle towns were, and still are, Abilene,
Dodge City, and Wichita. Their names suggest to most people the roughness associated with the American West, and they bring to mind the one-
story frame buildings with false fronts and gaudy signs, hitching posts,
board sidewalks, cowboys and horses, gamblers and cattlemen, blacksmiths and railroaders, merchants, land agents, prostitutes, vaqueros, and
a hot sun beating down on a dusty street lined with saloons and few other
business houses. The nineteenth-century Kansas cattle towns owe much of
their fame to eastern newspapermen and writers. These people found life
in the cattle towns quite different from that of the cities and towns in the
East. The cowboy, of course, was largely responsible for this. Easterners
were intrigued by cowboys, who wore six-guns, boots, large hats, and
spurs and earned their living on horseback. To the easterner, the cowboy's
life had much appeal. It was free and colorful and exciting, or so the
writers told their readers. And these writers, to feed the growing appetites
of their readers, did not hesitate to make cowboys and cattle towns appear
to be more than they really were.

Between 1866 and 1885, just about every town on a railroad in Kansas
shipped some Texas cattle. They all could have been called cattle towns at
one time or another, but they were not. Only about fifteen Kansas towns
had that label in varying degrees. Abilene, Dodge City, and Wichita, of
course, were prominent as cattle towns, but Newton, Caldwell, Brookville, Salina, Solomon, Ellsworth, Great Bend, Junction City, Waterville,
Chetopa, Coffeyville, and Baxter Springs also held that distinction. Some of

these frontier settlements were cattle towns for less than a year. Their survival depended on shipments of cattle, and such shipments depended on politics, the railroads, the line of settlement in Kansas, and the state legislature in Topeka. The westward push of settlement across the state caused the legislature to move the quarantine area or "deadline," as it was called, west of where farmers were settling on cheap land bought from the railroads or on government homesteads. Following the Civil War the quarantine area was changed six times—in 1867, 1872, 1876, 1877, 1879, and 1883—to protect the Kansas settlers' livestock from Texas fever. And each time the line was moved, the Texas cattle trade was forced to move farther west. Cattle towns died and others were born. If two or more cattle towns developed in an area, the strongest survived. During 1871, the year of greatest competition for the Texas cattle trade, ten Kansas towns were vying for the trade. That year more longhorns were driven north than at any other time in history, more than 700,000. (The table on page 200 shows the years of heaviest Texas cattle trade in fifteen Kansas towns.)

At times some of the cattle towns resembled the boom mining towns of California or the Rocky Mountains. They grew rapidly where a railroad and a Texas cattle trail came together, usually by someone's design. The presence of cowboys and vaqueros and cattlemen and cattle buyers, their pockets full of dollars, attracted honest merchants and professional

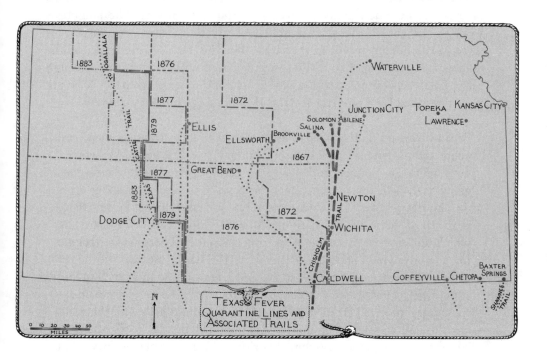

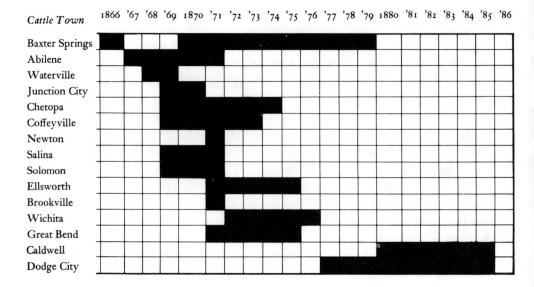

PEAK YEARS OF THE TEXAS CATTLE TRADE IN 15 KANSAS TOWNS

people, but they also lured characters with get-rich-quick schemes: gamblers, prostitutes, con artists, and others seeking something for nothing or for very little effort. The lanky long-legged bovines driven up the trails from Texas became symbols of wealth in the cattle towns. The longhorns were to the cattle towns what gold and silver or other precious metals were to the mining towns farther west. But the Texas cattle trade, unlike mining, was seasonal. The cattle towns boomed only from spring through early fall. Preparations for the anticipated 1874 cattle boom in Wichita were described by a reporter for the *Wichita Eagle* on May 28:

> Broad-brimmed and spurred Texans, farmers, keen business men, real estate agents, land seekers, greasers, hungry lawyers, gamblers, women with white sun bonnets and shoes of a certain pattern, express wagons going pell mell, prairie schooners, farm wagons, and all rushing after the almighty dollar. The cattle season has not yet fully set in, but there is a rush of gamblers and harlots who are 'lying in wait' for the game which will soon begin to come up from the south. There was a struggle for a while which should run the city, the hard cases or the better people. The latter got the mastery, and have only kept it by holding a 'tight grip.' Pistols are as thick as blackberries. The taxes are paid by the money received from whiskey sellers, gambling hells, and the *demi monde*, and thousands of dollars are obtained besides to further the interests of the town. Wichita flourishes off the cattle business, and

these evils have to be put up with; at least that is the way a large majority of the people see it. But notwithstanding this a man is safe in Wichita as anywhere else if he keeps out of bad company. The purlieus of crime there are no worse than in many eastern cities of boasted refinement and good order. But woe to the 'greeny' who falls into the hands of the dwellers therein, especially if he carries money. From these must come most of the stories of outrage at Wichita. They are entitled to little sympathy because they can find plenty of good company if they desire it.

The first herds of longhorns usually arrived by early June when the Kansas climate provided good grass and water for the cattle and bearable weather for the Texans who spent weeks galling their legs on their saddles as they drove their herds north. The annual boom in the cattle towns usually evaporated about the time the first frost coated the land in a glistening web of white, soon after the last drovers with their cowboys and vaqueros left to return to Texas and the cattle buyers returned east. The gamblers, pimps, and prostitutes also left to spend their winters in Kansas City, St. Louis, or other large cities.

Kansas cattle towns were something like resorts for the Texas drovers and cowboys. Their visits there might be equated to the modern vacation, and the cowboys and drovers usually let off steam when they reached them. It was only natural. After two or three months on the trail in dust or mud or both, with little sleep and a routine that must have been very tiring, they delivered their herds of longhorns and were paid for their labor, usually in cash. Suddenly they felt free, uninhibited, and rich by cowboy standards, with anywhere from $50 to $90 in accumulated wages. Before going into town, some cowboys might bathe in a nearby river, creek, or pond, or they might head straight for town, where for two bits they could use a tub with hot water in the back of a barber shop. A shave and a haircut followed, and then the purchase of some new clothes to replace the frayed, dirty, and smelly ones worn on the trail. In Abilene, a cowboy might buy new clothes at Jacob Karatofsky's Great Western Store. Karatofsky advertised dry goods, clothing, boots, shoes, hats, caps, and gents' furnishing goods. When Abilene died as a cattle town in late 1871, Karatofsky, a native of Germany, moved his store to Ellsworth and later to Wichita. Other merchants also followed the cattle trade from one town to another.

Another prominent merchant in the Kansas cattle towns was Mayer Goldsoll, a Russian immigrant, who first made his home in St. Louis. He established a general store called the Old Reliable House at Ellsworth about 1868. When the cattle trade went to Abilene instead of Ellsworth, he opened a branch in Abilene called the Texas store. He also opened branch

stores in other towns, including Denison, Texas. Goldsoll tried to follow
the cattle trade. In the late 1860s, he claimed his Ellsworth store had the
largest stock of groceries, liquors, cigars, and tobacco in western Kansas.
It probably did. Like most merchants, Goldsoll sold more groceries than
all other goods. It was not unusual for cattlemen arriving by train ahead of
their trail herds to buy groceries in bulk and send them by wagon south to
replenish the bins of their northbound chuck wagons. Still other groceries
were sold to drovers camped near the cattle towns waiting for word that
their herds had been sold. Once the railroad reached Wichita, that town
did a flourishing business with the Texans. Wichita became the first town
north of Texas on the Chisholm Trail. During the spring and summer of
1873, one grocery firm in Wichita had sales averaging $12,000 per month.[2]

Clothing was next on the list of the most popular goods sold. Most
cowboys bought new clothes when they reached the end of the trail. Many
also purchased new boots. The Texans seem to have preferred custom-
made boots. In Abilene, Tom C. McInerney employed as many as twenty
men in his boot shop during the summer months to meet the demand. His
boots were high-heeled, red-topped, with tooled Lone Stars and crescent
moons. They sold for $12 to $20 a pair. At Ellsworth, the Texans could
buy custom-made boots from John Mueller, who later moved his business
to Dodge City; if they could afford only store-bought boots they probably
got them in Reuben and Sheek's "gent's" furnishings. Two doors east was
J. Ringolsky & Co., called drovers' headquarters, which kept a general
line of clothing and supplies. Still another prominent establishment at Ellsworth was Jerome Beebe's general store with branches at nearby Wilson
and Brookville, Kansas. Beebe sold everything from high-grade groceries
and "wines and liquors for medicinal purposes" to Kirby's reapers and
Moline plows for farmers.

Kansas newspaper editors noted with more than passing interest the
dress of the Texas drovers and cowboys and vaqueros. One editor at
Baxter Springs wrote in June 1872: "A stranger to witness the number of
mustangs parading our streets, bearing upon their sides the map of Mexico,
and the jingling of hundreds of ornamental bells, vulgarly termed 'spurs,'
used to decorate the boot heels of the Mexicans and cow-drivers, and to
excite the risibilities of bucking ponies, and he can well imagine himself
in the old city of Mexico! These, however, are the concomitants of Texas
cattle. So, it's all right! bring on your cows!"[3]

That same year, on July 25, the *Ellsworth Reporter* noted:

Here you see in the streets men from every state, and I might say from
almost every nation—the tall, long-haired Texas herder, with his heavy
jingling spurs and pairs of sixshooters; the dirty, greasy Mexicans,

TEXAS LONGHORNS.

BY THE EARLY 1870S, ADVERTISING
had become an important tool for persons associated
with the cattle culture.

with unintelligible jargon; the gambler from all parts of the country, looking for unsuspecting prey; the honest emigrant in search of a homestead in the great free West; the keen stock buyers; the wealthy Texas drovers; dead beats; 'cappers'; pick-pockets; horse thieves; a cavalry of Texas ponies; and scores of demimonde.

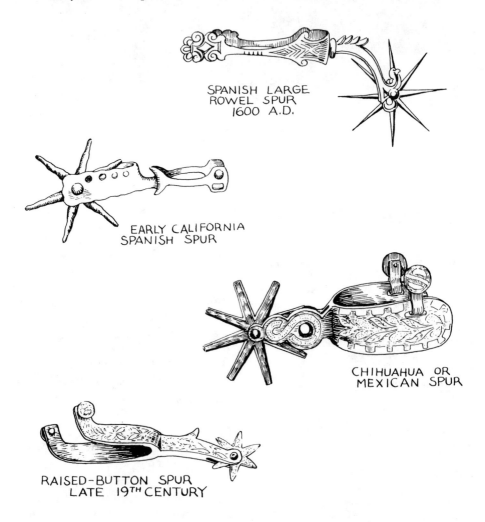

SPANISH LARGE
ROWEL SPUR
1600 A.D.

EARLY CALIFORNIA
SPANISH SPUR

CHIHUAHUA OR
MEXICAN SPUR

RAISED-BUTTON SPUR
LATE 19TH CENTURY

A decade later, in 1882, long after Baxter Springs and Ellsworth and other Kansas cattle towns had died, Kansas editors were still writing about the dress of the Texans. But the editors were a bit more blasé. One newspaper report from Wichita noted:

The typical cowboy wears a white hat, with a gilt cord and tassel, high-top boots, leather pants, a woolen shirt, a coat, and no vest. On his heels he wears a pair of jingling Mexican spurs, as large around as a tea-cup. When he feels well (and he always does when full of what he calls "Kansas sheep-dip"), the average cowboy is a bad man to handle. Armed to the teeth, well mounted, and full of their favorite beverage, the cowboys will dash through the principal streets of a town yelling like Comanches. This they call "cleaning out a town."[4]

The late Robert M. Wright described in his fine book entitled *Dodge City, the Cowboy Capital*, published in 1913, the last time some cowboys attempted to run the town of Dodge City and intimidate local lawmen. It was late one summer afternoon in the early 1880s, during what Wright called "quiet time in Dodge." City marshal Jack Bridges, a former deputy U.S. marshal, was taking his rest.

So the cowboys tanked up pretty well, jumped their horses, and rode recklessly up and down Front Street, shooting their guns and firing through doors and windows, and then making a dash for camp. But before they got to the bridge [south of Dodge City's business district, crossing the Arkansas River], Jack Bridges . . . was out with a big buffalo gun, and he dropped one of them, his horse went on, and so did the others. It was a long shot and probably a chance one, as Jack was several hundred yards distant.

There was big excitement in Dodge City following the shooting. Cattlemen protested, but Wright, who ran a large general store where he sold groceries and other goods to the Texans, took the position that it was justifiable homicide. Most Dodge City residents agreed. Wright, then the mayor of Dodge, finally convinced most of the Texans that his position was the right one. Never again, according to Wright, did the cowboys attempt to run the town.

The pattern of most cowboys arriving in Dodge City and the earlier cattle towns was similar. After cleaning up and buying new clothes, they were likely to seek some liquid refreshment in the saloons, usually those with Texas names. Many played poker or monte or other sporting games and visited the ladies of the night. But it is foolish to believe that all cowboys and vaqueros and drovers who came up the trails from Texas did all of these things when they arrived in a cattle town. Writers of articles, books, and Hollywood westerns have through the years depicted a certain sameness about the Texans and what they did—a stereotypical Texas cowboy who supposedly did not respect the law, who was immoral and dishonest. Such was not the case. Certainly there were some cowboys who matched this description, but most seem to have been honest men. Certainly many were more honest than some of the prominent cattle-town residents who sought to relieve the cowboys of their hard-earned cash.

In Baxter Springs, Coffeyville, and Chetopa, all located in southeast Kansas along the border with Indian Territory, cowboys and vaqueros were occasionally arrested for shooting off their pistols and fighting when drunk, and sometimes for gambling. Local ordinances against gambling were enforced in these border towns when local officers felt it was in their interest, either politically or economically. But contemporary newspaper accounts suggest that local residents, not the cowboys, were responsible for the more serious crimes. For instance, J. R. Boyd, mayor of Baxter Springs, shot and killed the city marshal, C. M. Taylor, during the summer of 1872. At the time Marshal Taylor was trying to serve the mayor with a warrant for assaulting a local businessman named Smith.[5] A few months later another local resident named Thomas Wells was shot and killed by the brother of a young woman with whom Wells supposedly had become "too intimate."[6] That same year at Coffeyville, about 55 miles west of Baxter Springs, the town's marshal was wounded by a woman of ill repute in a hotel room. A man passing the room and hearing the shot opened the door, rushed inside, and fired his pistol at the woman. She was killed instantly. The shooting occurred in a hotel on Coffeyville's main street, then known as "Red Hot Street."[7] Later, A. B. Clark, Coffeyville's mayor, ordered gambling stopped and all gamblers arrested. He was shocked when the majority of his town council were among those brought in. There were no cowboys involved.[8]

The character of Baxter Springs—the first cattle town in Kansas—Coffeyville, and Chetopa was different from that of Abilene, Ellsworth, Newton, Dodge City, and the other cattle towns farther west on the Kansas plains. The terrain east of Baxter Springs, for example, was wooded and similar to the Ozarks; the land around Coffeyville and Chetopa had a relatively eastern nature as well. It seems likely that the open plains acted upon the mood of the cowboys. An English writer, Charles Wentworth Dilke, described the effect of the land as "a kind of intoxication" in his book *Greater Britain*, published in 1868. After weeks on the trails from Texas, crossing wide expanses of land, the drives undoubtedly produced in many men what Kansan John J. Ingalls once called "a pathetic solemnity, born of distance, silence and solitude." There is little wonder then that the Texans let off steam in the cattle towns. They were like oases of civilization on the uncivilized plains. And since these prairie and plains cattle towns were newly settled frontier communities, law and order was slower to arrive than in the southeast Kansas cattle towns. Most of the merchants and professional people looked down on the gamblers and prostitutes and other disreputable characters, but these honest citizens were too busy

LOOKING EAST ALONG THE MAIN STREET OF DODGE CITY, KANSAS,
in 1872, about five years before the town
became a major cattle town. A railroad train is on the right.

LOOKING NORTH ALONG THE MAIN STREET OF NEWTON, KANSAS,
in 1871, the year Newton was considered by many cowboys and cattlemen
to be "the wickedest town in Kansas."

DODGE HOUSE IN DODGE CITY, KANSAS, 1874.
The hostelry contained 38 rooms, a restaurant, bar,
and billiard hall. For eight dollars a cowboy
could get a week's room and board.

THE INTERIOR OF THE LONGBRANCH SALOON,
one of Dodge City's most notorious establishments,
built in 1873.

trying to get established in their new towns to expel the undesirables. Eventually, however, those residents wanting a "decent" town were able to bring law and order in varying degrees, sometimes before the cattle trade and the undesirables had moved on.

Most of the cowboys involved in the trail drives from Texas were young and single. For some of them their arrival in the cattle towns far from home was something like modern young men going off to college or on a vacation with friends. They felt free, perhaps for the first time in their lives. They thought they were grown-ups and it was only natural that they wanted to do what they believed grown-ups did. These young cowboys undoubtedly heard and talked a great deal around their campfires during their long trail drives north about what went on in the cattle towns, and many on their first trip out seem to have sampled what the cattle towns had to offer. But after a week or two, or after they had gently been relieved of all or most of their hard-earned cash, they often became wiser, and on their second trip up the trail, if they made a second drive, they restricted their cattle-town activities to haircuts, baths, some new clothes, and perhaps other purchases to take back home to Texas. There were, of course, exceptions: those men who worked and saved their money during most of the year so they could spend it all during one or two weeks in town. But the cowboys who sought to repeat their wild cattle-town experiences time and again seem to have been the exception to the rule.

Some of the cattlemen, the owners of the herds, undoubtedly enjoyed the entertainments offered in the cattle towns, but most put business before pleasure. They sought to sell their longhorns for the best possible price. The recollections of many cattlemen are contained in *The Trail Drivers of Texas*. Their successes are noted. M. A. Withers, as an example, bought six hundred longhorn steers valued at $8 to $10 a head or $5,400 and drove them to Abilene in 1868. His expense was $4 a head. He sold the herd for $16,800, giving him a profit of $9,000. Another Texan named James F. Ellison drove about 750 longhorns to Abilene in 1869. He also made a profit of $9,000. As more and more Texas cattlemen let drovers take their herds north to market and the drovers trailed larger herds, profits increased, since the trailing expense per head was lower. One Texan made a profit of $15,000 from a herd sold at Wichita in 1872.

Someone once described the Kansas cattle towns as truly indescribable, adding that each cattle town can only be compared to itself. In a sense this was true not only of cattle towns but of all frontier settlements in the West. In appearance, however, most of the cattle towns were similar. There were few if any trees on the prairie and plains. The trees seen in these towns today were planted later. There was no public water supply other than nearby rivers, creeks, hand-dug wells, or cisterns designed to

catch and store rainwater. Public sanitation did not exist. There was no
indoor plumbing until the late 1880s, and then it was rare. Outhouses could
be seen behind most homes and business houses, most of which were of
frame construction like all other structures. A few sod houses appeared
during the early years of some cattle towns, and later, in towns like
Ellsworth, a few houses and business buildings were constructed of stone
found nearby. Most streets were wide. They were dirt—muddy when wet
or dusty when dry. The only sidewalks were in front of the larger business
houses. They consisted of board planks. The business buildings were
usually built facing the railroad tracks, especially the cattle town hotels.

Good accommodations became important in attracting the Texas
cattle trade. Joseph McCoy realized this when he built the Drovers Cottage
in Abilene. When the three-story structure, 40 by 50 feet with adjoining
stable, was completed early in 1868, it was the finest hotel on the plains.
The building cost $15,000 to erect and furnish. There were more than
forty spacious rooms plus a restaurant, bar, and billiard room. The Drovers
Cottage, "vaguely Italianate" but without the ornamentation, looked something like a box standing on the plains. It fronted the railroad tracks about
one block west of the stockyards. A long veranda provided patrons with
shade and comfort from the summer sun. One Abilene resident wrote: "On
its lordly porch strayed or sat lordly Texan drovers, eastern city cattle
buyers and commission agents, all exhaling an air of circumambient sub-
stantiality. Not to be omitted from this parade were at times leading
saloonkeepers, gamblers and individuals known to have killed a white
man."[9]

The Drovers Cottage changed hands three times between 1869 and
1870. When Moses B. George, a wealthy Texas cattle buyer, purchased the
hotel in the fall of 1870, he had the structure enlarged. By the spring of
1871 the Drovers Cottage measured 70 by 90 feet, contained nearly a
hundred rooms, and could stable fifty carriages and a hundred horses. By
1872, however, when it was obvious that the cattle trade would not be
returning to Abilene, George moved the hotel by flatcar to Ellsworth,
where it was in operation by May. George sold the hotel to James Gore
in 1873, but business soon declined because of competition from another
new hotel in Ellsworth called the Grand Central. Still another Ellsworth
hostelry was known as Beede's Hotel. Caldwell had the Moreland House,
advertised as "The Home of the Cowboy," while Wichita had eight
hotels and five boardinghouses during its peak cattle-trade days. One of
Wichita's better-known hotels was the Douglas Avenue House, a large
three-story brick structure. Dodge City had the Dodge House, a two-
story frame building containing thirty-eight rooms, a restaurant, a bar,
and a billiard hall. The chief competitor of the Dodge House was the

Western House, or Great Western Hotel. Rates were $1.50 per day or $8 per week for board and lodging.

While the hotels had bars, not very many cowboys patronized them. The hotel bars were for the cattlemen, cattle buyers, commission men, and owners of town businesses. Occasionally a cowboy might wander into a hotel bar, but most preferred the saloons. There were twice as many saloons as other businesses in the Kansas cattle towns. Most were long, narrow rooms, darkly lit, with small and not very fancy bars. There were a few tables and chairs in each. About the only shiny objects were cuspidors and perhaps a bartender's balding head. At night kerosene lamps provided yellowish light. Everything was dirty and smelly. The blend of tobacco, liquor, straw, horses, kerosene, and human sweat in the summer and the sometimes sizzling spit of tobacco juice on a hot stove in the fall or early spring left an unforgettable odor, one that many cowboys probably looked forward to on the long trail drives north, but one they often tried to forget after they had drunk or gambled away their wages and were headed back to Texas, their pockets empty and their heads aching.

Whiskey was the principal drink served in the earliest saloons of Abilene, Baxter Springs, and Waterville. A few of the better-known "bitters"—the generic term for liquors—were Squirrel, Old Crow, and McBryan, a very popular brand. As mentioned, Texans often called whiskey "Kansas sheep-dip," not to be confused with the real thing, advertised as "the only certain cure for Scab and its Prevention" in sheep.

One early resident of Abilene described his town's first saloons as "jerry-built affairs with hardly a cellar. The lumber used often warped badly, being more or less green. The structures stood propped up one or two feet above ground. Each had a front flare on which the owner boldly painted the name of his place."[10] Texas cowboys on their first trail drive to Abilene may have been surprised by the area of town where most of the saloons were located. It was more Texan than some Texas towns of the late 1860s. A Topeka newspaperman, visiting Abilene in August 1871, wrote that on the "north side of the tracks you are in Kansas, and hear sober and profitable conversation on the subject of the weather, the price of the land, and the crops. When you cross to the south side you are in Texas, and talk about cattle, varied by occasional remarks on 'beeves' and 'stocks.' Nine out of 10 men you meet are directly or indirectly interested in the cattle trade; five at least out of every 10 are Texans."[11]

At times the residents of "Kansas" Abilene probably wondered whether the righteous life that most had been taught to follow was really that good. They did avoid the temptations of Texas Street on moral grounds and because their pocketbooks were thin, but they dressed poorly, their wives worked hard, and their homes were mostly small frame houses that today would be called shacks. Inside, the furnishings were plain and simple. These "good" people lacked much in the way of worldly possessions, but they were optimistic. They taught their children to fear God and to live a righteous life. But since Abilene was small, these children could not help seeing the "sinful" people on Texas Street wearing better clothes and spending money and seemingly enjoying life each and every day. The contrast in the eyes of the children was undoubtedly a confusing one, especially after a schoolhouse was opened in the fall of 1869 adjacent to Texas Street. Many children walked Texas Street daily to and from school.

Some of these children undoubtedly noticed that the Alamo saloon on Texas Street did not have swinging doors to shelter customers inside from curious passersby outside. All other saloons did. But the Alamo had three sets of double-glass doors. Inside, it was the showplace of Abilene during the last years of the cattle trade there. One early resident remembered that there was an "ornate, domineering bar with its brass-mountings and colorful bottles of liquors" reflected in imposing mirrors. "Paintings, in remote but lascivious imitation of Titian, Tintoretto or Veronese, exhibiting nude women relaxed in beauty prostrate, seduced the Alamo's sporting life."[12] No other saloon in Abilene compared to the Alamo in 1871, but many had added ornately carved mahogany or walnut bars with polished glass mirrors on the walls.

A newspaperman from the *Kansas State Record* at Topeka spent an evening in the Texas portion of Abilene. In the August 5, 1871, issue, he wrote:

> At night everything is 'full up.' The 'Alamo' especially being a center of attraction. Here, in a well lighted room opening on the street, the 'boys' gather in crowds round the tables, to play or to watch others; a bartender, with a countenance like a youthful divinity student, fabricates wonderful drinks, while the music of a piano and a violin from a raised recess, enlivens the scene, and 'soothes the savage breasts' of those who retire torn and lacerated from an unfortunate combat with the 'tiger.' The games most affected are faro and monte, the latter being greatly patronized by the Mexicans of Abilene, who sit with perfectly unmoved countenances and play for hours at a stretch, for your Mexican loses with entire indifference . . . the two things somewhat valued by other men, viz: his money and his life.

Saloonkeepers seeking the cattle trade favored Texas names for their establishments. As mentioned, Abilene had an Alamo saloon. So did Dodge City and Newton. Abilene also had the Lone Star, the Old Fruit—a Texan slang expression for the "genuine article"—plus the Elkhorn, Applejack,

Hibernia, Bull's Head, and others. Abilene's Bull's Head saloon, built in 1871, was owned by Phil Coe and Ben Thompson, both Texans. Newton also had a Bull's Head saloon, along with the Side Track, Mint, and Do Drop In, names that do not seem very Texan. Abilene's Bull's Head saloon caused quite a controversy. Soon after it opened the proprietor had a bull painted across the outside front flare of the building. Stuart Henry, an early resident of Abilene, later described what happened:

> Spread across the surface appeared naively limned a big red bull in all its grandeur as depicted in livestock journals. . . . The painting produced an unexpected effect. . . . Though as far from any knowledge of art or desire for it as any people could well be, the picture made them instinctively revolt. Once again a baffling question almost as old as humanity! Bulls were frequently driven or led through the town without causing anybody a moment's thought, much less an objection, yet the image on that saloon stunned. It met with denunciation as immoral, degrading, hateful. And this in a cattle country whose present and future depended on stock breeding! . . . Bulls did breed before the public in that open 'God's country,' yet man with a brush was ignoble if he reproduced in paint the all-desired virility. The natural human cry: Nature is good, Art—indecent! So influential citizens, suddenly possessed of the thin-skinned susceptibilities of their mid-Victorian epoch, could not overlook the defiant animal on the Bull's Head. It must be considered an insult to the good women of the town, a shame in plain sight of children. To let the bull stand unobjected to or forbidden was held to be an outright 'knuckling under' to the Texans and to open the full road to unsupportable transgression. . . .

At first the proprietors, both Texans, refused to change the sign. They stood their ground. And with them the Texas cowboys chuckled at the reaction to the sign by the Kansans. What happened next is rather hazy, but about two weeks later it appeared that the controversy might erupt into violence. The proprietors then had the offending feature of the bull painted out. This satisfied the citizens of Abilene, but the Texans still chuckled, for, as Stuart Henry recalled, the "denaturing operation . . . left the outline still sketched to view."[13]

There is no question that most cattle towns during the 1870s had an overabundance of saloons for the worn and weary trail drivers. There were nineteen places licensed to sell liquor in Dodge City in 1876. The population of the town was only 1,200. During the summer months when the trail herds were arriving, all of the saloons had good business. But during the winter months they had to depend upon local residents. Then there was one saloon for roughly every sixty residents. The nicest and most popular saloon was the Saratoga, owned by Chalkley M. "Chalk" Beeson. He loved music and exercised good taste in providing entertainment—often a full orchestra—for his patrons. The Saratoga was high-toned compared to Dodge City's other saloons. It attracted the town's leading citizens, railroad men, cattle barons, and other prominent people. Beeson took the name of his saloon from the resort community of Saratoga, New York. Other prominent saloons in Dodge City included the Alamo, Beatty and Kelley's Alhambra, Mueller and Straeter's Old House, the rather plush Opera House saloon, and the Longbranch, built in 1873 by Charles Bassett, Ford County's first sheriff, and A. J. Peacock. Later, Chalkley Beeson bought it and William H. Harris became his partner. Today, thanks to the television program *Gunsmoke*, the Longbranch saloon is more famous than ever.

Although most cattle towns on the plains had ordinances against gambling, they were rarely enforced. Nearly all the saloons in Dodge City and elsewhere on the Great Plains offered gambling. It seems to have been considered fashionable on the plains, while in the rolling country of southeastern Kansas ordinances against gambling were generally enforced. In the towns where gambling was permitted, some saloons hired gamblers, but most let professional gamblers—transients for the most part—ply their trade. Fancy gambling equipment was not common, contrary to the impression sometimes conveyed by Hollywood westerns. Games of chance were pretty much limited to card games such as poker, monte, and faro, and a handful of dice games including chuck-a-luck, hazard, and keno, a game played something like bingo. Keno required many players and therefore was reserved for busy nights in the larger saloons. One Wichita saloon capitalized on the game's popularity in the early 1870s and called itself Keno Hall.

The professional gamblers usually won. The Texas drovers and cowboys usually lost. Robert Wright tells of one such instance in his book *Dodge City, the Cowboy Capital:* One day a cowboy, bent on having a good time, rode into town and headed for the Green Front saloon to do some gambling. In a short time he lost all his money. "Sore at his ill luck," the cowboy decided to prefer charges against the proprietor of the saloon "for running a gambling joint." The cowboy located Wright, then the mayor of Dodge City, introduced himself, and, according to Wright, presented his case with these words: "A feller in that 'ere Green Front has just robbed me of more'n sixteen dollars, an' I wants ter have 'im pulled." Wright replied, by his own account, "Been gambling, have you?" and called to Bill Tilghman, the city marshal, who was crossing the street: "Here, Bill, is a fellow that has been gambling. Run him in." "[T]hey hauled the prisoner to the police court," Wright noted, "where he was fined ten dollars and costs, as an object lesson to those who might presume to violate the anti-gambling ordinance of Dodge City." There were two standards in Dodge City.

Violence related to gambling was not uncommon. One Kansas newspaperman visited Ellsworth in late July of 1872 and reported:

Last Saturday evening about seven o'clock as I was walking down the street from supper, I heard three shots fired and saw a man rush out of a saloon and up the street with a six-shooter in each hand, he ran about half a block and fell, but immediately got up and went into another saloon; shortly after he entered two more shots were fired; then and there it ended. Everyone rushed to the spot and excitement ran high for a few minutes and every second man you met had a revolver in his hand. Finally the result was ascertained to be one man shot through the arm and lower part of the leg, another man shot through the leg close to the body, and a third with only a hole through the pants leg. The first two did the shooting. Both are gamblers and the whole thing arose over a game of monte. The third man was a mere spectator, and the shot that just missed him clearly unintentional, and should be a lesson to him to loaf in some better place.[14]

Of all the stories of the Kansas cattle towns, one involving a Texas cattleman by the name of Peppard is the most awesome. It was told by Robert Wright in an address delivered before the annual meeting of the Kansas State Historical Society in 1901. Peppard, Wright declared, was one cattleman whom the lawmen of Dodge City did not like to see come to town:

Invariably rows began then, and he was in all of them. While driving up a bunch of beeves to Dodge, so the story goes, Peppard's trail boss killed the negro cook. It has been said that the boss and Peppard were great friends and chums, and the boss killed the cook because Peppard wanted him killed. Anyway, a short time after they arrived at Dodge, Peppard and his boss fell out. The next morning Peppard saw him behind a bar in one of the saloons, and straightway procured a shot-gun loaded with buck, and turned it loose at the boss, who dodged behind the ice-chest, which was riddled. A very narrow escape for the boss it was. Peppard then took a man and dug up the dead negro, chopped off his head with an ax, brought it in a sack to within thirty miles of Dodge, when nightfall overtook them and they had to lay out. The negro had been dead two weeks, and it was very warm weather. Wolves were attracted by the scent, and made a most terrible racket around the camp-fire, and it was decidedly unpleasant for the two men. Peppard's man weakened first and said they must remove the head or the camp. Inasmuch as the head was the easier to remove, they took it a mile or two away. Then the wolves took it and the sack several miles further, and they had much difficulty in finding it. At last it was produced in court with the bullet-hole in the skull, and the perplexing question was sprung on the court as to its jurisdiction to hold an in-quest when only a fractional part of the remains was produced in court. The case was ably argued, *pro* and *con*. Those in favor of hold-ing the inquest maintained that the production of the head in court included the other necessary parts of the anatomy, and was the best evidence on earth of his demise, and that the bullet-hole was a silent witness of his taking-off. The opposition argued that if the court had jurisdiction to hold an inquest on the head, there was no reason why the courts of Comanche county and other localities could not do the same on any other fractional part of the anatomy which might be found scattered over their bailiwick. The court, after mature delibera-tion, decided to give continuance until such time as the rest of the remains could be produced in court. Peppard left town disgusted with the decision, and, for all I know to the contrary, the case is still docketed for continuance.

Joseph McCoy, the man who made Abilene a cattle town, reportedly did not drink. Yet he sometimes visited the better saloons and enjoyed observ-ing the Texans. In 1874, McCoy wrote of the cowboy dances he had wit-nessed a few years earlier in one of Abilene's saloons:

> The cow-boy enters the dance with a peculiar zest, not stopping to divest himself of his sombrero, spurs, or pistols, but just as he dis-mounts off his cow-pony, so he goes into the dance. A more odd, not to say comical sight, is not often seen than the dancing cow-boy; with the front of his sombrero lifted at an angle of fully forty-five degrees; his huge spurs jingling at every step or notion; his revolvers flapping up and down like a retreating sheep's tail; his eyes lit up with excite-ment, liquor and lust; he plunges in and "hoes it down" at a terrible rate, in the most approved yet awkward country style; often swing "his partner" clear off of the floor for an entire circle, then "balance all" with an occasional demoniacal yell, near akin to the war whoop of the savage Indian.[15]

The cowboy's dancing partners in many cattle towns were prostitutes. The local newspaper editors called them by various names, including soiled doves, sporting women, women of evil name and fame, frail sisters, calico queens, girls of the night, painted cats, sports, nymphs du prairie, and inmates of houses of ill fame. Prostitutes were not welcome in most Abilene saloons; however, in most of the other Kansas cattle towns it was not uncommon for the girls to work for the proprietor of the combination saloons and dance halls. Early in 1879 a Dodge City editor described one such establishment in his town as "a long frame building, with a hall and bar in front and sleeping rooms in the rear. The hall was nightly used for dancing, and was frequented by prostitutes, who belonged to the house and for benefit of it solicited the male visitors to dance. The rooms in the rear were occupied both during the dancing hours and after, and both day and night by the women for the purpose of prostitution."[16]

A historian friend of mine several years ago checked census records, police court dockets, city treasurers' reports of police judges, case files of district courts, newspapers, and other reliable sources and determined that most early Kansas cattle-town prostitutes were young, white, and unmarried. Each owned a small amount of personal property, but here, he observed, "any generalization must end. The girls were short or tall, fat or thin, pretty or homely. They came from good families and bad which they left behind in the East, or in England, Ireland, Germany, France, the Indian Nation, or just about any place that produced girls. Prostitution was a melting pot where the only general criterion was possession of a female body."[17]

The evidence seems to suggest that most girls did not migrate to new cattle towns as old towns died. In one instance, prostitutes did move but not by choice. Joseph McCoy wrote that in September of 1870 the prostitutes in Abilene were told to get out of town. Many of them left for Baxter Springs and Wichita. The ages of prostitutes in four Kansas cattle towns—Abilene, Ellsworth, Wichita, and Dodge City—never exceeded about twenty-three years on the average. Fourteen-year-old girls were recorded in Dodge City, and girls of seventeen, eighteen, and nineteen were the rule rather than the exception in nearly all Kansas cattle towns. The evidence suggests that most girls left the profession at a fairly youthful stage. Most probably retired into marriage.

Kansas laws labeled prostitution and brothel-keeping as misdemeanors punishable by fines up to $1,000 and county jail sentences up to six months, but none of the cattle towns used this authority. Most towns as they became organized passed local ordinances to deal with the situation. In most instances prostitutes were simply fined a few dollars. Baxter Springs probably had the steepest fines of the early cattle towns. One account in a Baxter Springs newspaper in September 1871 reported the disposition of four cases in police court. The terse published account reads:

Mollie Bowman for keeping house of ill-fame, $50.00 and costs.
Jennie Mitchell, inmate house of ill-fame, $30.00 and costs.
Nellie Wright, inmate house of ill-fame, $30.00 and costs.
Sallie Miller—keeping house of ill-fame, $50.00 and costs.[18]

In Abilene and Ellsworth the fine was $5 for girls and $10 for madams. It was $8 plus $2 court costs for girls in Wichita, while madams paid $18 plus $2 court costs. At Caldwell the girls were charged $5 plus $2 court costs. In nearly every cattle town on the prairie and plains no assessment was made if the girls were ill and unable to work. It was not uncommon in some towns for the girls to live with a prominent businessman or politician as his wife. This was particularly true in Dodge City, where James H. "Dog" Kelley, a restaurant owner and early mayor, lived with a woman called "The Great Easton." Bat and Jim Masterson at Dodge City in 1880 and William H. Harris, vice-president of a Dodge City bank, also lived with such girls.[19]

The files of the Kansas State Historical Society contain the names of more than six hundred girls who worked as prostitutes in Abilene, Wichita, Ellsworth, Hays, Dodge City, and Caldwell between 1870 and 1885. There were undoubtedly more girls, in these towns and others, whose names were not recorded. While many used their real names, others did not. They chose names that appealed to their Texas customers, southern names like Minnie, Katie, Hattie, Mattie, Annie, Fanny, and Jenny. But not all names sounded southern. There was one girl in Wichita called Tit Bit, while in Dodge City there was a Cuttin' Lil Slasher, Hambone Jane, and Dutch Jake. Other towns had girls with such names as Timberline, Sweet Annie, Wicked Alice, Fatty McDuff, Peg-Leg Annie, Kitty Kirl, the Galloping Cow, Lady Jane Gray, Roaring Gimlet, Little Lost Chicken, Cotton Tail (said to be a natural blonde), Irish Molly, and Big Nose Kate Elder.

As might be expected, there are many stories about these girls. One girl named Prairie Rose supposedly walked down the main street of Ellsworth wearing nothing but carrying two loaded pistols. She made the walk on a wager and apparently won. Another girl named Eve did the same thing in Wichita one evening in 1875, but her motives are unclear. Most recollections of the cattle-town prostitutes have been left by the residents. Recollections by the Texas cowboys who took advantage of the girls' services are almost nonexistent. Perhaps the frankest account by a Texas cowboy—and it is rather mild—was J. L. McCaleb's recollections of Abilene found in the first volume of *The Trail Drivers of Texas*. He wrote:

As it had been a long time since we had seen a house or a woman, they were good to look at. I wore a black plush hat which had a row of

COWBOYS, PROBABLY FROM TEXAS,
photographed in Kansas during the late 1870s.

TWO OF DODGE CITY'S "SOILED DOVES."
Left is "Squirrel Tooth Alice," whose nickname probably originated
from the prairie dog she often carried in her lap. Like many other
"nymphs of the prairie," she eventually left her profession to get married.
The woman on the right was called "Timberline" by her many customers.

small stars around the rim, with buckskin strings to tie and hold on my head. We went into town, tied our ponies, and the first place we visited was a saloon and dance hall. We ordered toddies like we had seen older men do, and drank them down, for we were dry, very dry, as it had been a long ways between drinks. I quit my partner, as he had a girl to talk to, so I went out and in a very short time I went into another store and saloon. I got another toddy, my hat began to stiffen up, but I pushed it up in front, moved my pistol to where it would be handy, then sat down on a box in the saloon and picked up a newspaper and thought I would read a few lines, but my two toddies were at war, so I could not very well understand what I read. I got up and left for more sights—you have seen them in Abilene, Dodge and any other place those days. I walked around for perhaps an hour. The two toddies were making me feel different to what I had felt for months, and I thought it was about time for another, so I headed for a place across the street, where I could hear a fiddle. It was a saloon, gambling and dance hall. Here I saw an old long-haired fellow dealing monte. I went to the bar and called for a toddy, and as I was drinking it a girl came up and put her little hand under my chin, and looked me square in the face, and said 'Oh you pretty Texas boy, give me a drink.' I asked her what she wanted and she said anything I took, so I called for two toddies. My, I was getting rich fast—a pretty girl and plenty of whiskey. My old hat was now away back on my head. My boss had given me four dollars spending money and I had my five-dollar bill, so I told the girl that she could make herself easy; that I was going to break the monte game, buy out the saloon, and keep her to run it for me when I went back to Texas for my other herd of cattle. Well, I went to the long-haired dealer and as he was making a new layout I put my five on the first card (a king) and about the third pull I won. I now had ten dollars and I thought I had better go and get another toddy before I played again. As I was getting rich so fast I put the two bills on a tray and won. Had now twenty dollars, so I moved my hat back as far as it would go and went to get a drink—another toddy, but my girl was gone. I wanted to show her that I was not joking about buying out the saloon after I broke the bank. After this drink things did not look so good. I went back and it seemed to me that I did not care whether I broke him or not. I soon lost all I had won and my old original five. When I quit him my hat was becoming more settled, getting down in front and I went out, found my partner and left for camp. The next morning, in place of owning a saloon and going back to Texas after my other herds, I felt—Oh! what's the use? You old fellows know how I felt.

In all of the recollections of the old-time drovers and cowboys gathered together in the monumental two-volume work *The Trail Drivers of Texas*, there is no mention of the word "prostitute." About the only published work that speaks frankly about such women is *We Pointed Them North*, E. C. "Teddy Blue" Abbott's recollections of his cowboy days as told to Helena Huntington Smith in the late 1930s. His experiences relate to the cattle-town women in Montana and on the northern plains.

Abbott was not ashamed to recall his experiences and to relate his observations of such women. The late J. Frank Dobie wrote in 1943 that Abbott's book "is franker about the women a rollicky cowboy was likely to meet in town than all the other range books put together. The fact that Teddy Blue's wife was a half-breed Indian, daughter of Granville Stuart, and that Indian women do not object to the truth about sex life may account in part for his frankness."[20]

Not all prostitutes in the cattle towns worked in dance halls. Some worked in brothels, or "sporting houses," often referred to as bawdy houses. Many people believe the term "red-light district" originated in Dodge City. It supposedly came from a sporting house called the "Red Light" because of a blood-red glass in the front door through which the light shone at night. The Red Light brothel was located in Dodge City's vice district south of the "deadline," or quarantine line, which in this case was the Santa Fe railroad tracks. Abilene's tenderloin district was often called the "Beer Garden" or "McCoy's addition" after the man who helped to make Abilene a cattle town. Ellsworth's district was called either "Nauchville" or "Scragtown," while in Newton—during 1871, its only year as a cattle town—the girls could be found in "Hide Park." It was a wild year. One Wichita newspaperman reported that Newton had ten bawdy houses "in full running order and three more under way." He added:

Plenty of rotten whiskey and everything to excite the passions was freely indulged in. . . . Rogues, gamblers, and lewd men and women run the town. I have been in a good many towns but Newton is the fastest one I have ever seen. Here you may see young girls not over sixteen drinking whisky, smoking cigars, cursing and swearing until one almost loses the respect they should have for the weaker sex. I heard one of their townsmen say he didn't believe there were a dozen virtuous women in town. This speaks well for a town claiming 1,500 inhabitants.[21]

One of the dance halls in Newton's Hide Park was operated by Perry Tuttle. It was the scene in August 1871 of the most deadly single act of violence recorded in any Kansas cattle town—an event often referred to as "Newton's General Massacre." The principal characters were a night policeman, Mike McCluskie (his real name was Arthur Delaney), his young friend Jim Riley, a Texas gambler called Bill Bailey (real name: William Baylor), and a Texas cattleman, Hugh Anderson, who with his father and brother had driven a large herd of longhorns up the trail to Newton.

On Friday, August 11, 1871, residents of Newton went to the polls to vote on a bond proposal. The gambler Bailey, who supposedly had killed two or three men in Texas, was hired as a special policeman to watch the polls. But Bailey drank heavily during the morning. When he began to badger election officials during the afternoon, Mike McCluskie intervened and removed Bailey from the polling area.

That night Bailey and McCluskie happened to meet in front of the Red Front Saloon, where a large election night crowd had gathered. Bailey was still drinking. When Bailey demanded that McCluskie set up the drinks for the crowd, McCluskie refused. Bailey cursed McCluskie and struck him with his fists. Then Bailey, apparently thinking twice about what he had just done, began to back away. It was too late. In a flash McCluskie pulled his six-gun and fired twice. The first shot missed its mark and lodged in the door of a nearby store. But the second shot struck Bailey in the right side, lodging below his heart.

Bailey was carried to the nearby Santa Fe Hotel, where Gaston Boyd, the town's only reputable doctor, tried to save his life. He failed. The Texas gambler died at eight o'clock the next morning, and was buried later that same day. When McCluskie was told of Bailey's death by his young friend Jim Riley, he left town. He wanted things to cool off even though he believed he would not be arrested for the killing. Most townspeople felt the shooting was justified.

But a small group of Texas cowboys felt differently. They had liked Bailey. He was one of their kind. He was a Texan. And as they drank in one of the saloons, they quietly swore to avenge his death. Their leader was Hugh Anderson, who had a reputation for recklessness, and had supposedly been involved in at least two gunfights in Texas. The Texans agreed to keep their intentions to themselves and to wait for McCluskie to return. It was then, they said, that they would even the score.

The next Saturday night, McCluskie slipped back into Newton and made his way to Perry Tuttle's dance hall in Hide Park. There, sitting at a corner table, he drank and gambled and laughed. Everyone was friendly, and McCluskie must have believed that everybody had forgotten about the killing of Bailey. But some of Hugh Anderson's friends, drinking at the bar, had seen McCluskie enter the dance hall. One of them hurried to tell

Anderson while the others walked over to McCluskie's table. One of the Texans sat down and began talking with McCluskie. The others stood nearby, smiling and joking as if nothing had happened.

A few minutes later, Hugh Anderson entered the saloon. McCluskie apparently did not see him until, six-shooter in hand, he walked up to McCluskie's table. Everyone moved back. The men had words, and Anderson fired his gun at McCluskie. The bullet hit McCluskie in the neck. He tried to stand up. He pulled his six-gun, pointed it at Anderson, and squeezed the trigger, but the cartridge did not go off. McCluskie fell to the floor, and Anderson fired another shot into his motionless body.

There are conflicting accounts of what happened next, but it is known that at about the time McCluskie was shot, his young friend Jim Riley entered the saloon. Suffering from a bad case of tuberculosis, young Riley had been befriended by McCluskie, and he felt close to the man lying on the dance hall floor. Apparently angered by what he saw, he turned and locked the door, pulled his gun, and began firing. The Texans pulled their guns and tried to return Riley's fire. When the shooting stopped and the smoke cleared, townsmen forced the saloon door open. Two men lay dead. Four others, including Anderson and McCluskie, were wounded. And before too many days passed, the death toll climbed to five. Three of the wounded men, including McCluskie, died.

Young Jim Riley somehow escaped the dance hall and fled Newton. Hugh Anderson was arrested for McCluskie's death, but Anderson's father and brother with the help of some friends were able to sneak him out of Newton on a train to Kansas City, where doctors treated his wounds. The town of Newton did not remain wild for long after the "massacre." Early in 1872, as the cattle trade was shifting to Wichita 25 miles away, the citizens of Newton formed a law-and-order committee and gave every gambler, prostitute, and outlaw twelve hours to get out of town. They all left. One shoddy character, sick in bed, was carried to the train on a cot to make his exit before the deadline.[22]

Some of Newton's undesirables went to Wichita and began to ply their professions in that town's tough district, which was called "Delano." It was located at the west end of the main street bridge across the Arkansas River. Delano consisted of two combination saloon-and-dance-halls. One was run by E. T. "Red" Beard, and the other by Joseph "Rowdy Joe" Lowe and his wife Kate. In a letter to his Topeka newspaper, the *Commonwealth*, S. S. Prouty reported that Rowdy Joe's was patronized "mainly by cattle herders though all classes visit it, the respectable mostly from curiosity." Prouty said the profits came from drinks. "No charge is made for dancing but it is expected that the males will purchase drinks for themselves and female partners at the conclusion of each

A QUIET-LOOKING ABILENE, KANSAS, IN 1875,
three years after the cattle trade moved on.

WATERVILLE, KANSAS, IN 1872,
a few years after its short-lived cattle-town days.
Located 100 miles west of the Missouri River on the Central Branch
of the Union Pacific, Waterville became a stopping point
for settlers arriving from the east. Notice the people standing
in line in front of the land office waiting to file
for a homestead.

dance."[23] Prouty did not speculate on what the female partners might be selling on the side.

Although most sporting houses were located in the rough districts of the cattle towns, there were a few in the better areas of the larger communities. In Wichita, one brothel was located on the town's main street. About 1876, near the end of Wichita's cattle-town days, the city fathers received a petition signed by several citizens calling for the brothel's closing. The petition, suffering from poor spelling and poor grammar, reads:

We the undersign petician youre Honorable Body to take immeditally Steps to Renain or Declar the inmates of the House Occupied by Mattie Wilson or Nonen as the Old Ozark Dollar on Douglas an between Main & Water St. a Newsence for the Reeasons that it is a injar to the Publick Business in that vicinity Endangers proety by Fire by inmates of sutch a House & that it is situated on One of the Main streets of the city & is a Public Nusence.[24]

Whether the petition had its desired effect is unknown.

There is no question that the cattle towns influenced the material culture of the Texas cattlemen, drovers, cowboys, and vaqueros. For some, the experience may have changed their views of people in other walks of life or simply reinforced them. For the cattlemen the cattle towns provided long-sought-after markets for Texas longhorns and profits that made them cattle barons. Their newfound wealth enabled many Texans to improve their standard of living, to travel, and to do things wealthy people did during the late nineteenth century. For the drovers, cowboys, and vaqueros the cattle-town markets created jobs driving the herds to Kansas. These men were paid for their work and usually spent all or most of their wages on new material possessions and/or fun in the cattle towns. Merchants, saloonkeepers, gamblers, prostitutes, and other people in the cattle towns benefited materially. They in turn provided new experiences for the Texans.

The Kansas cattle towns were mixing places for different types and classes of people from different geographic regions. But the railroads that helped to create the Kansas cattle towns, and brought the material goods that were sold to the Texans, also brought settlers. Most of these settlers, farmers determined to build their homes on the plains and prairies and till the land that was being grazed or crossed by the Texas longhorns, did not understand the Texas cattlemen, drovers, and cowboys or their system of cattle raising. Many Texans viewed the settlers as interlopers. Yet the law was on the side of the settlers. Most lawmakers in Washington did not understand the cattlemen's western system of cattle raising, which was tied to the semiarid conditions of the plains from Texas to Canada. The eastern laws relating to land and water rights were satisfactory in the East, but they were unsuited to the needs and conditions of the cattlemen in the West. As settlers, backed by the law, pushed across the central plains, cattlemen said "damn" and began either to adjust or to seek new regions where the grass was a little greener and the eastern ways had not yet arrived. For some cattlemen these new regions were to the north beyond Kansas.

•❖•

CHAPTER 11

On the Northern Ranges

*The cattle industry and the cattlemen were already estab-
lished in the mountains and in the Great Plains . . . before
the history of the trail herds moving north began.*

—CARL FREDERICK KRAENZEL[1]

RUNNING northeast from near Fort Laramie in southeast Wyoming to near the city of Valentine in north central Nebraska is nature's dividing line between the southern and northern plains. Traveling along this line you will notice that to the south the plains are notably flat with only an occasional valley, canyon, or butte. The grasses are mostly short—the blue grama (*Bouteloua gracilis*) and buffalo grass (*Buchloe dactyloides*) predominating. But to the north of the dividing line the plains are more rolling with frequent canyons and buttes and, as you move farther north, some mountains breaking the continuity of the plains. While short grasses like those to the south are dominant there, taller grasses like bluestem (*Agropyron Smithii*) and needle-and-thread grass (*Stipa comata*) may be seen growing in bunches. Scientists refer to the region south of the line as the Kansan Biotic Province and the region to the north as the Saskatchewan Biotic Province.[2] Such labels, however, are used only by scholars and scientists. Most people today, like the cowboys and cattlemen of the nineteenth century, simply refer to the regions as the southern and northern plains.

Winters on the northern plains generally are longer and colder than on the southern, but the weather is rarely consistent from winter to winter. Some years have heavy snowfall while in others the snowfall is light. Even temperatures vary from year to year, but one can be certain that in what is now Montana and portions of Wyoming, the Dakotas, and northwestern Nebraska, temperatures at some point will dip well below zero each winter.

In some areas thirty or forty degrees (Fahrenheit) below zero is not uncommon. Still, the duration of such temperatures varies from winter to winter and from one place to another.

Many explorers and military men who crossed the plains early in the nineteenth century believed that few animals or even man could survive the cold and snowy winters on the northern plains, then considered part of the Great American Desert. This belief may have contributed to the misconception that buffalo—the plains Indians' cattle—*migrated* to the southern plains to escape the northern winters. Such migrations never occurred. Buffalo on the northern plains wintered there, simply roaming in a broad circle of perhaps 300 miles seeking forage where they found it. Buffalo, unlike cattle, would paw and root through the snow for forage. Captive buffalo and wildlife including deer and elk still survive the northern winters, as do many cattle. And so does man, as he has done for centuries.

The first white man's cattle on the northern ranges were not Texas longhorns. They were eastern farm-raised cattle from places like Iowa, Missouri, and Illinois. They belonged to immigrants bound for the new territory of Oregon, beginning in 1843, most of them destined to become farmers and stockmen. Many took their family cows with them. These cattle were mostly of the Durham or shorthorn strain, capable of producing milk for the immigrants' children on the long journey to the Northwest. Once in Oregon, such cattle would be used as breeding stock. But many became footsore and worn out by the time they crossed what is now Nebraska. Some were left to die along the Oregon Trail, but others were traded for provisions or stronger cattle at such places as Fort Bridger in present Wyoming or at Fort Hall, a Hudson's Bay Company trading post on the Snake River in present-day Idaho.

Cattle trading at Fort Hall was very active between 1843 and the early 1850s. There, beginning in 1843, a fur trader named Richard Grant began swapping flour and other provisions for immigrants' worn-out cattle. By the fall of 1843, Grant and his two sons had gathered a sizable herd that they drove northward to the mountain valleys of what is now western Montana before winter set in. There the cattle survived winter's cold and snow. When spring came they were fat, and Grant and his sons trailed them back to Fort Hall, where one good animal was traded for two worn-out ones. After about a dozen years of repeating this process annually, Grant and his sons sold the herd, by then more than six hundred head, and retired from the cattle business.[3]

Richard Grant was one of the earliest cattle raisers in what is today Montana. But he was not a *rancher* in the Texas sense. He entered the business with little or no experience in cattle raising. Described as "a genuine British aristocrat," Grant may have learned from other fur traders that cattle could survive in the north. Or he may have observed that deer, elk, buffalo, and other wild game lived through the northern winters and surmised that cattle probably could do the same. Regardless, Grant's cattle found plenty of forage on the dried winter grasses blown free of snow. The June, pine, bluejoint, and bluestem grasses of the northern ranges suffer little from heat or cold. When frost comes each fall, most do not wilt. Because of the dry climate and the high protein content of these grasses, they cure into a dry feed that stays palatable and nutritious all winter long. They survive trampling, and in many areas the winter wind causes the snow to drift, leaving large areas of grassland exposed. As long as the grass is exposed, even in the coldest weather, cattle are able to keep in good condition. It is only when the snowfall is extremely heavy and there is little wind, causing the snow to cover the grasses at uniform depth, that cattle often die because they do not paw and root through the snow to find grass.

The same year Richard Grant was entering the cattle business in a small way at Fort Hall, explorer John C. Frémont came upon a herd of cattle on the plains about 35 miles northeast of where Denver stands today. Nearby were the adobe buildings of Fort Lupton, a trading post constructed a decade earlier by Lancaster P. Lupton. He was a former lieutenant in the United States army who had resigned in 1836 to become a fur trader along the eastern slopes of the Rocky Mountains. Lupton raised and sold cattle as a sideline to trading with the Indians. According to one account, he sold cows for $12, steers for $10, and calves for $4 a head. These cattle also survived the often vicious winters.[4]

By the 1850s other men had discovered that cattle could make it through the winters on the northern plains. Small pockets of cattle raising existed, in what is now Colorado and at several points along the Oregon Trail from Nebraska to Oregon, by the late 1850s. Granville Stuart, a West Virginian by birth, was soon doing what Richard Grant had done earlier. Stuart and his brother first went to the California gold fields with their father in 1852. Having had poor luck, they started back east in 1857. Near Salt Lake City they became alarmed at reports of Mormon hostility and turned north, crossing into what is now western Montana. In the spring of 1858 they found gold in the Deer Lodge Valley near Gold Creek. Although gold had been discovered in the area earlier, it was the news of the Stuart discovery that sparked the Montana gold rush of 1862. By then Stuart had taken some lame oxen from Fort Hall to western Montana. These cattle grew fat during the winter of 1860. They were driven back to Fort Hall the following spring and sold or traded for other lame cattle. Stuart's business grew rapidly because of the heavy influx of goldseekers.[5]

One of the goldseekers was a twenty-five-year-old Ohio-born over-land freighter named Nelson Story (sometimes spelled Storey). He was freighting goods between Denver and Leavenworth when he learned of the Montana gold strike. Having witnessed the earlier gold rush in the Rocky Mountains near modern Denver, Story realized there would be a demand for coffee, flour, cured pork, goldpans, bolts of cloth, kettles, molasses, shovels, and many other items in Montana. So he loaded two ox-drawn wagons and a string of eleven pack mules with supplies. With two helpers and his wife, Story headed for the Montana gold fields. Nelson Story's adventures at this point may seem insignificant to the culture of the cowboy, but Story was on the first leg of a journey that would eventually find him introducing Texas longhorns and Texas cowboys to Montana. How it happened is a fascinating tale.

Story's party arrived in the Montana gold fields in June 1863. Soon he and his wife opened a store in the new boom town of Virginia City. His wife helped to run the store and made dried apple, pumpkin, and berry pies. Miners paid $5 in gold dust for each pie. Story found time to locate his own gold claim, and he and his wife accumulated a great deal of gold dust from their business and claim. With more and more people coming into the region, Story realized there would be greater demand for beef, flour, coffee, and other provisions, and he decided to go to Texas and buy some cattle. But first, Story took $30,000 in gold dust and traveled by stage to Salt Lake City. From there he sent the gold dust by express coach to a New York City bank. Story followed by stage and railroad, and in New York converted his gold to paper money, realizing a profit of $10,000. He took a bank letter of credit and $10,000 in currency, which was sewn in his suit, and headed west to Leavenworth, Kansas, his old stamping ground. There he used the bank letter to open a checking ac-count. And in that city on the Missouri River, Story met two old friends. When he told them of his plans to go to Texas, buy a herd of longhorns, and drive the cattle to Montana Territory, his friends said they liked the idea and agreed to join him on the journey.

Was Nelson Story unique? Perhaps. But he was a veteran plainsman who knew the West. Unlike the newcomers pushing westward to get a new start and to forget the Civil War, he knew the vast distances that had to be covered on the plains and understood that distance could be con-quered in time. Story and his two friends arrived in Texas about June of 1866. They purchased a herd of cattle (one account says six hundred head, another a thousand, still another three thousand—which figure is correct is unknown), a wagon to haul provisions and gear, and extra horses. Then Story hired twenty-two cowboys experienced in trail driving. These cow-boys would be the first of many Texans to carry the customs and tech-niques of the Texas cattle culture to Montana Territory.

Story and his men began driving the cattle north in early August of 1866. They followed a known trail to the Red River, crossed the then swollen stream with some difficulty, and headed northeast across Indian Territory toward Baxter Springs, Kansas. Indians demanded a toll to cross their land, and men just outside the law demanded money to permit Story's herd to enter southeastern Kansas. Story apparently refused to pay the tribute and turned his herd west, entering Kansas some distance west of Baxter Springs. The herd was then trailed northeastward to a point where the drive hit the Oregon Trail in northeast Kansas. Story left his two friends in charge and hurried to Leavenworth, where he purchased three wagons and filled them with provisions. He also purchased more than two dozen new fast-firing rolling-block-action Remington rifles (probably Remington rolling-block conversions of Civil War model 1861/1863 percussion muzzle-loading rifled muskets) and ammunition. Hiring men to drive the wagons, Story led the way west until they reached the slow-moving cattle herd.

Story's party reached Fort Laramie in September 1866 and found several freighters waiting to follow the Bozeman Road north to Montana. Army officers had advised them not to attempt the journey alone, since the Sioux Indians were on the rampage all along the Powder River to the north. The officers warned Story that Indians would certainly attack his slow-moving herd. But Story's party and the other waiting freighters discussed their chances. All agreed that together they were a strong force, one the Indians would not likely attack. Thus they joined together and started north through Indian country. Although they saw Indians nearly every day, it was not until the group neared Fort Reno on the edge of the badlands that the Indians attacked. The battle was brief. Story's men, armed with their Remington rifles, easily fought off the Indians.

The group continued on to just south of Fort Kearny in what is today northeast Wyoming. Soldiers rode out from the post, which was then being constructed, and told Story to keep his herd 3 miles from the fort—the grass around the post was for army cattle. They also advised Story and the freighters that they could not continue north because of Indians. Story and the others appealed the order, but waited more than a week without receiving an answer. Disgusted with the army and determined to continue north, they finally moved the cattle and wagons around Fort Kearny under cover of darkness. They continued to travel only by night and kept the wagons and the cattle in a tight bunch during the day, while on constant guard for Indians. Three times Indians attacked, but each time they were driven off. As the herd and wagons neared the Big Horn River, they were hit by an early winter storm. Story issued extra clothing to his men. Many of the longhorns drifted with the storm, but when the sky cleared most

were found. Story and his men, dangerously chilled, continued on. Fortunately, the storm had forced the Indians to seek shelter.

Story and his party may have parted from the freighters at some
point after crossing into what is now Montana. History records that
Story's group trailed the cattle and wagons to a ford near the mouth of the
Stillwater River near modern Columbus, Montana, in late November. On
December 3, 1866, they entered Gallatin Valley. Although snow covered
the ground and it was very cold, Story ordered some of the cowboys to
cut down trees to construct a ranch building and corral. This became the
Story ranch, not far from modern Bozeman, Montana, a ranch that continued to operate into the early 1900s. But back in early December of 1866,
Story did not wait to see his ranch building and corral finished. Leaving
most of the men to finish the construction and to watch the cattle, Story
with a few cowboys cut out a small bunch of prime steers from the herd.
With the wagons leading the way, the party headed for Virginia City.
They arrived there on December 9, 1866, and the townspeople turned out
to welcome them.[6]

Thus ended Nelson Story's 2,500-mile trail drive, a drive that
brought Texas cowboys and longhorns into what is now Montana in 1866.
But the impact of that event would not be felt for another decade. Story's
cattle drive did not open the way for other Texas herds, since the most
direct route between Texas and Montana was through Indian country. The
Bozeman Trail was closed soon after Story took his herd over it. In 1868
the government made a treaty at Fort Laramie with Chief Red Cloud
barring stockmen from grazing their cattle on the rich grasslands north of
the Platte River in what is now eastern and northern Wyoming and
southern Montana. Thus the cattle raisers on the rolling plains and in the
mountain valleys of Montana Territory came to rely on cattle from Oregon
and the Northwest.

Despite the fact that they are often ignored by writers tracing the
development of the western cattle industry—perhaps because there was no
Joseph McCoy to popularize the subject or other writers to romanticize
it—the events concerning the movement of cattle from Oregon east during
the late 1860s and early 1870s were important to the cowboy culture of the
northern ranges. When immigrants had reached Oregon years earlier,
many became stockmen. Their cattle grew fat on the rich grasslands of
the Yakima, Snake, Columbia, and Willamette valleys, and by the late 1860s
there was a surplus of cattle in the Northwest. Stockmen began driving
them east to Idaho and western Montana to sell. By 1869, there was probably more good beef available than the miners in all the mining camps of
the northern Rockies could have consumed. And the quality of this beef
was high compared to that of the Texas longhorns or the Spanish cattle of
California.

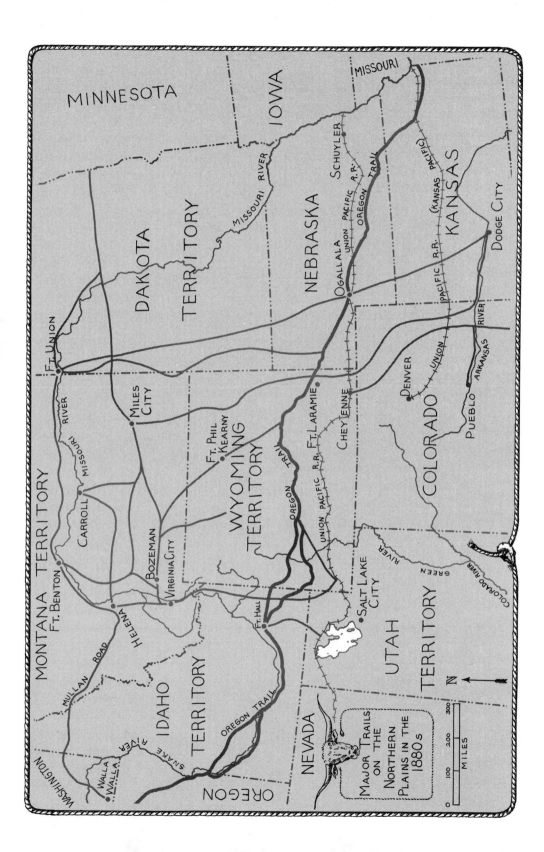

MINNESOTA

IOWA

MISSOURI

DAKOTA TERRITORY

MISSOURI RIVER

SCHUYLER

NEBRASKA

UNION PACIFIC R.R.

OREGON TRAIL

(KANSAS PACIFIC)

KANSAS

OGALLALA

UNION PACIFIC R.R.

DODGE CITY

FT. UNION

MILES CITY

MONTANA TERRITORY

MISSOURI RIVER

CARROLL

FT. PHIL KEARNY

WYOMING TERRITORY

FT. LARAMIE

CHEYENNE

UNION PACIFIC R.R.

DENVER

COLORADO

ARKANSAS RIVER

PUEBLO

FT. BENTON

BOZEMAN

VIRGINIA CITY

HELENA

OREGON TRAIL

OREGON TRAIL

UNION PACIFIC R.R.

SALT LAKE CITY

GREEN RIVER

COLORADO RIVER

MULLAN ROAD

FT. HALL

UTAH TERRITORY

IDAHO TERRITORY

SNAKE RIVER

WALLA WALLA

WASHINGTON

OREGON TRAIL

OREGON

NEVADA

MAJOR TRAILS ON THE NORTHERN PLAINS IN THE 1880s

N

0 100 200 300

MILES

From 1869 through 1875, more than 250,000 head of cattle were trailed east from Oregon along the Oregon Trail to Boise, across Little Camas and Big Camas prairies, and on across perhaps 100 miles of lava wasteland (now the Craters of the Moon National Monument), to where Idaho Falls stands today. At that point the trail turned north over Monida Pass into Montana Territory. Some cattle were also driven east over what was called Mullen Road, a trail from the Columbia River northeastward across northern Idaho into western Montana Territory. The trail was named for the young lieutenant who supervised its construction in the 1850s. These northern trails were more difficult to traverse for men, horses, and cattle than those running from Texas to Kansas. The roaring Snake River and several streams were harder to cross than the rivers on the southern plains, and nowhere in the south did cowboys have to pick their way through glass-edged lava as they did on the single northern trail. Then, too, temperature extremes in the north often made trail life more unbearable than in the south.

Texas cowboys, other than those who had come north with Nelson Story in 1866, had little opportunity to experience the hardships of the far northern drives during the late 1860s. None of the men operating the small ranches along the Oregon Trail in what is now Wyoming, Idaho, and Oregon appear to have worked as cowboys in Texas, nor were they familiar with the lore of the open range. The handling of cattle on the open range was simply unknown in the north until the 1870s. Most of the northern cattle farmers had small herds and knew the business of cattle raising only as it had been practiced along the Atlantic seaboard or on farms in the Middle West. A few may have observed California ranchos in operation, but if they had, they had adopted few of their practices. It seems doubtful that the cowboys brought north by Nelson Story—those who stayed—exerted any influence on Montana cattle-raising customs, except perhaps on Story's ranch.

But south of the forbidden grasslands of northern and eastern Wyoming and the western Dakotas the influence of the Texas cowboy was beginning to be felt. The Union Pacific Railroad, on its westward push toward the Pacific, reached what is now Cheyenne, Wyoming, late in 1867. That was the same year Joseph McCoy established Abilene as the first railhead market for Texas cattle in Kansas. While many of the longhorns driven to Abilene and later to other Kansas cattle towns were shipped east to market, many were sold as stock for the ranges of central and western Kansas, eastern Colorado, western Nebraska, and southeastern Wyoming Territory. Many a Texas cowboy helped to drive these herds beyond the boundaries of Kansas, where buyers fattened the animals on Nebraska, Kansas, or Colorado grasses. By the time the longhorns were ready for market, new cattle towns had sprung up. Kit Carson, a small settlement on the plains of eastern Colorado Territory named for the well-known mountain man, became something of a cattle town, but not on the scale of Abilene or Dodge City or Wichita. The Kansas Pacific line reached Kit Carson in 1869. When the railroad reached Denver the following year, that town became a major shipping point, with more than four hundred carloads of cattle shipped east the first year.

In wet years the high plains of eastern Colorado and northwest Kansas provide lush grasses for grazing. T. J. Burkett, a Texas cowboy, trailed a herd of longhorns into northeastern Colorado and south to near Deer Trail, 50 miles southeast of Denver, in the early 1880s. His reaction to the country probably was typical of that of other cow people of the day. "After leaving the Nebraska line we crossed over into Colorado, and there had the pleasure of feasting our eyes on the most beautiful range that was ever beheld by a cowboy. The grammas grass was half a knee high, and was mixed with nutritious white grass that was waist high, waving in the breeze like a wheat field. We drove up the Arickaree, a distance of about 100 miles, and had a picnic along this bubbling stream every day," wrote Burkett.[7]

To the east in western Kansas, D. W. "Doc" Barton and his brother Al, both Texans, introduced open-range ranching in 1872. They left southern Texas in February of 1872 with three thousand head of long-horns and headed north toward Kansas. But hostile Indians and outlaw bands of Mexican desperadoes forced the Barton brothers to abandon plans to drive their cattle straight north across Indian Territory. Instead they followed what became known as the Western or Pecos trail up the Pecos River valley in what is now New Mexico and on north into Colorado. Once they reached the Arkansas River near where Pueblo, Colorado, stands today, the Bartons and their fourteen cowboys turned the herd east and followed the river into southwestern Kansas.

On the site of modern Garden City, Kansas, the Barton brothers established their camp around the remains of a large cottonwood tree. Its giant trunk had been half burned and almost stripped of branches to furnish fuel for travelers following the Santa Fe Trail. Through the summer of 1872, the half-burned tree trunk served as their camp marker. It could be seen from many miles around. But in the fall of 1872 the Bartons built some dugouts along the banks of the Arkansas River near present-day Pierceville, Kansas. The dugouts became their ranch headquarters, and the Bartons grazed their longhorns from south of the Arkansas River to the Red River of Texas. In time, "Doc" Barton adopted the OS brand for his herd.

To the north of Kansas, along the Union Pacific line in Nebraska, few

DOAN'S STORE ON THE RED RIVER IN TEXAS
was a stopping point for many drovers and cowboys driving cattle north
in the late 1870s and '80s. It was near modern Vernon, Texas.

"TEXAS CATTLE IN A KANSAS CORN CORRAL."
Drawing by Frederic Remington,
in *Harper's Weekly*, April 1888.

cattle were shipped east by rail until 1869, when plans were made to construct adequate shipping facilities. The towns of Schuyler and Columbus both sought the stockyards. Schuyler, at the northern end of the Blue River trail, won the honor. In 1870 between forty thousand and fifty thousand longhorns were trailed north from Texas through Kansas to Schuyler, where they changed hands. By 1871, however, more and more settlers were arriving in the region, and the cattle trail was pushed west to Kearney. Two years later, in 1873, it shifted again, to the west to Ogallala, where it remained for more than a decade.

It was not unusual for Texas cowboys driving herds of longhorns to Abilene in the late 1860s and early 1870s to find themselves going beyond the northern border of Kansas. This happened to Richard "Dick" Withers, who eventually settled at Boyes, Montana. Withers was reared on his father's ranch north of Lockhart in Caldwell County, Texas. He made his first drive to Kansas at the age of eighteen years. He had traded a beef steer for a pair of goatskin leggings, bought a slicker and a pair of blankets, put a saddle on his bay horse named Buck, and added the 110 steers he had gathered to a larger herd owned by Colonel J. J. Myers. Withers sold his cattle at Abilene and returned to Texas. Then in 1870, after gathering more cattle on his own, he joined his father and another cattleman named J. W. "Bill" Montgomery and drove a large herd north.

They took two wagons on the drive and had two cooks to feed the cowboys, who were driving more than 3,500 head. They sold the cattle at Abilene on the condition that they be delivered in Idaho, beyond the Snake River. Montgomery and young Withers agreed to take the cattle to Idaho while his father returned to Texas. Many years later Withers recalled his experiences and the route that was followed:

We went from Abilene to the Big Blue river, from there to the South Platte, below South Platte City, going up that stream to Julesburg and crossed the river, from whence we went to Cheyenne. As we were working oxen we had to have them shod at Cheyenne, as the gravel had worn their hoofs off to the quick. After leaving Cheyenne we struck the North Platte river below Fort Fetterman. A few days before we got to Fetterman we made a long drive to water, and when we reached the water, there being no other herds there we turned our herd loose that night. During the night a herd of five hundred big fat steers came in, which were being driven to Fetterman, and the drivers, not knowing we were there, turned their herd loose also and mixed with our herd. The next morning we told them that as we were going to Fetterman they could cut them out when we reached that place. When we arrived at Fetterman we rounded up our herd for them and they went to cutting out, but as they were tenderfeet, they did not succeed very well and now and then one would come back on them. . . . When they were through cutting there were sixteen of those big fat steers in our herd which they could not cut out, and we told them our horses were 'all in,' and we could not cut them, so I made a trade with them, giving sixteen head of lean cattle for their fat ones, and they sure came in mighty handy. . . .

Withers and Montgomery and their cowboys drove the herd up the North Platte and struck across to Sweetwater, following the old California immigrant trail. They passed Enchanted Rock and Devil's Gate, two well-known landmarks. What happened next is told in Withers's own words:

There the cook broke one of the ox yokes and we could not get one, so we had to camp and cut down a small cottonwood tree to make a yoke with a dull axe and the king bolt of the wagon to burn the holes with. . . . We pulled out the next day, and all went well until we reached the Rocky Mountains. It was forty miles across these mountains and two hundred miles around, so we decided to go across them. This was in October and the weather had been good, but we were getting short of grub. The first night in the mountains it came a snow storm and twenty-five of our horses died and our cattle scattered considerably. All we could do was to push them in the old trail from each side and let them drift along. At this time our sixteen fat steers came in mighty handy, for when our supply of provisions gave out we began killing them. The meat would freeze in just a little while, so we lived on nothing but beef for over a month. We had no flour, salt or coffee, and nowhere to purchase these things. Only a few trappers and miners were in the country and they did not have enough to supply us. Our horses all gave out and we had to walk and drive our diminishing herd. We had plenty of money, but could not buy any horses because there were none to buy, however, one day a miner came along with eight big U.S. mules, and Bill purchased them. We thought those big mules would relieve our troubles, but when I saddled one of them and went after the cattle he did not last an hour, for he could not climb the mountains. We managed to secure a few more horses from miners, and after pushing on for another ten days we reached Salt Valley, where we layed over for several days while three of the men went back into the mountains to gather up the cattle we had left, numbering about three hundred head. Bill Montgomery pulled on with the herd, and I took a man and a pack mule and also went back into the mountains to try to gather more of the missing cattle. I found about fifty head of them and hired a trapper to take them to Ogden [Utah Territory], while I and my man returned to overtake the main herd which was about ten days ahead of us. We camped one night near a big lake on the trail, and next morning we found the tracks of a big grizzly bear in the snow within ten yards of where we slept. We had our heads covered up and I supposed he could not smell us as he passed our camp.

We did not overtake the herd until they reached Snake River. There Noah Ellis, who had taken one herd on to the man we had sold to, returned to us. From there on we had no trouble, but soon reached our destination, and delivered the cattle to Mr. Shelly. Bill Montgomery then bought one hundred and fifty mules from Shelly, paying $75 to $100 each for them and started them to Branyon to ship them to Missouri where he expected to sell them for good prices. I took the stage for Ogden to get the cattle I had sent there by the trapper, and when I arrived there I sold the cattle and went on to Branyon to meet Bill. I had to wait several days for him to arrive, and when he got there, Noah Ellis and I pulled out for Texas, arriving at Lockhart on Christmas Eve.[8]

In 1870 the assessment rolls of Wyoming Territory listed only 8,143 cattle. The following year almost four times as many cattle were driven into southeastern Wyoming. Most were Texas longhorns. Fifteen thousand of the lanky Texas cattle were owned by Dudley and John Snyder. Charles F. Coffee, a Texas cowboy, helped to drive one of their herds up the trail from the Red River. Coffee recalled that he and other cowboys "had to break the trail, fight Indians and scare buffaloes out of the way to keep them from stampeding our cattle." After the three-month drive to Cheyenne, the Snyders could sell only 1,200 steers from one herd in Wyoming Territory. So the cowboys drove the rest to Ross's Crossing on the Snake River in Idaho, where buyers were found. As Coffee recalled, the cowboys "struck some nice snow storms. To a Texas cowpuncher who had never seen snow, it looked like 'the other place' on the plains."[9]

Obviously the colder climate encountered by Coffee and other Texas cowboys necessitated a change in their dress. The Texans found a wool or flannel shirt more practical than the cotton shirt worn on the southern ranges. Wool absorbed body moisture during the daytime heat of the northern summers, so the cowboys were actually cool during hot days and much more comfortable on the cold nights in the north. The cowboys also found woolen pants good, although they preferred pockets that went straight down in front instead of down the side as they do in most men's trousers today. The reason was not fashion but practicality. Things like pocketknives, tobacco, and coins could slide out of side pockets when the cowboys sat on the ground. Front pockets prevented this. The first Texas cowboys in the north probably purchased or traded for woolens at one of the several army posts. As towns grew, merchants began to stock woolen goods for the northern cowboys, including among other things vests. Vests provided added warmth in cold weather, and vest pockets were handy places to carry cigarette papers, tobacco sacks, matches, short pencils, small note or tally books in which to keep records of brands, dates wages were due, or dates when mail orders from eastern stores were to arrive.

Northern cowboys usually carried a coat tied in a roll behind their saddles. Most coats were wool to provide added warmth should the late summer weather suddenly turn cold. And every cowboy had a slicker or oilskin raincoat rolled and tied behind his saddle. Some early slickers were constructed of canvas and painted on the outside. The slicker covered a man's legs while in the saddle and was often needed during the frequent summer rain squalls that were sometimes accompanied by intense electrical disturbances on the northern ranges.

Another difference in the dress of southern and northern cowboys was the shape of their hats. When the Texans arrived on the northern ranges they found that the wind was usually more intense and that they had difficulty keeping their wide-brimmed hats on their heads. Thus the wide-brimmed hat of the southern plains soon gave way to a narrow-brimmed one in the north. And most cowboys made a hatband of leather or braided horsehair to hold their hats tight on their heads.

The only item of wearing apparel that did not change significantly was the cowboys' boots. Northern cattlemen adopted Texas-style boots with little change. Most were handmade after the bootmakers arrived and set up their shops in Cheyenne, Billings, Miles City and the other northern cattle towns. If there was any difference in northern boots, it was in the ornamentation. Texas stars were not as common on the boots of northern cattlemen whose roots were in the north; instead they were heavily stitched with moroccan kid tops and calfskin vamps. The tops were rarely under full shinbone length of about 17 inches. This length enabled the northern cowboys to ford most of the streams and rivers without having water pour into their boots. By the late 1880s a good pair of handmade boots cost from $17 to $20. Most cowboys could afford such boots, even though the expense took a big chunk of one month's pay. A cowboy's average wage during the 1880s was $35 to $45 a month, depending upon the man's experience and ability.

During the early 1870s many Texas longhorns were trailed to Idaho, eastern Oregon, and northern Nevada. Most were destined for the region drained by the weaving Owyhee River, a 250-mile-long stream flowing northwest from northern Nevada across southwest Idaho and southeast Oregon to where its waters run into the Snake River. There, as in western Montana Territory, the demand for cattle had grown following the discovery of gold in the spring of 1863. Silver City, Idaho Territory, became a major trading center in the region. From there Con Shea and George T. Miller went to Texas in 1869 and drove a herd of longhorns back to Idaho. They were the first Texas cattle to arrive in that area. And in 1871, when many longhorns were being driven north by C. F. Coffee and other Texans, Miller and David Shirk were driving another herd of Texas cattle into Owyhee country. Shirk's reminiscences of his drives in 1871 and 1874 have been preserved. His experiences were similar to those of Coffee, Withers, and others who drove longhorns into the Northwest.[10]

The early 1870s found many longhorns growing fat on rich grasses in the valleys of the Chugwater and the Sibylee, and during the summer months in the high meadows of the Medicine Bow Mountains near Laramie and the Sierra Madre range running from southern Wyoming into northern Colorado. There were at least 100,000 cattle in southern Wyoming in 1871, although most were in small herds numbering a thousand head or less. Only two herds reportedly contained more than ten thousand head.[11] The open-range system of ranching was only in its infancy here, where cattle raisers found the buffalo grass of the plains especially appealing. Because of the dry climate and the high protein content of the slender blades, buffalo grass cured into a dry feed that stayed palatable and nutritious all winter long.

The early Wyoming cattle raisers did not take full advantage of the grasslands, however. Few were experienced stockmen. Most were men who had freighted or mined along the Sweetwater or had been merchants in the boom railroad towns of southern Wyoming. They turned to stock raising after the boom began to fade. As the longhorns were driven north, some of the Texas cowboys were induced to stay to work for the Wyoming cattle raisers. Other Texans saw the potential of the grasslands on the northern ranges and began to establish their own ranches. The Texans soon taught the lore and practices of the open-range system to the Wyoming ranchers.

By about 1875 most of the grassland of southern Wyoming had been stocked with cheap longhorns. Cattlemen were already eying the vast region of grassland over the divide of Teapot Dome, in the Powder River basin at northeastern Wyoming Territory, and even the area that is today central and eastern Montana. This country was still forbidden to the cattlemen of southern Wyoming and western Montana. It belonged to the Sioux, and the treaty of 1868 said cattlemen had to stay out. The turning

point came after the annihilation of Colonel George Armstrong Custer in
the battle of the Little Big Horn in 1876. A treaty with the Sioux and
Cheyenne, signed on September 26, 1876, at the Red Cloud Agency in
Nebraska, opened the vast region north of the Platte River and east of the
Bozeman Trail to cattle grazing, although most cattlemen waited to move
their cattle into the region until after the Indians were subdued and con-
fined to the reservations.

The mood of the Wyoming cattlemen preparing to invade eastern
and northeastern Wyoming is reflected in the following account by R. E.
Strahorn in his *Handbook of Wyoming and Guide to the Black Hills and
Big Horn Regions*, published at Cheyenne in 1877:

> . . . the Wyoming of today glows with a new life. Peace has dawned,
> so suddenly that the long fettered frontier has scarce awakened from
> its ten years of darkened dreaming. To realize that this grand area of
> nearly 100,000 square miles, crowded with all the bountiful resources
> of a coveted empire, is at once and forever emancipated from savage
> sway, may be easy in quiet New England, but not so where the keys to
> development have always been carried at the girdle of a hostile
> possessor. To define the thrill which permeates the frame of the first
> herdsman who pushes his flocks northward across the Platte River at
> staunch old Fort Fetterman, and sets his feet firmly upon 'Indian
> ground' might also be a prosy task in the East, but in the valleys of
> Wyoming it will meet an echoing tingle never to be forgotten.

To the north in western Montana, cattle raisers began to move east from
the Musselshell to look over the "empire" of grass that stretched as far
east as the eye could see. These men encountered buffalo hunters who were
already in the region killing the shaggies for their hides. The cattlemen did
not mind—the buffalo ate the grass they wanted for their cattle. And by
1883, the buffalo hunters had done their job on the northern plains as
thoroughly as the job had been done on the southern plains a decade
earlier. Buffalo hunting, as an occupation, came to an end in the United
States.

The opening of the new ranges in the north during the late 1870s
could not have come at a more opportune time. Cattlemen on the southern
plains were being forced farther west by the settlement of Texas and
Kansas. Since many cattlemen had been grazing their cattle on public
lands in these states, they had no choice but to move their ranching operations elsewhere as settlers moved onto their grazing lands. Some cattlemen
began eying the Texas panhandle. Charles Goodnight was the first rancher
to move into that region in 1876, and others followed. And cattlemen who

had earlier considered much of Arizona as worthless for cattle raising began to eye the area again. What is now Arizona had been included in the Territory of New Mexico until early 1863, when Arizona Territory was organized. Still other cattlemen began to move from Texas northward into what was then western Indian Territory, now Oklahoma, especially after cattle prices began to recover from the economic panic of 1873.

For many Texas cattlemen the northern ranges had special appeal. Until the late 1870s, most of these Texans had viewed the northern ranges only as a marketplace for their longhorns. Some of them went north to settle, but most remained in the south. Now the opening of large portions of Wyoming, Montana, and western Dakota territories became very attractive, especially to the Texans who had been grazing their cattle on public lands. The region was generally free of settlers, and in spite of the severe winters, many Texans began to leave their old ranges in the south to begin anew in the north. They took their customs, techniques, longhorns, cow ponies, and saddles with them.

The saddles used by the Texans were far better for working cattle than the hornless eastern rigs used by many northern cattle raisers. These eastern saddles—designed solely for riding—had been brought west over

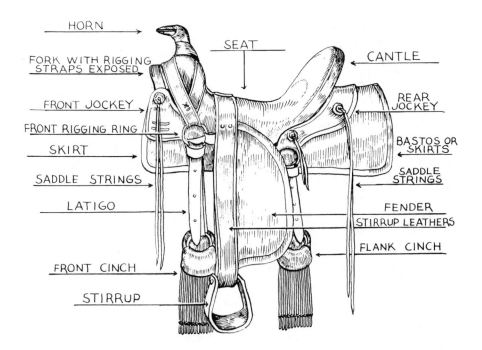

WESTERN SADDLE

the Oregon Trail. A few northern cattle raisers used old Spanish saddles. They had been brought from California to Oregon and then found their way east onto the northern ranges. They were better than the eastern rigs for working cattle, but the saddles from Texas were even better. The Texans coming north used the light Texas saddle developed in the 1850s or a modified Mexican-style *mochila* saddle.

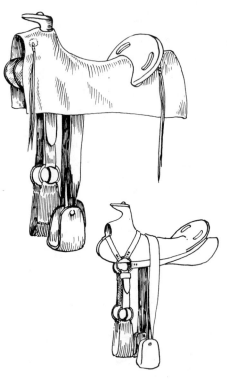

The light Texas saddle weighed only twelve or thirteen pounds. As has already been detailed (page 115), it had sidebars lined with square leather inner skirts and short outer skirts back of the cantle. The seat of rawhide was stitched on the tree. The stirrups were wide—the "box-car" variety. The Mexican saddle, the one brought north by perhaps a majority of the Texans, had the heavy Mexican tree with narrow straps, a horn smaller than in other Mexican saddles of the day, and a *mochila* covering. It was called a Mother Hubbard. The saddle, first developed about 1868, was similar to the earlier *mochila* saddle used in California and Texas, but the *mochila* was attached to the tree in the Mother Hubbard variation and could not be removed.

MEXICAN SADDLE WITH AND WITHOUT
MOCHILA COVERING

The saddle was literally one piece. On both saddles tie strings began to appear. These enabled the cowboys to carry extra equipment tied to their saddles.

The descriptions of early stock saddles may suggest that there were many different types of saddles. Stock saddles did vary in size, in height and angles of the horn and cantle, in whether the seat was short or long, wide or narrow, whether the horn was vertical or sloped upward at an angle, whether the stirrups were large or small, whether the saddle was held on the horse by one cinch or two, where the cinch(es) and rigging rings were located. And there were many other incidental details that made one saddle seem different from another. But fundamentally all stock saddles were and still are the same. And if a nineteenth-century cowboy spent time in any saddle, the chances were good that he would soon believe his saddle was the best—until he could afford to buy another. Nearly all stock saddles used by cowboys "gradually acquired tiny humps and hollows that registered with his anatomy, and induced both comfort and security of seat. These little mouldings, which suited well the owner, would often fight the contour of a stranger's legs."[12]

The location of a cinch and whether there was one or two depended upon the working habits of the cowboy in the saddle. The single-rigged or one-cinch saddle evolved directly from the vaquero's saddle in Mexico. The cinch usually was placed directly under the pommel. But when the vaquero became a roper the cinch was moved under the stirrup leathers or centered under the saddle. A cinch in such a position is known as a centerfire rig. And the single cinch was fine for the vaquero who used a long rope and then secured it quickly around the saddlehorn. But most Texas cowboys preferred a shorter rope tied to the saddlehorn. This method placed more strain on the saddle and resulted in the use of two cinches—one at the front of the saddle, the other at the rear.

What became known as the "plains saddle" had double rigging—two cinches. This saddle appeared by the middle 1870s. The half-seat and cantle were covered by one piece of leather. There were full skirts fully lined with sheepskin, and the rigging was stronger than that of most saddles of the day. The stirrups were narrow. The cantle cover was carried on back to form a projecting cantle rim that became known as the Cheyenne roll. The wooden saddlehorn was lower and sturdier than the Texas saddlehorn, and it was covered by leather, giving it added strength. The earliest plains saddle had caused problems. The tree was long, 15 to 17 inches. The men who built these saddles probably reasoned that the added length would provide extra leverage and in turn be better for heavy roping. The saddle did provide these advantages, but it also caused kidney sores on horses and chaffed the seats and legs of the cowboys using them.

OX BOW

STEEL

BRONCO

BOX

VISALIA

OLD SPANISH
SOLID WOOD

THIS UNIDENTIFIED SADDLEMAKER
plied his trade somewhere in Kansas in the 1870s. The saddle (inset)
was manufactured at Halsted, Kansas, in the early 1880s and shows much
of the gear used by a plains cowboy. Six-gun, spurs, quirt, and leggings
were part of the cowboy "uniform."

These problems, however, were corrected by about 1883. Much of the
credit for the development of the plains saddle goes to John S. and Gilbert
M. Collins, two brothers who owned saddlemaking shops in Cheyenne,
Omaha, Billings, and Great Falls during the late nineteenth century.[13]

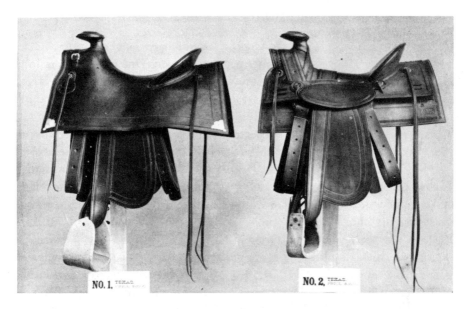

THESE TEXAS-STYLE SADDLES
were manufactured by Frank Meanea of Cheyenne,
with his own modifications. The one on the left, with the *mochila*
attached to the tree, is called a "Mother Hubbard." The saddle
on the right came to be known as a "Cheyenne saddle." Meanea
retained the essential features of the Texas saddle—double rigging,
with the front rigging straps up over the fork—but added
the Cheyenne roll cantle. He opened his saddle shop in Cheyenne in 1873
and died in 1928. The saddles sold for $35 each in the 1880s,
when this photograph was taken.

A WYOMING COWBOY WITH HIS SADDLED HORSE.

EXACTLY HOW MANY TEXANS moved to the northern ranges during the late
1870s and early 1880s is unknown, but many stayed. One of them was John
B. Kendrick, later to be governor and United States senator from
Wyoming. He drove some Texas cattle up the trail in 1879. His fine old
home, Trails End, in Sheridan, Wyoming, is now a museum.[14] Some of the
Texans may have been surprised at the large number of Oregon cattle on
the Wyoming ranges. More than 100,000 head had been moved eastward
in 1879, and nearly 200,000 in 1880, although countless thousands died
during the terrible winter of 1880–81. Blizzards swept across the plains
and temperatures reached record lows. In the spring and summer after the
great "die up," not more than 100,000 cattle were driven east from Oregon.
By then the great surplus of Oregon cattle was gone.

To restock the northern ranges, many Texas cattle were driven
north between 1881 and 1885. By then trail driving had become a
sophisticated business. Colonel Ike T. Pryor of San Antonio, whose recollections appear in *The Trail Drivers of Texas*, wrote that driving cattle
to the northern ranges "was reduced to almost a science, and large numbers
of cattle were moved at a minimum cost." To illustrate his point, Pryor
said he drove fifteen herds in 1884 from south Texas to points north of
Kansas.

It required a minimum of 165 men and about 1000 saddle horses to
move this entire drive. In other words, these cattle were driven in
droves of 3000 to each herd, with eleven men, including the boss, and
each man was furnished with six horses.

The salaries of these eleven men, including the boss, were $30.00
each for the ten men, including the cook, and $100.00 a month for the
boss. This gave an outlay of $400.00 a month, and estimating $100.00
for provisions, there was an expense of $500.00 a month to move a herd
of 3000 cattle 450 to 500 miles. Briefly speaking, in those days it was
possible to drive 3000 cattle 3000 miles for $3000.00, or in other words,
from South Texas to Montana a herd could be driven of 3000 head,
for not to exceed $3000.00. My average expense on the fifteen herds in
1884 was about $500.00 a month. The average distance traveled by
these herds was from 450 to 500 miles per month and when I had sold
and delivered all of these cattle to Montana, Dakota and Wyoming
ranchmen, I had lost 1500 head or 3 per cent.

Texas cattle were not the only cattle used to restock the northern ranges.
Eastern cattle, variously called "states cattle," "barnyard stock," or "pil-
grims," were shipped west by train. Between 1882 and 1884, as many cattle
were shipped west as east. But the eastern cattle created new problems on

the northern ranges. While they were more valuable than the Texas long-horns, eastern cattle could not withstand the vicious winters. Many carried pleuropneumonia, a serious disease in eastern cattle during the 1880s. The lanky longhorns adjusted to the winters on the northern ranges much better than the eastern cattle, although by the early 1880s the business-minded cattlemen seeking to improve their product were beginning to object to the longhorn. The days of these noble Texas cattle were num-bered, even among Texas cattle raisers.

The *Cheyenne Daily Leader*, on September 30, 1881, pretty much summed up the growing belief among many cattlemen that polled or horn-less cattle were "growing in favor all over the country." The newspaper reported: "In forsaking Texans for shorthorns, the stockgrowers were influenced by two considerations; To procure a milder animal, of greater beef-making capacity, and which should avoid the objection of long horns." The newspaper's writer pointed out that longhorns were objec-tionable because they interfered in the shipping of cattle, and they "teach cattle to become quarrelsome and offensive, a fact that is well-known to all who have aught to do with cattle."

While the popularity of Texas cattle declined in the north, the popularity of other Texan things did not wane. The open-range practices first introduced by Texans in southern Wyoming rapidly spread north-ward beyond the Platte and into western Dakota and Montana territories. Granville Stuart, the early Montana cattle raiser, witnessed the arrival of the cowboy culture. He wrote many years later:

It would be impossible to make persons not present on the Montana cattle ranges realize the rapid change that took place on those ranges in two years. In 1880 the country was practically uninhabited. One could travel for miles without seeing so much as a trapper's bivouac. Thousands of buffalo darkened the rolling plains. There were deer, antelope, elk, wolves, and coyotes on every hill and in every ravine and thicket. In the whole Territory of Montana there were but two hundred and fifty thousand head of cattle, including dairy cattle and work oxen.

In the fall of 1883 there was not one buffalo remaining on the range and the antelope, elk, and deer were indeed scarce. In 1880 no one had heard tell of a cowboy in "this niche of the woods" and Charlie Russell had made no pictures of them; but in the fall of 1883 there were six hundred thousand head of cattle on the range. The cow-boy, with leather chaps, wide hats, gay handkerchiefs, clanking silver spurs, and skin fitting high heeled boots was no longer a novelty but had become an institution.[15]

As the cowboys moved north from southern Wyoming and western Nebraska, one of them, perhaps a Texan, made up a song that caught the mood of the times:

> *Good-bye, old Paint, I'm leavin' Cheyenne,*
> *Good-bye, old Paint, I'm leavin' Cheyenne,*
>
> *I'm leavin' Cheyenne, I'm off to Montan;*
> *Good-bye, old Paint, I'm leavin' Cheyenne.*
>
> *Old Paint's a good pony, he paces when he can;*
> *Good-bye, old Paint, I'm leavin' Cheyenne.*
>
> *My foot's in the stirrup, my bridle's in my hand;*
> *Good-bye, young lady, my horse he won't stand.*
>
> *Good-bye, old Paint, I'm leavin' Cheyenne;*
> *Good-bye, old Paint, I'm leavin' Cheyenne.*[16]

But not all Texas cowboys who headed north could take the cold winters. Perhaps two out of every five stayed. They were probably the ones who realized that the winter weather could never be conquered—it had to be contended with. And they were the ones who set about to make the best of things as they found them. It seems to have been a matter of attitude. This is reflected in the words of another song written by an unidentified cowboy in the early 1880s. The words go like this:

> *Oh, I am a Texas cowboy*
> *Far away from home,*
> *If ever I get back to Texas*
> *I never more will roam.*
>
> *Montana is too cold for me*
> *And the winters are too long;*
> *Before the roundups do begin*
> *Our money is all gone.*
>
> *All along the Yellowstone*
> *'Tis cold the year around;*
> *You will surely get consumption*
> *By sleeping on the ground.*
>
> *Come all you Texas cowboys*
> *And warning take from me,*

And do not go to Montana
To spend your money free.

But stay at home in Texas,
Where work lasts the year around,
And you'll never catch consumption
By sleeping on the ground.[17]

For a time the northern ranges provided the cattleman with everything his frontier institution required: good grass, water, a natural increase in herds, and good prices for his cattle at accessible markets. The cattleman's successes did not go unnoticed in the East. The unparalleled industrial growth of the United States following the Civil War had created many men of wealth, especially in the Northeast. Some of these men were shrewd, ruthless speculators who made their fortunes by exploiting others. Many had made money in mining or railroading in the West. By 1880 the plains seemed to be the new promised land, and numerous investors, hearing of the fortunes being made in cattle raising, were eager to invest their ready capital in cattle.

Eastern newspaper reporters and writers in livestock journals had painted rosy pictures of the cattleman's successes on the northern ranges. Wealthy eastern businessmen and their counterparts in England and Scotland soon invested large sums of money in cattle companies organized in the East. They were attracted by accounts like the following one that appeared in *Breeder's Gazette*, published in Chicago on September 27, 1883. The story had been taken from a Denver newspaper:

A good sized steer when it is fit for the butcher market will bring from $45 to $60. The same animal at its birth was worth but $5.00. He has run on the plains and cropped the grass from the public domain for four or five years, and now, with scarcely any expense to his owner, is worth forty dollars more than when he started on his pilgrimage. A thousand of these animals are kept nearly as cheaply as a single one, so with a thousand as a starter and with an investment of but $5,000 in the start, in four years the stock raiser has made from $40,000 to $45,000. Allow $5,000 for his current expenses which he has been going on and he still has $35,000 and even $45,000 for a net profit. That is all there is of the problem and that is why our cattlemen grow rich.[18]

On the basis of such accounts eastern money poured into the West like water, and the capitalists came west not on horseback but in their Pullman cars decorated in plush red velvet and stocked with wine, Havana cigars, and the other trappings of the wealthy easterner. One of the better-known cattlemen to take advantage of outside capital was Alexander Hamilton Swan, a native of Pennsylvania. He came west as a young man and lived in Ohio and Iowa before moving farther west. In 1873, Swan and his brothers formed a cattle company, but it soon failed as a result of severe winter weather. In 1883, he started his own company with $3,750,000 in Scottish capital. The firm was called the Swan Land and Cattle Company, Ltd. The Scottish investors actually put up $2½ million. They later claimed that they had paid $800,000 too much, since the price was based upon 89,167 head of cattle while there were really only sixty thousand, and on 22,826 head of calves when the actual number was 1,600. Obviously, Swan was a shrewd businessman. He had sought this large amount of capital in order to buy land. At one point the company owned or controlled 600,000 acres reaching from Ogallala, Nebraska, to Fort Steele, Wyoming, and from the east–west Union Pacific tracks north to the Platte River. Swan helped to build stockyards at Council Bluffs, Iowa, and at Omaha, Nebraska.

John Clay, in his book *My Life on the Range*, described Alexander Swan as

> about six feet and an inch, and wherever he went he made an imposing figure. His face was close shaven, he had a keen eye, a Duke of Wellington nose, and gold teeth. While his manner was casual it was magnetic and he had a great following. At Cheyenne groups of men sat around him in his office and worshipped at his feet. In Chicago he was courted by bankers, commission men, breeders of fine cattle; in fact, all classes of people in the livestock business. The mercantile agencies rated him at a million, while I doubt, so far as the range is concerned, if he ever owned an honest dollar.

But Swan and many other cattlemen on the northern plains suffered a severe setback in the terrible blizzards of 1886 and 1887. Heavy snow and very cold temperatures reduced Swan's herds from 113,000 to 57,000 head, and in May of 1887, the almost legendary company went into receivership. Swan's own fortune was lost in the bankruptcy proceedings. After the company was reorganized, John Clay took over the management of Swan Land and Cattle Company and operated it on a reduced but successful basis. The ranch headquarters, built in 1876, may still be visited at Chugwater in southeastern Wyoming.

The terrible winter storms of late 1886 and early 1887 brought an end to the era of the open range and cattle kings on the northern plains. The vicious weather plus the overstocking of the ranges by men greedy for profits contributed to the collapse of many cattle empires. The problems of the cattlemen were compounded in many areas by the arrival of settlers. The railroad that brought eastern capital to the West also brought settlers who sought to make their homes close to the path of the iron horses, their link with eastern civilization. The Democratic administration in Washington in 1886 promised new homes in the West for poor men and declared that the farmer's frontier had *not* been stopped by what many eastern politicians called the "cattle barons" in the West. History began to repeat itself as grangers moved onto the northern ranges to claim their homesteads or to buy railroad land, just as they had done in Kansas.

So the age of the cattle kings and the open range on the northern plains gradually came to an end. But ranching would continue. Those men who would succeed in cattle raising turned to agriculture for help. They raised hay to feed their cattle during the winter months. The successful ranchers were those who also used care and sound business methods in the raising of cattle.

CHAPTER 12

Ranch House Culture

*Ownership of thousands of acres of land and herds of
cattle could well cause a man to want to build for the ages.
Perhaps his empire could pass from generation to generation, with his initial success buttressing a dynasty of
ranchers bearing the family name.*

—LEWIS ELDON ATHERTON[1]

EASTERN politicians of the late nineteenth century labeled the
western cattleman a "cattle baron" and accused him of blocking westward
settlement. Many settlers in the West did the same, but western politicians
—at least those with their roots in the cow country—defended the cattleman by saying he was simply a businessman trying to protect what was
rightfully his. Unfortunately, the writers of the period who had the opportunity to seek out the truth chose instead to write about the cattleman's
hired man on horseback—the cowboy. As a result, the true picture of the
cattleman of the late nineteenth century and his contributions have until
recently been overshadowed by the exploits—real and imagined—of the
cowboy.

Why nineteenth-century eastern writers chose generally to ignore the
cattleman is unknown. It may have been that these representatives of
magazines and newspapers viewed the cattleman as a businessman, an occupation that was commonplace in the booming industrial East. Then too,
the cattleman was often not as colorful as the cowboy seemed to be. A
few "cattle barons"—men like Captain Richard King and Abel Head
"Shanghai" Pierce—*were* colorful, and they did attract the attention of
some writers.

Captain Richard King, for instance, often traveled with his family
from their south Texas ranch to San Antonio, where they stayed in the
gracious Menger Hotel and usually occupied the same rooms. On one oc-

casion, Captain King arrived just ahead of his family and headed for the bar to have a drink. When he went upstairs, Mrs. King complained that she had ordered water for the pitcher on her washstand, and the water had not been delivered. King picked up the pitcher, walked to the balcony overlooking the lobby, and hurled the pitcher to the marble floor below, where it smashed into many pieces. He then called out to the desk clerk: "If we can't get any water up here, we don't need a pitcher." Several pitchers of cool water were quickly dispatched.[2]

And then there was the time when "Shanghai" Pierce arrived at a hotel in Hot Springs, Arkansas, without a reservation. After being told several times there was no room available, Pierce, bellowing in his out-of-doors voice, asked the manager if the hotel was for sale. The manager said he owned a half-interest and would sell it for $15,000. Without batting an eye, Pierce wrote out a check for that amount and went upstairs to one of *his* rooms.[3]

But such extravagant behavior was by no means typical among the majority of early Texas cattlemen, who tended to be rather conservative in their actions, especially off the range or trail. And eastern writers made little effort to understand them or their contributions. The writers failed to acknowledge, for example, that it was the cattleman who first settled many unpopulated regions and brought his own form of law and order. Instead the men with the pens in their hands saw the cowboy as the dominant and more colorful figure and missed the point that it was the cattlemen who were responsible for the cowboy's environment.

To understand the culture of the nineteenth-century cattleman, one must realize that the difference between cowboy and cattleman did not begin to emerge until good northern markets opened in Kansas following the Civil War. It was then that Texas cattle raisers began hiring extra young men to work their cattle on the open ranges and to round up and drive the mossy-horns to the Kansas railhead towns. It was then too, that the label "cowboy" became firmly attached to the hired man on horseback. At the same time, the man who owned the cattle became known as a "cowman" and, in time, "cattleman," and a distinct culture began to emerge from the ranch house, a culture that included much of the flavor of the business world in the East.

Most of these early cattlemen were self-reliant. Although of course no two were identical, most did have one thing in common—they started out with very little and stuck it out until they made good. Joseph McCoy, who knew many Texas cattlemen during the late 1860s and early 1870s, observed that the successful cattlemen of that period had received a thorough drilling in adversity during their youth. McCoy noted that they learned not only the "intrinsic value of a dollar but how to make and take care of one." These kind of men, wrote McCoy, "invariably make earth's most successful business men."[4]

One such Texan was Dan Waggoner, born in Tennessee in 1828. He moved to Texas with his family in the early 1840s. Dan's father was of German descent, and before his father's death in 1848, young Dan learned thrift and economy. In 1850, Dan Waggoner set out on his own with a wife and 242 longhorns. He established a ranch along Denton Creek in what is today Wise County in north-central Texas. The following year he purchased 15,000 acres near Cactus Hill on the Trinity River about 17 miles from where Decatur, Texas, stands today. Gradually he built his herd of Texas cattle, although Indians frequently ran off his stock. When the Civil War ended, Waggoner began branding his cattle with three D's in reverse, a brand easy to recognize but difficult to change. And by 1869 he was driving his longhorns north to Kansas, where he began to realize a good profit. As his wealth increased, Waggoner bought more land and expanded his ranch into Wilbarger, Foard, Baylor, Archer, and Knox counties in Texas. Waggoner once said that a cowman could afford neither to own nor to lease the land upon which his cattle ranged, but he bought land to protect his interests as settlers moved into north-central Texas. By 1895, Waggoner was a wealthy man with 45,000 cattle, 2,500 horses, 100,000 acres of deeded land purchased from the state of Texas, and 500,000 acres near Fort Sill, Indian Territory, just across the Red River to the north, leased from the government. When Dan Waggoner died in 1904, his ranch covered more than a million acres.[5]

Many Texas cowmen, including Waggoner, who prospered from the trail drives to Kansas invested some or all of their profits in land, in more cattle, and in their ranch houses. Some of these men constructed new ranch houses near their old ones and turned their former homes into storage buildings or bunkhouses. Cattlemen who were married usually were the first to build new houses to make life easier for their wives. Dan Waggoner built a castlelike stone house east of Decatur in the late 1870s, but it was the exception to the rule. Most new ranch houses were one-story and of wood frame or adobe construction. By today's standards most of these houses were rather primitive in appearance and comfort. Many had long verandas or porches, usually on the south, to catch the sun in the winter and the breeze in the summer, but the low roofs provided shade from the heat too. Inside one might find a parlor, dining room, large kitchen, the bedrooms (as many as needed), and perhaps a small room used by the cattleman as an office. Sometimes the office had an outside door for visitors.

The furnishings of these Texas ranch houses of the late 1870s might include a few pieces of furniture handed down to the cattleman and his wife by their parents. Store-bought furniture was becoming commonplace

THE LONE CONE RANCH NEAR TELLURIDE, COLORADO,
in the late 1870s or early 1880s. The rancher's wife is seated
near the ranchhouse door. To the left, holding the horses,
are her two daughters, identified only as Dolly and Kate.

THE SIMPLE HEADQUARTERS OF THE GRIMES RANCH
in Clark County, Kansas, in 1899. At left is a rather crude
but efficient horse corral, and at right are the ranch buildings. While some
cattlemen, particularly on the northern plains, had elaborate layouts,
this is typical of the facilities on the southern plains
in the 1880s and '90s.

by this time. The furniture was freighted to the ranch from stores in Fort Worth or San Antonio or elsewhere. And by the late 1870s many ranch houses sported lace curtains on the parlor windows, a sure sign of a woman in the house. The houses were lighted at night by candles or coal oil—kerosene—lamps. A few kitchens had hay-burning stoves, with spring-backed cylinders which were filled with hay. The springs pushed the hay into the fire until the cylinder magazine was empty. Meanwhile the other cylinder magazine was loaded and ready to go. But these hay-burners were not as common as wood-burning stoves. And the fireplace was still the reliable standby in most ranch houses, providing not only heat during the winter but an open fire for cooking.

While only sketchy details of a Texas cattleman's ranch house routine exist for the late 1870s, a reasonably accurate picture can be pieced together from fragments of letters, records, and recollections left by different cattlemen. The routine in a ranch house varied from day to day, week to week, and month to month, depending upon the ranching activities. But on most days at home, the cattleman was up early, usually before first light. The cowboy life led by most Texas cattlemen before they became ranchers had instilled in them early rising habits. The cattleman's wife—a majority of Texas cattlemen in the 1870s seem to have been married—might get up at the same time or even earlier to prepare a large pot of hot coffee while her husband was dressing. Then while his wife began to prepare breakfast, the cattleman might walk to the bunkhouse to make certain his cowboys were up and understood their jobs for the day. Before the ranch was fenced with barbed wire, not all of the cowboys would stay in the bunkhouse. Those assigned the task of line riding would spend their nights in line shacks. Thus perhaps only part of his force would be available. Or, if the cattleman preferred to avoid excessive familiarity with his hired hands, he might have a private chat with his foreman. It depended on how the cattleman viewed his domain, whether he saw himself as a feudal overlord or simply a friendly employer.

The cattleman, if he planned to join his cowhands on the range that day or perhaps ride to town to conduct business, would then saddle his own horse in anticipation of the day's activities. The cowboys, once dressed, would also catch and saddle their horses. By then the rancher's wife would have cooked the ham or sausages or steak, gathered and cooked some eggs, baked some fresh biscuits or corn bread, and set a large table in the ranch house kitchen or dining room with iron knives and forks and heavy ironstone plates, cups, and saucers, probably white in color. The cattleman, his foreman, and the cowhands all headed for the ranch house and sat down together for breakfast. Ranch house meals were usually quiet. Once the food was served, hardly a word was spoken. And

THE RANCH HOUSE AND BUILDINGS
of the Bar CC Ranch in Ochiltree County, Texas, in the late 1880s.

A CORNER OF THE DINING ROOM
was the business office of the LS Ranch in the Texas Panhandle.
C. T. Herring owned the ranch early in this century.

AN INDIAN TERRITORY RANCH IN THE LATE 1880S.

THE PLAIN RANCH HOUSE OF C. E. DOYLE,
an early cowman in Clark County, Kansas, probably in the 1880s.
Notice his name and brands painted above the door.

when someone had taken his last bite and last gulp of hot coffee, he excused himself and went outside, perhaps for a smoke or a chew of tobacco. Leaving the table immediately after eating was a habit formed by most cattlemen and cowboys on the trail or range, where work was always waiting. There were, of course, exceptions to this rule, especially if there were guests for breakfast or for any meal. By the early 1880s, cowhands on larger ranches were fed not by the cowman's wife but by a cook.[6]

The wife's routine with domestic chores varied from day to day— there was washing, ironing, cleaning, cooking, and, in spring and summer, tending a garden. There is no question that the wives of most cattlemen contributed a great deal to their husbands ranching operations. And any examination of ranch house culture would be remiss if it did not include the story of Lizzie Johnson, cattlewoman. Her full name was Elizabeth E. Johnson, and she was born in Missouri in 1843. She moved to Hays County, Texas, soon after her father had established the Johnson Institute there in 1852. It was the first school of higher learning west of the Colorado River. Lizzie began teaching at the school when she was sixteen. Later she left to teach in schools at Manor, Lockhart, and Austin. Quietly she saved her money and added to her income by writing stories for *Frank Leslie's Magazine*. As she accumulated money, she invested it. At one point she purchased $2,500 worth of stock in the Evans, Snider, Bewell Cattle Co. of Chicago. She earned 100 percent dividends for three years straight and then sold her stock for $20,000. On June 1, 1871, she invested the money in cattle and registered her own brand (CY) in the Travis County brand book along with her mark.

Lizzie Johnson's wealth continued to grow. So did her responsibilities. In the summer of 1879, at the age of thirty-six, she married Hezkiah G. Williams, a preacher and widower with several children. She continued to teach school in Austin, write magazine articles, and invest in cattle. She maintained control over her wealth, having had her husband sign a paper agreeing that all of her property remained hers. On his own, Hezkiah entered the cattle business in 1881, but he was a poor businessman who also liked to drink, and Lizzie had to keep pulling him out of financial trouble. At least twice Lizzie and Hezkiah traveled up the Chisholm Trail to Kansas. They rode behind the herd in a buggy drawn by a team of horses. This was about 1879, and Lizzie was the first woman to drive her own herd up the trail. For several years she and her husband, after coming up the trail, spent the fall and winter months in St. Louis, where Lizzie made extra money by keeping books for other cattlemen. When she died in 1924, at the age of eighty-one (her husband had died in 1914), Lizzie Johnson's estate totaled more than $200,000, including large holdings in Austin real estate.[7]

Lizzie Johnson and other Texans involved in the cattle business watched with interest as eastern and foreign capitalists invested in cattle ranches in Texas, Kansas, and portions of Nebraska, Colorado, and Wyoming during the late 1870s. Some of the easterners were undoubtedly attracted to ranching by the growing romance associated with the West, and cattle raising in particular. Ranching offered freedom, some risks and excitement, hunting, wildlife, and other things linked with what was left of the fading western frontier. The country from west Texas north was, for the most part, unspoiled by the white man. The opportunity to enjoy this land was undoubtedly an attraction, but *easy money* seems to have been the primary reason for most outsiders to invest in cattle ranching. Certainly an added incentive for the Scots and Englishmen was that American beef was beginning to threaten stockraising in the British Isles. By 1881, refrigerated beef was going to England at the rate of 110 million pounds a year. American beef was selling at a lower price in England than native beef. The Scots and British wanted a piece of the American action.[8]

Events in the West had first focused eastern attention on the growing western cattle industry in the late 1860s. The long cattle drives to the railhead towns in Kansas were unusual. They were news. Men in financial circles throughout the East began to pay more attention to western cattle when they saw cattle money flowing through the banks. The *National Live Stock Journal* reported in May 1871 that Kansas City banks had handled $3 million of cattle money in 1870, while $500,000 had passed through the banks at Omaha. And by 1871, Kansas City (with seven railroads) had four packing plants in operation. The stockyards there were built that year as well, along with a livestock exchange building. The development of a refrigerator car in the early 1870s also attracted attention. Within a few years other cities, including Omaha, Chicago, Wichita, Fort Worth, and St. Louis, had packing plants in operation, and names like Armour and Swift were becoming household words in the East where western beef was being enjoyed.

Books certainly had some effect on attracting attention to the cattle industry. The first book on western stock raising was Hiram Latham's *Trans-Missouri Stock Raising: The Pasture Lands of North America*, published by the Union Pacific Railroad at Omaha in 1871. The book was a collection of letters written by Latham to the *Omaha Herald*. Devised by the railroad as a promotional tool, it apparently did little to attract eastern or foreign investors to the western cattle trade. Reports of cattle losses from bad winter storms on the plains in 1872, and the economic panic of 1873, reduced the potential value of the book.

But then in 1874 came Joseph McCoy's *Historic Sketches of the*

Cattle Trade of the West and Southwest, which described not only the romantic cattle drives from Texas to Kansas and northward but the business of buying and selling cattle. As the book was being distributed, the cattle market was recovering from the panic of 1873 and cattle raising in the West again looked promising. A visitor to America, James MacDonald, may have visited with McCoy as he toured the American West soon after McCoy's work was published. MacDonald returned to the British Isles and wrote *Food from the Far West; or, American Agriculture with Special Reference to Beef Production and Importation of Dead Meat from America to Great Britain*, a book published in London and Edinburgh in 1878. The volume was widely read, and undoubtedly attracted Scots and Britishers to the American cattle business.

The year before MacDonald's book was published, John Adair became one of the first Englishmen to invest in American cattle. Educated as a diplomat, Adair preferred the world of business. In 1866 he established a brokerage house in New York City and became successful by placing British loans in America at high interest rates. About 1869 he married an attractive widow, Cornelia Wadsworth Ritchie, a member of a prominent eastern family. Both enjoyed sporting events and excitement, and in 1874 they went buffalo hunting on the plains of Kansas. Although Adair managed to shoot only his horse and no buffalo, he fell in love with the plains and within a year had moved his brokerage house to Denver. Before coming west, Adair—through one of his agents in Denver—had loaned $30,000 to Charles Goodnight, then trying ranching in Colorado. When Adair expressed an interest in cattle ranching, his agent recommended that he meet and talk with Goodnight. The two men got together, and Goodnight invited Adair and his wife to visit the Texas panhandle, where Goodnight was just starting a new ranching operation in the Palo Duro Canyon south of modern-day Amarillo.

The two men hit it off from the start, as did their wives, although they were from totally different backgrounds. Goodnight and his wife Mary Ann were plainspoken. They had experienced the hardships of frontier life, and had known bad times. In contrast, Adair was a debonair city man, and his wife, Cornelia, the daughter of a New York banking tycoon and the sister of a United States senator, was a lady of refinement. Adair agreed to invest nearly $500,000 in foreign money in Goodnight's ranching operation. The men became partners, with Goodnight agreeing to call the ranch the JA—Adair's initials—and to brand the cattle with a JA.

Goodnight began grabbing land, buying a little to gain control of a lot. He purchased only 24,000 acres of public land at 75¢ an acre, but by selecting alternate tracts he achieved control of all of Palo Duro Canyon.

The canyon was ideally suited for cattle ranching. It was well watered, with enough good grass for thousands of cattle, and beneath its rimrock the herds were sheltered from the winter blizzards sweeping down across the plains from the north. Soon the ranch headquarters was constructed; it had the size and appearance of a small frontier town. There were more than fifty buildings, including a stone house for the Adairs to use on their infrequent visits, a two-story house of logs and wood planks for the Goodnights, a large cookhouse—it was called a messhouse—plus a tin shop, blacksmith shop, and other necessary buildings for storage and to house the cowboys.

A Texas newspaper reporter who visited the ranch late in 1885 wrote:

> The mess-house is a large and very substantial structure. . . . Near this house is a dairy, where the butter is made and stored during the summer in sufficient quantities to last headquarters during the entire year. . . . A short distance from this house is the poultry yard and house where the largest and finest breeds of fowls are kept. They supply eggs by the gross for the residents of this village, and the cook who takes care of them says that at least 1000 chickens a year are appropriated for table use. . . . On the farm, some twenty miles from the headquarters . . . last year, 300 tons of hay were saved. . . . The water at this farm is strong with gypsum, very unpalatable to a stranger, and in warm weather can discount a double dose of Epsom salts. . . .[9]

Goodnight bought two thousand blooded bulls for $150,000 and began to improve the quality of his cattle. Within a few years after Goodnight and Adair became partners, they owned nearly 100,000 cattle, and John Adair cleared a profit of $512,000 from his $500,000 investment.

By then, the invasion of eastern and foreign capitalists had already occurred. It started very early in the 1880s, about the time (1881) General James S. Brisbin's book titled *The Beef Bonanza: Or, How to Get Rich on the Plains* was published in Philadelphia. Brisbin had spent twelve years in the West as a soldier. He actually knew very little about cattle raising, but wrote a superficially convincing book that was totally optimistic and uncritical about the "enormous" profits being made in cattle and sheep raising. He made wholesale borrowings from Hiram Latham's 1871 book *Trans-Missouri Stock Raising: The Pasture Lands of North America*, but his own material contains many inaccuracies. Brisbin would seem to have written the book to promote both stock raising and himself. He acted as a broker in sales of cattle and sheep ranches after the book was published.

Until now, little reference has been made to sheep and sheep ranching in the West. Certainly sheep were plentiful. Like cattle, they had been introduced by the Spanish, but as the western grasslands became overstocked with cattle *and* sheep, cattle ranchers began to object to the sheep that ate the grass the cowman wanted for their cattle. The cattlemen argued that sheep cropped the grass too short. And water holes, the cattlemen said, were often ruined by sheep. Some even claimed that cattle do not like the smell of sheep and would not cross land where sheep had grazed until the rains had washed away the sheep odor. In some areas, especially on the southern plains, there were cattlemen with deep-seated racial prejudices against the Mexican and Basque shepherds.

Cattleman John H. "Jack" Culley, onetime manager of the huge Bell Ranch in San Miguel County, New Mexico, witnessed conflicts between cowmen and sheep ranchers at first hand. In his book *Cattle, Horses & Men of the Western Range*, Culley wrote:

Certainly the prejudice against sheep among cattlemen in the early days was very strong. I think it came to us from the Texans, from whom we derived our range practice and much of our tradition. The Texan associated sheep with Mexicans, and from the day of the Alamo for many years nothing Mexican looked good to the Texans. Furthermore, with the exception of certain localities controlled at an earlier date by Spanish-Americans who owned large herds of sheep, and the Mormon territory, practically the whole range country owed its early permanent settlement and development to the cowman. . . .The cowman felt he had a right to call the country a cattle country and to regard the sheepmen as intruders. Irritation was increased by the fact that just when the cattlemen could believe their long continued efforts had succeeded in stabilizing the livestock business of the range country, sheep from California and Oregon were poured in on them in hordes. It spelled chaos—and war.

James Brisbin, in his book *The Beef Bonanza*, does not allude to conflicts between cattlemen and sheepmen. The serious conflicts were yet to develop, since the overstocking of the plains was only beginning. He did, however, make sheep ranching sound appealing by quoting numerous success stories. His stories relating to cattle ranching, however, dwarfed those of sheep. The accounts of successes in cattle ranching were designed to interest large and small investors alike. For the small investor, Brisbin quoted J. L. Brush of Weld County, Colorado, as saying: "I commenced eight years ago [probably early 1870s] with a capital of $400, and I now own, as a result of the increase and my own labor, 900 head of fine cattle, besides having made considerable investments in lands from money taken from the herd. I think the average profit on capital invested in cattle will not fall short of 40 per cent per annum over and above all expenses."[10] And there were other, similar stories for the small investor.

For those with big money, Brisbin wrote that General R. A. Cameron, another Colorado rancher, had a herd of five thousand cattle. Brisbin pointed out that the herd required

about eight herders, at an expense of $900 per annum for two, and $600 each per annum for six, including their food; total, $5,400. Allowing $2,100 for incidental expenses, including teams, horses, saddles, and shanties for the men, the grand expense would be $7,500, or $1.50 per head. Again, allowing one year for breeding, and four years for the growth of the calf, a full-grown, four-year-old steer, worth $20.00 to $30.00, would cost the breeder $7.50. A Texas yearling can be bought for from $7.00 to $10.00; a two-year-old from $12.00 to $15.00; and a cow for from $15.00 to $25.00. The difference is partly in quality but more in the time and place of purchase. New stock, just driven in, is always the lowest priced. A two-year-old heifer brought from Iowa or Missouri will bring $35.00, and the same grade of cows from $45.00 to $55.00. Excellent milkers will bring even more; a two-year-old Durham bull, three-fourths thoroughbred, ranges from $60.00 to $75.00, and a full-grown thoroughbred will bring from $200 to $500. In cattle-raising in Colorado, General Cameron puts the profits at 50 to 55 per cent per annum on the capital invested, over and above all expenses and losses of every kind.[11]

Such accounts—most related experiences of the late 1870s and early 1880s— could not help but attract attention in the East. Brisbin's book was widely circulated and drew more easterners and foreigners to the West. Coming from New York, Boston, Philadelphia, from Scotland and Britain, the wealthy newcomers brought their expensive tastes and ways to the cow country. Many of the new ranchers of the late 1870s and early 1880s had been educated in Ivy League schools. Diplomas from Dartmouth, Princeton, Yale, Columbia, and Harvard were not uncommon on ranch house walls. And from Texas northward into Montana a new cattle aristocracy developed.

The wealthy newcomers were not as evident in Texas and the Southwest, where cattle ranching had existed for many years. Cattlemen there remembered the bad years and tended to be careful with their growing wealth and conservative in their way of life. The new culture blossomed in all its glory in the more recently opened range country to the north where cattlemen had known only prosperity. It was particularly evident in Cheyenne, the city closest to the newly purchased ranches in Wyoming Territory and western Nebraska and Dakota Territory. The newcomers, seeking the companionship of others with the same education, upbringing, and wealth, began to congregate in Cheyenne. In June of 1880, twelve of these eastern-bred cattlemen, all members of the Wyoming Stock Growers' Association, organized what they called the Cactus Club. But they found Cheyenne's three major hotels—the Railroad House, the Inter-Ocean, and Tim Dyer's—lacking the creature comforts they desired, and by the summer of 1881 they had constructed a three-story mansard-roofed brick and wood building, with hardwood floors and thick carpets, at a cost of $25,000. It became known as the Cheyenne Club.

The facilities included a dining room, reading room, and billiard room on the first floor, six sleeping rooms upstairs, and a kitchen and wine room in the basement. Trained servants were brought from the East to wait on the members. The best liquors money could buy were shipped by train to Cheyenne, along with all sorts of delicacies to please the tastes of the wealthy cattlemen. The racks in the reading room contained the latest copies of *Harper's Weekly* and major eastern newspapers, including the New York *Tribune* and the Boston *Sunday Herald-Traveler*. Here and there were, naturally enough, copies of livestock journals, including the *Breeder's Gazette* published in Chicago.

The walls of the Cheyenne Club were decorated with many fine paintings by such well-known artists as Albert Bierstadt and Paul Potter, a seventeenth-century Dutch artist. The paintings reflected the tastes and upbringing of the members, although Potter's painting of a cow and bull became the center of a minor ruckus: Cattleman John Coble, who was connected with the Two Bar Ranch at Rock River, Wyoming, pulled his revolver and shot holes in the leg of the bull in the painting. Coble, who had been drinking, was suspended from membership in the club. He later claimed that he shot at the painting because it was a travesty on purebred stock. The painting ended up in the Wyoming State Museum at Cheyenne.

Coble was not the only cattleman expelled from the Cheyenne Club for offenses against decorum. Harry Oelrichs, whose imported sixteen-passenger four-horse coach (drag) with seats inside and on top was often parked outside the club, lost his membership for kicking a servant down the stairs—a most palpable violation of club rules. The club's by-laws formally spelled out the grounds for expulsion, which included:

Drunkenness within the precincts of the club to a degree which shall be offensive to members or injurious to the standing of the club.
Use of profanity or obscenity.
A blow struck in a quarrel within the precincts of the club.
Cheating at cards or any game in the club house.

The Cheyenne Club had other, general rules that reflected the cultural influences brought west by the new breed of educated and wealthy cattlemen. They included:

> Smoking of pipes will not be permitted in any of the public rooms of the club house.
>
> No wines or liquors or mineral waters may be served in the reading rooms.
>
> All games may be played in the rooms of the club house appropriate to the purpose, but no game shall be played for a money stake. No game shall be played on Sunday.[12]

Limited by charter to only two hundred members, the Cheyenne Club was exclusive. For nearly a dozen years its members were the social leaders in Cheyenne. Yet the club was not restricted to cattlemen with an eastern upbringing. Men who had never gone to college were members. Being a wealthy cattleman seems to have been the major consideration for membership.

Dressing in tuxedos for dinner was not uncommon, and the club was, as John Clay later wrote, "a cosmopolitan place." The new culture must have rubbed off on many a self-made cattleman. Many years after the club faded into history, Clay wrote: "Under its roof reticent Britisher, cautious Scot, exuberant Irishman, careful Yankee, confident Bostonian, worldly New Yorker, chivalrous Southerner and delightful Canadian all found a welcome home." Clay, an educated Scotsman, protected British investors in American cattle ranching for many years. He served as president of the Wyoming Stock Growers' Association and watched the Cheyenne Club grow during its early years. He described it as a "natural development." Clay added:

> While it was intended as a purely social home for the residents and non-residents, it became really the business center also. In the old Borderland we used to slip into a public house, old and dingy, and seal a bargain with a draw of 'Scotch,' and so in the above well furnished cafe many a bottle of 'Phiz' paved the way for a big trade. For herds of cattle were tossed about in the most reckless way. The year 1882 saw cowpunching in all its glory with a color of carmine around it. It was fashionable. The hunter for big game from European shores had told the wondrous tale of free grass and fat beef, or buffalo, elk and antelope, of a wild, free life with little restraint, of invigorating days under the shadows of mountains that almost matched the Alps, of champagne air that was a tonic to body and soul; and dangling before

SIXTEENTH STREET IN CHEYENNE,
Wyoming Territory, in 1868.

THE CHEYENNE CLUB.

CHARLES GOODNIGHT
late in life.

BY THE END OF THE 1880s,
many ranch managers were using a buckboard to tour their ranches. This
photograph was taken in Texas around the turn of the century by Erwin Smith.

them, as a result of these charming surroundings, was wealth and the ease and dignity that comes with it.[13]

The Cheyenne Club was without a doubt the most exclusive club in the cattle country during the 1880s, but it was not the only club where cattlemen could relax or conduct business. In 1885 a number of cattlemen, including a few who were members of the Cheyenne Club, established a club in Laramie, about 60 miles northwest of Cheyenne. But it never had the flair of the Cheyenne Club. Perhaps the closest rival was the Denver Club, housed in a large brownstone building on 17th Street in Denver. In 1885 an exclusive club was formed in Helena, Montana, but its membership included wealthy businessmen, mine owners, and operators as well as cattlemen. In time other clubs appeared in Kansas City, Fort Worth, and elsewhere, but none ever matched the Cheyenne Club, not even the famous Saddle and Sirloin Club later established in Chicago.

The arrival of the new culture on the plains inspired many wealthy cattlemen to hire ranch managers, men to administer the ranching operations. Having a manager enabled the owner to live a gracious life in the city, to travel, and to be free from the day-to-day problems of running a large ranch. Many cattlemen established homes in cities like Denver, Fort Worth, Kansas City, and Cheyenne, where they could enjoy the creature comforts of life yet be reasonably close to their cattle domains. By 1884, Cheyenne, population seven thousand, was credited with being the wealthiest city per capita in the world because of the permanent homes built there by many cattlemen.

Ferguson Avenue, now Carey Avenue, with its beautiful homes, large grassy lawns, shrubbery, and low iron fences, was known as "cattleman's row" in Cheyenne. Behind the large houses in numerous styles—there was everything from an Old English country house to a French villa—were coach houses or well-built barns to shelter the fine horses and carriages, phaetons, road wagons, and even a few buckboards. Several of the houses were designed by George Rainsford of New York City, said to have possessed "the best knowledge of horse breeding, the best sense of architectural proportion and the best command of profanity" in Wyoming Territory.

There is no question that the eastern culture influenced the self-made cattleman, especially on the northern plains, but it never really eliminated the western flavor of life, nor did it completely change the old-time cattleman. Most self-made cattlemen seem to have taken what they wanted from the eastern culture and rejected the rest.

An interesting story is told by Agnes Wright Spring in her delightful book *Cow Country Legacies*. It is about E. W. Whitcomb, who came west in the 1850s and started ranching on Chugwater Creek early in the 1860s.

Whitcomb married a Sioux Indian woman. In time, he became wealthy from ranching and built a large brick house several miles outside Cheyenne. As the area became settled and eastern culture arrived, his wife was still wearing moccasins and a blanket over her head and shoulders. Whitcomb gave his wife the choice of returning to her people on the reservation with a large number of ponies for security, or staying, as he hoped she would, and changing her Indian ways.

Mrs. Whitcomb decided to return to her people. Her husband gave her the promised horses and supplies, and she left. That night in camp, however, her Indian friends encouraged her to go back to her husband. In the morning she did, and she agreed to change her ways. Her husband soon built a large house for his wife on "cattlemen's row" in Cheyenne, but always kept a tepee in the front yard to humor his wife and her relatives. Agnes Wright Spring noted that Mrs. Whitcomb became one of the most gracious women in Wyoming, and she "kept the fine house according to the white housekeeper's standards."[14]

With wives hard to find during the early years, it was not uncommon for cattlemen to marry Indian women, especially on the northern plains. A few of them considered such alliances as nothing more than conveniences for sex, cooking, and housekeeping; when eastern civilization arrived, these men usually terminated their marriages out of fear that they would suffer socially or in business. But most cattlemen with Indian wives were faithful, regardless of consequences. Granville Stuart, the early Montana cattleman, remained loyal to his Indian wife, Aubony—she was often called Ellen—who bore him nine children. And John W. Prowers, an early Colorado cowman, remained married to Amache Ochinee, a daughter of the Cheyenne chief Ochinee. They were married in 1861. She wore her hair in braids throughout her life. She learned to speak English only after many years of marriage, but preferred to speak in her tribal tongue at home.

Most ranchers—except for those from the South who were steeped in the antebellum plantation tradition—preferred wives, whether white or Indian, of an independent nature who could take care of themselves. Most white wives came from the same social stratum as their husbands. This contributed to the stability of ranch marriages, in which family life became the center of social and economic activities. Some ranchers said they wanted wives with "spunk." It was not uncommon for wives to be actively involved in their husband's businesses. Eula Kendrick, wife of John B. Kendrick, kept the ranch records and handled much of the business correspondence on their huge ranch near Sheridan, Wyoming. She also accompanied him on business trips to distant cities.

The influence of women on both the self-made cattlemen and the wealthy new ranchers from the East was significant. The wives of the successful cattlemen had servants to maintain their city houses. This gave the women much time for social and cultural activities, including art lessons, reading, and especially music. Fiddles or violins were quite common throughout the cattle country from the earliest days. But as the cattlemen prospered and as eastern culture arrived, so did more sophisticated musical instruments, including pianos and pump organs. The first piano in Wyoming Territory was freighted across the plains by ox team from Missouri in 1864. It was owned by Bill Carter, an early cattleman, sutler at Fort Bridger, and judge. Many other pianos were in evidence in ranch houses by the late 1870s.

Moreton Frewen, who built one of the most elaborate ranch houses on the northern plains, had a piano shipped by railroad from the East to Rock Creek station more than 200 miles from his ranch, which was located on the Middle Fork of Powder River east of modern Kaycee, Wyoming. The piano was then freighted overland by wagon to his thirty-six-room ranch house constructed on high ground above a bend in the river. The piano was another touch of culture in a drawing room that was already lined with books. The piano was delivered in 1879, not quite two years before Frewen went to New York City to marry Miss Clara Jerome, sister of Jennie Jerome, who became Lady Randolph Churchill, mother of Sir Winston Churchill.

Perhaps the most prominent name closely linked to the cattleman's culture of the late nineteenth century is that of Theodore Roosevelt. In 1884, Roosevelt established two ranches in the Badlands of Dakota Territory. The future President of the United States intended to make ranching his regular business, but his coming west was something of a retreat from painful memories and political defeat in the East. Roosevelt's political hopes had vanished with the presidential nomination of James G. Blaine, a man Roosevelt bitterly opposed, and only a few months before heading west, Roosevelt's wife of four years died in childbirth. Within hours his mother had died too.

Roosevelt gave his all to ranching, and the life apparently agreed with him. Years later he wrote:

No life can be pleasanter than life during the months of fall on a ranch in the northern cattle country. The weather is cool; in the evenings and on the rare rainy days we are glad to sit by the great fireplace, with its roaring cottonwood logs. But on most days not a cloud dims the serene splendor of the sky; and the fresh pure air is clear with the wonderful clearness of the high plains. We are in the saddle from morning to night.

The long, low, roomy ranch-house, of clean hewed logs, is as comfortable as it is bare and plain. We fare simply but well; for the wife of my foreman makes excellent bread and cake, and there are plenty of potatoes grown in the forlorn little garden-patch on the bottom. We also have jellies and jams, made from wild plums and buffalo berries; and all the milk we can drink. For meat, we depend on our rifles; and, with an occasional interlude of ducks or prairie-chickens, the mainstay of each meal is venison—roasted, broiled, or fried.[15]

For many easterners, Roosevelt made cattle ranching in the West fashionable during the 1880s, especially after he beat up a bully in a hotel in Mingusville and tracked down a band of badmen who had stolen a boat from one of his ranches. He made ranching seem something special. But after three years of ranching in Dakota Territory, Roosevelt gave it up and returned east a refreshed and renewed man, ready to pursue a career in politics. Before that long career would take him to the White House, Roosevelt took time to write about his ranching experiences. In 1888, about a year after the terrible winter of 1886–1887 that ruined many a cattleman on the northern ranges, Roosevelt wrote what might be described as the epitaph of the cattle king and his culture:

The best days of ranching are over. . . . The great free ranches, with their barbarous, picturesque, and curiously fascinating surroundings, mark a primitive stage of existence as surely as do the great tracts of primeval forests, and like the latter must pass away before the onward march of our people; and we who have felt the charm of the life, and have exulted in its abounding vigor and its bold, restless freedom, will not only regret its passing for our own sakes only, but must also feel real sorrow that those who come after us are not to see, as we have seen, what is perhaps the pleasantest, healthiest, and most exciting phase of American existence.[16]

CHAPTER 13

Bunkhouse Culture

You never saw an old cowpuncher. *
They were scarce as hen's teeth.
Where they went to, heaven only knows.

—JOHN CLAY[1]

THE cowboy who rode north from Texas during the years following the Civil War was essentially a creature of circumstance. He was colorful because he was not typical. To the easterner unfamiliar with life in the West, the cowboy was someone new and unusual. He performed most of his daily work from the back of a cow pony. Armed to the teeth, he drove herds of cantankerous longhorns hundreds of miles up the trail to Kansas and beyond. The cowboy's hair was long, and his dress was different. His large-brimmed hat made him stand out. His unusual working tools were foreign to most easterners, as were the Spanish words he occasionally uttered. All these things made the cowboy a romantic figure in the eyes of people in the East.

The occupation of the cowboy in this hemisphere was already more than three centuries old when eastern writers discovered the man on horseback during the years following the Civil War. It was the long cattle drives from Texas to Kansas that sparked the writers' imaginations. Their stories relating how the lanky longhorns were trailed north by men on horseback, through bands of Indians and outlaws, were exciting. To many readers the stories offered escape from the memories of the war. Even cattle stampedes sounded rousing. Many young men were attracted to the

---

*The word "cowpuncher" was coined in Kansas during the 1870s. When cowboys helped to load cattle aboard railroad cars, they used metal-pointed poles to prod the longhorns into stock cars. The prod poles were about 6 feet long with a steel spike on the end. The cowboys who punched the cattle with the poles began referring to themselves as "cow punchers."

life of the cowboy. In addition to young Texans who fell naturally into the occupation, they came from Missouri and states to the east. Countless stories have been told about how young boys in their teens ran away from home to become cowboys after reading about life in the West in eastern newspapers, periodicals, and dime novels.

The story of one such boy, not yet a teen-ager, appeared in the *Democratic Leader* published in Cheyenne on February 1, 1885. The newspaper reported that two eastern detectives were in town searching for an eleven-year-old boy named Fred Shepard who had run away from his home in New York City. The boy's father, a wealthy banker, was offering a $10,000 reward for his son's safe return. The detectives told how young Fred had accumulated a choice library of dime novels containing cowboy stories. The last novel he had read was found on his desk, open at the place where a young cowboy detective unmasks his father's murderer "and carves him into mincemeat to quick music and while holding the minor villains in subjection with two revolvers in one hand." Scrawled at the bottom of the open page were the words: "I'm goin' West to be a cowboy detective." Fred had broken into his tin savings bank and taken $20 in dimes and quarters, gathered a few clothes, and then climbed out of his window and headed west.

What happened to young Fred is unknown. He may have become a cowboy. How many Freds or Williams or Georges or runaways with other names actually became cowboys also is unknown, but the recollections of cattlemen and old-time cowboys suggest that at least half of the young men becoming cowboys remained in that occupation for at least one year. George Saunders, a prominent member of the Old Trail Drivers Association in Texas, estimated in the early 1920s that some 35,000 men accompanied herds of longhorns up the trails between 1867 and the late 1880s. But, he noted, only about a third of these men participated in more than one drive.[2]

The payroll figures for one Texas ranch between 1885 and 1909 suggest that many young men quickly became disillusioned with the cowboy's life. The records of the Spur Ranch in west Texas show that some young men began working on April first and quit on the seventh, twelfth, or the fourteenth of the same month. A few left because they were homesick, others because the hard work was not as interesting or as romantic as the eastern literature of the day had suggested.[3]

The magazine articles and romantic dime novels even influenced the young men already working as cowboys. Some of these cowhands began to picture themselves as rugged individualists like the characters in the stories they read. But the majority did not seriously believe that their individual interests should take precedence over the interests of their

THE FIRST RAILROAD STOCKCARS WERE SMALL
compared to this 1889 model used by the Chicago, Rock Island,
and Pacific Railway Company.

COWBOYS PICKED UP THE NAME "COWPUNCHERS"
when they began prodding cattle to get the animals into railroad stockcars.

employers. Granville Stuart, an early Montana cattleman, wrote of the cowboys: "They were loyal to their outfit and to one another. A man that was not square could not long remain with an outfit. . . . Every man would sacrifice his life to protect the herd. If personal quarrels or disputes arose while on a roundup or on a drive, the settlement of the same was left until the roundup was over and the men released from duty, and then they settled their differences man to man and without interference from their comrades."[4]

The recollections and reminiscences of other nineteenth-century cattlemen and cowboys from Texas to Montana support Stuart's statement, as do many contemporary accounts. One observer writing in the *Texas Live Stock Journal* published at Fort Worth on October 21, 1882, described loyalty as "one of the most notable characteristics of the cowboy. . . . The man who is faithful to the interest of his employer, is naturally faithful in his friendships; and if the inner history of friendships among rough, and perhaps, untutored cowboys could be written, it would be quite as unselfish and romantic as that of Damon and Pythias."

The culture that developed among cowmen and cowboys on the open ranges of Texas constituted a kind of fraternity, loose but cooperative in certain important purposes of life. There on the frontier beyond organized society and written law, these men formulated laws of their own to meet their requirements. These laws were nothing more than an unwritten gentlemen's agreement to certain rules of conduct. And as the culture of this Texas cowboy spread northward across the unsettled plains, so did these rules of conduct.

The more important rules included:

A cowboy was expected to be cheerful even if he was tired or sick.
A cowboy was expected to have courage. (Cowards could not be tolerated in the cowboy culture because one coward might endanger the whole outfit in time of danger.)
No real cowboy was a complainer. (Complaints were associated with quitting, and no real cowboy was a quitter.)
A cowboy always helped a friend, but if the cowhand saw a stranger or even an enemy in distress, the rule said he was to render assistance as quickly as possible. (This mutual-help principle was essential to survival on the open range where everyone helped one another, especially during roundup time.)
A cowboy did the best he could at all times.

Ramon Adams, an authority on the old-time Texas cowboy, described some other rules of conduct in these words:

A standing rule in the old trail days was to awaken a man by speech and not by touch. The hardships and dangers of the drive frayed his nerves and he was apt to "come alive" with a gun in his hand. No firing of guns around a cow camp unless emergency demanded it was another unwritten rule.

Rude and unlettered though he might be, and treating his companions with a rough and ready familiarity, the cowboy yet accorded his neighbor the right to live the life and go the gait which seemed most pleasing to himself. One did not intrude upon the rights of others in the cattle country, and he looked to it very promptly that no one should intrude upon his.[5]

Womanhood on the open range was placed in high esteem because there were so few women at first. The cow country was a man's country, but as ranches developed and women arrived—most were the wives and daughters of ranchers—new rules developed. For instance, cowboys could show no interest in the women of the household, or even an appreciation for their hospitality except by eating heartily at their table. A cowboy was to respect good decent women and protect their character. But Oliver Wallis, an old-time rancher in the Medicine Bow Range of Wyoming, explained the rule in a different way when he wrote: "The old-time cowboy was most respectful of women as long as they kept their place. If they let down the bars, one of those boys would go the limit."[6]

The scarcity of women in the cow country undoubtedly contributed to the fact that most young cowboys were not married. But then, most cowhands were young men in their late teens or early twenties. Many were not yet ready to settle down. As a rule, cowboys did marry, but only after they began ranching for themselves or after they quit the cattle business altogether. When settlers moved into cattle country and towns grew, cowboys were able to locate "lady friends," as they were often called. Sometimes they were the daughters of farmers or young ladies from town. The focal point of their social life was the dance. The girls would dress in their Sunday best with calico and gingham dresses that nearly touched the ground. Whether the dance was held in town or at a ranch, the cowboys got decked out in the best clothes they owned. As the fiddler played, one of the men acted as caller for what could be described as a form of the modern square dance. It was a rompin', stompin' affair that might last until dawn.

Although cowboys believed in minding their own business, some would occasionally find themselves in trouble because they did not like the way another man was treating a woman, even his own wife. Ramon Adams summed up how the cowboy felt:

He was apt to be pretty touchy in protecting her character. He felt that a man was pretty low that would bring a woman into contact with dirt, or to allow her to touch it of her own accord. He placed her upon a high fence because he wanted to look up to her. He wanted her feminine with frills and fluffs all over. He had no use for those he-women who wore pants and tried to dress like a man.[7]

The good women in the cow country no doubt appreciated the cowboy's code as it applied to them, but there are few contemporary accounts by women who were there. Bulah Rust Kirkland, the daughter of a early Texas cowboy, did leave one record early in this century. She wrote:

> I believe I could walk along the streets of any town or city and pick out the real cowboy, not by his clothes especially, but because one can nearly always notice that he has a very open countenance and almost innocent eyes and mouth. He is not innocent of course; but living in the open, next to nature, the cleaner life is stamped on his face. His vices leave no scars or few, because old mother nature has him with her most of the time.[8]

In contrast to the scarcity of recollections from nineteenth-century ranch women, there are many stories about women told by cowboys. C. Boone McClure, the long-time director of the Panhandle-Plains Historical Museum at Canyon, Texas, recalled a story many years ago about a Texan who worked as a cowboy as a young man. He was given the duty of escorting a young lady on a sightseeing tour of a ranch. Accustomed to the rough and easy association of other cowboys, he dreaded the ordeal of conversing with an attractive young woman. The ranch manager assigned her a gentle horse, which the cowboys called "Old Guts" because of the constant rumbling of the animal's digestive organs. Truthful and yet discreet, the cowboy was thrown into considerable confusion when the young woman asked the name of her mount. The cowboy paused and then replied that he thought the horse was called "Old Bowels."

A cowboy was expected to saddle and unsaddle his own horses. Help was not appreciated unless the cowboy was injured. If he was hungry after a long day in the saddle, he took care of feeding his mount before filling his own stomach. A cowboy was expected to take good care of his horses. If they showed signs of abuse, the cowboy would most likely lose his job. As one old cowboy saying goes: "An empty saddle is better than a mean rider." When a cowboy signed with a new outfit and the boss pointed out to him the horses he was to ride, no information concerning the horses was given. This was taken as a good sign by the new hand. It meant the boss had confidence in the new cowboy's ability to handle horses. When a boss wanted a cowhand to quit, he would take the cowboy's favorite mount away from him. That was a sure sign he was being asked to quit before he had to be fired.

There was no formal punishment if a cowboy broke any of these unwritten rules, but if a violation was viewed as serious, the cowboy could become a social outcast. Other cowboys would refuse to speak to him. The rules, as they related to him, were ignored, and the cowboy usually moved on. If the cowboy had mistreated or insulted a good woman, however, chances were good that he would be killed sooner or later. The code of the cowboy culture was based on principles learned by men who spent much of their lives in the open. They sought to lead lives that were free from falsehood and hypocrisy. Their code had as high a standard as that of educated society in the East during the late nineteenth century.

WHEN SITTING AROUND A CAMPFIRE or loafing in a bunkhouse, cowboys might speak contemptuously of eastern fashion. Some cowboys could not understand how men in the East could work in celluloid collars, or wear black, narrow-brimmed bowler hats that did little to shade their eyes from the sun. But as early as 1867 cowboys in the American West were becoming as much the slaves of fashion as anyone in the East. Even today, style of dress is important to the cowboy.

For instance, in the 1950s a research and photographic team from *Life* magazine sought out J. Frank Dobie, who had spent time as a cowboy before settling down to teach at the University of Texas in Austin and to write books. The *Life* team arrived at Dobie's home one day and explained that they were doing a feature on "The Real Cowboy" and wanted to get his thoughts on the subject.

Angus Cameron, then Dobie's editor with an eastern publisher (and the man who looked over every word in this book), had come west to visit Dobie. Cameron later recalled that Dobie

gently led them to more workaday ideas about the life of a modern cowhand. He joshed them a little when he discovered that they thought the cowboy worked more for the love of it than the wages, and gave them a real steer when one of them queried, "Mr. Dobie, I understand that when you were a cowhand you stuffed your pants down into your boots. . . . Do you think the modern cowhand wears his pants on the outside of his boots because he's learned that he can better keep the dust and grit out in that way?" Dobie grinned, rumpled his white hair with a gnarled hand and answered, "Well, no. I reckon

THE COWBOY ON THE LEFT, IDENTIFIED AS JAMES M. KELLERMAN,
is wearing the typical dress of many cowboys during the 1870s.
He has a woven-leather quirt—a whip with a short stock
and two-to-four loose thongs—in his right hand. The two young Montana men—
Thomas Astou on the left, "Dogy" Taylor on the right—are wearing clothing
typical of cowboys on the northern ranges in the late 1880s.
Whether these men ever worked as cowboys is unknown, but several
years before this picture was taken, Taylor was tending bar
in a Miles City saloon.

these boys have noticed just like everybody else from all the western moving pictures they see these days that their silhouette just naturally *looks* better with the pants outside the boot."

One of the earliest mentions of conformity in dress among western cowboys was by General George Wingate. "No man, who can by any possibility avoid it, engages in any part of the business of cattle raising . . . without first procuring a white felt hat with an immensely broad brim, and a band consisting either of a leather strap and buckle, or a silk twist like a whip lash. . . . A cowboy must also have a pair of fancy chapareros, or overalls, made out of calf skin, or stamped leather. Boots with high French heels are indispensable," he wrote.[9]

uart, the Montana cowman, recalled in even more detail
cowboys in the late 1880s. "They wore the best clothes
buy and took a great pride in their personal appearance
ings," wrote Stuart.

ur outfit used to pay $25.00 a pair for made-to-order
hen the best store boots in Helena were $10.00 a pair.
Their trappings consisted of a fine saddle, silver mounted bridle, pearl-
handled six shooter, latest model cartridge belt with silver buckle, silver spurs, a fancy quirt with silver mountings, a fine riata sometimes
made of rawhide [most probably Manila hemp], a pair of leather
chaps, and a fancy hatband often made from the dressed skin of a
diamond-backed rattlesnake. They wore expensive stiff-brimmed light
felt hats, with brilliantly colored silk handkerchiefs knotted about their
necks, light colored shirts and exquisitely fitted very high heeled riding boots.[10]

Stuart's description seems to suggest that *all* cowboys in Montana in the
late 1880s wore identical outfits, but such was not the case. Each man chose
his own dress, although it generally conformed to what had evolved as the
cowboy "uniform," the dress best suited to the work he performed. Many
of the jobs traditionally associated with trail drives, cow hunts or roundups, and the open range remained essential to the cowboy's occupation

LOW CROWNED, BROAD BRIMMED HATS FROM MEXICO, WERE CALLED POBLANOS 1750

BIG FLOPPY BRIMMED HATS ADOPTED BY THE GRINGO OF TEXAS 1820's

J.B. STETSON INTRODUCED BOSS OF THE PLAINS RAW EDGE 1870's

THE MONTANA PINCH BECAME POPULAR IN THE 1880's

POPULAR AT THE TURN OF THE CENTURY HIGH CROWN WIDE BRIM

1920's THE MOVIES INFLUENCED SIZE. THE TEN GALLON HAT

STETSON'S COLUMBIA-STYLE POPULAR IN 1930's 1940's

WIDE BRIM AND LOW CROWN POPULAR WITH THE RODEO CROWD

ALSO THE HIGH CROWN AND WIDE BRIM IS BACK TODAY

after the open-range system began to give way to landownership and ranches with fenced boundaries. It is true that once a ranch was fenced with barbed wire, the line rider's daily chore of patrolling the ranch's artificial boundary lines was eliminated; no longer, unless a fence had been broken, did anyone have to drive wandering cattle back to their respective ranges. Nonetheless, some cowboys still had the occasional job of riding the fence line to check on the condition of the wire and the posts and gates. And cowboys continued to be amateur veterinarians—some were nearly as competent as those with "Doctor" before their names—treating sick cattle and horses they came upon with medicine carried in their saddlebags.

One thing did change. Most cowboys no longer had to sleep and eat in the crude shacks or dugouts near the lines, and they found themselves spending many nights in the bunkhouse located at ranch headquarters. Just where and when the word "bunkhouse" originated is unknown. Like so many other terms that are a part of the cowboy's culture, it probably evolved as the cowboys molded words to suit their needs. The bunk-house was the bachelor living quarters on a ranch. Cowboys also knew the bunkhouse by other names, including "doghouse," "shack," "dump," and occasionally "ram pasture." If gambling took place inside its four walls, a bunkhouse was often called a "dicehouse." If the bunkhouse a rancher provided was especially drafty and poorly constructed, the cowboys might refer to it as a "dive," a name they also reserved for a very dirty saloon. Even line shacks and dugouts were sometimes called bunkhouses.

The label cowboys applied to their bunkhouse was often a revealing reflection of their employer and of his attitude toward those who worked for him. The cattleman who believed in taking care of his men would provide good accommodations, but the rancher who had little concern for their comfort might not even provide bunks—just a building. The cow-boys would then bed down on the wood floor, if one existed. As might be expected, such cattlemen had a bad reputation among cowboys, and would experience a considerable turnover in men.

The furnishings even in the better bunkhouses were not elaborate, and they varied from ranch to ranch and from region to region. On the southern plains one might find bunks and mattresses for each cowboy, plus a table and a few chairs in the middle of the room near a wood stove. The first cowboy up in the morning would stoke the fire to take the chill off the air. On hot summer nights, when the cowboys were not range-riding, they usually laid their bedrolls on the ground outside the bunk-house to catch the breeze. On the northern plains, where most summer nights were cool, the cowboys slept inside when not on the range. Most bunkhouses on the northern plains had fireplaces or at least a wood stove to provide not only warmth but a place to keep a pot of coffee hot. On smaller ranches the cowboys might cook in their bunkhouses, but most large ranches provided a cook or messhouse where the cowboys ate their meals around large tables. The quality of food served up by a ranch cook was often a determining factor in keeping good cowboys.

One ranch cook, Oliver Nelson, was hired on in the summer of 1882 to cook for the hands on the T5 Ranch in the Cherokee Strip southwest of modern Carmen, Oklahoma. Nelson was hired in a Kansas border town to the north and told to take a wagonload of supplies to the ranch. The supplies aboard that wagon tell us much about the needs and eating habits of the T5 cowboys. Nelson's inventory included "forty pounds Climax Plug, twenty pounds Bull Durham, and several caddies [small boxes] and packs of smoking tobacco; a dozen .45 Colt single-action pistols and twenty boxes of cartridges; a roll of half-inch rope; ten gallons of kerosene and a caddy of matches; one hundred pounds of sugar, one 160-pound sack of green coffee, five hundred pounds of salt pork, twenty sacks flour, two hundred pounds beans, fifty pounds country dried apples, a box of soda, and a sack of salt."[11]

When he arrived at the T5 Ranch, Nelson's first meal for the cowboys consisted of bread, bacon, flour gravy, coffee, and a cup of sugar. He prepared the meal in what was a combination kitchen-and-bunkhouse, although it was not large enough to house a bunk for each cowboy. Some hands slept on the beds of nearby wagons during the warm months. Nelson's description of this kitchen-and-bunkhouse is vivid and paints a realistic picture of conditions in Indian Territory in the early 1880s. He wrote:

> The cabin, thirty feet by sixteen, lay east and west; it had doors in the north and south, fastened by old-fashioned string latches; a sash window east of each door, and one in the west end. The walls were of cedar poles ten inches thick. The roof was of split cedar covered with four inches of mud and about twelve inches of earth; it rested on two parallel ridge poles about five feet apart, which were supported in the center by two upright posts set in the dirt floor.
>
> In the northwest corner was a double bunk, pullman style, with poles for springs and hay for feathers; it was apt to have seam squirrels (lice), but no bedbugs. In the northeast corner was a cupboard with four shelves; here were tin plates and cups and iron handled knives and forks, four sixteen-inch ovens, and a fry pan. Between the two doors was a twelve-foot table, with boxes around it for chairs. There was a fireplace with a stick chimney, and an iron hook hanging in the center to hang a four-gallon coffee-pot on; a coffee-grinder was nailed to the

side of the fireplace, and below the grinder was a shelf for a three-gallon sour dough jar. Under the window in the west was a box desk to hold extra pistols, tobacco, or anything the boys didn't want to drag around. Then we had a gun rack in the southwest corner, and half a dozen guns.[12]

Oliver Nelson was probably typical of many ranch cooks in the 1880s. The food he prepared was simple but filling. And coffee was much in demand. Between August 1882 and August 1883, Nelson used up thirteen 160-pound sacks of coffee. But he didn't know everything about cow camp cooking when he went to work on the T5 Ranch. There he learned about what cowboys call "mountain oysters":

There was about eight hundred bulls with the through herd, one, two, and three years old. One day Nigger Henry brought in half a peck of the clippings (testicals) from the bull pen, and poured them in my dishpan. I bawled him out, and dumped them in the creek. When the boys sat down to supper they said, "Henry, where's the oysters?" "Mistah Olivah done trowed dem in de creek." I came near getting into trouble. I said, "Fellers, I never heard of eating such. I thought Henry was putting up a job on me. I'll cook anything you'll bring in to eat, only let me in on it." There was some sour talk, but we eat our bacon for supper. The next day we had a big "oyster" fry, which kept up four weeks.[13]

Every ranch cook had his problems at one time or another. William Pendleton Ricketts, a native of Kentucky who grew up in western Missouri, became a cowboy in Wyoming Territory about 1876. Late in life he recalled a story about a Swedish cook at the Quarter Circle Block Ranch:

One evening after supper the cowboys, while sitting around in front of the kitchen, saw a skunk come into the back door and look around. When the cook saw him he became excited. One of the cowboys told the cook to leave the skunk alone, that he will leave. But the cook said: "Me scald him, me scald him." Seizing a teakettle the cook proceeded to carry out his threat. Every time the hot water fell on him the aroma flew, and around and around the Swede and the skunk went. That kitchen wasn't used any more that summer.[14]

When a ranch outfit went on spring or fall roundup, the cook loaded the chuck wagon with supplies and rode out on the range to cook for the

THE BUNKHOUSE ON THE "OW" RANCH ON HAT CREEK IN WYOMING
during the 1880s. Five of the cowboys are providing musical entertainment
while the men left of center are practicing with boxing gloves.
The man standing in the doorway is probably the ranch foreman.

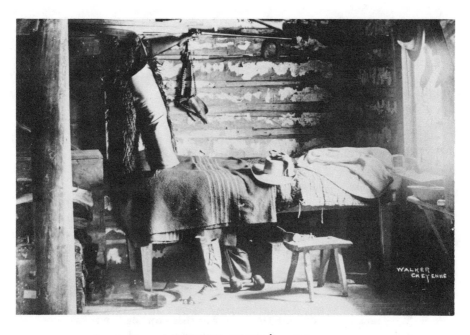

A WYOMING COWBOY'S BUNK,
probably in the corner of a ranch bunkhouse, around the early 1880s. Two rifles,
a pistol, and the cowboy's "woollies," or chaps, hang from the log wall.
Note the barbells on the floor to the left of the stool.

FIVE KANSAS COWBOYS AND A RANCH COOK
(with frying pan) pose outside the cook house on the Open C Ranch
in Clark County, Kansas, during the 1880s.

ON HOT SUMMER NIGHTS IT WAS NOT UNCOMMON FOR COWBOYS
to place their bedrolls on the ground outside the bunkhouse to catch
the breeze. These cowboys have done just that. They were working for the
W. D. Boyce Cattle Company along the Cimarron River
in western Kansas and eastern Colorado around 1880.

cowboys. By the late 1880s many large outfits, especially on the southern plains, used an additional wagon to carry bedding, branding irons, ropes and hobbles, and things the cowboys could not carry on their horses. In an emergency the bedwagon—cowboys often called it the "hoodlum" wagon—could carry an injured cowboy to town and a doctor. Usually only the larger outfits ran a bedwagon. The smaller outfits had sufficient room on their chuck wagons for the bedding and other things.

The normal makeup of a ranch outfit on the range included a cook, a horse wrangler, ten to fifteen cowboys, and the wagon boss, the man in charge of the outfit on the range. Everyone took orders from him. He designated the territory to be covered by the cowboys. The horse wrangler was the man in charge of the *remuda*, the horses used by the outfit. (The literal meaning of the Spanish word *remuda* is "change" or "replacement"; *remuda de caballos* means "relay of horses.") Being a horse wrangler was often the first job performed by a young man starting out as a cowboy. Of course, he had to be able to ride and handle horses, since he usually rounded them up three times a day. He would start in the morning by herding them into a bunch near where the cowboys were working so that the cowhands could change from their roundup horses to their cutting horses, mounts highly trained for cutting out cattle from a herd. He would gather the horse herd again about noon near the chuck wagon so the cowboys could change mounts again. The wrangler's last roundup was late in the afternoon so that the hands could catch their night mounts—horses that were best suited for night riding because of their eyesight. These night mounts were used occasionally to check the herd but most of the time were staked near the chuck wagon where the cowhands slept in their bedrolls on the ground so they would be handy in case of a stampede. Each time the wrangler rounded up the horses, he usually placed a rope corral around them. Such a corral consisted of lariat ropes tied together until they circled the herd. The rope corral was elevated about 4 feet off the ground by poles or rods.

The work of the cowboy during roundups or between the spring and fall roundups depended in part on where he was. If he was working on the southern plains in the spring of the year, the cowboy would gather and feed weak stock, generally cows and calves or cows heavy with calf. If the winter had been mild and food plentiful, little feeding would be required. But if the stock were weak they would be fed or moved to a better pasture with good grass. On some days a cowboy might be told to ride fence to make certain there were no broken wires through which cattle could wander onto another ranch. At other times he might be told to ride the range. This meant he should look for any unbranded calves and injured or crippled cattle. If any cattle with a freshly exposed injury were found, the cowboy had to doctor the injury to keep the screwworms out.

Screwworms were and are a serious problem on the southern plains from June until late September, the very warm months. Blowflies will blow or lay their eggs in open wounds, and swarms of screwworms will attack the area the same day. If an animal is not caught and doctored within a day or so, the worms will do much damage. Cowboys usually carried a bottle of screwworm remedy. Most still do so today. If they have none, the cowboy locates some dry cow chips, crushes some in his hands and tamps the manure into the wound to shut off the air from the worms. Without air the screwworms will die.

While riding range that was open or fenced, the cowboy also checked on the water supply. Where no running creeks or rivers or natural spring-fed water holes existed, raising cattle was difficult until windmills appeared in the early 1880s. In most areas of the southern plains the water table lies too far beneath the surface to be reached by a dug well. Windmills were not used until well drilling was perfected in the late 1870s. Then the windmills—they were first used by railroads in the West—could tap the underground water, which enabled ranchers to construct dirt-tank reservoirs to hold water for their cattle. A range-riding cowboy was expected to check on the condition of ranch windmills and to make certain they were operating properly. If not, he was expected to try to repair them. The famous XIT Ranch in the Texas panhandle erected its first windmill in 1886, soon after the ranch was established. By 1900 the ranch had 335 windmills in operation on its ranges.[15]

On the southern plains such work continued through the hot summer months. Cowboys also scattered the bulls to different parts of the ranch where they could do what nature endowed them to do. And whenever a cowboy found a sleeper—a calf that had been earmarked by a rustler who intended to come back later and steal the animal—he would stop and range-brand it. Since some state laws prohibited the carrying of a running iron, the cowboy might carry a stamp iron bearing the brand of his outfit. But these were heavy and rather awkward, and it was not unusual for a cowboy to carry a branding ring made of copper. The ring was a few inches wide, and any type of brand could be run with it. The cowboy built a hot fire, heated the ring, and using two wooden sticks for handles he drew the brand on the animal.

Fall work on the southern plains was the roundup. The calves were gathered for shipment to feeders who would fatten them for baby beef. The old cows and dry or barren ones were also gathered and shipped for slaughter. The balance of the cowboy's fall and winter chores on the southern plains consisted of range and fence riding, checking on the water supply for stock, plus herding the bulls and placing them in an isolated pasture for winter. Of course, the cowboys continued to look after their horses and break new mounts for the coming spring.

Many of these routine tasks were also performed by cowboys on the northern plains. But the colder climate and the different character of the land often demanded that the cowboy perform still other jobs. For instance, in the spring a northern cowboy might ride bog and pull weak stock out of bog or mud holes. As on the southern plains, cowboys had to feed the weak cattle, especially the cows and calves. And as in the south, northern cowboys had to check the water supply. In many areas of the northern plains water was not the problem it was in the south. Melting snow filled water holes and streams in the spring. But cowboys often had the job of cleaning out water holes filled with debris carried by the thawing snow. Because of the shortness of the spring and summer on the northern ranges, there might be only three weeks between the time the spring roundup work was done and the fall roundup work began. Some cowboys in the north took short vacations then to enjoy the warm temperatures of summer, but others became hay slayers, as they called themselves, and cut hay for winter feed. The raising of hay became commonplace in the north and many areas of the south following the terrible winter of 1886–87. Not all cowboys enjoyed cutting hay with a scythe. It was performed on foot and not from the saddle.

Fall work normally began with the roundup of beef cattle for shipment to market. At that time, calves born since the spring roundup were branded and marked. This work often continued until the first snowfall. By then the bulls were gathered so they could be fed during the winter months, and calves were rounded up and weaned in order to give their mothers a better chance of surviving the cold winter months.

Fewer cowhands were needed on northern ranches during the winter months than in the south. The best hands—usually the older men who had proved themselves—were given winter jobs. They would gather weak cows and calves, feed bulls and weak cattle, cut ice to open water holes, haul firewood, and ride the range to check the other cattle. Many line shacks remained in use on the northern ranges even after the arrival of barbed wire. The shacks provided cowboys with shelter should they be caught on the range by a sudden blizzard. Some cowboys might spend much of the winter in a line shack close to the cattle. After each storm a cowboy would ride the range to check on the condition of cattle and their drift. Most cowboys with winter jobs on northern ranches were given at least two mounts to ride. They were called their "winter horses," and each animal had to be capable of carrying a cowboy holding a calf while at the same time driving a weak cow being brought in to feed.[16]

By the middle 1880s, there was a difference between the horses found on Texas ranches and those in Montana. An unnamed newspaper reporter, apparently quite familiar with the cowboy's life on both northern and

southern ranges, wrote of the two regions' respective advantages and disadvantages in the July 25, 1885, issue of *Kansas Cowboy* published at
Dodge City. He wrote from somewhere in Montana:

> It would delight the heart of the average Texas cowboy to be hired by
> a Montana cowman, and there shown the horses from which he was
> to select his mount—great big tallowy horses as sleek as livery horses,
> and very few of them but what are gentle as a dog. And I may add
> that when a Montana cowboy gets back from a season's roundup, that
> his horses are still fat. In the first place he has plenty of them and
> these men do not allow their hands to dash those horses around just
> for the fun of the thing. And the cattle here are too different from
> what they are in Texas, that there is really very little hard riding to do.
> Boys who have worked on both ranges say that while the average
> Texas cow pony cannot compare with his Montana brother as to
> looks, yet when it comes to doing hard work and a heap of it, he is
> far superior to the latter. He is quicker and harder, and better adapted
> to just such work. . . . Live! Why, these cowboys live higher than any-
> body. They have every thing to eat that money can buy, and a cook
> with a paper cap on to prepare it. The cook is so neat and polite that
> you could eat him if you were right hungry. . . . Cowboys get about
> the same wages here that they do in Texas, but one dollar in Texas will
> buy as much as three in Montana, and the boys only get work three or
> four months in the year.

A HORSE FOR A COWBOY was, needless to say, essential. And it is understandable that there was a close relationship between man and beast. The horse
was the cowboy's constant companion. Each cowboy had stories of the
ability, skill, and understanding of his favorite horse. And every horse had
a name that could be traced to the animal's disposition or markings, or
perhaps to an incident in which it had been involved. Most cowboys
wanted horses of solid colors—bays, browns, sorrels, duns, and blacks—but
no paints. A paint horse may have been the favorite of western fiction
writers and Indians, but few cowboys acknowledged that one had ever developed into a fine cutting horse. Some cowboys would ride paints into
town to see their lady friends, but for working cattle a solid-color horse
with some breeding was preferred.

E. C. "Teddy Blue" Abbott told the story of his favorite horse in
his recollections, *We Pointed Them North*. He related how one morning
he watched Bill Charlton, a fellow cowboy, trying to ride a "half-broke
horse." Charlton could not ride very well.

TEXAS COWBOYS BREAKING NEW MOUNTS.
Above: At a roundup camp on the OR Ranch in Texas.
Below: "A settin' on his tree."
Both photographs by Erwin Smith.

The horse cut up some, and Bill got mad and spurred him. At that time [in the 1880s] they all had these Mexican spurs with long rowels and bells on them, and a long hook—a cinch hook it was called—on top of the rowell; this was to hook into them leather bands, when a horse was bucking, and keep you from being throwed. Now Bill accidentally ran this hook into the cinch ring, and it caught there, and the horse bucked him off. He would have been kicked to death in a minute. I was riding a green horse myself, but I got alongside Bill's horse and grabbed the cheek strap and throwed myself out of the saddle. But my own spur caught on the cantle, and there I was stretched out for about a second between them two horses. Then I got loose and dropped to the ground, and got the cinches unbuckled and the saddle off and Bill out of it.

Bill Charlton, Abbott recalled, was "pretty well shaken up." Charlton thanked him and said: "What have I got you want?" Abbott thought a moment and replied: "Give me that little bay horse." Charlton gave Abbott the horse he had just ridden and Abbott named him "Billy" after Charlton. The horse was then about ten years old. Abbott worked with him. "He was a wonderful rope and cut horse, but I thought so much of him I never used him much, only to ride him to town. That was the reason he lasted so long," recalled Abbott, who considered Billy his top horse for twenty-six years. The horse died when he was thirty-six years old on Abbott's ranch in Fergus County, Montana.

    The task of breaking wild, never-before-ridden horses was one job common to all cowboys, whether on the northern or southern plains. And there was no easy way to do it. First they had to catch the horse with a rope. "Most any bronc is a ticklish proposition to handle when first caught," wrote Will James, the cowboy turned artist, in his book *Cowboys North and South*. "It's not always meanness, it's fear of the human. They only try to protect themselves. Sometimes by going easy and having patience according, a man can break one to ride without bucking, but even at that, the meanest bucking horse I ever saw was gentle to break, and never made a jump till one day he got away and run with the wild bunch for a couple of years." Will James and many other cowboys preferred horses that bucked when first ridden. "I figgers it's their mettle showing when they do," observed James, adding: "It's the right spirit at the right time—every horse what bucks is not a outlaw, not by a long shot. I've seen and rode many a good old well-broke cow horse what had to have his buck out in the cold mornings, just to kind of warm hisself up on the subject and settle down for the work ahead."

*   *   *

FOUR COWBOYS FROM THE THREE CIRCLE RANCH IN TEXAS
take time out from their chores to play a game of hearts on the range.
Photograph by Erwin Smith.

COWBOYS, APPARENTLY DURING A ROUNDUP,
in the Oklahoma Panhandle in the 1880s, bathing in a water hole.
The chuck wagon is on the rim of the hill behind the cowboys,
and one of the horses is in the water with them.

WHILE THE BREAKING OF BRONCS was often difficult and dangerous, cowboys sometimes did it for fun. When their chores were done and they had time, several cowhands might make a contest out of breaking a particularly wild bronc. Or they might hold a competition to determine which cowboy was the best roper. Such contests were likely to occur whenever two or more cowhands got together during their free time. Eventually the contests became organized and became the foundation for the modern rodeo.

COWBOYS NOT GIVEN JOBS on northern ranches during the cold winter months might hole up in a nearby town until spring or wander south in hopes of finding work on a ranch in Kansas, Indian Territory, Texas, or elsewhere in the Southwest. The wandering cowboy in the West was *not* a myth. Numerous accounts attest to the wanderlust that characterized many cowboys. Even ranch records document this. Many years ago, William Curry Holden went through the records of the Spur Ranch, which once covered about half a million acres in the Texas counties of Garza, Kent, Dickens, and Crosby. The ranch was established in that area of West Texas in 1883 by the Espuela Land and Cattle Company of Fort Worth, sold to an English syndicate two years later, and sold to the S. M. Swenson interests in 1907 and named the SMS Ranch. Of the 901 different cowboys employed between 1885 and 1909, only 3 percent worked as many as five seasons and 64 percent remained only one season.[17]

Why cowboys moved on is anyone's guess. Some may have been running from the law, others searching for something or hoping their luck would get better elsewhere. Perhaps the vast open spaces acted like a magnet and drew the restless cowboy beyond the horizon. The plains undoubtedly had an effect on the mind of the cowboy, as suggested in a little-known cowboy song sung on the SMS Ranch early in this century. Written by John R. Craddock, who was raised in Dickens County, the song is titled "The Wandering Cowboy." The words capture the mood of the cowboy:

> *I am a wandering cowboy,*
> 　*From ranch to ranch I roam;*
> *At every ranch when welcome,*
> 　*I make myself at home.*

> *Two years I worked for the Double L,*
> 　*And one for the O Bar O;*
> *Then drifted west from Texas,*
> 　*To the plains of Mexico.*

There I met up with a rancher
  Who was looking for a hand;
So when springtime greened the valleys,
  I was burning the Bar S brand.

I worked on through the summer,
  Then early in the fall,
Over the distant ranges,
  There came the old, old call.

So I drifted to Arizona,
  To work for Uncle Bob,
A-tailing up the weak ones
  On a winter feeding job.

But the ranch camp grew too lonely,
  With never rest or change;
So I saddled up one morning
  And struck for a distant range.

One night in wild Wyoming,
  When the stars hung bright and low,
I lay in my tarp a dreaming
  Of the far off home ranch-o,

When the cottonwood leaves are whispering,
  In the evening soft and low;
'Tis there my heart's a-turning,
  And homeward I must go.

It is now I'm tired of rambling.
  No longer will I roam
When my pony I've unsaddled
  In the old corral at home.[18]

The saving of a few dollars was often reason enough for a cowboy to quit and move on. Certainly cowhands did not become wealthy punching cattle. Branch Isbell, a Texas cowhand, went to work in 1872 for $20 per month "by the year, work or play. I had the privilege of trading horses, and at the end of a year I had $150 in cash and five good ponies—more clear profit than I ever afterwards saved at wages varying from $50 to $125 per month."[19] Wages increased a little by the 1880s on most ranches from Texas northward. The records of the Spur Ranch indicate that in 1885 the monthly wage averaged $38.72, but that dropped to $32.24 in 1890. During the 1890s the average monthly wage ranged between $32 and $33. A first-class cowhand on the Spur Ranch received $35; top hands, $40 and $45; trail bosses, $50 and $65; and range foremen or wagon bosses, $125. Usually a wagon cook received the wage of a top hand, while the cook at the ranch headquarters got 50 a month or the same as the trail boss. Wages on the northern ranges ran about the same.[20]

Most cowboys were able to save a little money, but after several months of hard ranch work the temptation of going to town and shooting all or most of their wad was great. Bill Oden saw this happen quite often in the late 1880s and 1890s. Born in Alabama, Oden came to Texas at the age of fourteen. Three years later he became a cowboy in San Saba County and a year later moved onto the plains of West Texas. In his recollections, Oden wrote:

> The old-time cowhand would stay on the ranch for six or eight months, exposed to the rigors of winter and the torrid heat of the desert sun, doing honest labor for his boss. . . . When there was nothing of importance to be done on the ranch, he was at liberty to go to town. He would put his horse in the livery stable, stop at the best hotel in town and charge to the ranch [the ranch would then withhold future wages to pay the bill], and stay as long as he wanted to. As he would usually load up on bug juice when he hit town, his money would usually give out in eight or ten days, and he would saddle up and head for the ranch, to make the boss an excellent hand for another eight or ten months.[21]

THE QUOTE BY JOHN CLAY at the beginning of this chapter suggests that he never saw an old cowboy. Undoubtedly, to be sure, there were some. It is a fact, however, that most men quit cowpunching after ten or fifteen years. The work was rough. And sleeping in the open and not taking care of health or injuries would often create a "stove-up" cowboy, one who spent the rest of his life nursing poor health. James Emmit McCauley, a Texan, was one such. Before his death in 1924, McCauley wrote his story. He recalled, in part:

> I have done as most cowpunchers do after they have got too stove up to ride. For a man to be stove up at thirty may sound strange to some people, but many a cowboy has been so bunged up that he has quit riding that early in life. Now at thirty I went back to my early rais-

TEXAS COWBOYS ARRIVING IN TASCOSA
to quench their thirst at a bar.
Photograph by Erwin Smith.

INSIDE THE SALOON AT TASCOSA
LS Ranch cowboys drink at the bar.
Photograph by Erwin Smith.

A ROUNDUP OUTFIT SOMEWHERE ON THE SOUTHERN PLAINS
during the late 1880s.

A COWBOY FUNERAL IN TEXAS IN THE 1880s.

ing. When I realized I could no longer follow the long-horned cattle I determined not to work for wages any longer. In just a little less than a month after I left the hospital I had married a girl I had known for ten years or longer. I found my little capital had went down until I was worth less than $500. I've been married now three years and I have 320 acres of land and it would take $5,000 to get me to move. I consider I have done better than I possibly could have done working for wages. Besides, I have two little ones to bless our home, a boy two years old and a girl most a year old. All in all I got out of cowpunching is the experience. I paid a good price for that. I wouldn't take anything for what I have saw but I wouldn't care to travel the same road again, and my advice to any young man or boy is to stay at home and not be a rambler, as it won't buy you anything. And above everything stay away from a cow ranch, as not many cowpunchers ever save any money and 'tis a dangerous life to live.[22]

James McCauley was one of the more fortunate cowboys if one believes John Clay's comment that "the ordinary cowboy usually degenerated, drifted, disappeared, or worse still, became a saloonkeeper." Since Clay was a cattleman, he no doubt had some basis for his observation. He had known many cowboys on the northern ranges during the 1880s and 1890s. In his classic *My Life on the Range*, Clay described the cowboys in one outfit as "a lot of ruffians full of fight, more especially when there was booze on tap, but they were honest, loyal and capable." Of the cowboys in another outfit, he wrote that they "had capacity, but they were light fingered, treacherous, inclined to gamble, and held human life as of little value. And still it was a pleasure to see them work. They swept round a herd with an easy grace and careless abandon, yet never missing a point."[23]

By the early 1880s the type of cowboys hired by a ranch outfit usually reflected the views of the cattleman who employed them. He wanted men who agreed with his way of thinking. The cowboys, to keep their jobs, had to abide by the rules of the rancher. Charles Goodnight had three rules for his cowhands: no gambling, no drinking, and no fighting. Such unwritten but clearly stated ranch codes evolved from the unwritten rules of the trail-driving days, when a drunken man could cause havoc and where cowboys had more important things to do than gamble or fight. The rules reflected the old open range code of behavior and practice on the frontier.

The growing business of cattle ranching firmly established the cowboy in the category of labor by the early 1880s, while the rancher or cattleman was clearly management. The cattlemen were acquiring wealth from the natural propagation of cattle and the hard labor of the cowboys.

The old-time practices of fraternity between cowmen and cowboys were changing. The cowboy's unwritten rule concerning loyalty was not as strong on some ranches as it had been a decade earlier. For one thing, foreigners from Britain and Scotland owned ranches, and in the eyes of many cowboys the easterners who had invested in cattle were also foreigners. They brought their ideas and ways to the cow country and were diluting the once-strong fraternity that had existed between cowmen and cowboys. The gap between many ranch owners and their laboring men on horseback became wider and wider.

The cowboy's displeasure with changes over which they had no control was first voiced in the Texas panhandle in 1883, soon after the large ranchers in the region organized the Panhandle Cattlemen's Association. One purpose behind the establishment of this and other such associations throughout the West was to eliminate rustling. But the panhandle cattlemen began calling a halt to many of the old practices, including the one permitting cowboys to keep a brand and run a few head of cattle and stock horses on their employer's ranch. Many cowboys did not like the change. A number were convinced that the ranchers cared little about the cowboy and his welfare, and that some were taking advantage of the cowhands.

Early in the spring of 1883 the outfits of three large ranches—the LX, the LIT, and the LS, all in the Canadian River country of the Texas panhandle—happened to come together near the mouth of Frio Creek east of modern Hereford, Texas. The outfits had been rounding up cattle that had drifted south during the winter. All of the men enjoyed a meal together and then began talking about their wages and the *new* rules being imposed on all cowhands. Everyone voiced dissatisfaction. Since their employers had organized an association, it was only natural that the cowboys began to talk about having their own organization. Before the three outfits broke camp they had formed a loose organization and issued a proclamation, the original of which ended up in the Panhandle-Plains Historical Museum at Canyon, Texas.

The proclamation, announcing what was the first cowboy strike in the American West, reads:

We, the undersigned cowboys of Canadian River, do by these presents agree to bind ourselves into the following obligations, viz—First, that we will not work for less than $50 per month, and we furthermore agree no one shall work for less than $50 per month, after 31st of March.

Second, good cooks shall also receive $50 per month.

Third, anyone running an outfit shall not work for less than $75 per month. Anyone violating the above obligations shall suffer the consequences. Those not having funds to pay board after March 31st will be provided for 30 days at Tascosa.

The ultimatum was signed by twenty-four men, including the wagon bosses for the LX, the LIT, and the LS ranches—Roy Griffin, Waddy Peacock, and Tom Harris. The cowboys set April 1, 1883, as the date for their strike.

Exactly what happened next is a bit clouded, but individual negotiations occurred between cattlemen and some of the cowboys involved. A few hands were fired and found themselves afoot, something no self-respecting cowboy could fathom. Many of the striking cowboys gathered at Tascosa, where they drank and talked and drank some more. A few near-violent acts occurred, but no one is believed to have been killed as a direct result of the strike. The cattlemen did not suffer from the cowboys' absence because of the influx of many young men looking for work. Within a week or two the striking cowboys seem to have sensed failure, and the strike ended less than a month after it started. Some of the striking cowboys returned to work, but others left the country.[24]

The strike undoubtedly caused some concern among cattlemen, and some ranchers began to establish written rules for their hands. Probably the first large ranch to do so was the XIT Ranch. The management drafted a code of twenty-three regulations called "General Rules of the XIT Ranch" early in 1888. These rules represented a radical departure from anything then in practice on the southern plains, and they provide important insights into the changing cowboy culture of the late 1880s. The rules were:

No. 1

Whenever a person is engaged to work on the ranch, the person so engaging him will fill out and sign a blank, giving the name of the party employed, for what purpose employed, the amount of wages he is to receive, the date he will begin work, and deliver the same to the person employed, who must sign the counterpart of such contract, which must be forwarded to headquarters at the first opportunity; and no one will be put upon the Company's pay roll, or receive any pay until this is complied with.

No. 2

Employees, when discharged, or on leaving the Company's service, are required to bring or send to the headquarters office, a statement from the person under whom they were at work, showing the day they quit the Company's service, and no settlement will be made with any employee, until such statement is furnished.

No. 3

Employees discharged from or leaving the service of the Company are expected to leave the ranch at once and will not be permitted to remain more than one night in any camp.

No. 4

The wages due any employee will not be paid to any other person without a written order from the employee to whom such wages are due.

No. 5

No person in charge of any pasture, or any work on the ranch, or any contractor on the ranch, will be permitted to hire any one who has been discharged from the Company's own accord, with the intention of getting employment at some other place on the ranch, [nor can anyone] be so employed except by special agreement, made beforehand between the person in charge of the outfit he leaves and the one in charge of the outfit he wishes to work for.

No. 6

Private horses of employees must not be kept at any of the camps, nor will they be allowed to be fed grain belonging to the Company. No employee shall be permitted to keep more than two private horses on the ranch and all such horses must be kept in some pasture designated by the ranch manager.

No. 7

No employee shall be permitted to own any cattle or stock horses on the ranch.

No. 8

The killing of beef by any person on the ranch, except by the person in charge of the pasture, or under his instruction, is strictly forbidden. Nor is the person in charge of a pasture allowed to have beef killed, unless it can be distributed and consumed without loss. And all hides of beef killed must be taken care of and accounted for. It shall be the duty of each person having beef killed to keep a tally of the same and report the number, age and sex killed to headquarters every month.

No. 9

The abuse of horses, mules or cattle by any employee will not be tolerated; and any one who strikes his horse or mule over the head, or spurs it in the shoulder, or in any other manner abuses or neglects to care for it while in his charge, shall be dismissed from the Company's service.

No. 10

Employees are not allowed to run mustang, antelope or any kind of game on the Company's horses.

No. 11

No employee of the Company, or of any contractor doing work for the Company, is permitted to carry on or about his person or in his saddle bags, any pistol, dirk, dagger, sling shot, knuckles, bowie knife or any other similar instruments for the purpose of offense or defense. Guests of the Company, and persons not employees of the ranch temporarily staying at any of its camps, are expected to comply with this rule, which is also a State law.

No. 12

Card playing and gambling of every description, whether engaged in by employees, or by persons not in the service of the Company, is strictly forbidden on the ranch.

No. 13

In case of fire upon the ranch, or on lands bordering on the same, it shall be the duty of every employee to go to it at once and use his best endeavors to extinguish it, and any neglect to do so, without reasonable excuse, will be considered sufficient cause for dismissal.

No. 14

Each outfit of men that is furnished with a wagon and cook is required to make its own camping places, and not impose on the other camps on the ranch unnecessarily.

No. 15

Employees are strictly forbidden the use of vinous, malt, spiritous, or intoxicating liquors, during their time of service with the Company.

No. 16

It is the duty of every employee to protect the Company's interests to the best of his ability, and when he sees they are threatened in any direction to take every proper measure at his command to accomplish this end, and as soon as possible to inform his employers of the danger threatened.

No. 17

Employees of neighboring ranches on business are to be cared for at all camps, and their horses fed if desired (provided there is feed in the camp to spare); but such persons will not be expected to remain on the ranch longer than is necessary to transact their business, or continue their journey.

No. 18

Bona fide travelers may be sheltered if convenient, but they will be expected to pay for what grain and provisions they get, at prices to be fixed from time to time by the Company, and all such persons must not remain at any camp longer than one night.

No. 19

Persons not in the employment of the Company, but freighting for it, are not to be furnished with meals for themselves or feed for their teams at any of the camps on the ranch, but are expected to come on the ranch prepared to take care of themselves.

No. 20

Loafers, "sweaters [men who sweated as a result of their great efforts to avoid work]," deadbeats, tramps, gamblers, or disreputable persons, must not be entertained at any camp, nor will employees be permitted to give, loan or sell such persons any grain, or provisions of any kind, nor shall such persons be permitted to remain on the Company's land anywhere under any pretext whatever.

No. 21

No person or persons, not in the employment of the Company, shall be permitted to hunt or kill game of any kind, inside of the ranch inclosure, under any pretext whatsoever, and all employees are instructed to see that this rule is enforced. Employees of the Company will also not be permitted to hunt or kill game except when necessary for use for food.

No. 22

It is the aim of the owners of this ranch to conduct it on the principle of right and justice to every one; and for it to be excelled by no other in the good behavior, sterling honesty and integrity, and general high character of its employees, and to this end it is necessary that the foregoing rules be adhered to, and the violation of any of them will be considered just cause for discharge.

No. 23

Every camp will be furnished with a printed copy of these rules, which must be nailed up in a conspicuous place in the camp; and each and every rule is hereby made and considered a condition and part of the engagement between the Company and its employees, and any employee who shall tear down or destroy such printed rules, or shall cause the same to be done, shall be discharged.

By Order of the Company,

Abner Taylor
Manager.[25]

J. Evetts Haley, in his book *The XIT Ranch of Texas*, observed that there was 'much infringement of these rules, particularly that of carrying guns, but those governing liquor and gambling were rigidly enforced."

Not surprisingly, several of the XIT ranch's twenty-three written rules incorporated elements of the earlier, unwritten code of the cowboy. Yet the fact that the ranch management found it necessary to include them in the printed rules suggests that numerous cowboys were no longer living by the code. By the late 1880s many of the old-time cowboys were gone. Younger men had taken their places. The earlier traditions of the cowboy culture were simply not as strong as they once were because of outside influences brought to the cattle country by the impersonal world of big business and the things associated with civilization along the Atlantic seaboard. By 1890 there is no question that the old-time traditions of the cowboy's way of life were beginning to vanish, from Texas to Montana. They had originated on the frontier, and the frontier had disappeared with the arrival of what the old-timers called the "devil's hatband."

CHAPTER 14

⸻•●•⸻

End of the
Open-Range Culture

They say that Heaven is a free range land
Good-by, Good-by, O fare you well;
But it's barbed wire fence for the Devil's hat band
And barbed wire blankets down in Hell!

—OLD COWBOY SONG[1]

THERE is something menacing about a long stretch of barbed-wire fence. For one who is native to the West, such a fence still looks unfriendly and suggests in no uncertain terms that one should stay on one's own side. And when the wind whistles through the frail-appearing metallic wire—it is much stronger than it appears—dulled by cold and heat, the fence sounds forbidding. Yet it is hard to imagine that "bob wahr," as many westerners call it, had such a great impact in the West during the last century and brought an end to the frontier and the era of the open range. Today, more than a century after its invention, barbed wire remains an unnatural barrier that in the West hints at the hardness of the land. It is not difficult to imagine how this wire was viewed by cowboys and cattlemen brought up on the open range. Barbed wire was *not* in harmony with the land. The sharp barbs cut horses, cattle, and men, but, more important, the wire restricted movement. It is understandable why many cowboys began referring to barbed wire as the "devil's hatband" when it first appeared in the late 1870s.

Fences, of course, were nothing new in the 1870s. Early colonists in America had built fences from split logs, boards and stones. English common law brought to America endorsed a "fence livestock in" concept, placing the burden of responsibility on the stock owner to control his livestock. Settlers along the Atlantic coast found plenty of wood and stone with which to construct fences. But as their descendants pushed westward onto the prairies and plains, wood became scarce. There were few trees. Some settlers found stone to build their fences, but others sought substitute materials. In time, many farmers turned to planting thick hedges of thorny Osage orange, or *bois d'arc*. The remnants of these hedgerows may still be seen today in many areas of Kansas, Nebraska, and elsewhere on the plains.

Wood also was scarce in the cattle country of Texas, but few cattlemen sought substitutes, since they grazed their longhorns on the open ranges. Aside from small corrals, these cattlemen had little need for fences. During the late 1860s and early 1870s most Texas cattlemen thought the ranges would always be free and open. But a handful of Texans located in south Texas believed that full ownership of the land was the only guarantee of complete control of the water and grass for their cattle. One of these cattlemen was Mifflin Kenedy.

Kenedy's ranch was the first ranch of any size to be fenced in the West. The fencing occurred soon after Kenedy and Captain Richard King dissolved their ranching partnership. Kenedy enclosed 131,000 acres with a board fence constructed of creosoted cypress posts and hard pine planks which were brought on order by ship from Louisiana and transported by wagon from the Texas coast to his ranch. Richard King also enclosed his ranch with a similar type of fence costing $500 to $1,000 a mile to construct. Not far away was another ranch owned by a woman wealthy enough to enclose her 90,000 acres with a continuous board fence. And a few smaller ranches in south Texas were also fenced by the early 1870s at a cost of several hundred dollars a mile. But fenced ranches in Texas and elsewhere on the broad expanse of plains and prairies of the West were the exception to the rule. They were not in character with the wide open space, and they were not needed.

One purpose in fencing the larger south Texas ranches was to tell outsiders not to trespass. Bands of outlaws, frequently roaming back and forth across the Rio Grande, inhabited the region. But the primary reason for the fences was that they enabled cattlemen to control their stock. Kenedy, King, and a few other cattle raisers wanted to begin livestock breeding programs to improve the quality of their cattle. Fences to keep stray cattle out were necessary for such programs.[2]

The open-range system of cattle raising was not conducive to such control. Most cattle grazed on public land used by more than one rancher. It was unthinkable to fence an open range. After all, the open-range system was dependent upon cooperation among ranchers and the mutual-help principle, especially at roundup time. Even if open-range ranchers had

wanted to fence their ranges of the late 1860s and early 1870s, the cost
of erecting board fences would have been prohibitive. But cattlemen began
to think more about fences as increasing numbers of settlers began pushing westward into cow country. It was open-range ranchers along the
eastern edge of the cattleman's frontier—particularly in Kansas and
Nebraska—who first felt the pressure to control their cattle. More and
more frequently, farmers turned to the law when cattle overran their
fields. Both Kansas and Nebraska passed herd laws making it mandatory
for cattlemen to restrain their herds from wandering at will over the
prairies and plains. This was a blow to the very heart of the open-range
system, and most cattlemen viewed such legislation with disgust.

The majority of cattlemen, especially in Texas, believed that farmers
should fence their land to keep cattle out. This belief reflected Spanish
law in what had been New Spain and early Texas. That law had traditionally held that the landowner must fence his land if he wished to protect
his crops from cattle on the open range. The herd laws, however, reflected
English common law brought to the plains and prairies by the settlers.
Herd laws placed the burden of responsibility on the cattlemen, even when
cattle broke through fences or otherwise got loose.

In most instances, cattlemen lost out in legal battles deriving from
herd laws. They lost because the more numerous settlers gained control of
the political process by electing their own representatives to state legisla-
tures and to Congress. What happened from Texas northward during the
1870s was a repeat of what had happened a decade earlier in California.
Ranching had dominated California's agricultural interests through the
1860s, and it followed traditional Spanish law. The open-range concept
was universal. The California Trespass Act of 1850 had made it clear that
if settlers did not want cattle destroying their crops, orchards, and vineyards, the farmers were responsible for erecting fences to keep livestock
out.

California farmers living in areas with good annual rainfall solved
the problem of fencing by growing hedges of willows, sycamores, or alder
at little expense. California law said a hedge fence was lawful if it was
"five feet high and sufficiently close to turn stock." A stone fence also
was lawful if it was 4½ feet high, while a rail fence had to be 5½ feet
high. But in dry areas of California where hedge fences would not grow
easily or where stone and wood were not plentiful, few farmers could
afford to buy and transport lumber or other fencing materials. In these
areas many people found it impossible to farm, and they left the land to the
cattlemen. Not until 1872, two years before barbed wire appeared on the
market, was the trespass law removed from the statute books in California.
By then the influx of farmers was so great that California politicians

realized they could no longer remain partial to large landowners, namely the cattlemen.[3]

As state lawmakers in the cattle country east of the Rocky Mountains began passing measures defining the relative rights of cattlemen and farmers, open-range cattlemen were obliged to have cowboys patrol the boundaries of their ranges to keep cattle from trespassing on other people's property. This demand increased the number of range riders and line riders assigned to patrol the boundaries. They followed imaginary "lines" that divided their outfit's cattle from those on the other side of the line or from a settler's property. When cattle began to wander across the line, it was their duty to turn them back.

Reginald Aldridge, an Englishman who came to America in 1877 and became a cowboy and rancher in southern Kansas, Indian Territory, and Colorado, spent time as a line rider. "It is not hard work," he recalled, "but decidedly monotonous, riding by yourself for so many hours every day. A good line-rider ought to be able to see if any cattle have left the range by the tracks they leave on the ground as they pass out, and must then follow up the trail and bring them back. The chief difficulty I always found was to distinguish between the old and the fresh trails, unless there had been sufficient rain to wash out the old tracks."[4]

Line riders often lived in dugouts or small shacks thrown up on the edge of the open ranges. The life of a line rider was lonely. On many days he saw no other human being. A big event in his daily or weekly routine came when he met another line rider or when a wagon from his outfit brought a supply of groceries. The line rider would then stop and exchange news and sometimes cigarettes or a pipe full of tobacco. His job was most difficult in periods of drought, whether in Texas or Montana. When water holes and streams dried up on a range, it was difficult and often impossible to hold back thirsty cattle in search of water.

Then came the invention of barbed wire in 1873, and in a few short years the face of the West began to change. At first, Texas cattlemen did not use it. Many were suspicious of barbed wire. Henry D. McCallum, a leading barbed-wire historian, wrote in his book *The Wire That Fenced the West* that "Texans were dubious about any innovation from the North. Although the War between the States had been over for ten years, they still suspected that this might be another Yankee scheme to benefit the industrial North at the expense of the agricultural South." Barbed wire was invented in Illinois, and in the eyes of most Texas cattlemen, Illinois was in the East. And the fact that a *farmer*, Joseph Farwell Glidden, was credited with inventing barbed wire also was suspicious.

As with anything or anyone famous, legends have grown up around how Glidden came upon the idea of barbed wire. One story recounts how he and some friends visited a county fair in De Kalb County, Glidden's home area, and saw an exhibit put up by Henry W. Rose, which consisted of a strip of wood about an inch square and about 16 feet long. Into the wood Rose had driven some sharp barbs, leaving the points sticking out. The blocks of wood were hung on smooth wire. As cattle and other livestock tried to crawl through the wire fence, they were stopped by the sharp points that pricked their hides. Borrowing this idea, so the story goes, Glidden created *his* barbed wire.

Another story, perhaps tied to the first, relates how Glidden's wife asked her husband to put up a fence around her flower garden to protect it from dogs. Glidden first tried smooth wire without success. Then he borrowed his wife's coffee grinder to use as a reel for the smooth wire and, with the aid of an old grindstone to bend it, placed short pieces of wire with sharp points around the smooth wire. How many strands and how they were spaced are questions still unanswered, but the fence kept the dogs out of his wife's garden. It may have been that Glidden got the idea for the fence from Henry Rose's exhibit. Regardless, Glidden was granted a patent on his barbed wire on November 24, 1874.[5]

An important feature of Glidden's "Winner," as his first barbed wire is called, was that the barbs or spur wires were held in place by two wires that were twisted around the barbs. This made the wire not only durable but readily adaptable to mass production. Barbed wire could be produced cheaply, but the low cost was not its only advantage. Barbed-wire fencing took little room. Aside from the wooden posts to which the wire was attached—stone posts were used in some areas of Kansas and elsewhere when wood posts could not be obtained—the barbed wire did not touch the soil or shade vegetation. It could withstand high winds and not cause snow to drift during the winter.

The year Glidden was granted his barbed-wire patent he formed a partnership with a neighbor, Isaac L. Ellwood, and built a small factory in De Kalb. By late 1874 they were producing barbed wire. They hired Henry Sanborn as a salesman. Sanborn sold some wire in Illinois and then headed west and south into Texas. There he sold ten reels of barbed wire to a merchant in Gainesville, and later sold a carload to a hardware store in Austin. But Sanborn found it difficult to convince ranchers and farmers of the merits of the new fencing. Most Texans, for reasons already mentioned, not only rejected barbed wire as something northern, but opposed it because the barbs could injure their cattle and horses. Will James (not to be confused with the cowboy-artist of more recent times) spent his early years as a Texas cowboy before turning writer. James witnessed the introduction of barbed wire on his home range in Texas. Later, in his classic *Cow-boy Life in Texas, Or, 27 Years a Maverick*, James wrote that the first thing that aroused the indignation of cattle people "was the terrible destruction of stock caused from being torn first on the wire and the screw worm doing the rest."

Henry Sanborn, of course, tried to talk down such disadvantages. While he is credited with having sold the first barbed wire in Texas, it was John Warner Gates who apparently convinced many Texans of the advantages of the new fencing. Gates, early in 1876, when he was about twenty years old, was hired by Glidden and Ellwood. By summer he was heading for Texas. Exactly where he went or whom he visited is hazy. He apparently had little success until he arrived in San Antonio late in the year. There, after failing to talk visiting ranchers and farmers into using barbed wire, Gates, borrowing a technique from the medicine shows that were then commonplace throughout the Southwest, hit upon the idea of giving a demonstration to show the effectiveness of the new fencing.

Gates obtained permission from city officials to build a corral on one of San Antonio's plazas, probably Military Plaza. As people watched the corral being built, their curiosity became more intense. When the corral was completed, Gates had twenty-five longhorns—some accounts say there were as many as 135 head—driven into the barbed-wire enclosure. A large crowd gathered. Gates, acting as master of ceremonies, described the advantages of the new fencing. The longhorns milled around inside the corral. One old-timer's story tells how two men with flaming torches were sent inside to frighten the longhorns into pushing against the wire. Another story tells how Gates arranged to use only docile longhorns. At any rate, his demonstration convinced many farmers and ranchers of the value of his product. By dusk, he supposedly had more orders than he could fill.[6]

The bare facts may suggest that Gates was simply a good businessman. He was, but John Gates was more than that. He is described as a brash young man, a good talker as well as a showman. These qualities contributed to his success in the middle 1870s. And Gates, not one to be held back, was soon manufacturing barbed wire on his own. His small operation grew rapidly, and bigness soon became Gates' trademark. A gambler at heart, he earned the nickname "Bet-a-Million" Gates. The nickname, according to most versions of the story, was earned one rainy day when Gates and Isaac Ellwood were traveling by train from Chicago to Pittsburgh. There were not enough men to play cards. A bored Gates watched heavy drops of rain run down the windowpane. Suddenly Gates offered Ellwood a bet that one particular raindrop would reach the bottom of the windowpane before the others. Ellwood took the bet and the game was on, with stakes as high as a thousand dollars on each raindrop. Before the train reached Pittsburgh, Gates had won what most men would have considered a fortune—along with the nickname "Bet-a-Million." His maneuvering in the world of business later made him chairman of the board of directors of the powerful American Steel & Wire Company. Still later,

Gates entered a tiny oil business, developed the city of Port Arthur, Texas, as an oil-shipping center and built up the Texas Company, better known today as Texaco. He died in 1911, thirty-five years after his first truly successful business promotion of barbed wire in San Antonio.

However, not all of the cattlemen who watched Gates's barbed-wire demonstration were persuaded to use the new fencing. Abel H. "Shanghai" Pierce, the south Texas rancher, refused to buy, saying he did not want any type of fencing that would cut up his cattle. But Pierce, like other cattlemen who were at first opposed to it, in time accepted this inexpensive fencing and installed it on his ranch.

The earliest barbed-wire fences constructed by open-range cattlemen did not fully enclose their grazing land. The fences were east–west "drift fences" designed to keep northern cattle from drifting onto the southern ranges. Perhaps the earliest such drift fence was constructed by Major Andrew Drumm along the northern edge of what was then called the Cherokee Strip, a huge corridor of land laid out by the government as a travelway for Cherokee Indians going west to hunt buffalo. Located in the northwestern part of Indian Territory, the Strip was 60 miles wide and 250 miles long. But the Cherokees never found much use for the land. Drumm had made a small fortune in the California gold fields and in stock raising near San Francisco. He had helped to organize one of San Francisco's pioneer meat-packing companies, Willoughby Bros. & Drumm, before returning east. When the cattle-town markets of Kansas opened, Drumm added to his wealth by buying cheap cattle in Texas and driving them north to sell. Following the Chisholm Trail through Indian Territory, including the Cherokee Strip, Drumm was impressed with the grassland. By 1870 he had established a ranch in the Strip, and soon other cattlemen, including E. M. Hewins of Cedarvale, Kansas, and a Colonel Evans of St. Louis, had placed their cattle on the Strip's rich grasses.

Drumm and a partner, Andy Snyder, ran as many as fifty thousand head under the U brand. Soon after Glidden's barbed wire came on the market, Drumm and Snyder erected a drift fence along the northern boundary of their 150,000-acre range. Some accounts suggest that the fence stretched for nearly 200 miles. By 1881, other drift fences with three or four strands of barbed wire had appeared along the northern edge of the Texas panhandle. The *Dodge City Times* on November 6, 1884, reported: "The longest line of fencing in the world will be the wire fence extending from Indian Territory west across the Texas Pan-Handle and thirty-five miles into New Mexico. The total length being 200 miles, 84 miles of this fence is already under contract. Its course will be the line of the Canadian river and its purpose is to stop the drift of northern cattle."

This long fence was not continuous. Each cattleman put up his fence along his portion of the range where he thought it would best serve the purpose. Therefore, portions of the fence did not always connect. The cost of erecting the "drift fence" ranged from $200 to $400 a mile, depending upon the roughness of the terrain crossed and the cost of transporting wire and posts to the range. This fence saved the grass of the Canadian region for Texas cattle during the vicious winter of 1884, but when the spring of 1885 arrived there were dead cattle along nearly the entire length of each fence line. They had drifted south with the storms. When they reached the drift fences, they could go no farther. Starved or frozen to death, they stacked up behind the fences like wood on a pile.

Many cattlemen from Texas northward into Montana had begun using barbed wire by the early 1880s. Most did so to protect the land they owned and land they hoped they could own. The invasion of settlers into cattle country usually was accompanied by the building of barbed-wire fences by both cattlemen and farmers. Cattlemen with foresight had purchased land and water rights, but those lacking the ability to anticipate the changes suddenly started to grab as much land as they could obtain. These open-range cattlemen who might not otherwise have used barbed-wire turned to the cheap fencing to enclose land they did not own. Some ranchers exploited the law in an effort to gain control of land. In New Mexico, Wyoming, and elsewhere there were cattlemen who induced their cowboys to file homestead claims on land that was part of their open range. For a price, the cowboys turned title to the land over to their rancher bosses. In this manner cattlemen gained ownership of land they had been using for years as open range. Charley Coffee, a Texas trail driver turned Wyoming rancher, found another way to beat the invasion of farmers. "We couldn't shoot, for they weren't like Indians, so the only way I could get even was to go into the banking business," recalled Coffee, who made generous loans at high interest rates to struggling farmers and took mortgages on their homesteads. In time, Coffee was able to foreclose on much of the land and return it to grazing.[7]

The increased demand for barbed wire in the West is reflected in the following figures:

> 1874—5 tons made and sold
> 1875—300 tons made and sold
> 1876—1,420 tons made and sold
> 1877—6,431½ tons made and sold
> 1878—13,327½ tons made and sold
> 1879—25,188½ tons made and sold
> 1880—40,250 tons made and sold[8]

It should be emphasized that Glidden's barbed wire was not the only type produced during the late nineteenth century. Many authorities believe there are more than four hundred types of barbed wire. Some were invented before 1867 when the first United States patents were issued. And even before Joseph F. Glidden received his patent in November 1874, his friend Isaac L. Ellwood had obtained a patent for what is called "Ellwood Ribbon." It is a wide metal strip with four-point sheet-metal barbs. Ellwood received his patent in February 1874, nine months before Glidden obtained his. Ellwood, however, never produced his wire commercially. He recognized the superiority of Glidden's wire and helped to produce it.

During the latter half of the 1870s and early 1880s, a rash of other patents were issued for countless variations of barbed wire. Some had two barbs around one piece of wire, while others consisted of two wires with sheet-metal barbs of associated shapes and sizes. One patent issued in August 1878 was for a three-hundred strand wire with simple tacks held in place by the twisted strands. Many inventors hoped to cash in on the

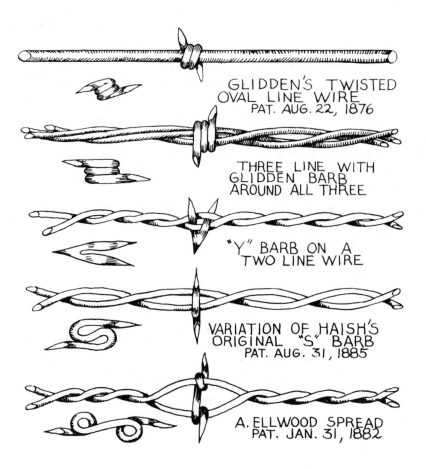

GLIDDEN'S TWISTED
OVAL LINE WIRE
PAT. AUG. 22, 1876

THREE LINE WITH
GLIDDEN BARB
AROUND ALL THREE

"Y" BARB ON A
TWO LINE WIRE

VARIATION OF HAISH'S
ORIGINAL "S" BARB
PAT. AUG. 31, 1885

A. ELLWOOD SPREAD
PAT. JAN. 31, 1882

growing demand for barbed wire, but Joseph Glidden's simple wire barb twisted onto double-strand wire remains even today the most popular. It is easier to handle than most other types.

The stringing of a barbed-wire fence was and is a more complex process than one might imagine. During the late 1870s and early 1880s ranchers fencing their land began by having a surveyor mark the boundary lines of their ranches with stakes, piles of rock, or mounds of earth. usually at intervals about 30 feet apart. On these marks the fence posts were erected. But first a rancher had to find suitable posts. Many cattlemen insisted on cedar or locust posts. Some liked Osage orange or *bois d'arc*, woods that last in the ground for many years. Pine, cottonwood, and a few other softwoods would suffice if the ends were dipped in creosote to ward off rot and occasional termites. Once the rancher obtained the posts, each about 6 feet long, they were taken to the range or pasture by wagon and one post would be tossed to the ground near each marker left by the surveyor. If the ground was hard, as it generally was, a bucket of water to loosen the soil was poured on the spot where the post hole was to be dug. Sometimes barrels of water had to be freighted 20 miles or more for this purpose. Then a 2-foot hole was dug, the post set in the ground, and loose dirt packed around the base of the post. Once a line of posts was erected, a load of barbed wire would be brought to the site by wagon.

Barbed wire came wound on large wooden spools. Before the cowboys could handle the wire, they had to put on heavy leather gloves, some with long sleeves to protect their lower arms. Most cowboys carried bandages and some iodine in their saddlebags or in the wire wagon, since it was unusual not to be scratched handling barbed wire. A spool of the wire was then rigged on a crosspole at the back of the wagon. When the loose end of the wire was unwound, twisted around the first post about one foot from the ground, and made secure, the wagon moved along the line of posts for perhaps 200 yards unreeling the wire. The back of the wagon was then jacked up on one side. The barbed wire on the ground was cut free from the spool and attached to the axle of the jacked-up wheel. When the elevated wheel was turned, the wire was pulled taut. The wagon was now in a position to pull the wire next to the line of posts. Patent wire stretchers appeared later, but most cowboys found the wagon wheel technique easier to use. Once the wire was taut, a cowboy moved along the posts, stapling the wire to each post. The wire was stapled on the side of the posts facing into the pasture, so that the wire was pressed against the posts and not the staples when stock ran into the fence. After the first strand of wire was attached to the posts, the process was repeated for each strand of wire on the fence. And each new strand was placed higher on the posts. Four- and five-strand fences were and still are very common in cattle country.

Joseph Glidden and Henry Sanborn built a four-strand fence on their Frying Pan ranch in the Texas panhandle in the early 1880s. Their fence posts were 20, not 30, feet apart. A special order of extra-heavy Glidden barbed wire was sent from the factory to the nearest railroad terminal 250 miles from the ranch, then transported by wagon to the ranch. The fence cost $39,000 to build. It was 150 miles long, enclosing the 125,000-acre ranch. Later the size of the ranch was doubled. Once the barbed wire was installed, Sanborn, who directed the ranch operations, placed 1,500 head of cattle on the land to demonstrate the effectiveness of barbed-wire fencing. Although Glidden and Sanborn purchased the ranch in 1881, Glidden visited the Frying Pan only once in 1884. He wanted no part of ranching in his old age and left the ranch management to Sanborn.

The Frying Pan was large, but not the largest ranch in Texas by 1883. A report in the *Dodge City Times*, September 27, 1883, gave that honor to Charles Goodnight's ranch in the panhandle. Goodnight's spread consisted of 700,000 acres (the King Ranch then totaled only 614,140 acres), and it required 250 miles of barbed-wire fence to enclose. By the late 1880s, however, even Goodnight's ranch and its fencing was small compared to that of the XIT Ranch along the western side of the Texas Panhandle. The XIT was established in 1885 by the firm of Taylor, Babcock, and Company (they were called the Capitol Syndicate because they received 3,050,000 acres of Texas land in return for building the state capitol at Austin). By the fall of 1886, the owners of the XIT had put up more than 780 miles of barbed-wire fence. The west line fence, with many jogs, ran 260 miles long, beginning at the northwest corner of Texas and running south 150 miles without a turn. The east line was 275 miles long. In all, fence riders checked 575 miles of outside fence around the XIT. It took more than 300 carloads of material to build the fence, at a cost of $181,000. By the late 1890s cross fences divided the ranch into ninety-four pastures. The ranch then had about 1,500 miles of fence, according to J. Evetts Haley, who wrote the classic *The XIT Ranch of Texas*. Haley observed that the fence building required more than 100,000 posts, five carloads of wire stays, and one carload of staples. "So many gates were necessary in the corrals and along the fences, that the first general manager just ordered a carload of gate hinges," wrote Haley. More than 110,000 cattle were placed on the ranch by late 1886.

There is no question that barbed wire caused problems for man and beast. Will James remembered that when the first fence was put up on his home ranges in Texas, cattle

would run full tilt right into it, and many of them got badly hurt; and when one got a scratch sufficient to draw blood, worms would take hold of it. Some men would come into a range, where the stock had regular rounds or beaten ways, and fence up several hundred acres right across the range, and thus endanger thousands of cattle and horses. After the first three years of wire fences, I have seen horses and cattle that you could hardly drive between two posts, and if there was a line of posts running across the prairie, I have seen a bunch of range horses follow the line out to the end and then turn. But, in a few years, the old tough-hided cow found a way to crawl through into a corn field if the wire was not well stretched and the posts close together. The man who had horses cut up and killed by the wire often felt like cutting it down, and in many instances did. . . .[9]

Most cattle and horses eventually adjusted to the presence of barbed wire. Animals born behind such fencing learned early to respect it. But some cattlemen and cowboys never did accept the fencing. Barbed wire meant change that was difficult to accept. It had the effect of denaturing many of the beliefs of cow people. In 1884, for instance, one Texas trail driver spoke the thoughts of many cowboys and cattlemen when he looked back over a ten-year period. He wrote:

In 1874 there was no fencing along the trails to the North, and we had lots of range to graze on. Now there is so much land taken up and fenced in that the trail for the most of the way is little better than a crooked lane, and we have hard times to find enough range to feed on. These fellows from Ohio, Indiana, and other northern and western states—the "bone and sinew of the country," as the politicians call them—have made farms, enclosed pastures, and fenced in water-holes until you can't rest; and I say, Damn such bone and sinew! They are the ruin of the country, and have everlastingly, eternally, now and forever, destroyed the best grazing land in the world. The range country, sir, was never intended for raising farm-truck. It was intended for cattle and horses, and was the best stock-raising land on earth until they got to turning over the sod—improving the country, as they call it. Lord forgive them for such improvements! It makes me sick to think of it. I am sick enough to need two doctors, a druggery, and a mineral spring, when I think of onions and Irish potatoes growing where mustang ponies should be exercising, and where four-year-old steers should be getting ripe for market. Fences, sir, are the curse of the country![10]

Not all homesteaders, however, could afford barbed-wire fencing. Those settlers who had spent most of their money to come west turned furrows with their plows around their claims. Cattlemen knew that legally a furrow was the same as a fence, but their cattle did not. Many cattle not yet behind

barbed wire wandered over the furrows and were shot and killed or
wounded by farmers. Violence usually followed, as in an incident that occurred in 1877 only a few years after the invention of barbed wire. The
place was Custer County, in west-central Nebraska. The principal characters were Print Olive, a Texan who had moved north with his brothers
to ranch along the Platte River, and two homesteaders named Luther
Mitchell and Ami Ketchum.

Rancher Print Olive settled in the region first. By the middle 1870s
he and his brothers had more than 25,000 head of cattle grazing on the
rich grasslands of Custer County. Unfortunately, the rich black earth that
produced fine grass was also perfect for farming. Soon the farmers arrived,
and the conflict between the two cultures began. Print Olive, who had a
fierce temper, was not willing to compromise. He tried to frighten the
homesteaders by cutting their fences, destroying their crops, and driving
cattle across their plowed fields. The two homesteaders, Mitchell and
Ketchum, retaliated by killing some of the cattle belonging to the Olive
brothers. When Print's brother Bob, a deputy sheriff, tried to arrest
Mitchell and Ketchum, he was shot and killed. The homesteaders were
arrested, but before they could receive a formal hearing both men were
kidnapped by the Olives and lynched. Then two of the Olives' cowboys,
according to one account, doused the homesteaders' bodies with whiskey
and set them on fire. Print Olive and one of his cowboys were tried, con-
victed of the murders, and sentenced to life in prison. However, they were
released two years later on order of the Nebraska Supreme Court because
their trial had not been held in Custer County, the scene of the murders.
A new trial was ordered but never held, and Olive returned to ranching.
Later, in the summer of 1886, Olive was murdered in Trail City, a cattle
town just across the Kansas border in eastern Colorado.[11]

Other acts of violence associated with barbed-wire fences took place
in the late 1870s and 1880s. In some areas, especially Texas, fence cutting
reached the proportions of a war during the drought of the summer and
fall of 1883. Many cattlemen had difficulty finding water and grass for their
cattle. Most of the ranchers owned or leased the land they fenced, but some
had enclosed public land in addition to their own. Still other ranchers
began stringing barbed-wire fences around farms and small ranches belonging to other people in an effort to grab every possible acre of grassland for their cattle. Times were hard. Fences blocked many public roads,
cutting off schools and churches and interfering with the delivery of the
mail. Men began to cut fences, and soon ranchers were hiring men to do
the job. More than half of the counties in Texas reported the cutting and
wrecking of fences and the burning of pasturelands by late 1883. The most
serious damages occurred in a wide swath down the center of Texas from

the Red River south. West of that region was still the cattleman's frontier in Texas.

Much of the fence cutting was done at night by armed bands of men calling themselves Javelinas, Blue Devils, or Owls among other names. After cutting fences and in many instances pulling fence posts from the ground, the fence cutters would leave warnings against rebuilding. Most such warnings were ignored. In a few cases ranchers or their cowboys were waiting when fence cutters arrived, and gunfights followed. News of such violence spread beyond the borders of Texas. The *Dodge City Times* in Kansas reported on October 4, 1883:

> Blood was shed in the southern part of Clay county [Texas] on the 14th inst. over the cutting of Sherwood's fence. A man named Butler, said to be a leader in the cutting business, was killed and several others wounded—supposed to have been done by parties guarding the fence or by line riders. If we are not misled by a similarity of names, Butler's land and home are within the inclosure made by Sherwood. When the news reached Henrietta [Texas] a large party of stockmen armed themselves and went to the scene of action. Intense excitement prevailed, and it was thought other collisions must take place. It is evident that since the state is powerless in the premises, the stockmen will defend their property to the bitter end. It looks inevitable that a terrible clash must be the outcome of the present deplorable condition of things in the troubled district.

Perhaps half-a-dozen men were killed in battles between fence cutters and ranchers defending their property. By the fall of 1883 damage to fences in Texas was estimated at $20 million, at least $7 million in Brown County alone. Politicians did not want to tackle the problem and tried to ignore it until Texas Governor John Ireland called a special session of the state legislature on January 8, 1884. The session was heated. Numerous petitions were introduced, and fence cutting was debated for hours. When the special session ended, the lawmakers had made fence cutting a felony punishable by one to five years in prison. At the same time, however, the fencing of public lands, or lands belonging to others, knowingly and without permission was made a misdemeanor, and builders of such fences were ordered to remove them within six months. Builders who had built fences across public roads were ordered to place a gate every 3 miles and to keep the gates in repair.

The actions of the Texas lawmakers brought an end to wholesale fence cutting, but the problem continued in Texas, especially during years of drought. Texas Rangers were sent after fence cutters in several

counties, including Brown and Navarro. Ranger Ira Aten, the son of a
circuit-riding Methodist preacher, was responsible for putting a stop to
the fence cutting in Brown and Navarro counties. In 1886, Aten posed as
a wandering cowboy and got a job on a small ranch owned by one of the
fence cutters in Brown County. In time, Aten learned that the head of the
Brown County fence cutters was none other than a local lawman. Aten
arranged for other Texas Rangers to be waiting when the gang made a
fence-cutting raid near Pecan Bayou. The Rangers surprised the four men
and ordered them to surrender. They refused and began firing. The
Rangers returned the fire, and when the smoke cleared two of the fence
cutters were dead and two others were wounded.

Not quite two years later, Aten was sent into Navarro County about
60 miles south of Dallas to put a stop to fence cutting there. In a letter
to his Ranger captain dated August 31, 1888, Aten reported what he had
learned while posing as a laborer:

The fence-cutters here are what I would call cowboys or small cowmen that own cattle from 15 head all the way up to perhaps 200 head
of cattle and a few cow ponies, etc. Some have a hundred acres of
land, and some more, and some not so much and perhaps a little field in
cultivation. They hate the Grangers as they call them [farmers] for it
is the Grangers that have the pastures. . . . In fact they hate everybody
that will fence land either for farming or pasture. They are a hard lot
of men in here, and they are thieves as well as fence-cutters. . . . Small
pastures that would not support but milk cows and work horses for a
very small farm have been cut time and again until the owners have
not the means to put up the wire any more and now all pastures are
down and this is called free-range country. Many have took down
their wire and rolled it up to save it from being cut. . . . The fence-
cutters themselves have told me that while a man was putting up his
fence one day in a hollow a crowd of wire-cutters was cutting it back
behind him in another hollow back over the hill. They delight in telling all such things and most of it is true also. The good citizens hold
the wire-cutters in dread for they know they would not hesitate a
moment to murder them.[12]

To stop the fence cutters in Navarro County, Ranger Aten decided to
place small bombs at regular intervals along some of the fence lines. The
bombs were constructed by stuffing dynamite into shotgun barrels and
then concealing the barrels under fences. But the Texas adjutant general
learned of Aten's plan and ordered that the bombs not be used. Aten ignored the order, planted the bombs, and instructed ranchers who had been

FOUR MEN RE-ENACT FOR THE CAMERA
how settlers probably cut 15 miles of barbed-wire fence
on the Brighton Ranch, Custer County, Nebraska, in 1885.

A LINE SHACK ON THE PITCHFORK RANCH IN WYOMING.
The cowboy at right is saddling up after a snowstorm
to check for wandering cattle.

victims of the fence cutting on how to use them. Aten was called to Austin, where the governor, who had learned that Aten had disobeyed orders, told him in no uncertain terms to remove the bombs. Aten returned to Navarro County and removed the bombs by exploding them. The explosions were heard for miles around. As word spread through the county that a Ranger had set the bombs, the fence cutting came to an abrupt halt.[13]

From the southern plains northward, local and state governments and many officials of federal land offices sought to prevent the fencing of public land. But cattlemen continued to enclose thousands of acres of government land from Texas to Montana. Transcripts of hearings by U.S. senators in Washington tell how mail delivery was stopped by illegal fences in western Nebraska during the early 1880s. The Brighton Ranch was one of several Nebraska outfits involved in fencing public land. To the south in Kansas a few cattlemen enclosed entire counties in western and southwestern areas, while in Dakota Territory the Marquis de Morés fenced a large chunk of public land, as did the Carlisle Cattle Company, a Wyoming ranching operation backed by English capital. There was even an attempt to fence pasturelands in the public domain in Nevada. And in New Mexico two companies were organized for the purpose of fencing large tracts of public lands to keep others out. But the cost of fencing in New Mexico made their task difficult. A three-strand barbed-wire fence with posts 33 feet apart cost $110 per mile. This meant it cost about $10 per head to keep cattle on the enclosed range.

Ab Blocker, the well-known Texas cattleman, had problems with fenced public land, but he was on the receiving end. In 1885, Blocker joined a drive heading toward a ranch near Deer Creek, Colorado. As the herd came to what is today the southern boundary of the Oklahoma panhandle, they ran smack into barbed-wire fence. Squatters had erected the fences and refused to let the Texas longhorns pass. The settlers, with no legal claim to the land, maintained that the Texas cattle would infect their farm cattle with Texas fever. Ab and his brother John Blocker rode to Camp Supply, Indian Territory, and spent about $60 on telegrams to Washington. As Ab Blocker recalled in *The Trail Drivers of Texas*, someone in the Department of Interior (that Department had authority over Indian Territory) finally advised the Blockers to cut the barbed wire and proceed. The government also ordered the cavalry to stand by in case of trouble. Ab and John Blocker returned to their herd. Ab took a hand ax and chopped down the single strand of barbed wire that blocked their access. The Blocker brothers continued their trail drive to Colorado without interference.

In some areas cattlemen fenced land set aside for public schools.

Cowmen even entered areas of public timber in Wyoming, northwest Nebraska, and New Mexico and cut down trees to obtain fence posts. It is easy to understand why farmers and small cattle ranchers were furious. The government land office in Washington supported farmers. N. C. McFarland, the public land commissioner, reported on April 5, 1883, that his office had no objection to cattlemen grazing their cattle on public land or cutting hay there until farmers arrived so long as the land was left open to all. But his statement was ignored by most cattlemen. He then advised settlers to cut all fences barring them from public land that they wished to homestead. Since his office had no judicial authority, however, cattlemen continued to ignore his orders. It was not until early 1885 that Congress passed a law designed to speed prosecution of those who fenced public land, although it had no effect in Texas, where the state had retained all public land when it joined the Union. The *Annual Report of the General Land Office* for 1886 cited illegal fences in the older and more established counties of Montana and Wyoming. Laramie County, Wyoming, had the most offenders—ten large cattle companies, including the Swan Land and Cattle Company with 130 miles of illegal fence.

Lawsuits against the ranchers did not seem to bother them as much as rustlers, many of whom posed as fence cutters to steal unbranded calves. Ranchers who fenced their herds often neglected to brand their calves before they were weaned. It was easy for a rustler to cut a pasture fence, drive the weaned calves to his ranch, and brand them as his own, although since cows and calves have a strong instinct for finding each other even when miles apart, this sometimes caused problems. To prevent reunions, rustlers might cut the muscles supporting the calf's eyelids, making the animal temporarily blind, or they would apply a hot iron between the toes to make the calf's feet too sore for walking. In a few cases rustlers split the calf's tongue to prevent suckling should the calf and mother meet. And it was not unusual for a rustler to kill a calf's mother to eliminate any possibility of mother and calf meeting again in this world.

Prosecuting rustlers in Texas, and in the cattle country northward through Kansas and Nebraska into Wyoming, the Dakotas, and Montana, was often difficult. Evidence was not easy to obtain. In Wyoming, some cowboys had quit their jobs on the big ranches, filed homestead claims, and built their own herds allegedly at the expense of their former employers. Several big ranchers brought rustling charges against the new cowmen. Jurors, however, seemed to show more sympathy for the cowboy-turned-rancher than for the wealthy absentee owners of the big ranches, and managers of absentee-owned ranches consequently made little effort to stop the rustling—perhaps hoping the problem would go away. It did not. By the late 1880s rustling had become such a problem in eastern Wyoming that several of the large ranchers, including some of the absentee-owners, organized and hired detectives to eliminate the rustlers.

Several of the alleged rustlers were killed, including James "Jim" Averill and a woman known as "Cattle Kate." Her real name was Ella Watson. A not-so-attractive prostitute, she supposedly accepted stolen calves from rustlers as the price for spending the night in her arms at her house on the Sweetwater in Carbon County, Wyoming. Averill's claim was next to Kate's. He had built a small combination general store and saloon and served as postmaster in the tiny community. Cattle Kate and Averill reportedly were lovers and partners in what several large Wyoming ranchers believed was a highly questionable cattle business. Kate kept the cattle she and Jim received in a corral on her claim. But their careers came to an abrupt end one day early in 1889 when six men rode up and hanged both of them from a tree near Kate's cattle corral.

Other small ranchers, including Tom Waggoner, died in a similar manner, apparently on orders of George B. Henderson, the man hired by the large ranchers to put a stop to the rustling. Whether all or any of the small ranchers killed were in fact rustlers is unknown; they may have been nothing more than competition to the big ranchers. The violence might have run its course had not Henderson been shot by an ambusher and killed. This apparent retaliation by someone other than the large ranchers put into motion what historians have called the Johnson County War. The conflict also has been called the TA War, the Little and Big Cattlemen's War, the Rustlers' War, the Invasion, and the Regulators' War, depending upon who is describing the conflict. Regardless of the label, the large ranchers set in motion plans to invade what they believed was the stronghold of the alleged rustlers, Johnson County, Wyoming, 250 miles northwest of Cheyenne. The drama, since depicted by Hollywood films at least half-a-dozen times, began to unfold in the spring of 1892.

Four prominent cattlemen—George W. Baxter, Tom Smith, Frank M. Canton, and R. M. Allen—went to Denver, where they hired some ex-sheriffs, former U.S. marshals, and a few other trusted gunmen. Some of these cattlemen, perhaps others, continued on to Texas, where they enlisted the services of a few more lawmen handy with carbines and pistols. All of these hired "guardsmen," as the cattlemen called them, were given an advance of "hush and travel" money and told to meet in Denver in early April. The committee of four cattlemen, representing the large cattle companies and the powerful Wyoming Stock Growers' Association to which the larger and frequently absentee-owned companies belonged, next arranged for a special train to transport the guardsmen north to Cheyenne on April 5, 1892.

Late that afternoon the special train made the short journey north from Denver to the railroad yards at Cheyenne, a run of a little more than an hour's time. At Cheyenne three stock cars were added to the train and loaded with seventy-eight hand-picked, high-priced, and grain-fed horses branded with the letter *A* on their shoulders. A flat car carrying a camping outfit plus three Studebaker wagons was added to the train. The engineer then moved the train to a remote place in the Cheyenne railroad yards, where it sat with the blinds drawn in the chair car. Curious people could not see the twenty-two "guardsmen" inside, but a perceptive observer was probably suspicious of the mysterious train.

Two days earlier the Wyoming Stock Growers' Association had ended its annual meeting in Cheyenne. For several weeks before the meeting, the association's secretary had been gathering a list of the names of supposed rustlers. Members had been invited to send nominations to the secretary, who appears to have accepted a member's word that any man nominated was a rustler. The secretary then passed the names to the association's executive committee, which in turn decided on the names that should go on a final list of wanted men. Although the Wyoming Stock Growers' Association has never admitted that the project had their official sanction, the members' involvement was considerable. As the special train stood in the railroad yard at Cheyenne, the expedition was preparing to take the law in Johnson County into their own hands. It should be pointed out that court records in the county leave little doubt that law enforcement there had broken down because the rustlers had used political influence and force for their own benefit. That was wrong. It was also wrong, however, for the cattlemen to try to take over the reins of law.

When the special train pulled out of Cheyenne that night, nineteen cattlemen and five stock detectives had joined the twenty-two hired gunmen or "guardsmen" already aboard the train. The train moved north toward Casper. At about four o'clock in the morning on April 6 the train quietly slowed to a stop in the Casper railroad yards just east of the town of six hundred souls. The men got off the train and unloaded the wagons, horses, and gear. A few more cattlemen reportedly joined the little army that had arrived by train. Major Frank Wolcott, a onetime receiver of the United States Land Office and United States marshal, was in command. Wolcott was a member of the executive committee of the Wyoming Stock Growers' Association. Still being as quiet as possible so as not to awake the people of Casper, the little army moved north, avoiding the town. About 6 miles north of Casper the men stopped and built campfires to prepare breakfast. All went well until their wagons pulled into the makeshift camp. The noise frightened several horses belonging to the cattlemen and "guardsmen," and the animals ran off, with several men giving chase. Snow soon began to fall. Perhaps these things were signs of what was to follow.

The small army, however, managed to move on and reach a friendly ranch about 65 miles north of Casper. There the men spent the night.

Word had reached Major Wolcott before he and the army reached the ranch that several rustlers had been seen at the KC Ranch on the road between Casper and Buffalo. The modern community of Kaycee is located on the spot where the ranch headquarters once stood, near where the Middle Fork of the Powder River comes out of the foothills of the Big Horns and Hole-in-the-Wall country, but in 1892 only the headquarters, a poorly cared-for log-and-frame cabin, stood on the spot.

Some accounts tell how the cattlemen's army orignally planned to go to Buffalo, Wyoming, the seat of Johnson County, and take charge of the courthouse and the weapons of the local militia that were stored there. Once in Buffalo, according to the account of J. Elmer Brock, the gunmen proposed to call a mass meeting of the citizens of Johnson County to offer amends and obtain help from the honest people, and then post a list of the alleged rustlers and give them twenty-four hours to get out of the country. But word that some of the wanted men were only about 18 miles to the north was too much for them. They decided to deal with the wanted men first.

Early on the morning of April 9, 1892, the cattlemen surrounded the crude headquarters of the KC Ranch. As the first faint rays of daylight appeared in the east, they captured Bill Jones, one of two trappers who had sought shelter in the ranch house the night before. Jones was taken prisoner as he walked from the house to the nearby stream to get water. When he did not return, the other trapper—William Walker—came looking for him. Walker also was captured. That left only two men in the ranch house—Nick Ray and Nate Champion, both on the invaders' wanted list. Other men who reportedly had been at the ranch had left well before the invaders arrived.

Presently, Nick Ray went outside to see what had happened to the trappers. He had not gone more than a few steps from the door before the invaders opened fire. Mortally wounded, Ray struggled back to the door, where Nate Champion, attracted by the gunshots, dragged him inside. That left Champion to hold off the invaders single-handedly. Ray died a few hours later, and before the sun began its westward swing, Champion was wounded several times. At about four o'clock that afternoon the invaders loaded a wagon with pitch pine and hay, pushed it up to the cabin, and set fire to it. The ranch house caught fire quickly, and Champion ran from the blazing structure toward a nearby ravine. He was shot down in his tracks about 200 yards away. One account relates how the invaders pinned a crude sign on Champion's chest that read "Cattle Thieves Beware."

The wagon used to burn out Nate Champion had been taken at about three o'clock in the afternoon from O. H. Flagg and his stepson, Alonzo

Taylor, who were passing the KC Ranch on a road. Both Flagg and Taylor escaped from the "guardsmen" in a hail of bullets and made their way to the ranch of John R. Smith, where Flagg was to have joined delegates preparing to leave for the state Democratic convention in Douglas. Flagg gathered a party of men and they started for the KC Ranch. But in the meantime Torrence Smith, a rancher living 4 miles north of the KC Ranch, had heard the firing and ridden south to investigate. Convinced the law was being violated, Smith started for Buffalo. Along the route he alerted other ranchers. At about 7:30 P.M., Smith arrived at Buffalo, where Sheriff Red Angus first learned of the gunmen. Angus called upon the local company of the National Guard for help. The commander refused. Sheriff Angus then tried to organize a posse but was able to find only six saddle horses. With six men he headed toward the KC Ranch. There the bodies of Nick Ray and Nate Champion were found. The army had left.

On Sunday morning, April 10, while Sheriff Angus was still at the KC Ranch, O. H. Flagg and his party of men rode into Buffalo and reported that the gunmen had gone to the TA Ranch owned by Dr. Harris about 13 miles south of Buffalo. "Couriers were sent out in different directions calling on men to come to town, and on Sunday evening at 8:30 a party of 49 men rode quietly out of Buffalo toward the south. This party elected A. S. Brown their leader and arrived at the TA about midnight," reported *The Buffalo Bulletin* in the weekly newspaper's first account of the invasion, published on April 14, 1892. "Pickets were at once posted around the buildings at a safe distance and the party then awaited daylight. Just before daylight the posse took position in sheltered places on all sides of the ranch. As soon as the posse hove in sight of the building shots were fired by the besieged cattlemen and the battle was then on."

Later in the day Sheriff Red Angus and forty additional men arrived at the TA Ranch from Buffalo. Angus took command, and as word of the invasion spread, other reinforcements arrived from Johnson and nearby Sheridan counties. The posse seems to have been made up of honest law-abiding citizens and perhaps some of the rustlers, all opposed to the unlawful invasion by the "cattle barons," as they called the large ranchers.

Although the cattlemen had cut the telegraph wires running south from Buffalo when they first arrived in the area, the wires were soon repaired. Wyoming's acting governor, Amos Barber, in Cheyenne received a telegram from Buffalo describing the state of affairs. Barber wired the President of the United States for help. President Benjamin Harrison replied by sending three troops of the Sixth United States Cavalry from Fort McKinney, about 25 miles from Buffalo. They arrived at the TA Ranch just as the trapped army was constructing dynamite bombs in an effort to end the two-day siege.

The cavalry "advanced on the fortifications waving a flag of truce," reported the *Buffalo Bulletin* in its first account. "Major Wolcott, commanding the cattle barons' party issued from the fortifications, refused to surrender to Sheriff Angus, but surrendered to Colonel Van Horn. . . . An examination of the buildings showed that the fortifications constructed by the cattlemen were well nigh impregnable, and that the storming of them would have entailed a heavy loss of life upon the besiegers. . . . The party was nearly out of provisions, all that was visible, in fact, was one loaf of cornbread and the hind quarters of a calf."

No one had been killed during the siege of the TA Ranch. The cattlemen and their "guardsmen" were taken to Fort McKinney and later to Fort D. A. Russell near Cheyenne. The story of the local proceedings that dragged along for about a year appear to have favored the large ranchers. No court action was ever taken, and the gunmen eventually went free. The wealthy cattlemen involved reportedly contributed $1,000 each to pay the costs of the action, more than $100,000, according to several accounts. But the complete list of those who paid has never been uncovered.

While the wealthy cattlemen who sponsored the army did escape prosecution, their actions became a political football and split the people of Wyoming. Most residents of the state seem to have sided with the people of Johnson County. Before the election of 1892, Democrats and Populists succeeded in convincing most voters that "the Republican Ring Gang of Cattle Barons of Cheyenne" had been responsible for the army. In truth, both Republicans and Democrats had taken part in the action, or at least had backed it; the army was not a political matter. But the Republican political machine in Wyoming suffered defeat at the polls and a Democratic governor was elected.[14]

The arrival of barbed-wire fences and the closing of the open ranges did not always contribute to violence, but in nearly each instance where the fences were erected, it marked the beginning of the end of the cowboy's open-range culture. Certainly the coming of civilization, including eastern business practices, brought other things that changed the cowboy's and cattleman's way of life, but it was the barbed-wire fence that could be seen and touched. Barbed-wire fencing signified the end of the old ways and the beginning of the new. It was something that affected each cowboy and cattleman, and others living in the West as well. This fact is perhaps best mirrored in a story told by Charles Goodnight, the pioneer rancher in the Texas panhandle.

Late in the 1870s Goodnight learned that a religious group that opposed liquor had started a settlement (it would later become Clarendon, Texas) near his ranch. One day soon after the settlers arrived, Goodnight decided to ride over and view the new community. As he neared their camp, Goodnight saw the new arrivals talking to a band of Pueblo Indians from what is now New Mexico. Unfortunately, the Pueblos spoke Spanish but no English. The settlers did not understand Spanish.

Nearing the group, Goodnight realized that the settlers believed the Indians to be fierce Comanches. The old Pueblo chief did not understand this and kept telling the settlers that he and his people were peace-loving and meant no harm. In Spanish the chief added that if the settlers would talk to the rancher who lived nearby, meaning Goodnight, he would vouch for the Indians. The settlers did not understand this.

The shouting match grew louder and was about to erupt into violence when Goodnight thought he had better make his presence known. As he moved toward the Indians and settlers, the old Pueblo chief recognized Goodnight, who later recalled: "I never saw anyone's face brighten up so much as this old chief's did." Goodnight then explained to the settlers that the Pueblos were peaceful. As the settlers relaxed, the Indian chief told Goodnight that he and his people had been trading with the Kiowas in Indian Territory and had decided to take a different route back to Taos. But at that point the chief asked Goodnight, "How do we get back to Taos?"

"You surely know the way back to Taos. Haven't you lived in this country all your life?" replied Goodnight.

Whereupon the chief cried out: "Alambre! alambre! alambre! todas partes!" ("Wire! wire! wire! everywhere!") Barbed wire had so changed the lay of the land in the Indians' eyes that even they were confused.[15]

Epilogue

The feel for the cowboy is everywhere; the symbol of the cowboy is just as pervasive.

—JOE B. FRANTZ[1]

THE golden age of the real cowboy in the American West was gone as the twentieth century dawned. Yet a cowboy culture was still glowing brightly in the minds of Americans. While this culture still permeates our society, it is not the culture of the real nineteenth-century cowboy. Rather it is a blend of fact and imagination, and it is rooted in the writings of men like Ned Buntline (whose real name was Edward Zane Carroll Judson), Colonel Prentiss Ingraham, Samuel S. Hall, Gerald Carlton, and other popular writers of the last century. These men produced romantic and adventurous stories about the West to capitalize on the public's curiosity about the frontier. The popularity of these fictional tales became so great that more and more of them were written to satisfy the public's craving. By the 1870s the cowboy was an integral part of this literature.

Just after the twentieth century began, Owen Wister, a Harvard graduate who had visited the West, added to what was becoming the myth of the cowboy with his novel *The Virginian*. But there are no cattle in the story, and the life of the cowboy is not portrayed with any accuracy. The novel firmly established the gunfight between the hero and the villain as a western theme and used for the first time the line: "When you call me that, smile!" *The Virginian* even included a romance for the cowboy hero. During the book's first fifty years, it sold more than 1,600,000 copies, not counting foreign translations and paper reprints. In the early years of this century Zane Grey, a New York dentist, also turned to writing westerns, and before long Frederick Schiller Faust—one of his many pen names was Max Brand—joined the growing number of writers who were keeping the mythical cowboy culture alive.[2]

Soon another form of entertainment was adding to the misconceptions: the Wild West show. William F. "Buffalo Bill" Cody and W. F. Carver took the first such show on the road in 1883. Cody, already a hero of dime novels, included in his repertoire demonstrations of shooting, bucking broncos, roping and riding wild steers, horse races, a re-creation of the Pony Express, an attack on the Deadwood stagecoach, and numerous other acts supposedly depicting life in the West. The Wild West show was entertainment, and its development closely paralleled that of the rodeo—usually pronounced "*roh*-dee-oh" among cowboys. Unlike the Wild West show, the rodeo (from the Spanish *rodear*, meaning "to surround or encircle") was a competition testing the skills of cowboys in such activities as bronc riding and roping. Rodeos developed as celebrations—the earliest were held on the Fourth of July—in Deer Trail, Colorado (1869), Cheyenne, Wyoming (1872), and Pecos, Texas (1883). The people of Prescott, Arizona, supposedly awarded the first trophy to a rodeo winner in 1888.

The Wild West shows that toured not only the West but many eastern cities and even foreign countries added to the myth of the cowboy. For instance, the Miller Brothers' 101 Ranch Wild West Show—organized by Joseph, Zack, and George Miller—included an event that became known as "bulldogging" (now it is called steer wrestling). Bill Pickett, a Texas cowboy of black and Indian descent, is credited with having developed this technique. Pickett would ride his horse (named Spradley) alongside a longhorn steer, drop to the steer's head, and twist the head slowly toward the sky. He would then bite the steer's upper lip, something few if any old-time cowboys would have thought of doing. The technique has been traced back to 1881, when Bill Pickett, then eleven years old, noticed a bulldog being used to work cattle; it was holding a cow motionless by biting the animal's upper lip. The dog's teeth apparently were painful to the sensitive membranes of the cow's lip. Pickett later tried biting a calf's lip and found that the animal stopped resisting. He used this method to hold cattle being branded before he joined the 101 Ranch show. He became something of a legend before he died from injuries received while breaking horses on the 101 Ranch near Ponca City, Oklahoma, in 1932. That was about a year after the 101 Ranch show, the last of the great Wild West shows, folded.

By then the rodeo had replaced the Wild West show as the largest form of live western entertainment. Some events, like roping and bronc riding, had of course originated with the *ranching cowboy*, a term used to separate the modern ranch hand from the professional rodeo performer who may never have been a working cowboy on a ranch. Bull riding, however, originated solely as rodeo entertainment. And the professional rodeo entertainer is just that, an entertainer.

Long before the Wild West show was a thing of the past, the western theme had been introduced into the infant medium of film. W. K. L. Dickson's vignette titled *Cripple Creek Barroom* was produced in 1898 by the Edison Company. And next came *The Great Train Robbery*, a longer film, produced near Dover, New Jersey, in 1903. The film seems to have been the blueprint for all westerns to follow. It was produced something like a modern documentary. Such films were "characterized by sincerity of sentiment and a poetic spirit," according to one authority, who noted that the audiences of these early westerns were made to feel that they were witnessing "not merely casual entertainment but, rather, a serious and dignified visual discussion of an era which had already passed into the nation's heritage."[3]

Names like "Bronco Billy" Anderson and William S. Hart soon became well known, but the age of "cowboy stars" did not develop until the 1920s, when Hoot Gibson, Fred Thomson, Ken Maynard, Bob Steele, Buck Jones, Harry Carey, Jack Hoxie, Tom Mix, and Art Acord appeared on the silver screen. Acord, like Mix, had been a rodeo performer, but Mix, who joined the Miller Brothers' 101 Ranch Wild West Show after serving during the Spanish-American War, had also been a lawman in the Southwest. William S. Hart, although born in Newburgh, New York, in 1870, had worked as a cowboy in Kansas and had been caught in the crossfire of a gun battle between a sheriff and two gunmen in Sioux City. By the early 1930s, however, William S. Hart's movies had been overshadowed by the new cowboy stars and a new approach to the making of westerns.

Hollywood writers had by then taken a closer look at the real cowboy and his culture. Much of the old-time cowboy's unwritten code was resurrected and embellished. In time, the western—on film and in print—was transformed into an assembly-line product that continued to glamorize the cowboy and his culture. The cowboy became a simple human being with all the strengths and weaknesses of the people who watched and read the westerns, and the cowboy always won out over evil. Rarely did the moviegoer or reader of westerns find the cowboy working cattle. The cowboy, especially as portrayed in films, became more like a Boy Scout than the old-time cowhand whose culture has been depicted in this book.

Gene Autry, who first made his way into films carrying a guitar in 1935, followed what he later described as the "Ten Commandments of the Cowboy," which are rather similar to the Scout oath: A cowboy must not take unfair advantage, even when facing an enemy. He must always tell the truth, and be gentle with children, elderly people, and animals. He must not advocate or possess racially or religiously intolerant ideas. He must help people in distress, be a good worker, keep himself clean in thought, speech, action, and personal habits. He must respect women, parents, and his nation's laws. He must neither drink nor smoke. And the cowboy was first, last, and always a patriot.[4]

The golden age of the cowboy with a "good guy" image continued through the 1940s and into the 1950s. In addition to Gene Autry, such figures as George O'Brien, Roy Rogers ("King of the Cowboys"), Larry "Buster" Crabbe, Alfred "Lash" LaRue, Charles Starrett ("the Durango Kid"), John "Duke" Wayne, Randolph Scott, Joel McCrea, and Bob Steele became household names. They appeared larger than life on the silver screen, and the cowboy created by the Hollywood writers became even more entrenched in American culture.

The growth of television following World War II brought the Hollywood cowboy to life in still another medium. Many of the old film cowboys toppled, however, as their industry refused to recognize television. Gene Autry and William Boyd ("Hopalong Cassidy") bought up the rights to all of their films and sold them to television, and the myth continued. "The Lone Ranger," successful on radio, was brought to television in 1949. Starring Clayton Moore and Jay Silverheels, the series lasted until 1956. And "Gunsmoke," another successful radio western, made its appearance on television in 1955 starring James Arness as Matt Dillon, U.S. marshal. The series continued until 1975, when it went off the air after nineteen years, then the longest run of any series on television.

As television grew, so did the number of westerns. Richard Boone became a Western TV star in the series "Have Gun, Will Travel" (1956–1963). In 1972 he returned in the Western series "Hec Ramsey," which lasted two years. The new breed of television western stars included Lorne Greene as Ben Cartwright in the series "Bonanza" (1959–73); Dale Robertson in "Tales of Wells Fargo" (1956–62), "Iron Horse" (1966–68), and "Death Valley Days" (1965–70). There was Clint Eastwood in the series "Rawhide" (1960–67) and Robert Fuller in "Laramie" (1959–62) and "Wagon Train" (1957–65). Clint Walker represented the cowboy image as the rugged Cheyenne Bodie in the series "Cheyenne" (1956–63). And there was Steve McQueen in the series "Wanted: Dead or Alive" (1958–61); Gene Barry in "Bat Masterson" (1957–61); Jack Lord in "Stoney Burke" (1962–63); and James Garner in "Maverick" (1956–60).

Most of the new breed of western stars on television retained some of the "good guy" traits of the film cowboys of the past, and they generally won in the end, just like these earlier counterparts in the movies. By the 1960s, however, the film industry, returning to westerns, was beginning to produce some pictures with an "anti-hero" theme. Others sought to humanize the cowboy. These films had stars, but they did not always portray the "good guy." Yet the films continued to convey the spirit of the mythical cowboy already rooted in the American culture. In the 1960s and

'70s such films included John Ford's "The Man Who Shot Liberty Valance" (1962); Sam Peckinpah's "Ride the High Country" (1962); Elliott Silverstein's "Cat Ballou" (1964), starring Lee Marvin as a drunken gunfighter and former cowboy; George Roy Hill's "Butch Cassidy and the Sundance Kid" (1969); Henry Hathaway's "True Grit" (1969), starring John Wayne; Sam Peckinpah's "The Wild Bunch" (1969); Arthur Penn's "Little Big Man" (1970); Philip Kaufman's "The Great Northfield, Minnesota, Raid" (1971); and John Milius' "The Life and Times of Judge Roy Bean" (1972), starring Paul Newman as the legendary "hanging judge" and "law west of the Pecos."

The writers of films, television programs, and books, however, have not been the only ones to contribute to the myth of the cowboy. Many historians have done so as well, by omission and default. They simply ignored the cowboy and his culture and did nothing to correct popular misconceptions. One prominent historian, Frederic Logan Paxson, ignored not only the cowboy and his culture but also the cattle trade, in his survey history titled *The Last American Frontier* published in 1910. Paxson does not so much as mention the cowboy. So the main purveyors of the cowboy and his culture were not the historians but the popular media, and most of what they have related has reflected a mythical hero on horseback, not the true cowboy of the nineteenth century.

Perhaps the first major attempt to correct the misconceptions was launched by Philip Ashton Rollins, a native of New Hampshire, who at the age of five spent four months with Jim Bridger, the famous scout and mountain man, and as a teen-ager rode twice with trail herds from Texas to Montana. Rollins built a fine collection of books, pamphlets, and manuscripts about the cowboy that are today housed at Princeton University. He wrote *The Cowboy, His Characteristics, His Equipment, and His Part in the Development of the West*, published in 1922. The book is a factual account of the old-time cowboy and his way of life. Since then other writers, including a growing number of historians, have sought to tell the truth about the cowboy. Yet, while most people are now willing to acknowledge that the real cowboy and his culture were not what westerns have projected, the mythical cowboy culture lives on.

The real American cowboy *was* colorful. He *was* a romantic figure, even before writers embellished his life and culture. He was a human being seeking his place in the sun like countless other people since the dawn of civilization. His culture developed out of the conditions of his time and place, and it should be recognized for what it really was—an important page in the history of the settlement of the American West.

But a mythical cowboy culture still survives alongside the real one, and it is in evidence today in cities and towns across America. From

BY THE 1880s, BEING A COWBOY WAS ALREADY "ROMANTIC."
Left: A young man from either Denver or Cheyenne
in his new cowboy outfit. It is not
clear whether he was a real cowboy or an early version of the
drugstore variety. Sometimes the photographer
even provided the clothes.
Right: Three Dodge City businessmen dressed as cowboys to have their
picture taken, apparently to impress some Eastern friends.

Bangor to Santa Barbara, from Portland to Palm Beach, it may be seen in all its glory. More and more young people and even many of their elders have adopted the fashions of the cowboy—western hats and boots, western-cut clothing, western belts and buckles actually unlike those worn by real cowboys a century ago. And in many parts of the country the pickup truck with a rifle hanging in a rack in the back window has become the cow pony of the modern cowboy. From the radio speaker inside blasts the sound of country music, and the bumper sticker may read: "Cowboys Do It Better!" More and more Americans seem to be grabbing for bits and pieces of this mythical cowboy culture.

Why?

Are they trying to avoid becoming a cog in a machine over which they have no control? Are they searching for some satisfying identity that suggests rugged individualism in our highly legislated society? Are they seeking the frontier experience through imitation? Are they looking for a new frontier?

Through the years, politicians have sought to substitute other frontiers for Americans to conquer. Henry A. Wallace proposed a "new frontier" in 1934—one at which "free-booter democracy of the purely individualistic type" would give way to the cooperative efforts of a new breed of frontiersmen "whose hearts are aflame with the extraordinary beauty of the scientific, artistic, and spiritual wealth now before us." But Wallace was not successful. Neither was John F. Kennedy, who in 1960 laid similar plans to conquer a "new frontier of uncharted areas of science and space, unsolved problems of peace and war, unconquered pockets of ignorance and prejudice, unanswered questions of poverty and surplus."

Future politicians will undoubtedly propose other substitute frontiers for Americans to conquer, since we seem to yearn for the frontier experience. It has become an American tradition. The reality, however, may be that Americans are dissatisfied with the trappings of modern civilization—big cities, masses of people, man-made pressures and problems, and the frustrations of a mechanical society. The cowboy symbolizes the free life, closely tied to the out-of-doors and Nature. The impact of land, the grass, the rivers and streams and gushing springs, the color of the sky and the clouds, the climate and the weather—these things are characteristic of the real *and* the mythical cowboy cultures.

Ironically, the very thing that destroyed the real cowboy's culture during the last century was the culture of the man in business and industry, deeply rooted in the East. This culture, requiring homes, churches, and cities and towns, had a sense of permanence about it and required the support of institutions and government. It arrived on the prairies and plains with settlers who sought to extend this culture. They succeeded. It is a paradox, however, that the business culture that now stretches from the Atlantic to the Pacific still believes in the mythical culture created by its writers, and too many Americans are shaping their lives after the images of that mythical culture, one that never existed.

Notes

Chapter One: The Spanish Roots

The historical and cultural development of the cattle industry in New Spain has not received the attention it deserves in the United States. One reason is the language barrier. Another is the fact that many Spanish documents and archival records in Spain and in Mexico have not been fully explored by scholars. Yet the cattle industry in New Spain had a tremendous influence on the early cattle industry in the United States. Several volumes may someday be written on the subject.

This chapter only attempts to convey to the reader the roots and the foundations on which the cowboy culture of the American West was built.

Unless otherwise cited, my sources for this chapter have been William H. Dusenberry's *The Mexican Mesta: The Administration of Ranching in Colonial Mexico* (Urbana: University of Illinois Press, 1963); François Chevalier's *Land and Society in Colonial Mexico: The Great Hacienda* (Berkeley and Los Angeles: University of California Press, 1963), trans. from French by Alvin Eustis and ed. by Lesley Byrd Simpson; Richard J. Morrisey's unpublished Ph.D. dissertation "The Establishment and Northward Expansion of Cattle Ranching in New Spain" (Berkeley: University of California, 1949) and his subsequent articles "The Northward Expansion of Cattle Ranching in New Spain, 1550–1600," *Agriculture History*, Vol. XXV (1951), and "Colonial Agriculture in New Spain," *Agriculture History*, Vol. XXXI (1957); and Donald D. Brand's "The Early History of the Range Cattle Industry in Northern Mexico," *Agricultural History*, Vol. XXXV (1961), which is presented in outline form with bibliographical suggestions. These efforts constitute the major scholarly works relating to the early development of the cattle industry in Mexico.

Of general help was Peter Gerhard's *A Guide to the Historical Geography of New Spain* (London: Cambridge University Press, 1972), Vol. 14 in the Cambridge Latin American Studies; *Bolton and the Spanish Borderlands* (Norman: University of Oklahoma Press, 1964), ed. by John Francis Bannon; Herbert I. Priestley's *The Mexican Nation: A History* (New York: Macmillan, 1926); and Julius Klein's *The Mesta: A Study in Spanish Economic History, 1273–1836* (Cambridge: Harvard University Press, 1920), Vol. 21 in the Harvard Economic Studies series.

The quote from John Bartlett Brebner comes from his book *The Explorers*

of North America, 1492–1806 (New York: Macmillan Co., 1933). The quote
from José de Acosta appeared in his *Historia Natural y Moral de las Indias*
(Sevilla, 1590), as cited by Robert M. Denhardt: *The Horse of the Americas*
(Norman: University of Oklahoma Press, 1975). Bernal Díaz del Castillo's
quote came from his *Historia verdadera de la conquista de la Nueva España*
(Mexico City, 1904), edited by Genaro García. The quote from Father Alonso
Ponce's unidentified secretary was cited by Lesley Byrd Simpson: *Exploitation
of Land in Central Mexico in the Sixteenth Century* (Berkeley: University of
California Press, 1952). And the quote of Muñoz Camargo was found in
François Chevalier's *Land and Society in Colonial Mexico: The Great Hacienda*,
already cited.

1. Samuel E. Morison, *Admiral of the Ocean Sea* (Boston: Little, Brown and
Co., 1942), Vol. II, pp. 49–50.

2. John E. Rouse, *The Criollo: Spanish Cattle in the Americas* (Norman:
University of Oklahoma Press, 1977), pp. 23–29.

3. Arnold R. Rojas, *Bits, Bitting and Spanish Horses* (Goleta, Cal.: Kimberly
Press, 1970), p. 45.

4. Robert M. Denhardt, "The Horse in New Spain and the Borderlands,"
Agricultural History, Vol. XXV (1951), p. 145. See also Robert M. Denhardt,
The Horse of the Americas (Norman: University of Oklahoma Press, 1975),
pp. 53–63; J. Frank Dobie, *The Mustangs* (Boston: Little, Brown and Co.,
1952), pp. 21–23.

5. Charles W. Hackett, ed., *Historical Documents Relating to New Mexico,
Nueva Vizcaya, and Approaches Thereto, to 1773* (Washington: Carnegie Institution, 1923), Vol. I, p. 41. See also Rouse, *The Criollo*, pp. 23–29.

6. Rouse, *The Criollo*, pp. 14–19, 216–217, 219, 224.

7. Cortés also reserved for himself the broad valley of Oaxaca, about 500
miles southeast of Mexico City, ringed by mountains and having a semiarid,
temperate-to-cool climate. Later, he took a well-watered region of fertile valleys
called Cuernavaca located to the south of Mexico City. Some writers have
suggested that Cortés named Cuernavaca because of some link with a cow or
cattle (*vaca*). Donald D. Brand, "The Early History of the Range Cattle Industry in Northern Mexico," observed that Cuernavaca is a "corruption of a
Nahuatl name that means something like 'near the woods.' I do not know who
first perpetrated the bastard etymology of Cuernavaca: however, among the
writers whose lead has been followed rather slavishly are Paul I. Wellman, *The
Trampling Herd* (New York, 1939), 21, who places the Cow's Horn hacienda
of Cortés in Cuba, and J. Frank Dobie, *The Longhorns* (Boston, 1941), 3, who
has Cortés stock his great Cow Horn (Cuernavaca) estate in Mexico from a
hacienda in Cuba. Among the numerous followers are Charles Wayland Towne
and Edward Norris Wentworth, *Cattle & Men* (Norman, 1955), 119, who com-
pound the error by writing of Cortés' splendid place in the Oaxaca Valley
named Cuernavaca, Cow's Horn (now a picturesque town south of Mexico
City). It would tax even Aladdin's wonderful lamp to move the town of
Cuernavaca to the Valley of Oaxaca."

8. Manfred R. Wolfenstine, *The Manual of Brands and Marks* (Norman:

University of Oklahoma Press, 1970), pp. 5, 42–45; see also Oren Arnold and John P. Hales, *Hot Irons: Heraldry of the Range* (New York: Macmillan, 1940), p. 28. The practice of branding dates back to the Chinese. There is biblical evidence that Jacob, the great herdsman, branded his stock. Branding has been traced back to 2780 B.C. in Egypt. Paintings depicting the branding of cattle have been found in several Egyptian tombs. In New Spain, before Cortés branded any cattle, his force of Spaniards and Tlaxcalan allies enslaved many Tepeacan Indians. "They were branded on cheeks and lips with the letter G (for *guerra*, war) and portioned out, one-fifth for the king, one-fifth for Cortés, the remainder to be sold." See William W. Johnson, *Cortés* (Boston: Little, Brown and Co., 1975), p. 156.

9. *Actas de Cabildo*, Vol. II, p. 3, as cited by Dusenberry, *The Mexican Mesta*, pp. 46–47. According to Dusenberry, the brands of the owners in the vicinity of Mexico City are reproduced in the *Actas de Cabildo*, Vol. II, pp. 196–210. The origin of the Mesta can be traced to local meetings of Castilian stockmen during the early Middle Ages. They met two or three times a year to enforce the ordinances of the town charter pertaining to the pastoral industry, mostly sheep raising. These gatherings were called *mestas*, probably because strays were *mezclados*. See Klein, *The Mesta*, pp. 9–10.

10. J. Lloyd Mecham, *Francisco de Ibarra and Nueva Vizcaya* (Durham: Duke University Press, 1927), pp. 29–30. Coronado's story is detailed in Herbert E. Bolton, *Coronado, Knight of Pueblos and Plains* (Albuquerque: University of New Mexico Press, 1949). In 1521 Ponce de León attempted to establish a colony on the west coast of Florida. He brought with him a small herd of Andalusian cattle, the first such animals brought to what is today the United States. What happened to these cattle is unknown. For the story of the development of the cattle industry in Florida, see Joe A. Akerman, *Florida Cowman: A History of Florida Cattle Raising* (Kissimmee: Florida Cattlemen's Association, 1976).

11. The word *vaquero* represents a combination of the Spanish word *vaca*, meaning "cow," with the suffix *ero*, meaning "one engaged in a given occupation or activity." See Ramon Adams, *Western Words* (Norman: University of Oklahoma Press, 1944), p. 172.

12. Records and documents describing the dress of the early vaquero in New Spain are sparse. Artifacts in the Edward Larocque Tinker Collection, Humanities Research Center, University of Texas, Austin, provided some guidance, as did Fay E. Ward, *The Cowboy at Work* (New York: Hastings House, 1958); Glenn R. Vernam, *Man on Horseback* (New York: Harper and Row, 1964); Ruth E. Kilgour, *A Pageant of Hats, Ancient and Modern* (New York: Robert M. McBridge Co., 1958); and Edward Warwick, Henry C. Pitz, and Alexander Wyckoff, *Early American Dress* (New York: Benjamin Blom, 1965).

13. Lee M. Rice and Glenn R. Vernam, *They Saddled the West* (Cambridge: Cornell Maritime Press, 1975), pp. 2–3. See also Vernam, *Man on Horseback*, pp. 238–240, and Ward, *The Cowboy at Work*, pp. 193–194, 207–208.

14. Dobie, *The Mustangs*, p. 22.

15. J. Frank Dobie, "The First Cattle in Texas and the Southwest Progenitors of the Longhorns," *Southwestern Historical Quarterly*, Vol. XLII (1939), p. 172, citing Nicolas Rangel, *Historia del Toreo en México* (Mexico City, 1924).

16. Basil Hall, *Extracts from a Journal Written on the Coasts of Chili, Peru, and Mexico* (Edinburgh: Archibald Constable and Co., 1824), Vol. I, pp. 158–164.

17. Chevalier, *Land and Society in Colonial Mexico*, p. 112.

18. Lesley Byrd Simpson, *Exploitation of Land in Central Mexico in the Sixteenth Century* (Berkeley and Los Angeles: University of California Press, 1952), pp. 2–3.

19. *Ibid.*, pp. 1–2.

Chapter Two: Moving North

1. Morrisey, "The Northward Expansion of Cattle Ranching in New Spain," p. 121. Literally the term "Anglo-America" implies people of English, Scotch, and perhaps Irish ancestry. People from Germany and elsewhere in northern Europe were involved in the early cattle industry of the western United States. The term "Anglo-American" should not be used in contrasting the backgrounds of people from northern Europe, including the British Isles, to those of Spain.

2. Herbert Ingram Priestley, *The Mexican Nation: A History* (New York: Macmillan, 1923), pp. 136–149, 171–173.

3. The most complete study of the hacienda system is François Chevalier's *Land and Society in Colonial Mexico*, trans. from French by Alvin Eustis and ed. by Leslie Byrd Simpson. The translation, however, does not include the voluminous footnotes published in the Paris edition, 1952. Another work that includes material on haciendas in New Spain is *Haciendas and Plantations in Latin American History* (New York and London: Holmes and Meier, 1977), ed. by Robert G. Keith. The collection includes François Chevalier's "The North Mexican Hacienda," taken from *The New World Looks at Its History* (Austin: University of Texas Press, 1963). These works were consulted.

4. Jo Mora, *Californios* (Garden City: Doubleday and Co., 1949), p. 127.

5. Frank Gilbert Roe, *The Indian and the Horse* (Norman: University of Oklahoma Press, 1955), pp. 376–379.

6. There are numerous accounts of how the name "Texas" originated. A letter written by Father Damian Massanet to Don Carlos de Siguenza contains the story of the Indians greeting the padres with the word "Thechas!" Father Massanet, however, used the spelling "Tejas" in a letter he later wrote. The letter is reproduced in *The Quarterly of the Texas State Historical Association*, Vol. II, pp. 281–312, and later reprinted as an appendix in Robert Carlton Clark's *The Beginnings of Texas 1684–1718* (Philadelphia: Porcupine Press, 1976). The spelling "Tayshas" is given in Joe B. Frantz's excellent popular history *Texas: A Bicentennial History* (New York: W. W. Norton and Co., 1976), p. 10.

7. Fray Gaspar José de Solís's account may be found in "Diary of Fray Gaspar José de Solís, in the Year 1767–68," *Southwestern Historical Quarterly*, Vol. XXXV (July 1931), p. 56. Translated by Margaret Kenney Kress, the diary makes note of "many Spanish cattle, unbranded and without owner, because the first person who entered when these lands were discovered and conquered, was Captain León (of glorious memory). On the bank of these rivers he left a bull and a cow, a horse and a mare, and this is the reason why there are so many cattle and horses unbranded and wild." Richard J. Morrisey, in his unpublished Ph.D. dissertation "The Establishment and Northward Expansion of Cattle Ranching in New Spain," pp. 176–179, notes that Alonso de León took 200 cattle, 400 horses, and 150 mules on the journey. J. Frank Dobie includes the story in *The Mustangs*, p. 98, citing Father Massanet's letters as the source. The story is told by other writers, including Sandra L. Myres in her fine article "The Spanish Cattle Kingdom in the Province of Texas" in *Texana*, Vol. IV, No. 3 (Fall 1966), p. 235. Robert C. Clark, in *The Beginnings of Texas*, makes no mention of Captain de León's *deliberately* leaving cattle and horses at various streams. He does write that Captain de León relaxed his control on the return journey and "animals were so carelessly attended that numbers of horses and mules were lost . . . ," p. 26.

8. James Wakefield Burke, *Missions of Old Texas* (South Brunswick and New York: A. S. Barnes and Co., 1971), pp. 134–137.

9. François-Xavier Martin, *The History of Louisiana, from the Earliest Period* (New Orleans: François-Xavier Martin, 1827), p. 363.

10. Fray José Franco López, *The Texas Missions in 1785* (Austin: St. Edwards University, 1940), pp. 12–20.

11. Odie B. Faulk, *The Last Years of Spanish Texas, 1778–1821* (The Hague: Mouton and Co., 1964), pp. 88–89.

12. Herbert E. Bolton, *The Padre on Horseback* (San Francisco: The Sonora Press, 1932), p. 64.

13. Junior Jean Wagoner, *History of the Cattle Industry in Southern Arizona, 1540–1940* (Tucson: University of Arizona, 1952), p. 19. Carlos III was responsible for expelling the Jesuits from the Spanish empire in 1767. All Jesuit missionaries and other "Black Robes," as they were called, were arrested, dispossessed, taken to Vera Cruz, and transported to prison in Spain.

14. The best surveys of early cattle ranching in Arizona are Wagoner's *History of the Cattle Industry* and Richard J. Morrisey, "The Early Range Cattle Industry in Arizona," *Agricultural History*, Vol. XXIV (1950).

Chapter Three: The Californiano Culture

1. Arnold R. Rojas, *The Vaquero* (Charlotte and Santa Barbara: McNally and Loftin, 1964), p. 24.

2. Ramon Adams, *The Rampaging Herd* (Norman: University of Oklahoma Press, 1959), lists 2,651 books and pamphlets relating to the men and events in

the cattle industry, but only 81 of them are listed under California. Under the listing for Texas there are 439; Wyoming, 201; Montana, 172; and Kansas, 145. Although Adams was a Texan and more familiar with publications relating to the cattle industry of Texas and areas to the north, his bibliography is reasonably complete for California and other regions. Unfortunately, writers and historians —often there is a great difference—have ignored much of the history, even the colorful and romantic aspects, of the California cattle industry. The important published works consulted were: Robert Glass Cleland, *The Cattle on a Thousand Hills: Southern California, 1850–1870* (San Marino: The Huntington Library, 1941), a superb piece of scholarship but thin on California cattle drives; Richard Henry Dana's 1840 masterpiece *Two Years Before the Mast* (Boston: Houghton Mifflin Co., 1911 edition), with much material on the hide and tallow trade of early California; William Heath Davis's 1889 classic *Seventy-five Years in California* (San Francisco: John Howell, 1967 and best edition); Jo Mora's *Trail Dust and Saddle Leather* (New York: Charles Schribner's Sons, 1946) and his *Californios*, both rich in personal observations but thin on citing sources; and Arnold R. Rojas's equally delightful and important works, *Last of the Vaqueros* (Fresno: Academy Library Guide, 1960), *The Vaquero*, and *Bits, Bitting and Spanish Horses*. Of some value were L. T. Burcham's article "Cattle and Range Forage in California, 1770–1880," *Agricultural History*, Vol. XXXV (1961); Dane Coolidge's *Old California Cowboys* (New York: E. P. Dutton and Co., 1939), and Helen Bauer's *California Rancho Days* (Garden City: Doubleday and Co., 1953).

3. Herbert Eugene Bolton, *Fray Juan Crespi: Missionary Explorer on the Pacific Coast, 1769–1774* (Berkeley: University of California, 1927), pp. 264–265.

4. Mora, *Californios*, pp. 30–33. Unfortunately, Mora does not provide his source for the figures quoted.

5. This letter is now in the private collection of Floyd E. Risvold at Minneapolis, Minnesota.

6. H. T. Lilliencrantz, "Recollections of a California Cattleman," *California Historical Society Quarterly*, Vol. XXXVIII (1959), p. 341.

7. Denhardt, *The Horse of the Americas*, p. 292.

8. Randolph B. Marcy, *The Prairie Traveler* (New York: Harper and Brothers, 1859), pp. 119–120.

9. Cleland: *The Cattle on a Thousand Hills*, p. 14.

10. The seeds of Mexican independence were planted in 1808 when Napoleon I conquered Spain. He placed his brother, Joseph Bonaparte, on the Spanish throne. This left the Spanish colonies without a recognized European ruler. In 1810, Father Miguel Hidalgo y Costilla, a priest in the town of Dolores, called upon his Indian followers to rise up against the Spanish. Hidalgo's followers won several victories, but their leader was captured and executed. Late in 1820, Iturbide became leader of the rebels and defeated the Spanish, proclaiming himself emperor of Mexico.

11. Clarence W. Gordon, "Report on Cattle, Sheep, and Swine, Supplementary to Enumeration of Live Stock on Farms in 1880," *Report on the*

Productions of Agriculture. Tenth Census (Washington: Department of Interior, 1883), Vol. III, p. 1029.

12. *Ibid.*, p. 1029, citing M. Duplot de Mofras, *Exploration du territoire de l'Oregon, des Californies et de la mer Vermeille, 1840, 1841, 1842,* pp. 320–321. The figures for 1834 and 1842 come from this source. The incomplete figures for 1830 were found in Davis, *Seventy-five Years in California*, pp. 282–283.

13. George W. B. Evans, *Mexican Gold Trail: The Journal of a Forty-Niner* (San Marino: The Huntington Library, 1945), pp. 176–177.

14. Davis, *Seventy-five Years in California*, p. 108.

15. Erwin Gustav Gudde, ed., "Edward Vischer's First Visit to California," *California Historical Society Quarterly*, Vol. XIX (1940), pp. 205–206.

16. Davis, *Seventy-five Years in California*, p. 222.

17. Gudde, ed., "Edward Vischer's First Visit to California," p. 209.

18. Harvey L. Carter, "Ewing Young," *The Mountain Men and the Fur Trade of the Far West* (Glendale: The Arthur H. Clark Co., 1965), Vol. II, pp. 379–401, is a biography of Young. See also *The Diary of Philip Leget Edwards* (San Francisco: Grabhorn Press, 1932), a reprint of Edwards's experiences published in serial form in 1860.

19. Cleland, *The Cattle on a Thousand Hills*, pp. 44–45, citing Walter A. Hawley, *The Early Days of Santa Barbara* (Santa Barbara, 1920), pp. 95–96.

20. Tracy I. Storer and Lloyd P. Tevis, Jr., *California Grizzly* (Lincoln: University of Nebraska Press, 1978), p. 120.

21. Andy Russell, *Grizzly Country* (New York: Alfred A. Knopf, 1968), pp. 108–109. A personal book rich in observation.

22. Davis, *Seventy-five Years in California*, p. 172.

23. Storer and Tevis, *California Grizzly*, pp. 150–151.

Chapter Four: The Texian Culture

1. The term "Texian" is generally used to refer to a citizen of Mexican Texas or of the Republic of Texas. "Early colonists and leaders in the Texas Revolution . . . used Texian . . . but in general usage after annexation Texan replaced Texian." See *The Handbook of Texas* (Austin: The Texas State Historical Association, 1952), Vol. II, p. 768.

2. J. Frank Dobie, *Guide to Life and Literature of the Southwest* (Dallas: Southern Methodist University Press, 1952), p. 89.

3. Burke, *Missions of Old Texas*, pp. 55–56. The author provides a chronological catalog of Texas missions.

4. Rouse, *The Criollo*, p. 91.

5. David Woodman, Jr., *Guide to Texas Emigrants* (Waco: Texian Press, 1974), pp. 168–170, is a reprint of the 1835 edition published in Boston. This 192-page guide was originally published by the Galveston Bay and Texas Land Company, organized in New York City in late 1830 to promote settlement of

lands in eastern Texas. Although a promotional piece and generally positive in tone, it provides an interesting commentary on life in Texas in the early 1830s.

6. Clarence W. Gordon, "Report on Cattle, Sheep, and Swine," Vol. III, p. 965. Gordon provides the estimate of percentages of "native American" and Spanish cattle in Texas in 1830. Unfortunately, he lists no source for his information. The reference to French cattle refers to French-Canadian cattle brought to Louisiana by the Acadians when they were expelled from Canada in 1755. These cattle were used as dairy animals. As the French settled the grasslands of southwest Louisiana, beginning about 1730, they obtained Spanish cattle from east Texas and perhaps elsewhere. The French-Canadian cattle, in time, were absorbed by the population of Spanish cattle. Brand registration began in Louisiana about 1739. See Rouse, *The Criollo*, pp. 78–79.

7. Rouse, *The Criollo*, pp. 192–193. Texas longhorns of today, according to Rouse, are "very fair representatives of the old Texas cattle, but, on good pasture and under controlled breeding for fifty years, they have undoubtedly increased both in body and horn size. The larger horn probably results from specific selection for that feature. The most prized individuals in the present herds often have horns that surpass many of those seen in old photographs of the northern drives."

8. A brief biographical sketch of James Taylor White may be found in *The Handbook of Texas*, Vol. II, p. 894. The sketch notes that White "came to Texas as early as 1819." Joseph Eve, however, in a letter written April 26, 1842, observed that White "moved here nineteen years ago," i.e., in 1823. See Joseph Milton Nance, "A Letter Book of Joseph Eve, United States Chargé d'Affaires to Texas," *Southwestern Historical Quarterly*, Vol. XLIII (1940), p. 488. An earlier reference to White may be found in Woodman's *Guide to Texas Emigrants*, pp. 62–63. White is mentioned by several contemporary writers, including Dobie, *The Longhorns*, p. 29, and Wayne Gard, *The Chisholm Trail* (Norman: University of Oklahoma Press, 1954), pp. 22–23.

9. Woodman, *Guide to Texas Emigrants*, p. 34.

10. *Ibid.*, 179–184. Gordon, "Report on Cattle, Sheep, and Swine," Vol. III, p. 965, contains much historical material on cattle in Texas. It includes the statement: "In 1842 the driving of cattle to New Orleans began." This often-used source is obviously not correct, since William Wilson wrote in his letter of Aug. 18, 1834, that cattle were then being driven to New Orleans. That is eight years earlier than the date in the government report. And there is little doubt that James Taylor White drove cattle to New Orleans from southeast Texas much earlier than 1834.

11. Mary Austin Holley, *Texas* (Austin: The Steck Co., 1935), p. 145, is a reprint of the original 1836 edition.

12. Woodman, *Guide to Texas Emigrants*, p. 119.

13. *Ibid.*, pp. 60–61.

14. I. C. Madray, *A History of Bee County with Some Brief Sketches About Men and Events in Adjoining Counties* (Beeville: Beeville Publishing Co., 1939), p. 5.

15. Vernam, *They Saddled the West*, pp. 9–11.

16. Frederick Law Olmsted, *A Journey Through Texas* (Austin and London: University of Texas Press, 1978), p. 54, is a reprint of the 1857 edition.

17. William D. Edwards, *The Story of Colt's Revolver* (Harrisburg: Stackpole Books, 1953), p. 99.

18. Gordon, "Report on Cattle, Sheep, and Swine," Vol. III, p. 965. See also Joseph M. Nance, *After San Jacinto* (Austin: University of Texas Press, 1970), p. 45–53.

19. J. Frank Dobie, *A Vaquero of the Brush Country* (Dallas: The Southwest Press, 1929), p. 5.

20. Joseph G. McCoy, *Historic Sketches of the Cattle Trade of the West and Southwest* (Kansas City: Ramsey, Millett and Hudson, 1874), p. 11.

21. Francis L. Fugate, "Origins of the Range Cattle Era in South Texas," *Agricultural History*, Vol. XXXV (1961), p. 157, citing Charles Adams Gulick, Jr., and Winnie Allen, eds., *The Papers of Mirabeau Buonaparte Lamar* (Austin, 1924), No. 1447, Vol. III, pp. 106–107.

22. Nance, *After San Jacinto*, pp. 64–66. A biographical sketch of Mabry Gray may be found in *The Handbook of Texas*, Vol. I, p. 723. A more interesting sketch of Gray's life may be found in J. Frank Dobie's "Mustang Gray: Fact, Tradition, and Song," *Tone the Bell Easy* (Austin: Texas Folklore Society, 1932), pp. 109–123.

23. Nance, *After San Jacinto*, p. 65.

24. William Banta and J. W. Caldwell, Jr., *Twenty-seven Years on the Texas Frontier* (Council Hill, Okla.: L. G. Park, 1933), pp. 4–7, is a revised and rewritten narrative by William Banta, taken from Banta's 1893 manuscript.

25. Gordon, "Report on Cattle, Sheep, and Swine," Vol. III, p. 965.

26. *Ibid.*, p. 985. Gordon cites 100,000 cattle in Texas in 1830 and 330,114 cattle in 1850. The figure 240,000 for 1845 is my own estimate.

Chapter Five: The Mixing of Cultures

1. J. Evetts Haley, ed., "A Log of the Texas-California Cattle Trail, 1854," *Southwestern Historical Quarterly*, Vol. XXXV (1932), pp. 208–209. Haley's introduction provides a brief sketch of early Texas trail drives to California.

2. Sheldon G. Jackson, *A British Ranchero in Old California* (Glendale and Azusa: The Arthur H. Clark Co., 1977), pp. 134–139.

3. Richard H. Dillon, ed., *California Trail Herd* (Los Gatos: The Talisman Press, 1961), pp. 49–124. This is the first publication of Loveland's diary. Dillon's 35-page introduction provides an interesting survey of California trail drives.

4. Cleland, *The Cattle on a Thousand Hills*, p. 144, citing the Los Angeles *Star*, Sept. 18, 1852.

5. The Missouri *Republican* (St. Louis), May 8, 1854.

6. Jotham Meeker's diary in the manuscript division, Kansas State Historical Society, Topeka.

7. New York *Daily Tribune*, Nov. 18, 1852.

8. Gordon, "Report on Cattle, Sheep, and Swine," Vol. III, p. 1071.

9. Arkansas *Gazette*, June 6, 1850.

10. Haley, ed., "A Log of the Texas-California Cattle Trail," p. 209, citing the Houston *Telegraph*, March 8, 1849.

11. *Fort Smith Elevator*, June 2, 1899.

12. Olmsted, *A Journey Through Texas*, pp. 273–275.

13. Haley, ed., "A Log of the Texas-California Cattle Trail," Vol. XXXV, pp. 211–237, 290–316, and Vol. XXVI (1932), pp. 47–66. Bell's log is published in three installments between January and July.

14. Cleland, *The Cattle on a Thousand Hills*, pp. 142–143, citing Charles Nordhoff, *California for Health, Pleasure, and Residence* (New York, 1873), p. 153.

15. *Ibid.*, p. 147.

16. *Ibid.*, citing the Los Angeles *Star*, April 26, 1856.

Chapter Six: Texas Trails North

1. James W. Freeman, ed., *Prose and Poetry of the Live Stock Industry of the United States* (Denver and Kansas City: Franklin Hudson Printing Co., 1905), p. 393.

2. "Notes and Documents," *Southwestern Historical Quarterly*, Vol. L (1946), pp. 96–97. Alva Fitzpatrick's letter is printed in full.

3. Freeman, ed., *Prose and Poetry of the Live Stock Industry*, p. 392; James Cox, *Historical and Biographical Record of the Cattle Industry and the Cattlemen of Texas and Adjacent Territory* (Saint Louis: Woodward and Tiernan Printing Co., 1895), p. 35. and *The Handbook of Texas*, Vol. I, p. 883, and Vol. II, pp. 235, 299.

4. Chris Emmett, *Shanghai Pierce: A Fair Likeness* (Norman: University of Oklahoma Press, 1953), p. 29.

5. J. Frank Dobie, *Life and Literature of the Southwest* (Dallas: Southern Methodist University, 1952), p. 126, citing a stapled pamphlet entitled *Hobo of the Rangeland* by Robert Beverly of Lovington, New Mexico.

6. Gordon, "Report on Cattle, Sheep, and Swine," Vol. III, p. 1029.

7. Thomas Candy Ponting, *Life of Tom Candy Ponting: An Autobiography* (Evanston: The Branding Iron Press, 1952), p. 20–42. Introduction and notes are by Herbert O. Brayer. Ponting's autobiography first appeared in pamphlet form published by Ponting at Decatur, Illinois, in 1907. Twenty-five copies were printed.

8. New York *Daily Tribune*, July 4, 1854.

9. George Squires Herrington, "An Early Cattle Drive from Texas to Illinois," *Southwestern Historical Quarterly*, Vol. LV (1951), pp. 267–269.

10. Vernam, *Man on Horseback*, pp. 317–322.

11. Rice and Vernam, *They Saddled the West*, pp. 5–11.

12. Savannah (Missouri) *Sentinel*, Nov. 22, 1851.

13. Cox, *Historical and Biographical Record of the Cattle Industry*, pp. 71–72.

14. St. Louis *Intelligencer*, Oct. 30, 1854.

15. *Daily Democratic Press* (Chicago), Oct. 11, 1854.

16. *Revised Statutes of the State of Missouri, 1930*, Vol. II, pp. 1004–1005.

17. C. C. Spalding, *Annals of the City of Kansas* (Kansas City: Van Horn and Abeel's Printing House, 1858), citing the *Western Journal of Commerce* (Kansas City), Jan. 9, 1858.

18. Dolph Shaner, *John Baxter of Baxter Springs: Picturesque Character of Frontier Days* (Baxter Springs: The Baxter State Bank, 1955), pp. 1–5.

19. *Missouri Statesman* (Columbia), June 24, 1859.

20. *General Laws of the Territory of Kansas, 1859*, pp. 621–622.

21. Dallas *Herald*, May 18, 1859.

22. Wayne Gard, "The Shawnee Trail," *Southwestern Historical Quarterly*, Vol. LVI (1953), p. 367.

23. *Laws of Missouri, 1860–1861*, pp. 25–28.

Chapter Seven: The Civil War and Change

1. Freeman, ed., *Prose and Poetry of the Live Stock Industry*, p. 549.

2. Cox, *Historical and Biographical Record of the Cattle Industry*, p. 300.

3. *Ibid.*, pp. 299–302.

4. J. Marvin Hunter, ed., *The Trail Drivers of Texas* (San Antonio: Jackson Printing Co., 1920–1923), Vol. II, pp. 161–162.

5. Cox, *Historical and Biographical Record of the Cattle Industry*, pp. 306–307.

6. E. Merton Coulter, *The Confederate States of America 1861–1865* (Baton Rouge: Louisiana State University Press, 1950), p. 246, citing Jefferson D. Bragg, *Louisiana in the Confederacy* (Baton Rouge, 1941), p. 83, and *Whig and Public Advertiser* (Richmond, Va.), Nov. 8, 1861.

7. Coulter, *The Confederate States of America*, p. 246, citing the *Hinds County Gazette* (Raymond, Miss.), Sept. 17, 1862.

8. Hunter, ed., *The Trail Drivers of Texas*, Vol. I, pp. 239–241.

9. *Ibid.*, Vol. II, p. 18.

10. *Ibid.*, Vol. I, pp. 433–436.

11. Cox, *Historical and Biographical Record of the Cattle Industry*, p. 412.

12. Hunter, ed., *The Trail Drivers of Texas*, Vol. I, pp. 162–163.

13. Coulter, *The Confederate States of America*, p. 245, citing *Southern Confederacy* (Macon, Ga.), Dec. 31, 1864.

14. Hunter, ed., *The Trail Drivers of Texas*, Vol. I, pp. 436–437.

15. Cox, *Historical and Biographical Record of the Cattle Industry*, pp. 58–59.

16. Hunter, ed., *The Trail Drivers of Texas*, Vol. I, pp. 436–437.

17. *Ibid.*, pp. 387–388.

18. Akerman, *Florida Cowman*, pp. 88–89, citing a 1940 interview with an unidentified Confederate veteran by Theodore Lesley at Tampa, Florida.

Chapter Eight: On the Open Range

1. Clara M. Love, "History of the Cattle Industry in the Southwest," *Southwestern Historical Quarterly*, Vol. XIX (1916), p. 383.

2. Lee Moore et al., *Letters from Old Friends and Members* (Cheyenne: Wyoming Stock Growers' Association, 1923), pp. 33–34. Moore, a former Texas trail driver, later moved to Wyoming to become a foreman on a Wyoming cattle ranch during the 1880s. Still later he became secretary of the Wyoming Board of Live Stock Commissioners.

3. Hunter, ed., *The Trail Drivers of Texas*, Vol. I, pp. 162–163.

4. James C. Shaw, *North from Texas: Incidents in the Early Life of a Range Cowman in Texas, Dakota and Wyoming* (Evanston: The Branding Iron Press, 1952), p. 5. Shaw wrote his recollections about 1930 while living near Orin, Wyoming. They were published in a small 43-page pamphlet entitled *Pioneering in Texas and Wyoming* in 1931. His recollections subsequently were reprinted in serial form in the Douglas, Wyoming, *Budget*, a newspaper. The best edition of his recollections is that of Branding Iron Press (1952), ed. by Herbert O. Brayer, whose introduction and notes are helpful.

5. Dobie, *The Longhorns*, pp. 44–49. See also *The Handbook of Texas*, Vol. II, p. 162, and Gard, *The Chisholm Trail*, p. 12. Most works relating to the history of the western cattle industry contain references to the origin of the word "maverick."

6. The best history of the King Ranch is Tom Lea's *The King Ranch* (Boston: Little, Brown and Co., 1957), a two-volume work. Another interesting study is Frank Goodwyn's *Life on the King Ranch* (New York: Crowell Co., 1951).

7. Cox, *Historical and Biographical Record of the Cattle Industry*, pp. 299–301. The story about Chisum's ranch house dining table was told by John A. Lomax. It may be found in his *Cow Camps & Cattle Herds* (Austin: The Encino Press, 1967), p. 48.

8. Philip Ashton Rollins, *The Cowboy* (New York: Scribner's Sons, 1922), p. 15.

9. One of the best reference books on brands and marks is Wolfenstine's *The Manual of Brands and Marks*. The book was edited by Ramon F. Adams, the well-known bibliographer and western historian.

10. Hunter, ed., *The Trail Drivers of Texas*, Vol. I, pp. 176–177.

11. *Ibid.*

12. W. M. French, "Ropes and Roping," *The Cattleman*, Vol. XXVI (1940), p. 23.

13. As mentioned in the text, little has been written about roping techniques.

W. M. French's 1940 article in *The Cattleman* magazine was helpful. Some material on roping was found in Ward's *The Cowboy at Work*. Both French and Ward were cowboys. The definitive book on stock roping has yet to be written.

14. Wolfenstine, *The Manual of Brands and Marks*, pp. 50–51.

15. Arnold and Hale, *Hot Irons*, p. 72.

16. *Handbook of Texas*, Vol. I, p. 310.

17. Freeman, ed., *Prose and Poetry of the Live Stock Industry*, p. 608.

18. Hunter, ed., *The Trail Drivers of Texas*, Vol. I, pp. 302–325.

19. Dobie, *A Vaquero of the Brush Country*, pp. 218–219.

20. J. Evetts Haley, *Charles Goodnight, Cowman and Plainsman* (Boston: Houghton Mifflin Co., 1936), pp. 121–122.

21. Many writers have touched on the chuck wagon and the cowboy cook, but the most complete study to date is Ramon Adams's *Come an' Get It: The Story of the Old Cowboy Cook* (Norman: University of Oklahoma Press, 1952). I have relied heavily on Adams. His quote may be found on pp. 21–22.

22. Hunter, ed., *The Trail Drivers of Texas*, Vol. I, p. 176.

23. Dobie, *A Vaquero of the Brush Country*, p. 110.

24. Hunter, ed., *The Trail Drivers of Texas*, Vol. I, p. 177.

Chapter Nine: Trail Herds to Railheads

1. Charles Moreau Harger, "Cattle-Trails of the Prairies," *Scribner's*, Vol. XI (1892), p. 742.

2. Gordon: "Report on Cattle, Sheep, and Swine," Vol. III, pp. 976–977.

3. *Ibid.*

4. *Texas Almanac* for 1870, pp. 124–126.

5. Dobie, *A Vaquero of the Brush Country*, pp. 20–29.

6. McCoy, *Historic Sketches of the Cattle Trade*, p. 20.

7. Hunter, ed., *The Trail Drivers of Texas*, Vol. II, pp. 137–140.

8. *The Republic* (St. Louis), Aug. 7, 1892.

9. George Crawford Duffield, "Driving Cattle from Texas to Iowa, 1866," *Annals of Iowa*, Vol. XIV (1924), pp. 243–262. I have improved the capitalization, spelling, and punctuation that appear in the original diary and as published in the *Annals of Iowa*.

10. *The Republic* (St. Louis), Aug. 7, 1892.

11. *Laws of Kansas*, 1867, Sess. 7, pp. 263–267.

12. McCoy, *Historic Sketches of the Cattle Trade*, p. 44. See also Robert R. Dykstra, *The Cattle Towns: A Social History of the Kansas Cattle Trading Centers* (New York: Alfred A. Knopf, 1968).

13. McCoy, *Historic Sketches of the Cattle Trade*, p. 50.

14. *Ibid.*, pp. 50–51.

15. Topeka *State Journal*, March 8, 1913.

16. McCoy, *Historic Sketches of the Cattle Trade*, p. 54.

17. Wichita *Eagle*, March 1, 1890.

18. In 1871 the Texas legislature in Austin enacted a law requiring that all persons purchasing cattle for driving to market across the northern limits of the state were to use a road brand. The law called for a "large and plain mark" to be "branded on the left side of the back behind the shoulder." See *Laws of Texas*, 1871, Sess. 12, p. 119.

19. Gordon, "Report on Cattle, Sheep, and Swine," Vol. III, p. 1071.

20. John A. Lomax, *Cow Camps & Cattle Herds* (Austin: Encino Press, 1967), p. 37. This work was written in 1945 as a contribution to an anthology of regional American folklore. The anthology was never published. The manuscript was located in 1962 and later published by Encino Press in an edition limited to 750 copies.

21. John A. Lomax, *Cowboy Songs and Other Frontier Ballads* (New York: Sturgis & Walton Co., 1911), p. xix. This work was first published in 1910.

22. *Ibid.*, pp. 22–23.

23. *Ibid.*, pp. 18–19.

Chapter Ten: Where the Trails Ended

1. Floyd B. Streeter, *Prairie Trails and Cow Towns* (New York: Devin Adair Co., 1963), p. 69. First published in 1936.

2. *Wichita Eagle*, June 26, 1873.

3. *The Cherokee Sentinel* (Baxter Springs), June 22, 1872.

4. Daniel W. Wilder, *The Annals of Kansas* (Topeka: Kansas Publishing Co., 1886), p. 94.

5. *Oswego Independent*, July 6, 1872.

6. *Ibid.*, Aug. 31, 1872.

7. *The Cherokee Sentinel* (Baxter Springs), June 22, 1872.

8. Alfred T. Andreas, *History of the State of Kansas* (Chicago: A. T. Andreas, 1883), p. 1574.

9. Stuart Henry, *Conquering Our Great American Plains: A Historical Development* (New York: E. P. Dutton and Co., 1930), p. 98.

10. *Ibid.*, p. 61.

11. *The Kansas State Record* (Topeka), Aug. 5, 1871.

12. Henry, *Conquering Our Great American Plains*, p. 267.

13. *Ibid.*, pp. 82–85.

14. *Manhattan* (Kansas) *Nationalist*, Aug. 2, 1872.

15. McCoy, *Historic Sketches of the Cattle Trade*, pp. 139–141.

16. *Dodge City Globe*, Feb. 17, 1879.

17. Joseph W. Snell, *Painted Ladies of the Cowtown Frontier* (Kansas City: Kansas City Posse of the Westerners, 1965), p. 11. This work was limited to 250 bound copies.

18. *The Cherokee Sentinel* (Baxter Springs), Sept. 1, 1871.

19. Snell, *Painted Ladies*, p. 9.

20. Dobie, *Guide to Life and Literature of the Southwest*, p. 60.

21. *Wichita Tribune*, Aug. 24, 1871.

22. The story of the "General Massacre" in Newton was pieced together from several original sources, including news accounts in the *Kansas Daily Commonwealth* (Topeka), Aug. 22, 23, and 27, 1871; the *Abilene Chronicle*, August 24, 1871; and the *Emporia* (Kansas) *News*, Aug. 25, 1871. Judge R. W. P. Muse's "History of Harvey County Kansas, for One Decade—from 1871 to 1881" in *Edward's Historical Atlas of Harvey Co., Kansas, 1882*, provided additional information. A longer version of this story appears in my *True Tales of the Old-Time Plains* (New York: Crown Publishers, Inc., 1979), pp. 99–103.

23. *Daily Kansas Commonwealth* (Topeka), Oct. 15, 1872.

24. Snell, *Painted Ladies*, p. 10.

Chapter Eleven: On the Northern Ranges

1. Carl Frederick Kraenzel, *The Great Plains in Transition* (Norman: University of Oklahoma Press, 1955), p. 105.

2. Lee R. Dice, *The Biotic Provinces of North America* (Ann Arbor: University of Michigan Press, 1943), pp. 24–27.

3. Ernest Staples Osgood, *The Day of the Cattleman* (Minneapolis: University of Minnesota Press, 1929), p. 12. Grant is mentioned in passing by Osgood, whose book is one of the earliest and best accounts of the cattle industry on the northern plains. Additional material on Grant was found in Vol. IX, *The Mountain Men and the Fur Trade of the Far West* (Glendale: The Arthur H. Clark Co., 1972), pp. 165–186.

4. John C. Frémont, *The Exploring Expedition to the Rocky Mountains, Oregon and California* (Buffalo: George H. Derby and Co., 1850), p. 133. An interesting biographical sketch of Lancaster P. Lupton by Ann W. Hafen may be found in Vol. II, *The Mountain Men and the Fur Trade of the Far West*, pp. 207–216.

5. Granville Stuart, *Forty Years on the Frontier* (Cleveland: The Arthur H. Clark Co., 1925). This two-volume set of Stuart's recollections, ed. by Paul C. Phillips, contains Stuart's story. The chapter on cattle raising in Vol. 2 is excellent.

6. Grace Raymond Hebard and E. A. Brininstool, *The Bozeman Trail* (Cleveland: The Arthur H. Clark Co., 1922), pp. 229–235. Other bits and pieces of Nelson Story's life were located in Vol. II of Stuart's *Forty Years on the Frontier*, p. 98, and Paul I. Wellman's *The Trampling Herd* (New York: Carrick & Evans, 1939), pp. 95–100.

7. Hunter, ed., *The Trail Drivers of Texas*, Vol. II, pp. 366–367.

8. *Ibid.*, Vol. I, pp. 277–281.

9. Charles F. Coffee et al., *Letters from Old Friends and Members* (Cheyenne: Wyoming Stock Growers' Association, 1923), p. 25.

10. Martin F. Schmitt, ed., *The Cattle Drives of David Shirk from Texas to the Idaho Mines, 1871 and 1873* (Portland: Champoeg Press, 1956). Schmitt's

introduction includes background on other early cattle drives in Owyhee country. This volume, limited to 750 copies, includes Shirk's later experiences as a cattleman in eastern Oregon. Shirk's original manuscript and related papers are in the University of Oregon Library.

11. *The Report of the Commissioner of General Land Office, 1871*, p. 263.

12. Rollins, *The Cowboy*, p. 133.

13. Vernam, *Man on Horseback*, pp. 322–323.

14. Mae Urbanek, *Ghost Trails of Wyoming* (Boulder: Johnson Publishing Co., 1978), p. 97. The author includes some material on the Texas cattle trail in Wyoming in her book. See also Struthers Burt, *Powder River Let 'Er Buck* (New York: Farrar and Rinehart, 1938).

15. Stuart: *Forty Years on the Frontier*, Vol. II, pp. 187–188.

16. The author of these words is unknown. A longer and slightly different version does appear in *American Cowboy Songs* (New York: Robbins Music Corporation, 1936), ed. by Hugo Frey.

17. Stephen Paullada, *Rawhide and Song* (New York: Vantage Press, 1963), pp. 174–175. See also J. Evetts Haley, *The XIT Ranch of Texas* (Chicago: The Lakeside Press, 1929), p. 139.

18. Quoted from the *Denver Journal of Commerce* (no date listed) in the *Breeder's Gazette* (Chicago), Vol. IV (Sept. 27, 1883), p. 421, as cited by Osgood, *The Day of the Cattleman*, p. 86.

Chapter Twelve: Ranch House Culture

1. Lewis Eldon Atherton, *The Cattle Kings* (Bloomington: Indiana University Press, 1961), p. 95.

2. Lea, *The King Ranch*, Vol. I, pp. 344–345.

3. Emmett, *Shanghai Pierce*, p. 7. This is the best biography of Pierce to date.

4. McCoy, *Historic Sketches of the Cattle Trade*, p. 290.

5. Cox, *Historical and Biographical Record of the Cattle Industry*, pp. 516–517.

6. This partial description of the cattleman's daily routine in the late 1870s was pieced together from many sources, including *The Trail Drivers of Texas* (1920–1923), the biographies *Charles Goodnight* and *George W. Littlefield* by J. Evetts Haley (1936 and 1943), and material found in *Prose and Poetry of the Live Stock Industry*, ed. by James W. Freeman.

7. Emily Jones Shelton, "Lizzie E. Johnson: A Cattle Queen of Texas," *Southwestern Historical Quarterly*, Vol. L (1947), pp. 349–366.

8. Lewis Nordyke, *Great Roundup: The Story of Texas and Southwestern Cowmen* (New York: William Morrow & Co., 1955), pp. 96–97.

9. *Galveston* (Texas) *News*, Jan. 10, 1886, as quoted in Haley, *Charles Goodnight*, pp. 327–328.

10. General James S. Brisbin, *The Beef Bonanza; Or, How to Get Rich on the Plains* (Philadelphia: J. B. Lippincott and Co., 1881), p. 43.

11. *Ibid.*

12. Agnes Wright Spring, *Cow Country Legacies* (Kansas City: The Lowell Press, 1976), pp. 18–19.

13. John Clay, *My Life on the Range* (New York: Antiquarian Press, Ltd., 1961), p. 74. This is a reprint of the 1924 first edition privately printed in Chicago.

14. Spring, *Cow Country Legacies*, p. 9.

15. Theodore Roosevelt, *The Wilderness Hunter* (New York: G. P. Putnam's Sons, 1893), Vol. I, p. 24.

16. Theodore Roosevelt, *Ranch Life in the Far West* (Flagstaff: Northland Press, 1968), p. 16. This volume contains a facsimile of six articles written by Roosevelt that appeared in 1888 in *Century Magazine*. The material quoted appears in the article titled "Ranch Life in the Far West."

Chapter Thirteen: Bunkhouse Culture

1. Clay, *My Life on the Range*, p. 84.

2. Hunter, ed., *The Trail Drivers of Texas*, Vol. I, p. 412. Unfortunately, Hunter does not provide his source for the figures mentioned.

3. William C. Holden, "The Problem of Hands on the Spur Ranch," *Southwestern Historical Quarterly*, Vol. XXXV (1932), p. 199.

4. Stuart, *Forty Years on the Frontier*, Vol. II, p. 182.

5. Ramon F. Adams, *The Cowman & His Code of Ethics* (Austin: Encino Press, 1969), pp. 11–12. This work was issued in an edition of 850 copies.

6. C. L. Sonnichsen, *Cowboys and Cattle Kings: Life on the Range Today* (Norman: University of Oklahoma Press, 1950), p. 46.

7. Adams, *The Cowman & His Code of Ethics*, p. 13.

8. Hunter, ed., *The Trail Drivers of Texas*, Vol. II, p. 492.

9. General George Wingate, "My Trip to the Yellowstone," *American Agriculturist*, Vol. XLV (1886), p. 152.

10. Stuart, *Forty Years on the Frontier*, p. 181.

11. Angie Debo, ed., *The Cowman's Southwest, Being the Reminiscences of Oliver Nelson freighter, camp cook, cowboy, frontiersman in Kansas, Indian Territory, Texas and Oklahoma, 1878–1893* (Glendale: The Arthur H. Clark Co., 1953), p. 98.

12. *Ibid.*, pp. 102–103.

13. *Ibid.*, pp. 112–113.

14. William P. Ricketts, *50 Years in the Saddle* (Sheridan, Wyoming: Star Publishing Co., 1942), pp. 16–17.

15. Terry G. Jordan, "Windmills in Texas," *Agricultural History*, Vol. XXXVII (1936), p. 81.

16. The description of the work and routine of the cowboy in the late nineteenth century was pieced together from numerous sources. Most recollections of the cowhands include references to their work and daily routine.

17. Holden, "The Problem of Hands on the Spur Ranch," p. 198.

18. John R. Craddock, "Songs the Cowboys Sing," *Texas and Southwestern Lore* (Austin: Texas Folk-Lore Society, 1927), pp. 190–191. This work is Vol. VI in the publications of the Texas Folklore Society ed. by J. Frank Dobie.

19. Hunter, ed., *The Trail Drivers of Texas*, Vol. II, pp. 21–22.

20. Holden, "The Problem of Hands on the Spur Ranch," pp. 197–198.

21. Bill Oden, *Early Days on the Texas-New Mexico Plains* (Canyon, Tex.: Palo Duro Press, 1965), p. 32. Oden's recollections, edited by J. Evetts Haley, are those of an ordinary cowboy.

22. James Emmit McCauley, *A Stove-up Cowboy's Story* (Dallas: Southern Methodist University Press, 1965), p. 72. McCauley's recollections were first published by the Texas Folklore Society in 1943.

23. Clay, *My Life on the Range*, pp. 83–84.

24. The *Fort Worth Gazette*, March 25 and 29, 1883, contains news stories relating to the strike. Ruth A. Allen's *Chapters in the History of Organized Labor in Texas* (1941) and the 1887 federal report on *Strikes and Lockouts* issued by the U.S. Commissioner of Labor contain additional information on the cowboy strike. The most comprehensive account, however, is a chapter devoted to the strike contained in John L. McCarty's fine book *Maverick Town: The Story of Old Tascosa* (Norman: University of Oklahoma Press, 1946), pp. 107–114.

25. A copy of the printed rules may be seen at the Panhandle-Plains Historical Museum in Canyon, Texas.

Chapter Fourteen: End of the Open-Range Culture

1. Walter P. Webb, *The Great Plains* (Boston: Ginn and Co., 1931), p. 295, citing Edwin Ford Piper's *Barbed Wire and Wayfarers*.

2. Attempts to improve the longhorn breed did not begin with Mifflin Kenedy or Richard King. About 1848, Colonel Thomas J. Shannon imported two cows and a bull from Queen Victoria's own herd of Durham cattle. They were shipped to New Orleans and hauled in wagons to North Texas. Shannon and a few other Texans realized that the tough, angular Texas longhorns were not the best of beef cattle; they did not have the weight, the docility, or the low feeding-cost factor that many other cattle had. The first year after the Missouri, Kansas, and Texas Railway reached Texas in 1872, the line delivered 200 carloads of breeding stock to Texas ranchers.

3. Cleland, *The Cattle on a Thousand Hills*, pp. 85–87.

4. Reginald Aldridge, *Life on a Ranch: Ranch Notes in Kansas, Colorado, the Indian Territory and Northern Texas* (London: Longmans, Green, and Co., 1884), p. 145.

5. Henry D. and Frances T. McCallum, *The Wire That Fenced the West* (Norman: University of Oklahoma Press, 1965). This well-written work provides the most comprehensive examination of the invention of barbed wire and its history to date.

6. *Ibid.*, pp. 68–72.

7. Coffee et al., *Letters from Old Friends and Members*, pp. 25–29.

8. Webb, *The Great Plains*, p. 309. I have converted Webb's listing of pounds to tons.

9. Will James, *Cow-boy Life in Texas, Or, 27 Years a Mavrick* [sic] (Chicago: Donohue, Henneberry & Co., 1893), pp. 108–109.

10. Freeman, ed., *Prose and Poetry of the Live Stock Industry*, p. 686.

11. A. O. Jenkins, *Olive's Last Round-Up* (Loup City. Neb.: Sherman County Times, 1930). This rare little booklet contains the story of Isom Prentice "Print" Olive (1840–1886). Olive left Nebraska after the terrible winter of 1885–86 and moved to Trail City, Colorado. He was murdered there in the summer of 1886 by Joe Sparrow, a former cowhand, who owed him $10.

12. Webb, *The Great Plains*, p. 314, citing that the original letter was in the files of the Texas adjutant general's office in Austin.

13. Harold Preece, *Lone Star Man* (New York: Hastings House, 1960). This well-researched biography of Aten recounts in much detail the fence-cutting incidents in Brown and Navarro counties of Texas. Aten died at the age of ninety in 1953.

14. Much has been written about the Johnson County War. The first, and rarest, book-length account is Asa Shinn Mercer's *The Banditti of the Plains; or, The Cattlemen's Invasion of Wyoming in 1892*, believed to have been printed in Denver or Cheyenne in 1894. As soon as the book was published, nearly all copies were impounded by a Cheyenne court in a libel suit and ordered to be destroyed. The author's Cheyenne print shop was burned, and he was ordered to leave the state. Many members of the Wyoming Stock Growers' Association and their sympathizers sought to locate and destroy every copy; even the copyright copies in the Library of Congress reportedly vanished. Nonetheless, some copies did survive. The book has been reprinted at least four times.

15. Harley True Burton, *A History of the JA Ranch* (New York: Argonaut Press Ltd., 1966), p. 93. This is a reprint of the author's 1927 thesis presented to the faculty of the graduate school of the University of Texas, Austin.

Epilogue

1. Joe B. Frantz, "Cowboy Philosophy," *The Frontier Re-examined*, ed. by John Francis McDermott (Urbana: University of Illinois Press, 1967), p. 180.

2. A valuable bibliographic profile of early western fiction may be found in Jeff C. Dyke's *Western High Spots* (Flagstaff: Northland Press, 1977). See also Albert Johannsen's *The House of Beadle and Adams and Its Dime and Nickel Novels* (Norman: University of Oklahoma, 1950).

3. William K. Everson and George N. Fenin, *The Western, from Silents to the Seventies* (New York: Penguin Books, 1977), p. 25.

4. *Ibid.*, pp. 20–21.

A Bibliography
for the General Reader

The sources cited in the text plus the annotated notes that follow the Epilogue provide sufficient source identification for the scholar and serious student of the cowboy. The general reader wishing to do further reading on cowboys, cattlemen, and specific aspects of the cowboy culture and the cattle trade will find the following selected bibliography useful as a guide.

Barbed Wire

Clifton, Robert T. *Barbs, Prings, Points, Prickers, & Stickers: A Complete and Illustrated Catalogue of Antique Barbed Wire.* Norman: University of Oklahoma Press, 1970.

Crouch, Amos. *Antique Wire Illustrated.* Chandler, Oklahoma: Antique Wire Sales, 1978.

Glover, Jack. *"Bobbed" Wire.* Wichita Falls, Tex.: Terry Brothers Printers, 1966. An illustrated guide to the identification and classification of barbed wire.

———. *More "Bobbed" Wire.* Wichita Falls, Tex.: Terry Brothers Printers, 1967. A sequel to the author's 1966 guide.

McCallum, Henry D. and Frances T. *The Wire That Fenced the West.* Norman: University of Oklahoma Press, 1965.

Wendt, Lloyd, and Kogan, Herman. *Bet a Million! The Story of John W. Gates.* Indianapolis: Bobbs-Merrill Co., 1948. The story of the introduction of barbed wire in Texas.

Brands

Ford, Gus L., ed. *Texas Cattle Brands.* Dallas: Clyde C. Cockrell Co., 1936.

Gard, Wayne. *Cattle Brands of Texas.* Dallas: First National Bank, 1956.

Hale, John P. *Hot Irons: Heraldry of the Range.* New York: Macmillan Co., 1940. The best early book on brands.

Haley, J. Evetts. *The Heraldry of the Range*. Canyon, Tex.: Panhandle-Plains Historical Society, 1949. Texas Panhandle.

Ward, Hortense W. *Cattle Brands and Cow Hides*. Dallas: Story Book Press, 1953.

Wolfenstine, Manfred R. *The Manual of Brands and Marks*. Norman: University of Oklahoma Press, 1970. Perhaps the most complete book yet written on the subject.

Note: In most western stock-raising states the stock growers' associations and/or state governments have published brand books containing all registered brands in their states. Such books began to appear late in the nineteenth century. Many copies may be found in libraries in western states.

Cattle

Allen, Lewis F. *American Cattle: Their History, Breeding, and Management*. New York: O. Judd and Co., 1868.

———. *History of the Short-Horn Cattle: Their Origin, Progress, and Present Condition*. Buffalo: Privately printed, 1872.

Dobie, J. Frank. *The Longhorns*. Boston: Little, Brown and Co., 1941. Since reprinted many times.

Laude, G. A. *Kansas Shorthorns: A History of the Breed in the State from 1857 to 1920*. Iola, Kan.: Laude Printing Co., 1920.

Miller, T. L. *History of Hereford Cattle*. Chillicothe, Missouri: T. E. B. Sotham Publisher, 1902.

Ornduff, Donald R. *The Hereford in America*. Kansas City: Privately printed, 1957.

Rouse, John E. *The Criollo: Spanish Cattle in the Americas*. Norman: University of Oklahoma Press, 1977.

Sanders, Alvin H. *A History of Aberdeen-Angus Cattle*. Chicago: New Breeder's Gazette, 1928.

———. *Short-Horn Cattle*. Chicago: Sanders Publishing Co., 1900.

———. *The Story of Herefords*. Chicago: Breeder's Gazette, 1914.

Ward, William F. *Breeds of Beef Cattle*. Washington: Government Printing Office, 1915.

Cattlemen

Athearn, Robert G. *Westward the Briton*. New York: Charles Scribner's Sons, 1953. Much on Englishmen who became western cattlemen.

Atherton, Lewis E. *The Cattle Kings*. Bloomington: Indiana University Press, 1961. A survey of the better-known nineteenth-century western cattle kings.

Bronson, Edgar B. *Reminiscences of a Ranchman*. Chicago: McClurg Publishing, 1910. Honest and to the point.

Casement, Dan D. *The Abbreviated Autobiography of a Joyous Pagan.* Manhattan, Kan.: Privately printed, 1944. A rare little pamphlet by a well-known Colorado and Kansas cowman who knew how to write.

———. *Random Recollections.* Kansas City: Walker Publications, 1955.

Clay, John. *My Life on the Range.* New York: Antiquarian Press, 1961. A reprint of the 1924 first edition that was privately printed in Chicago.

Coffee, Charles F., et al. *Letters from Old Friends and Members.* Cheyenne: Wyoming Stock Growers' Association, 1923.

Dobie, J. Frank. *Cow People.* Boston: Little Brown and Co., 1964. Sketches of Texas cattlemen, including Shanghai Pierce, Ab Blocker, Ike Pryor, and others.

Emmett, Chris. *Shanghai Pierce: A Fair Likeness.* Norman: University of Oklahoma Press, 1953.

Gressley, Gene M. *Bankers and Cattlemen.* New York: Alfred A. Knopf, 1966.

Haley, J. Evetts. *Charles Goodnight, Cowman and Plainsman.* Boston: Houghton Mifflin Co., 1936. One of the best biographies of a cattleman ever written. Reprinted.

———. *George W. Littlefield, Texan.* Norman: University of Oklahoma Press, 1943.

———. *Jeff Milton: A Good Man with a Gun.* Norman: University of Oklahoma Press, 1948.

Holden, William C. *Rollie Burns; Or, An Account of the Ranching Industry on the South Plains.* Dallas: Southwest Press, 1932. Good on ranching in the 1870s through the early 1890s in West Texas.

Hunt, Frazier. *Cap Mossman, Last of the Great Cowmen.* New York: Hastings House, 1951.

———. *The Long Trail from Texas: The Story of Ad Spaugh, Cattleman.* New York: Doubleday, Doran and Co., 1940.

Jenkins, A. O. *Olive's Last Round-up.* Loup City, Neb.: Sherman County Times, 1930. A rare little pamphlet about a Nebraska cowman of questionable character.

Lang, Lincoln A. *Ranching with Roosevelt.* Philadelphia: J. B. Lippincott Co., 1926.

Mercer, Asa Shinn. *The Banditti of the Plains.* Denver (or Cheyenne?): Privately printed, 1894. The cattlemen's invasion of Wyoming in 1892. Reprinted several times.

Ornduff, Donald R. *Casement of Juniata.* Kansas City: Lowell Press, 1975.

Ponting, Thomas C. *Life of Tom Candy Ponting: An Autobiography.* Evanston, Ill.: The Branding Iron Press, 1952.

Sandoz, Mari. *The Cattlemen: From the Rio Grande Across the Far Marias.* New York: Hastings House, 1958.

Stone, William H. *Twenty-four Years a Cowboy and Ranchman.* Hedrick, Oklahoma Territory: W. H. Stone Publishers, 1905. Reprinted.

Stuart, Granville. *Forty Years on the Frontier.* Cleveland: The Arthur H. Clark Co., 1925. Two vols. A pioneer cattleman's recollections of Montana and the northern plains.

Treadwell, Edward F. *The Cattle King.* New York: Macmillan Co., 1931. The life of Henry Miller.

Warren, Nellie F. and Patricia N., eds. *Conrad Kohrs: An Autobiography.* Deer Lodge, Mont.: Platen Press, 1977. A pioneer cattleman's recollections, delayed nearly fifty years in publication.

Cattle Ranches

Allred, B. W., and Dykes, J. C., eds. *Flat Top Ranch: The Story of a Grassland Venture.* Norman: University of Oklahoma Press, 1957. The story of modern conservation ranching in Bosque County, Texas.

Burns, Robert H., et al. *Wyoming's Pioneer Ranches.* Laramie: Top-of-the-World Press, 1955. Early ranches of Wyoming.

Burton, Harley T. *A History of the JA Ranch.* Austin: Press of Von Boeckmann-Jones Co., 1928. A master's thesis at the University of Texas on Charles Goodnight's Texas panhandle ranch. Reprinted in New York (1966).

Cattle Ranches and Cattle Raising on the Plains. Boston: Henry W. Brooks and Co., 1881. Author unknown. Early survey of ranching.

Cleland, Robert G. *The Irvine Ranch of Orange County, 1810–1950.* San Marino, Cal.: The Huntington Library, 1952.

Collings, Ellsworth. *The 101 Ranch.* Norman: University of Oklahoma Press, 1937. The story of Colonel George Miller's great Oklahoma ranch.

Elliot, W. J. *The Spurs.* Spur, Tex.: The Texas Spur, 1939. A history of the Spur Ranch.

Ellis, George F. *Bell Ranch as I Knew It.* Kansas City: Lowell Press, 1973. With historical overview by Donald R. Ornduff.

Gipson, Fred. *Fabulous Empire.* Boston: Houghton Mifflin Co., 1946. The story of the 101 Ranch in Oklahoma.

Goodwyn, Frank. *Life on the King Ranch.* New York: Thomas Y. Crowell Co., 1951.

Haley, J. Evetts. *The XIT Ranch of Texas and the Early Days of the Llano Estacado.* Chicago: The Lakeside Press, 1929. Reprinted.

Hill, Joseph J. *The History of Warner's Ranch, and Its Environs.* Los Angeles: Privately printed, 1927. A well-known California ranch.

Holden, William C. *The Spur Ranch.* Boston: Christopher Publishing House, 1934. Texas.

Lea, Tom. *The King Ranch.* Boston: Little, Brown and Co., 1957. Two vols. The story of the famous south Texas ranch.

Nordyke, Lewis. *Cattle Empire: The Fabulous Story of the 3,000,000 Acre XIT.* New York: William Morrow and Co., 1949.

Pearce, William M. *The Matador Land and Cattle Company.* Norman: University of Oklahoma Press, 1964. A fine history of the Scottish-owned ranches.

Williams, J. W. *The Big Ranch Country.* Wichita Falls, Tex.: Terry Brothers Printers, 1954. A wordy but interesting survey of many Texas cattle ranches.

Cattle Towns

Dykstra, Robert R. *The Cattle Towns: A Social History of the Kansas Cattle Trading Centers.* New York: Alfred A. Knopf, 1968.

Henry, Stuart. *Conquering Our Great American Plains.* New York: E. P. Dutton and Co., 1930. Much on early Abilene, Kansas.

Jelinek, George. *Ellsworth, Kansas, 1867–1947.* Salina, Kan.: Consolidated, 1947. A pamphlet containing some material on Ellsworth as a cattle town.

McCarty, John L. *Maverick Town: The Story of Old Tascosa.* Norman: University of Oklahoma Press, 1946.

Snell, Joseph W. *Painted Ladies of the Cowtown Frontier.* Kansas City: Kansas City Posse of the Westerners, 1965. An interesting study of prostitutes in Kansas cattle towns.

Streeter, Floyd B. *Prairie Trails & Cow Towns.* Boston: Chapman and Grimes, 1936. Kansas cattle towns. Reprinted.

Wright, Robert M. *Dodge City, the Cowboy Capital, and the Great Southwest in the Days of the Wild Indian, the Buffalo, the Cowboy, Dance Halls, Gambling Halls, and Bad Men.* Wichita: Wichita Eagle Press, 1913.

Cowboys

Abbott, E. C., and Smith, Helena Huntington. *We Pointed Them North: Recollections of a Cowpuncher.* New York: Farrar and Rinehart; 1939. Abbott—"Teddy Blue"—was reared in Nebraska and was a cowboy on the northern ranges. A candid recollection.

Adams, Andy. *The Log of a Cowboy.* Boston: Houghton Mifflin Co., 1903. Written as a novel without a plot. Fiction, but a true-to-life narrative.

Benton, Frank. *Cowboy Life on the Sidetrack.* Denver: Western Stories Syndicate, 1903. Cowboys and railroads.

Biggers, Don H. *From Cattle Range to Cotton Patch.* Abilene, Tex.: Press of the Abilene Printing News, 1908. A cowboy in west Texas.

Black, A. P. "Ott." *The End of the Long Horn Trail.* Selfridge, N.D.: Selfridge Journal, 1936. From Texas to the Dakotas.

Blasingame, Ike. *Dakota Cowboy: My Life in the Old Days.* New York: G. P. Putnam's Sons, 1958. The author went from Texas to the Dakotas in 1904. A vivid and candid recollection of ranch life in the Dakotas until 1912.

Brooks, Bryant B. *Memoirs of Bryant B. Brooks, Cowboy, Trapper, Lumberman, Stockman, Oilman, Banker, and Governor of Wyoming.* Glendale: The Arthur H. Clark Co., 1939.

Choate, Julian E., Jr., and Frantz, Joe B. *The American Cowboy.* Norman: University of Oklahoma Press, 1955. Good survey. Thoughtful.

Cook, James H. *Fifty Years on the Old Frontier, as Cowboy, Hunter, Guide, Scout, and Ranchman.* New Haven: Yale University Press, 1923.

Coolidge, Dana. *Arizona Cowboys.* New York: E. P. Dutton and Co., 1938.

———. *Old California Cowboys.* New York: E. P. Dutton and Co., 1939.

———. *Texas Cowboys.* New York: E. P. Dutton and Co., 1937.

Crissey, Forrest. *Alexander Legge, 1866–1933.* Chicago: Privately printed, 1936. Much on Nebraska and Wyoming cowboy life.

Debo, Angie, ed. *The Cowman's Southwest.* Glendale: The Arthur H. Clark Co., 1953. The reminiscences of Oliver Nelson.

Dobie, J. Frank. *A Vaquero of the Brush Country.* Dallas: Southwest Press, 1929. John Young's recollections.

Donoho, Milford H. *Circle-Dot: A True Story of Cowboy Life Forty Years Ago.* Topeka: Crane and Co., 1907.

Erskine, Mrs. Gladys. *Broncho Charlie: A Sage of the Saddle.* New York: Thomas Y. Crowell Co., 1934.

Fridge, Ike. *History of the Chisum War; Or, Life of Ike Fridge.* Electra, Tex.: J. D. Smith, 1927. Fridge went to New Mexico with Chisum in 1869. The narrative covers 1869 through 1880.

Gipson, Fred. *Cowhand: The Story of a Working Cowboy.* New York: Harper and Brothers, 1953.

Guernsey, Charles A. *Wyoming Cowboy Days.* New York: G. P. Putnam's Sons, 1936.

Haley, J. Evetts. *Life on the Texas Range.* Austin: University of Texas Press, 1952. The photographic art of Erwin E. Smith in Texas.

Halsell, H. H. *Cowboys and Cattleland.* Nashville: Parthenon Press, 1937. Texas.

Hinkle, James F. *Early Days of a Cowboy on the Pecos.* Roswell: Privately printed, 1937. New Mexico and West Texas.

James, Will. *Lone Cowboy: My Life Story.* New York: Charles Scribner's Sons, 1930. One of eight books written and illustrated by this one-time cowboy.

James, Will S. *Cow-boy Life in Texas, Or, 27 Years a Maverick* [sic]. Chicago: Donohue, Henneberry and Co., 1893. Texas.

Johnston, Harry V. *My Home on the Range: Frontier Life in the Bad Lands.* St. Paul: Wells Publishing Co., 1942.

———. *The Last Roundup.* Minneapolis: H. V. Johnston Publishing Co., 1949.

Jones, J. O. *A Cowman's Memoirs.* Fort Worth: Texas Christian University Press, 1953.

King, Frank M. *Mavericks: The Salty Comments of an Old-time Cowpuncher.* Pasadena: Trail's End Publishing Co., 1947. King was the author of three other books touching on the West. Each contains some material on cowboys.

Lomax, John A. *Cow Camps & Cattle Herds.* Austin: Encino Press, 1967.

———. *Cowboy Songs and Other Frontier Ballads.* New York: Sturgis and Walton Co., 1911. This work first appeared in 1910.

McCauley, James E. *A Stove-up Cowboy's Story.* Austin: Texas Folklore Society, 1943. Reprinted in 1965.

Melton, A. B. *Seventy Years in the Saddle.* Kansas City: Warden Printing Services, 1948.

Mora, Jo. *Trail Dust and Saddle Leather.* New York: Charles Scribner's Sons, 1946. Much on California cowboys.

———. *Californios.* Garden City, N.Y.: Doubleday and Co., 1949.

Post, Charles C. *Ten Years a Cowboy.* Chicago: Rhodes and McClure Publishing Co., 1886. Probably the second book written about the cowboy.

Rojas, Arnold R. *California Vaquero.* Fresno: Academy Library Guild, 1953.

———. *Last of the Vaqueros.* Fresno: Academy Library Guild, 1960. California.

Rollins, Philip A. *The Cowboy.* New York: Charles Scribner's Sons, 1922. An early attempt to correct some of the popular misconceptions about the cowboy and his life.

———. *Gone Haywire: Two Tenderfoots on the Montana Cattle Range in 1886.* New York: Charles Scribner's Sons, 1927.

———. *Jinglebob: A True Story of a Real Cowboy.* New York: Charles Scribner's Sons, 1927.

Rolt-Wheeler, Francis W. *The Book of Cowboys.* Boston: Lothrop, Lee and Shepard Co., 1921.

Russell, Charles M. *Back-Trailing on Old Frontiers.* Great Falls, Mont.: Cheely-Raban Syndicate, 1922.

———. *Good Medicine: The Illustrated Letters of Charles M. Russell.* Garden City, N.Y.: Doubleday, Doran and Co., 1929.

———. *"Paper Talk" Charlie Russell's American West.* New York: Alfred A. Knopf, 1979. Ed. by Brian W. Dippie and published in association with the Amon Carter Museum of Western Art at Fort Worth, Texas.

———. *More Rawhides.* Great Falls, Mont.: Montana Newspaper Association, 1925.

———. *Rawhide Rawlins Stories.* Great Falls, Mont.: Montana Newspaper Association, 1921.

———. *Trails Plowed Under.* Garden City, N.Y.: Doubleday, Page and Co., 1927. This book is composed of stories published earlier in Russell's *Rawhide Rawlins Stories* and *More Rawhides.*

Rye, Edgar. *The Quirt and the Spur: Vanishing Shadows of the Texas Frontier.* Chicago: W. B. Conkey Co., 1909.

Sears, Gen. W. H. *Notes from a Cowboy's Diary.* Lawrence, Kan.: Privately printed, [n.d.]. Sears worked for a time as a cowboy in western Kansas and eastern Colorado.

Siringo, Charles A. *A Texas Cowboy.* Chicago: Umbdenstock and Co., 1885. The first autobiography of a cowboy. The rare first edition is much sought after. The book has been reprinted.

Thorp, Nathan H. *Story of the Southwestern Cowboy, Pardner of the Wind.* Caldwell: Caxton Printers, 1945.

Equipment, Gear, and Techniques

Alley, John. *Memories of Roundup Days.* Norman: University of Oklahoma Press, 1934. Contains some material on roundup techniques on the southern plains.

Angell, George T. *Cattle Transportation.* Boston: Massachusetts Society for the Prevention of Cruelty to Animals, 1872. Interesting report on transporting cattle in railroad cars.

Bennett, Russell H. *The Compleat Rancher.* New York: Rinehart and Co., 1946. How to run a cattle ranch.

Byers, Chester. *Roping: Trick and Fancy Rope Spinning.* New York: G. P. Putnam's Sons, 1928.

Coe, Charles H. *Juggling a Rope.* Pendleton, Ore.: Hamley and Co., 1927.

Ortega, Luis. *California Hackamore (La Jáquima). An Authentic Story of the Use of the Hackamore.* Sacramento: News Publishing Co., 1948.

Rice, Lee M., and Vernam, Glenn R. *They Saddled the West.* Cambridge, Md.: Cornell Maritime Press, 1975.

Vernam, Glenn R. *Man on Horseback.* New York: Harper and Row, 1964. An excellent survey on the tools of the cowboy from before the advent of the Texas cowboy.

Ward, Fay E. *The Cowboy at Work.* New York: Hastings House, 1958. A fine survey of the cowboy's work, techniques, and use of tools.

General Surveys

Brown, Dee, and Schmitt, Martin F. *Trail Driving Days.* New York: Charles Scribner's Sons, 1952. A combination of words and historic photographs.

Dale, Edward E. *The Range Cattle Industry.* Norman: University of Oklahoma Press, 1930. Reprinted.

Freeman, James W., ed. *Prose and Poetry of the Live Stock Industry of the United States.* Denver and Kansas City: Franklin Hudson Printing Co., 1905. Reprinted in 1959.

Hill, J. L. *The End of the Cattle Trail.* Long Beach: George W. Moyle Publishing Co., [n.d].

Osgood, Ernest Staples. *The Day of the Cattleman.* Minneapolis: University of Minnesota Press, 1929. Reprinted.

Pelzer, Louis. *The Cattlemen's Frontier.* Glendale: The Arthur H. Clark Co., 1936.

Schlebecker, John T. *Cattle Raising on the Plains, 1900–1961.* Lincoln: University of Nebraska Press, 1963.

Wellman, Paul T. *The Trampling Herd.* New York: Carrick and Evans, 1939. An interesting and well-written narrative.

Horses

Beery, Jesse. *A Practical System of Colt Training; Also the Best Methods of Subduing Wild and Vicious Horses.* Lima, Ohio: Parmenter Printing Co., 1896. Some early techniques.

Camp, Charles. *Muggins, the Cow Horse.* Denver: Welsh-Haffner Printing Co., 1928. The story of an unusual cow horse.

Denhardt, Robert M. *The Horse of the Americas.* Norman: University of Oklahoma Press, 1975. Excellent survey.

Dobie, J. Frank. *The Mustangs.* Boston: Little, Brown and Co., 1952. Reprinted many times.

Gorman, John A. *The Western Horse.* Danville, Ill.: The Inter-State, 1939. Reprinted in 1944.

Muller, Dan. *Horses.* Chicago: Reilly and Lee Co., 1936.

Ortega, Luis. *California Stock Horse.* Sacramento: News Publishing Co., 1949.

Rarey, J. S. *The Modern Art of Taming Wild Horses.* Portland: Democratic Standard Office, 1858. A fascinating book but difficult to locate.

Roe, Frank G. *The Indian and the Horse.* Norman: University of Oklahoma Press, 1955. Some material on cowboys and their horses. Good background on the horse.

Rojas, Arnold R. *Bits, Bitting and Spanish Horses.* Goleta, Cal.: Kimberly Press, 1970. Good on history.

Wyman, Walker D. *The Wild Horse of the West.* Caldwell: Caxton Printers, 1945. Reprinted.

Regional Histories

Akerman, Joe A., Jr. *Florida Cowman: A History of Florida Cattle Raising.* Kissimmee: Florida Cattlemen's Association, 1976.

Baber, Daisy F. *The Longest Rope: The Truth About the Johnson County Cattle War as told by Bill Walker.* Caldwell: Caxton Printers, 1940. Wyoming.

Bauer, Helen. *California Rancho Days.* Garden City, N.Y.: Doubleday and Co., 1953.

Blanchard, Leola H. *Conquest of Southwest Kansas.* Wichita: Wichita Eagle Press, 1931. Some material on ranching.

Briggs, Harold E. *Frontiers of the Northwest.* New York: Appleton-Century Co., 1940. Much on the cattle industry in the Northwest.

Brown, Mark H., and Felton, W. R. *The Frontier Years.* New York: Henry Holt and Co., 1955. Much on ranching on the northern plains. Emphasis on the early photographs of L. A. Huffman.

———. *Before Barbed Wire.* New York: Henry Holt and Co., 1956. Sequel to *The Frontier Years.*

Burt, Struthers. *Powder River Let 'Er Buck*. New York: Farrar and Rinehart, 1938. Heavy on the northern plains, with emphasis on northeastern Wyoming.

Cleland, Robert G. *The Cattle on a Thousand Hills*. San Marino: The Huntington Library, 1941. Reprinted.

Cox, James. *Historical and Biographical Record of the Cattle Industry and the Cattlemen of Texas and Adjacent Territory*. Saint Louis: Woodward and Tiernan Printing Co., 1895. Reprinted in two vols. in 1959.

Culley, John H. *Cattle, Horses, and Men of the Western Range*. Los Angeles: The Ward Ritchie Press, 1940. New Mexico and the Southwest.

Dana, Richard H. *Two Years Before the Mast*. New York: Harper and Brothers, 1840. Much on the early hide-and-tallow industry in California. Reprinted many times.

Davis, William H. *Seventy-five Years in California*. San Francisco: John Howell, 1967. This is the best edition, a reprint of the scarce 1889 first edition.

Goff, Richard, and McCaffree, Robert H. *Century in the Saddle*. Denver: Colorado Cattlemen's Centennial Commission, 1967. The first 100 years of the Colorado Cattlemen's Association.

Gress, Kathryn. *Ninety Years Cow Country: A Factual History of the Wyoming Stock Grower's Association with Historical Data Pertaining to the Cattle Industry in Wyoming*. [Cheyenne?]: Wyoming Stock Growers' Association, 1963.

McCoy, Joseph G. *Historic Sketches of the Cattle Trade of the West and Southwest*. Kansas City: Ramsey, Millett and Hudson, 1874. Reprinted.

Nordyke, Lewis. *Great Roundup: The Story of Texas and Southwestern Cowmen*. New York: Morrow and Co., 1955. Much on Texas and the early cattlemen's associations.

Rainey, George. *The Cherokee Strip: Its History*. Enid, Okla.: Published by the author, 1925. Reprinted.

Schatz, August H. *Opening a Cow Country*. Ann Arbor: Edwards Brothers, 1939. Much on western South Dakota.

Wagoner, Junior Jean. *History of the Cattle Industry in Southern Arizona, 1540–1940*. Tucson: University of Arizona, 1952.

Webb, Walter P. *The Great Plains*. Boston: Ginn and Co., 1931. Contains an interesting chapter on the cattle trade, with emphasis on Texas and the Southwest.

Rodeos

Clancy, Frederick "Foghorn." *My Fifty Years in Rodeo, Living with Cowboys, Horses, and Danger*. San Antonio: Naylor Co., 1952.

Gard, Robert E. *Midnight, Rodeo Champion*. New York: Duell, Sloan and Pearce, 1951. A history of a famous rodeo bucking horse.

Gillespie, A. S., and Burns, R. H. *Steamboat—Symbol of Wyoming*. Laramie: University of Wyoming, [n.d.].

Kegley, Max. *Rodeo: The Sport of the Cow Country*. New York: Hastings House, 1942.

Lamb, Gene. *R-O-D-E-O Back of the Chutes*. Denver: Bell Press, 1956.

McCombs, R. V. *"Watch the Chutes!" The Story of a Roundup*. Boston: Gorman Press, 1930. The story of rodeo.

Terry, Cleo Tom, and Wilson, Osie. *The Rawhide Tree*. Clarendon, Tex.: Clarendon Press, 1957. The story of Florence Reynolds.

Westermeier, Clifford P. *Man, Beast, Dust: The Story of Rodeo*. Denver: World Press, 1947.

Trails and Trail Driving

Brayer, Garnet M., and Oliver, Herbert. *American Cattle Trails, 1540–1900*. Bayside, N.Y.: American Pioneer Trails Association, 1952.

Dillon, Richard H., ed. *California Trail Herd*. Los Gatos, Cal.: The Talisman Press, 1961. The diary of Cyrus C. Loveland on the trail drive to California in the 1850s.

Gard, Wayne. *The Chisholm Trail*. Norman: University of Oklahoma Press, 1954. Reprinted. A fine book.

Hunter, J. Marvin, ed. *The Trail Drivers of Texas*. San Antonio: Jackson Printing Co., 1920, 1923, 1924. Two Vols., but Vol. I was corrected and issued as "revised Vol. I" in 1924. The whole was reprinted in one Vol. in Nashville in 1925. Reprinted again in 1963. Recollections of Texas trail drivers.

Potter, Jack M. *Cattle Trails of the Old West*. Clayton, N.M.: Leader Publishing Co., 1935. Some material on trails and trail driving. Reprinted.

Ridings, Sam P. *The Chisholm Trail*. Guthrie, Okla.: Co-Operative Publishing Co., 1936.

Schmitt, Martin F., ed. *The Cattle Drives of David Shrik from Texas to the Idaho Mines, 1871 and 1873*. Portland: Champoeg Press, 1956.

Skaggs, Jimmy M. *The Cattle-trailing Industry*. Lawrence, Kan.: University of Kansas, 1973. Interesting survey.

Index

Grateful acknowledgment is made to the following for permission
to use illustrations from their collections:

Panhandle-Plains Historical Museum: Illustrations on pp. 161 (above), 259 (below),
270 (above)
University of Wyoming, Western History Research Center: Illustrations on pp. 247
(below), 269, 277 (below), 287 (above)

Grateful acknowledgment is made to the following for permission
to use previously published material as source for some
of the drawings in this book:

Jack Glover: Illustrations on page 316 first appeared in Jack Glover's *Bobbed Wire
Bible*. Reprinted by permission of Jack Glover.
Harper & Row, Publishers, Inc.: Illustrations on pages 17 (saddle), 18, and 49 are
adapted from *Man on Horseback* by Glenn R. Vernam: Figure 71 (page 162), Figure 74
(page 165), and Figure 133 A & B (page 312). Copyright © 1964. Reprinted by per-
mission of Harper & Row, Publishers, Inc.
Hastings House, Publishers, Inc.: The illustrations of rope throws with directional
arrows, on pages 148, 149, 150, 151, 152, and 153, are adapted from drawings by Fay
Ward from *The Cowboy at Work*, copyright © 1958, by permission of Hastings House,
Publishers, Inc.

Grateful acknowledgment is made to the following for permission
to use previously published textual material in this book:

Antiquarian Press: Excerpts from John Clay, *My Life on the Range*, copyright 1924.
The Arthur H. Clark Co.: Excerpts from Granville Stuart, *Forty Years on the Frontier*,
copyright 1925, and from Angie Debo, editor, *The Cowman's Southwest, Being the Reminiscences of Oliver Nelson freighter, camp cook, cowboy, frontiersman in Kansas, Indian Terri-
tory, Texas and Oklahoma, 1878—1893*, copyright 1953.
California Historical Society Quarterly: Excerpts from "Edward Vischer's First Visit
to California," edited by Erwin Gustav Gudde, which appeared in Volume XIX
(1940).
Elsevier-Dutton Publishing Company, Inc: Excerpts from Stuart Henry, *Conquering
Our Great American Plains*, copyright 1930, 1958 by Stuart Henry.
Florida Cattlemen's Association: Excerpts from Joe A. Akerman's *Florida Cowman:
A History of Florida Cattle Raising*, copyright © 1976.
Iowa State Historical Society: Excerpts from George Crawford Duffield's diary,
"Driving Cattle from Texas to Iowa, 1866," in the *Annals of Iowa*, Volume XIV (April
1924): 243—262. Original diary is in the collections of the Division of Historical
Museums and Archives, Iowa State Historical Department.
Floyd E. Risvold: The letter from Father Serra to Captain Don Fernando de Rivera y
Moncada, July 27, 1776. From Mr. Risvold's private collection.
George W. Saunders: Excerpts from Volumes I and II of *Trail Drivers of Texas*, copy-
right 1920 and 1923.
Southern Methodist University Press: Excerpts from James Emmit McCauley, *A
Stove-up Cowboy's Story*, copyright 1943 by the Texas Folklore Society.
Southwestern Historical Quarterly: Excerpts from James Bell's diary (1854), edited by
J. Evetts Haley, which appeared in Volumes XXV and XXVI (1932). By permission
of Texas State Historical Society.
The Talisman Press: Excerpts from Cyrus Loveland's diary, edited by Richard H.
Dillon in *California Trail Herd*, copyright © 1961.
Wyoming Stock Growers' Association: Excerpts from Lee Moore et al., *Letters from
Old Friends and Members*, copyright 1923.